WHITHER THE WEST?

On a variety of international legal matters, relations between the US and European countries are evolving and even diverging. In an ever-changing world, understanding the reasons for this increasing dichotomy is fundamental and has a profound impact on our understanding of world dynamics and globalization and, ultimately, on our awareness of where the West is going. This interdisciplinary volume proposes new frameworks to understand the differences in approach to international law in the US and Europe. To explain the theoretical and historical underpinnings of the diverging views, the expert essays present new research and develop innovative conclusions. They assess and explore issues such as the idea of sovereignty, constitutional law, the use of force, treaty law and international adjudication. Leading authorities in different disciplines including law and political science, the contributors engage in a new dialogue and develop a new discourse on inter-Atlantic views.

Chiara Giorgetti is Professor of Law at Richmond Law School, Virginia. She is an elected member of the American Law Institute, Vice President of the American Branch of the International Law Association and Chair of the Academic Council of the Institute for Transnational Arbitration. She clerked at the International Court of Justice and has acted as counsel in inter-state boundary disputes, claims commission and international investment arbitrations.

Guglielmo Verdirame is Professor of International Law at Kings College London. He has previously held positions at the Universities of Cambridge and Oxford, was a visiting scholar at Harvard Law School and Director of Studies for Public International Law at The Hague Academy of International Law. He is the author of *The UN and Human Rights: Who Guards the Guardians?* (2011).

ASIL STUDIES IN INTERNATIONAL LEGAL THEORY

Series Editors

Mark Agrast, ASIL
Mortimer Sellers, University of Baltimore

Editorial Board

Samantha Besson, Université de Fribourg
Allen Buchanan, Duke University
David Kennedy, Harvard University
Jan Klabbers, University of Helsinki
David Luban, Georgetown University
Larry May, Vanderbilt University
Mary Ellen O'Connell, University of Notre Dame
Onuma Yasuaki, Meiji University
Helen Stacy, Stanford University
John Tasioulas, University College London
Fernando Tesón, Florida State University

The purpose of the ASIL Studies in International Legal Theory series is to clarify and improve the theoretical foundations of international law. Too often the progressive development and implementation of international law has foundered on confusion about first principles. This series raises the level of public and scholarly discussion about the structure and purposes of the world legal order and how best to achieve global justice through law. This series grows out of the International Legal Theory project of the American Society of International Law. The ASIL Studies in International Legal Theory series deepens this conversation by publishing scholarly monographs and edited volumes of essays considering subjects in international legal theory.

Books in the series

International Law as Behavior
Edited by Harlan Grant Cohen and Timothy Meyer

Space and Fates of International Law: Between Leibniz and Hobbes
Ekaterina Yahyaoui Krivenko

Why Punish Perpetrators of Mass Atrocities?: Purposes of Punishment in International Criminal Law
Edited by Florian Jeßberger and Julia Geneuss

The Challenge of Inter-Legality
Edited by Jan Klabbers and Gianluigi Palombella

The Nature of International Law
Miodrag A. Jovanović

Reexamining Customary International Law
Edited by Brian D. Lepard

Theoretical Boundaries of Armed Conflict and Human Rights
Edited by Jens David Ohlin

Human Rights in Emergencies
Edited by Evan J. Criddle

The Theory of Self-Determination
Edited by Fernando R. Tesón

Negotiating State and Non-State Law: Global and Local Legal Pluralism
Edited by Michael A. Helfand

Jus Post Bellum and Transitional Justice
Edited by Larry May and Elizabeth Edenberg

Normative Pluralism and International Law: Exploring Global Governance
Edited by Jan Klabbers and Touko Piipaerinen

The Future of International Law: Global Government
Joel P. Trachtman

Morality, Jus Post Bellum, and International Law
Edited by Larry May and Andrew T. Forcehimes

Global Justice and International Economic Law: Opportunities and Prospects
Edited by Chios Carmody, Frank J. Garcia, and John Linarelli

Parochialism, Cosmopolitanism, and the Foundations of International Law
Edited by Mortimer Sellers

The Role of Ethics in International Law
Edited by Donald Earl Childress III

The New Global Law
Rafael Domingo

Customary International Law: A New Theory with Practical Applications
Brian D. Lepard

International Criminal Law and Philosophy
Edited by Larry May and Zachary Hoskins

Whither the West? International Law in Europe and the United States
Edited by Chiara Giorgetti and Guglielmo Verdirame

Whither the West?

INTERNATIONAL LAW IN EUROPE AND THE UNITED STATES

Edited by

CHIARA GIORGETTI

University of Richmond

GUGLIELMO VERDIRAME

King's College London

CAMBRIDGE
UNIVERSITY PRESS

University Printing House, Cambridge CB2 8BS, United Kingdom

One Liberty Plaza, 20th Floor, New York, NY 10006, USA

477 Williamstown Road, Port Melbourne, VIC 3207, Australia

314–321, 3rd Floor, Plot 3, Splendor Forum, Jasola District Centre, New Delhi – 110025, India

79 Anson Road, #06–04/06, Singapore 079906

Cambridge University Press is part of the University of Cambridge.

It furthers the University's mission by disseminating knowledge in the pursuit of education, learning, and research at the highest international levels of excellence.

www.cambridge.org
Information on this title: www.cambridge.org/9781107190115
DOI: 10.1017/9781316996836

© Chiara Giorgetti and Guglielmo Verdirame 2021

This publication is in copyright. Subject to statutory exception and to the provisions of relevant collective licensing agreements, no reproduction of any part may take place without the written permission of Cambridge University Press.

First published 2021

A catalogue record for this publication is available from the British Library.

ISBN 978-1-107-19011-5 Hardback

Cambridge University Press has no responsibility for the persistence or accuracy of URLs for external or third-party internet websites referred to in this publication and does not guarantee that any content on such websites is, or will remain, accurate or appropriate.

Contents

About the Authors	*page* ix
Acknowledgements	xiii

**Introduction: W[h]ither the West? The Divided West
and the Shifting Grounds of International Law**
Chiara Giorgetti and Guglielmo Verdirame · 1

I · THE IDEA OF INTERNATIONAL LAW IN THE DIVIDED WEST

1 **International Lawyers and Legal Forms
Transatlantic Denials**
Jean d'Aspremont · 13

2 **Are We (Americans) All International Legal Realists Now?**
Harlan Grant Cohen · 33

3 **Are Liberal Internationalists Still Liberal?**
Guglielmo Verdirame · 53

4 **The New, New Sovereigntism or How the European Union
Became Disenchanted with International Law and Defiantly
Protective of Its Domestic Legal Order**
Mark A. Pollack · 73

II · SPECIFIC AREAS IN INTERNATIONAL LAW: WHITHER THE WEST?

1 **International Law and Constitutional Law:
Is There a Final Arbiter?**

viii *Contents*

5 Authority and Dialogue
State and Official Immunity in Domestic
and International Courts
Chimène I. Keitner   115

6 Treaty Conditions and Constitutions
Walls, Windows, or Doors?
Edward T. Swaine   146

    2 International Adjudication and the Development
of International Law

7 International Courts and Tribunals in the USA
and in Europe
The Increasingly Divided West
Chiara Giorgetti   175

8 Unravelling a Paradox of Shared Responsibility
The Disconnection between Substantive and Adjudicate Law
Andre Nollkaemper   202

    3 International Law and the Use of Force

9 Divergent Views on the Content and Relevance of the Jus
ad Bellum in Europe and the United States?
The Case of the US-Led Military Coalition against
"Islamic State"
Tom Ruys and Luca Ferro   231

About the Authors

JEAN D'ASPREMONT is Professor of International Law at Sciences Po School of Law. He also holds a chair of Public International Law at the University of Manchester where he founded the Manchester International Law Centre (MILC). He is General Editor of the Cambridge Studies in International and Comparative Law and Director of Oxford International Organizations (OXIO). He is a member of the Scientific Advisory Board of the *European Journal of International Law* and series editor of the Melland Schill Studies in International Law.

HARLAN GRANT COHEN is Gabriel M. Wilner/UGA Foundation Professor in International Law and Faculty Co-Director of the Dean Rusk International Law Center. Cohen is a member of the Board of Editors of the American Journal of International Law (ASIL) and a member of the American Law Institute. He was a member of ASIL's executive council, served as co-chair of the society's 106th Annual Meeting and currently serves as chair of ASIL's International Legal Theory interest group. Cohen's scholarship has appeared in the George Washington, Tulane, Iowa and New York University law reviews and the Yale, Berkeley, NYU and Michigan journals of international law, among other places. He is a graduate of Yale University and New York University School of Law, where he was a Florence Allen Scholar and was inducted into the Order of the Coif. Prior to joining the Georgia Law faculty in 2007, he was a Furman Fellow at NYU and worked at the law firm Cleary Gottlieb Steen & Hamilton.

LUCA FERRO is a postdoctoral researcher at the Ghent Rolin-Jaequemyns International Law Institute of Ghent University (Belgium) and a former Visiting Scholar at the Columbia Law School (New York City, USA). He defended his doctoral dissertation in 2019, which was entitled *International 'Intervention' in Theory and in Practice* and devoted to assessing the legality of foreign involvement in the internal and external affairs of States through a varied set of case studies. While his research focuses primarily on topics of general public international law, the law of armed conflicts and international criminal law, he is also interested in international legal theory and methodology.

CHIARA GIORGETTI is Professor of Law at Richmond Law School. She is an expert in public international law, international adjudication and international arbitration. She has authored over forty publications on these topics, including eight authored and edited books and dozens of book chapters and articles. Giorgetti is an elected member of the American Law Institute, Vice-President of the American Branch of the International Law Association, and Chair of the Academic Council of the Institute for Transnational Arbitration. Giorgetti served as a member of the Executive Council and Executive Committee of the American Society of International Law and co-chaired ASIL Annual Meeting. She is also the co-founder of ASIL's interest group on International Courts and Tribunals. Prior to joining the Richmond Law faculty in 2012, Giorgetti worked in the international arbitration groups of White & Case in Washington, DC, and at Lalive in Geneva and served as counsel in several state to state disputes, including on matters of territorial and maritime boundaries and compensations for international law violations. She clerked at the International Court of Justice in The Hague and worked extensively with the United Nations in New York and Somalia. Giorgetti holds a JSD and LLM from Yale Law School, a MSc from the London School of Economics and a Laurea in Law from Bologna University.

CHIMÈNE KEITNER is Alfred and Hanna Fromm Professor of International and Comparative Law, University of California Hastings College of the Law. She is a leading authority on international law and civil litigation, and served as the 27th Counselor on International Law in the US Department of State. She has authored two books and dozens of articles, essays and book chapters on questions surrounding the relationship among law, communities and borders, including issues of jurisdiction, extraterritoriality, foreign sovereign and foreign official immunity, and the historical understandings underpinning current practice in these areas. Professor Keitner holds a bachelor's degree in history and literature with high honors from Harvard, a JD from Yale, where she was a Paul & Daisy Soros Fellow, and a doctorate in international relations from Oxford, where she was a Rhodes Scholar. Professor Keitner has served on the Executive Council of the American Society of International Law and as Co-Chair of the ASIL International Law in Domestic Courts Interest Group. She is a member of the American Law Institute and an Adviser on the ALI's Fourth Restatement of the Foreign Relations Law of the United States. She is also a founding co-chair of the International Law Association's Study Group on Individual Responsibility in International Law.

ANDRÉ NOLLKAEMPER is Dean and Professor of Public International Law at the Faculty of Law of the University of Amsterdam. He is also external Legal Advisor to the Minister of Foreign Affairs of the Netherlands, Member of the Permanent Court of Arbitration, President of the European Society of International Law and Member of the Royal Netherlands Academy of Arts and Sciences. In 1999, he established the Amsterdam Center for International Law (ACIL), which has become a center of excellence at the University of Amsterdam and ranks amongst the top institutions for international law in the Netherlands. His practical experience includes cases before the European Court on Human Rights, the Special Court for Sierra Leone, the International Criminal Tribunal for the Former Yugoslavia, the Extraordinary Chambers in the Courts of Cambodia, courts of the Netherlands and consultancy for a variety of international and national organizations. From 1998 to 2010 he was of-counsel at Bohler, attorneys in Amsterdam.

MARK A. POLLACK is Professor of Political Science and Law and Jean Monnet Chair at Temple University, in Philadelphia, where he also serves as Director of Global Studies. He received his PhD from Harvard University, and taught at the University of Wisconsin-Madison and the European University Institute in Florence, Italy before coming to Temple. He is the author of two books, *The Engines of European Integration* (Oxford University Press, 2003), and co-author (with Gregory C. Shaffer) of *When Cooperation Fails* (Oxford University Press, May 2009). He is also editor or co-editor of eight books, including most recently *Interdisciplinary Perspectives on International Law and International Relations* (with Jeffrey L. Dunoff, Cambridge University Press, 2013), and *Policy-Making in the European Union*, 7th edition (with Helen Wallace and Alasdair Young, Oxford University Press, 2015). His most recent work on international courts has appeared in journals such as *The American Journal of International Law*, the *European Journal of International Law*, the *Michigan Journal of International Law* and the *International Journal of Constitutional Law*.

TOM RUYS is a Professor of International Law at Ghent University, where he heads the Ghent Rolin-Jaequemyns International Law Institute (GRILI). He has authored several publications, including the monograph '*Armed Attack' and Article 51 of the UN Charter: Evolutions in Customary Law and Practice* (Cambridge University Press, 2010), which was awarded the Lieber Prize by the American Society of International Law, as well as *The Use of Force in International Law: A Case-based Approach* (co-edited with O. Corten; Oxford University Press, 2018). Ruys is co-editor-in-chief of the *Journal of the Use of Force and International Law* and of the *Military Law and Law of War Review*.

EDWARD SWAINE is Charles Kennedy Poe Research Professor at George Washington (GW) Law School, where he teaches and writes in the areas of international law, foreign relations law, international antitrust and contracts. He is the co-author of *Foreign Relations and National Security Law: Cases, Materials and Simulations* (4th ed. 2011) (with Franck, Glennon and Murphy) and has published work in the *American Journal of International Law, Columbia Law Review, Duke Law Journal, Harvard International Law Journal, Stanford Law Review, University of Pennsylvania Law Review, Virginia Journal of International Law, William and Mary Law Review* and *Yale Journal of International Law*, among others. Professor Swaine joined the GW faculty in 2006, after serving as the Counselor on International Law at the US Department of State. Before entering academia, Professor Swaine practiced law at the Brussels office of Cleary, Gottlieb, Steen and Hamilton and served as a member of the civil appellate staff at the US Department of Justice. He is a graduate of Yale Law School, where he was the Editor-in-Chief of the *Yale Law Journal*, and Harvard College. Professor Swaine is a reporter for the American Law Institute's Restatement of the Law (Fourth), Foreign Relations Law of the United States, and an elected member of the American Law Institute. He is a member of the Advisory Committee on Public International Law for the US State Department, a past member of the Executive Council of the American Society of International Law and former co-chair of the International Law in Domestic Groups interest group.

GUGLIELMO VERDIRAME QC is Professor of International Law at King's College London where he is appointed jointly by the Department of War Studies and the Dickson Poon School of Law. Professor Verdirame is the author of *The UN and Human Rights: Who Guards the Guardians?* (2011, Cambridge University Press), Winner of the Biennial ACUNS Book Award, and of *Rights in Exile* (Berghahn Books, 2005), as well as numerous articles and chapters in books. Before joining King's, he was a lecturer in the Faculty of Law at the University of Cambridge and a fellow of the Lauterpacht Centre for International Law (2003–11); a junior research fellow at Merton College, Oxford (2000–3); and a research officer at the Refugee Studies Centre at the University of Oxford (1997–8). Professor Verdirame was a visiting professor at Columbia Law School (2015) and a visiting fellow at Harvard Law School (2007). Professor Verdirame has practiced as a Barrister at Twenty Essex chambers in London since 2006, and was appointed Queen's Counsel in 2019. He specializes in public international law cases, especially investment arbitrations, interstate disputes as well as cases before the English courts involving international law issues.

Acknowledgements

We are grateful to the International Legal Theory Group of the American Society of International Law (ASIL) and especially Mortimer Sellers for accepting our proposal for a symposium and for their continuous support in our effort. Thank you to Richmond Law School and Dean Wendy Perdue for providing generous funds to sponsor the symposium and to the staff of Tillar House for hosting us in their beautiful location.

Our thanks to all the contributors for sharing with us their thoughtful ideas and for their patience as we finalized this manuscript. Thank you also to the staff of Richmond Law Library for checking and editing drafts and to editors and staff at Cambridge University Press for their hard work turning the manuscript into a book and for their patience during the process of completion.

CG & GV

My thanks and love go, as always, to Alexander and Charlotte for all the joy they bring.

CG

Introduction

W[h]ither the West? The Divided West and the Shifting Grounds of International Law

Chiara Giorgetti and Guglielmo Verdirame

This book has its origins in a seminar which took place on 6–7 May 2015 at Tillar House, the headquarters of the American Society of International Law in Washington, DC. The title of the seminar, which was organized under the auspices of the International Legal Theory Group of the American Society, was "Whither the West? Debates on Concepts of International Law in Europe and America". As organizers, our purpose was to gather a group of scholars based in Europe and North America to reflect on the state of the field, both in a general sense and in relation to specific issues.

While this was only five years ago, May 2015 almost feels like a different era in terms of international law. Barack Obama was still President of the United States; Xi Jinping was China's leader but had not yet consolidated his power; Russia had not intervened in Syria; and the United Kingdom had not voted to leave the European Union. Of course, there was already a profound sense of uncertainty, resulting from the financial crisis, the economic rise of China and the West's strategic failures in places where it had projected military power since the beginning of the century, that is, Iraq, Afghanistan and Libya.

That sense of crisis and uncertainty has only deepened since 2015. Some may dispute the relevance of the "West" as a geopolitical or cultural reference point for exploring this crisis, and our question "Whither the West?" was designed to include this kind of critique. But, for better or for worse and with all its many implications, the system of international law that emerged from World War II was largely the product of the political West; and indeed not for nothing, the instrument that first outlined its key features was called the Atlantic Charter. So "whither the West?" since then, what can be learnt and what can be built in a new and more inclusive system of international law?

2   *Introduction*

Developments since 2015 have also spawned a rich literature, including among international law scholars on these issues. Two strands of scholarship have only very recently emerged and though they did not, as such, receive the attention they would perhaps deserve if a similar debate were not to take place at the time our manuscript is sent to the printing press, they are still worth mentioning: first, there is a growing body of publications on the impact of populism on international law.[1] Second, other scholars have been focusing on a different challenge to liberal internationalism, namely the rise of what Tom Ginsburg calls "authoritarian international law."[2] Moreover, others have also explored how international law is understood and interpreted differently in different countries and regions of the world.[3]

In this book, we explore the divide – if such it is – between the USA and European views of international law in two steps. We first explore the theoretical dimension, and then focus on specific issues in international law, such as the relationship between international law and domestic law, the approach to international adjudication and the law on use of force.

Professor Jean d'Aspremont begins the theoretical section with a chapter on "International Lawyers and Legal Forms: Transatlantic Denials." Looking at both sides of the Atlantic, d'Aspremont challenges the narrative that pits international legal formalists against non-formalists and the common assumption among international lawyers according to which Europeans are more wedded to formalism – generically understood as the acknowledgement of the constraining role of legal forms – than their realist American counterparts. He explores two sides of the narratives, the "East Atlantic tale" and the "West Atlantic tale," with the aim of showing that both Europeans and Americans continue to demonstrate attachment to legal forms. The only significant differences between them lie in the way in which they seek to reinvent formalism and the role of legal forms.

D'Aspremont argues that both American and European international lawyers live in denial of their continuous engagement with legal forms, and in fact European and American international lawyers' engagement with formalism is a common denominator of the European and American traditions of

---

[1] H. Krieger, "Populist Governments and International Law," 2019 *European Journal of International Law* 30(3) 971–96; J. E. Nijman, "Populism and International Law: Which Backlash? Which Rubicon," 2018 *Netherlands Yearbook of International Law* 3–18; Eric Posner, "Liberal Internationalism and the Populist Backlash," *University of Chicago Public Law & Legal Theory Paper Series*, No. 606 (2017).

[2] See Tom Ginsburg, *Lauterpacht Lectures*, (Cambridge, 2019), https://upload .sms.csx.cam.ac.uk/media/2939251

[3] Anthea Roberts, Paul B. Stephan, Pierre-Hugues Verdier, and Mila Versteeg (eds.) Comparative International Law (2018) and Anthea Roberts, Is International Law International? (2017).

Introduction 3

international law. Indeed, he claims "we may all be formalists after all." Notwithstanding variations in their engagement with legal forms and in the agendas behind their respective projects of renewal, formalism unites rather than divides European and American international lawyers.

In his contribution, Professor Harlan Cohen takes a different path and focuses on features that may be common among American international lawyers. He addresses the claim that American-trained international lawyers are legal realists and its consequence in "Are We (Americans) All International Legal Realists Now?."

Cohen begins his exploration noting that legal realism can be defined by (1) empiricism, (2) an orientation towards process, practice and institutional choice rather than doctrine, (3) anti-formalism, (4) instrumentalism, (5) and pragmatism. He explores the origin of realism and argues that a wide range of schools of American legal thought drew from various aspects of legal realism (sometimes taking it in opposing directions), including the Legal Process School of Hart and Sacks, Law and Society, Critical Legal Studies and Law and Economics. He observes that various schools of modern American international law also instantiate the key characteristics of legal realism. Some schools, like the Policy Science School of Myres McDougal and Harold Lasswell and its progeny the New Haven School and "New" New Haven School (or Transnational Legal Process) are direct, explicit descendants of the legal realists. Others have their origins in other intellectual streams, like American International Relations scholarship. Over time, however, the various strands have converged and have become mutually reinforcing. International relations scholarship has been refracted through legal realism; American international law scholarship has borrowed from constitutional law scholarship already suffused with realism. He concludes that American legal realism has always had counterparts in other parts of the world, and one could question whether the thick lines between realism and positivism look much thinner and more porous in actual practice.

In the chapter "Are Liberal Internationalists Still Liberal?," Guglielmo Verdirame argues that liberal internationalism has undergone a largely undetected yet profound transformation in the last decades. As a result of an often unquestioning embrace of supranationalism and globalization, liberal internationalists have slouched towards cosmopolitanism. Yet, cosmopolitanism is a view of the international political order that is at odds with liberal internationalism properly understood. Today's liberal internationalists, like cosmopolitans, regard world government as both an aspiration and an inevitability. The idea of self-government, which was central to the liberal internationalism of the UN Charter, plays little or no role in this world view. This transformation of liberal internationalism is more evident in Europe, where supranationalism is not merely an ideology but the defining legal and political principle of the EU.

In "The New, New Sovereigntism, or How the Europe Union Became Disenchanted with International Law and Defiantly Protective of Its Domestic Legal Order", Professor Mark A. Pollack attacks the comfort zone of liberal internationalists from a different angle. He questions the transatlantic dichotomy that pictures the USA and the EU as divided in their attitudes towards international law, with the "Normative Power Europe" embracing international law and the "Exceptionalist New Sovereigntist US" as opposing any incursion of international law into the US legal order.

Instead, in his chapter, he documents the rise of what he names the "new, new sovereigntism" emanating from Europe. He does not, however, locate this new sovereigntism on the far right, but within pro-European parties and movement and primarily on the left and center-left of the political spectrum, that is those that seek to defend EU laws and EU legal order against the intrusion of a growing body of public international law to which they object.

These objections, Professor Pollack argues, are based on the claims that international-law making and interpretation are procedurally flawed, and that some international legal norms are antithetical to fundamental rights in Europe and, above all, that the European legal order must be protected. Pollack explores this European version of sovereigntism by focusing on three recent developments in international law: (1) the Anti-Counterfeiting Trade Agreement, which was rejected by EU institutions for failing to protect the rights of EU citizens; (2) the proposed Transatlantic Trade and Investment Partnership with the USA and the Comprehensive Economic and Trade Agreement with Canada, both of which have been denounced by political leaders and civil society for their secrecy as well as for alleged corporate domination of investor-state dispute settlement; and (3) the Union's long-running rejection of, and defiant non-compliance with, the WTO rulings on hormone-treated beef and genetically modified foods, which the EU found to be inconsistent with the Union's precautionary principle as well as the will of the people. Pollack finds that new European sovereigntism is not identical to its American sovereigntism, as it comes primarily from the left and center rather than the right, it objects to different features and fields of international law, seeks to defend different bodies of domestic law, and for the most part engages with the international legal order more constructively than American sovereigntism. He also stresses that this is a genuinely new phenomenon: for decades, Europe has been characterized by a mainstream, consensual and almost uncritical enthusiasm for international law, seen as legitimate in process as well as in content, and welcome in the EU legal order.

Introduction

Contemporary Europe, particularly on the left, has lost this uncritical acceptance of international law and has replaced it with a growing conviction that at least some parts of international law are objectionable both in process and in substance, and that domestic European rules and values must be defended against it. He concludes by highlighting the peril of ignoring the rise of this new European skepticism for all international law proponents.

In the second part of this book, several authors engage with the – perceived or real – divide of US/European concepts of international law in selected areas. First, the chapters by Chimène Keitner and Edward Swaine consider the relations between international law and constitutional law. Chiara Giorgetti and André Nollkaemper then explore issues related to international adjudication. Finally, Tom Ruys and Luca Ferro examine issues related to the use of force in international law.

In "Authority and Dialogue: State and Official Immunity in Domestic and International Courts," Chimène Keitner begins by noting that States have taken different approaches to incorporating relevant jurisdictional immunities into their domestic legal systems. Some common law countries, such as Canada and the United Kingdom, have adopted foreign state immunity acts that codify jurisdictional immunities as a matter of domestic law. The United States' domestic state immunity act codifies foreign state immunity, but not foreign official immunity. Other civil law countries, such as Italy, apply rules of foreign state immunity based on customary international law more directly.

She then assesses how domestic courts have adjudicated disputes related to jurisdictional immunities by interpreting and applying their domestic laws against the backdrop of international law and the customary international law norms that govern the contours of foreign state and foreign official immunity. In particular, she focuses on two challenges brought before international tribunals to immunity determinations made by domestic courts in Europe: a challenge brought by individual claimants before the European Court of Human Rights to the United Kingdom's determination that Saudi Arabia was entitled to jurisdictional immunity from civil claims for torture (*Jones v. United Kingdom*), and a challenge brought by Germany before the International Court of Justice to Italy's determination that Germany did not enjoy jurisdictional immunity from civil claims for World War II–era crimes (*Germany v. Italy*). Both of these cases pitted the right of access to a judicial remedy against the norm of state immunity. Domestic courts in Canada and Italy subsequently considered these international decisions in reaching their own conclusions about the scope of foreign state immunity under their domestic statutes. The Canadian Supreme Court's decision in *Estate of Kazemi v. Iran* illustrates normative coalescence around a conception of immunity based on a domestic statute and reinforced by international jurisprudence. By contrast, the Italian Constitutional Court's Judgment 238/2014 illustrates that international decisions can also provoke "legal protectionism" – the attempt to shield domestic norms and institutions from foreign or international "imports." This examination draws important conclusions, and Keitner finds that immunity cases defy categorization along a European/ North American divide. More consequentially, it is identifying the source of applicable norms (such as customary international law, a regional human rights convention or a domestic statute) that shapes the doctrinal paths available to judges in reaching a particular result.

In "Treaty Conditions and Constitutions: Walls, Windows, or Doors," Professor Edward Swaine examines the relationship between domestic constitutions and treaties. He notes that states frequently seek to interpose reservations, understanding, declarations or other "treaty conditions" that seek to change the international legal effect of a treaty for the state. The chapter considers three ways in which conditions based on constitutional claims can describe the relationship between the domestic and international domains, and that is: by establishing walls, windows or doors He also pays particular attention to the "reservations dialogue" described by the International Law Commission in its Seventeenth Report on Reservation to Treaties. That dialogue reveals different dispositions toward such conditions, including as between the United States, which has employed them heavily, and European states, which have been the most innovative in assessing them. While that dialogue continues to evidence the walls, or barriers, that persist between constitutions and treaties, possibilities for renovation exist.

Chiara Giorgetti examines international courts and tribunals in the USA and in Europe in "International Courts and Tribunals in the USA and in Europe: The Increasingly Divided West." She starts by pointing out that the general view pictures European countries as strong supporters of international adjudicatory institutions, while the USA has generally been more skeptical about international courts and tribunals. While this has historically been accurate for international courts whose jurisdiction cover human rights and international criminal law issues, the USA's position vis-à-vis international courts and tribunals has generally been more pragmatic than ideological. The positions of the USA and Europe have generally been similar in relation to tribunals examining issues related to trade and investment, for example.

More recently, however, the situation has seen consequential changes, with the USA showing more opposition towards all international courts and tribunals, including on matters of international economic law. The election of President Trump has resulted in a profound antagonism towards international courts and tribunals, and multilateral institutions more generally, in both words and facts, in line with the America First doctrine. Differently, European countries, guided in large part by the European Union, have broadly maintained their support for international courts and tribunals, including trade related courts, and have voiced their desire for substantial changes in investor-state dispute resolution mechanisms. In both cases, European countries have not tried to dissociate from those courts, but rather, have argued for stronger, clearer and more permanent dispute resolution mechanisms.

Professor André Nollkaemper explores the paradox that exists in the adjudication of shared responsibility in "Unravelling a Paradox of Shared Responsibility: The Disconnection between Substantive and Adjudicate Law." He examines how international courts have applied principles of state responsibility in the context of situations of shared responsibility between multiple parties, and concludes that when this occurs international adjudication becomes less suited as a process for implementing such responsibility.

He points out that international courts rarely apply even well-established principles of state responsibility, such as dual attribution, aid and assistance or direction and control. At the same time, courts have been unable or unwilling to develop principles of shared responsibility that are still controversial, and that reflect different conceptions about what the substantive law of responsibility is or should be, such as joint and several responsibility. Nollkaemper notes that the substantive law of international responsibility is slowly adjusting to its increasingly relational nature, but that the procedures of international adjudication in many respects are not well suited for incorporating this relational nature. There are considerable differences between states, in terms of their willingness to submit themselves to adjudication of shared responsibility claims, even within "the west," as a result of which responsibility will often will be shared between some states, but not all. He poignantly observes that the role of international adjudication in relation to shared responsibility differs widely – both between international courts and between states – in terms of the willingness of states to subject themselves, or make use of, international adjudication. An interesting example is given by the adjudication of claims in relation to extraordinary rendition. Whereas European states, such as Macedonia and Poland, were found responsible by the European Court of Human Rights in relation to their (shared) responsibility, the USA has always resisted attempts to be subjected to adjudication for their leading role in extraordinary rendition. The somewhat paradoxical conclusion is that reconstructing responsibility in a relational sense, based on the fact that when acting together they can achieve things they cannot achieve alone, underpins the development of substantive law of shared responsibility, but at the same time reduces the possibility that it may be resolved through adjudication. He concludes that in cases of concerted action the conduct of one actor often cannot be disconnected from that of other actors, and this may both justify shared responsibility, and may limit the power of international courts to effectively adjudicate shared responsibility claims. The development of the substantive law of responsibility can call for the renewal and change of procedural law. In the end, this connection ultimately rests on the idea that it is a task of procedural law to transmit substantive obligations or rights. In particular, relatively confined cases of shared responsibility in international courts may extend their power beyond individual actors that directly caused harmful effects, and may exercise jurisdiction to co-responsible parties.

In "Divergent Views on the Content and Relevance of the Jus ad Bellum in Europe and the United States? The Case of the US-Led Military Coalition against 'Islamic State'," Tom Ruys and Luca Ferro study the idea that Americans and Europeans hold different views on global security and the role of international laws and institutions in this respect. They start by pointing out that claims of a transatlantic divide on *jus ad bellum* are not new. Generally, it is considered that the EU side demonstrates a stronger adherence to the traditional positivist approach to international law, while US scholars are more open to policy-oriented methodologies. This translates into different views of the actual content of the UN Charter rules on the use of force, for example of the permissibility of self-defense against attacks by non-State actors, calls for new exceptions to the prohibition of the use of force and in relation to controversial issues, such as the legality of the anticipatory self-defense.

Ruys and Ferro offer a critical look at the alleged gap by means of a case-study, notably from the perspective of the recourse to force by the US-led military coalition fighting against the so-called Islamic State (IS) in Iraq and Syria. At first sight, this case would seem to confirm the existence of transatlantic divide pertaining to the *jus ad bellum*, more specifically in relation to the legality of self-defense against attacks by non-State actors and to the validity of the so-called unable and unwilling test. A closer analysis of the intervening States' positions, however, reveals a gradual acceptance of the more expansionist interpretation of the legal framework first put forward by the United States. Ruys and Ferro look at the legal arguments presented by the intervening States between the commencement of Operation Inherent Resolve in September 2014 and mid-2017 with a view to justifying their military operations in Iraqi and Syrian territory. The purpose is not to assess the intrinsic validity of these arguments, but rather to test their divergence or convergence. In the end, the case of the US-led military coalition against IS strikes is one where European States, as well as several other western States, originally steered clear from murky legal grounds only to find themselves ultimately embracing an extensive reading of the right of self-defense, and relying for the first time, whether explicitly or implicitly, on the controversial "unable and unwilling" doctrine to justify military operations abroad. At the end, they infer that though the issue remains open to debate, one cannot ignore the acquiescent attitude of numerous UN Member States, nor the more critical, or outright condemnatory position of several others (such as Russia). Nor can one *a priori* dismiss the suggestion that the Assad regime's own record of war crimes and human rights violations precluded the need for consent from the *de jure* government and turned the coalition against IS into a *sui generis* case, as some have suggested.

These thoughtful and in-depth contributions illuminate different aspects of international law in "the West" and they analyze key concepts that pertain to how international law is seen and develops in a variety of essential fields in Europe and the USA.

Any gathering that has as its theme a divide runs the risk of overstating, or even inventing, any such divide. The contributors to this book shunned this temptation and painted instead a more complex and nuanced picture – one where differences in both legal traditions (e.g., the influence of legal realism in America) and political institutions (e.g., the role of European institutions) are not denied, but where commonalities are also considered and where it is shown that the differences themselves can sometimes evolve in perhaps surprising ways (e.g., the tensions between European and international legal orders leading to a distinctly European version of sovereigntism). Moreover, as questions like immunity show, the boundary demarcating different approaches may not be the Atlantic but, rather, one between common law and civil law or depends on the particular statutory framework that has been adopted.

So whither the West? We would identify three sets of questions as determinative of the direction, or directions, in which the relationship between Western democracies and international law will evolve in coming years and decades.

First, there are questions about the relationship between the domestic order and international plane. Will an accommodation between the revival of self-government as a political ideal and the international order emerge that enables both to flourish? Or will that revival lead to a resurgence of populist and even nationalist sentiments that will fundamentally destabilize international law? How will the tension, if we can call it such, between renewed nationalism and globalisation play out?

Second, the attitude towards international dispute settlement will play a key role in shaping the future. The growth of international dispute settlement in recent decades was nothing short of astonishing. But how will the various tensions that have emerged be resolved? Within the trade regime, but also between the European legal order and international arbitration? Contributions to this book have considered the International Criminal Court (ICC), the dispute settlement mechanism of the World Trade Organization and investment arbitration in detail and, there too, tensions have emerged. Will the West pursue a systematic reform of international dispute settlement aimed at its expansion, as globalists would wish? Or will the West move towards a more selective approach – one where certain mechanisms of dispute settlement are supported, others reformed, and others perhaps abandoned? Is the divide between Europe and the US noted in this book long-lasting? What will the consequences be for the development of dispute settlements regimes?

Third, there are the questions regarding the response of the West to its relative economic and political decline. Will the "new normal" be a return to a more traditional, less ambitious type of international law on the basis that a more integrated and semi-supranational international law would have been viable (if it was) only as long as democracies were on the rise? But would this less ambitious international law, even if it is on the cards, be capable of governing globalization and dealing with climate change, health crises and other global threats?

This book is the first piece of a larger puzzle that we would like to build to understand how international law as an *international* discipline can work and the role it can play in building a better and more just system. Similar studies could focus on other parts of the world and then eventually address differences and commonalities highlighted throughout the different regions.

I

THE IDEA OF INTERNATIONAL LAW IN THE DIVIDED WEST

1

International Lawyers and Legal Forms

Transatlantic Denials

Jean d'Aspremont[*]

Whilst in a constant quest for the sophistication of their craft,[1] international lawyers relish simplistic repetitive narratives. They continuously represent the world that they inhabit as undergoing cataclysmic changes calling for the intervention of international law, itself portrayed as being in a state of crisis and in need of renewal.[2] It is noteworthy that international lawyers' simplistic narratives are not limited to the image they want to project about the world and international law. Their simplistic historical narratives also pertain to the way in which they represent themselves as a group of professionals and the configuration thereof.[3] Indeed, when it comes to representing themselves, international lawyers generally indulge in some Manichaeism of sort as they portray their discipline as fractured along very binary lines: the centre versus the periphery, orthodoxy versus self-reflectivity, reform versus rehabilitation, the critical versus the non-critical, the scholars versus the practitioners, the idealists versus the realists, the autonomists versus the pluralists, the unitarians versus the fragmenters, etc.[4]

---

[*] Professor of Public International Law, University of Manchester; Professor of International Legal Theory, University of Amsterdam; and Director of the Manchester International Law Centre (MILC).

[1] *See* the remarks of Anne Peters, *Realizing Utopia as a Scholarly Endeavour*, 24 Eur. J.J. of Int'l L. 533 (2013).

[2] This is not new. *See* J. d'Aspremont, 'Jenks' Ethic of Responsibility for the Disillusioned International Lawyer', Amsterdam Law School Research Paper No 2016–63, (October 28, 2016). *See generally* David Kennedy, *When Renewal Repeats: Thinking Against the Box*, 32 N.Y. U. J. Int'l L. & Pol. 335 (2000).

[3] Several models have been resorted to in order to conceptualise the community which international lawyers may compose: community of practice, epistemic community, interpretative community. For a review of the use of these various models *see* J. d'Aspremont, *The Professionalization of International Law, in* INTERNATIONAL LAW AS A PROFESSION 19 (Jean d'Aspremont et al., 2017).

[4] It is not without paradox that these binary narratives of self-representation seem to have been exacerbated by three decades of critical thinking.

This chapter grapples with one of these mundane self-representations, namely the narrative that pits formalists against non-formalists and that locates the dividing line between them somewhere in the Atlantic Ocean. It particularly seeks to challenge the common assumption among international lawyers according to which Europeans are more wedded to formalism than their American counterparts who, as the story goes, have successfully emancipated themselves from the straitjackets of legal forms.[5] The following sections thus take issue with this common self-representation whereby the Europeans are the (naive) believers in formalism and the Americans the (realistic) deniers of formalism. Such a narrative, it is argued here, does not do justice to the subtle and complex role ascribed to legal forms on each side of the Atlantic. This chapter accordingly sheds light on the two deceptive dimensions of this common narrative about formalism with the aim of showing that both Europeans and Americans continue to demonstrate attachment to legal forms, the only significant differences between them lying in the way in which they seek to reinvent formalism and the role of legal forms. This chapter ultimately makes the point that both American and European international lawyers live in denial of their continuous engagement with legal forms.

After a few general considerations on what is meant by legal forms, formalism and formal modes of legal reasoning and their origins, in Section 1.1 this chapter discusses the two sides of the narrative whereby Europeans are held to be formalists and American non-formalists. It starts with the European dimension of the story, which it calls 'the East Atlantic tale' (Section 1.2). It continues with the American side of the narrative, which it calls 'the West Atlantic tale' (Section 1.3). This chapter ends with a few observations on the denial of international lawyers as to the entrenchment of formalism in their argumentative practice and thought, a notion which they have nowadays elevated into a 'villain' of international legal thought (Section 1.4).

---

[5] *See generally* the remarks of Guglielmo Verdirame, '*The Divided West':International Lawyers in Europe and America*, 18 Euro. J. of Int'l L. 553 (2007). For a comprehensive account of all the facets of this narrative and with an emphasis on French legal scholarship, *see* Emmanuelle Jouannet, *French and American Perspectives on International Law*, 58 Me. L. Rev. 291 (2006) 11 ('Of course in France, too, the formalist, positivist view can be criticized or presented in a more nuanced form, but it still seems to me to be the dominant model for conceptualizing international law'). *See also* Serge Sur, *Impérialism et droit international en Europe et en Amérique*, in LE DROIT INTERNATIONAL ET L'IMPÉRIALISME EN EUROPE ET AUX ÉTATS-UNIS (H. Ruiz Fabri & E. Jounn eds., 2006). For an emphatic criticism of instrumentalism, *see* Martti Koskenniemi, *What Is International Law For?*, in INTERNATIONAL LAW 89 (Malcolm D. Evans ed., 2003); Richard H. Pildes, *Conflicts between American and European Views of Law: The Dark Side of Legalism*, 44 Va. J. Int'l L. 145, 148 (2003) (focusing on the resort to law and institution).

Three preliminary caveats are warranted at this stage. First, there is inevitably a great deal of oversimplification inherent in speaking of an 'American tradition' or a 'European tradition'. It is conspicuous that each of them comprises a myriad of variants and that their borders are porously defined. Such oversimplification is, however, a prerequisite for any comparative exercise, as the one attempted here.[6] Second, the following observations do not seek to pass any judgement as to the possible superiority of formal or non-formal modes of reasoning. There is no meta-theoretical perspective according to which one would be better than the other.[7] These are two different modes to create authoritative legal arguments without one having a priori ascendency on the other, other than different costs.[8] The third caveat warranted at this stage is meant to situate the argument. The remarks that followed are very much informed – and prejudiced – by a specific European understanding of the American tradition of international law. Even the very idea of an American 'tradition' of international law can possibly denote a very European take on how international law is thought and practised on the other side of the Atlantic.[9] Yet, I believe that such distortion can enrich – rather than invalidate – the following discussion by refreshing some common self-representations at work in American academia.

1.1 THE TERMS OF THE NARRATIVE: LEGAL FORMS, FORMALISM AND FORMAL MODES OF LEGAL REASONING

Formalism in legal thought is understood broadly here. It refers to the conferral of a constraining role to legal forms, that is to pre-agreed formal signals. So understood, formalism in legal thought is certainly not a contemporary creation.[10] By some accounts, it dates back to the

---

[6] For a similar caveat, *see* G. Verdirame, *'The Divided West': International Lawyers in Europe and America*, 18 Eur. J. of Int'l L. 553, 555 (2007).

[7] M. Koskenniemi, *Letter to the Editors of the Symposium*, 93 Am. J. Int'l. L. 351 (1999).

[8] Of course formal and non-formal modes of reasoning come with different costs. The former often provide false determinacy whilst the latter tend to impede the possibility to distinguish law and non-law and undermine the autonomy of legal reasoning. In that sense, the only weighing possible between formal modes of legal reasoning and non-formal modes of legal reasoning is limited to their costs in terms of false determinacy and autonomy of law. This is an evaluation I have attempted to do elsewhere. *See* J. d'Aspremont, FORMALISM AND THE SOURCES OF INTERNATIONAL LAW (2011), esp. chapter 2 and chapter 5. *See also* J. d'Aspremont. *The Politics of Deformalization in International Law*, 3 Goettingen J. of Int'l L. 503 (2011).

[9] *See however* Mark Janis, THE AMERICAN TRADITION OF INTERNATIONAL LAW. GREAT EXPECTATIONS 1789–1914 (2004).

[10] On the various understandings of Formalism, *see* J. d'Aspremont, FORMALISM AND THE SOURCES OF INTERNATIONAL LAW (2011), esp. chapter 1.

Scholastic school.[11] Yet, it is with the Enlightenment and the reinvention of international law along the lines of the liberal doctrine of politics that legal forms acquired the centrality that is attributed to them in international legal thought and practice – and which is contested in some parts of the world. Such liberalism is grounded in the idea that political freedom can only be preserved by a social order that does not pre-exist and must accordingly be projected and legitimised.[12] This liberal paradigm has important implications on both how law and modes of legal reasoning are understood, as well as the role of legal forms. Indeed, when applied to law, liberalism aims at reducing law to a 'legal-technical instead of ethico-political matter'[13] whereby rules are formal as well as objectively and content-independently[14] ascertained by virtue of legal forms, that is, some carefully designed and pre-agreed formal signals. From this liberal perspective – which has been called liberal legalism[15] or, more simply legalism[16] – such

---

[11] By advocating a bipartite classification of law, based on the distinction between natural and positive law, Aquinas – who coined the term 'positive law' – and later Hugo Grotius – who allegedly excised theology from the *jus gentium* of Vitoria and Gentili by construing international law by reference to both its source and its content, although they still abided by a substantive conception of validity, also resorted to a pedigree test to identify law. On this point, *see* J. Finnis, *The Truth in Legal Positivism*, in THE AUTONOMY OF LAW: ESSAYS OF LEGAL POSITIVISM 195, 199 (R. P. George ed., 1996); *see also* J. Finnis, *On the Incoherence of Legal Positivism*, in A COMPANION TO PHILOSOPHY OF LAW AND LEGAL THEORY 134, 136–9 (D. Patterson ed., 1999); *see also* A. D'Amato, *What 'Counts' as Law?*, in LAW-MAKING IN THE GLOBAL COMMUNITY 83, at 88 (N. G. Onuf ed., 1982); B. Bix, *Natural Law Theory*, in A COMPANION TO PHILOSOPHY OF LAW AND LEGAL THEORY 233–40 (D. Patterson ed., 1999).

[12] On the possibility to distinguish between two dimensions of liberalism, *see* Chantal Mouffe, THE RETURN OF THE POLITICAL 123–4 (1993) (drawing on Hans Blumenberg, THE LEGITIMACY OF THE MODERN AGE).

[13] M. Koskenniemi, FROM APOLOGY TO UTOPIA – THE STRUCTURE OF INTERNATIONAL LEGAL ARGUMENT 82 (2006).

[14] It is content-independent because ascertainment is generated in a way that does not hinge on the substance of the institution whose membership to the legal order is tested. On the notion of content-independence, *see* Noam Gur, *Are Legal Rules Content-Independent Reasons?* 5 Problema – Anuario de Filosofia y Teoria del Derecho 275 (2001). For some classical discussion, *see* H. L. Hart, ESSAYS ON BENTHAM 243–68 (1982) and J. Raz, THE MORALITY OF FREEDOM 35–7 (1986). *See also* Fabio P. Schecaira, LEGAL SCHOLARSHIP AS A SOURCE 26–7 (2013).

[15] F. Hoffman, *International Legalism and International Politics*, in THE OXFORD HANDBOOK OF THE THEORY OF INTERNATIONAL LAW 954–84, 961 (A. Orford & F. Hoffmann eds., 2016). For a different use of liberalism in international legal thought by reference to a certain configuration of the international society as a collection of liberal democracies, *see* D. Joyce, *Liberal Internationalism*, in THE OXFORD HANDBOOK OF THE THEORY OF INTERNATIONAL LAW 471–87 (A. Orford & F. Hoffmann eds., 2016).

[16] J. N. Shklar, LEGALISM, LAW, MORALS, AND POLITICAL TRIALS viii, 1–28 (1964).

legal forms are instrumental in ensuring that law does not collapse into a programme of governance and successfully displace politics.[17]

Unsurprisingly, this reduction of law to a legal-technical matter distinct from politics and morality by virtue of legal forms made its way into international legal thought,[18] both in the United States and in Europe.[19] Such transposition to international law was made possible, for instance by virtue of an analogy between the State and the individual of the liberal doctrine of politics.[20] This move gave rise to what has been called classical international legal thought.[21] The rise of modern international law in the nineteenth and twentieth century that accompanied the professionalisation of the discipline[22] perpetuated the liberal structure of legal thought mentioned above[23] and the

---

[17] R. M. Unger, KNOWLEDGE AND POLITICS 76–81 (1975); M. Koskenniemi, FROM APOLOGY TO UTOPIA – THE STRUCTURE OF INTERNATIONAL LEGAL ARGUMENT 71 (2006); M. Koskenniemi, *The Politics of International Law,* 1 Eur. J. Int'l L. 4, 4–5 (1990). T. O'Hagan, THE END OF LAW? 183 (1984); Paul W. Kahn, THE CULTURAL STUDY OF LAW. RECONSTRUCTING LEGAL SCHOLARSHIP 16–18 (1999; Judith N. Shklar, LEGALISM – LAW MORALS, AND POLITICAL TRIALS 8–9 and 16–23 (1986); Olivier Corten, LE DISCOURS DU DROIT INTERNATIONAL. POUR UN POSITIVISME CRITIQUE 45–67 (2009).

[18] On the distinction between primitive international legal thought, classical international legal thought, and modern international legal thought, *see* David Kennedy, *Primitive Legal Scholarship,* 27 Harv. Int'l L. J. 1 (1986). On the transposition of the liberal paradigm to international law, *see also* the remarks of Judith N. Shklar, LEGALISM – LAW MORALS, AND POLITICAL TRIALS 123–43 (1986).

[19] On the idea that both sides of the Atlantic espouse the view of international law as distinct from power, which is inherited from the Enlightenment, *see* Martti Koskenniemi, *International Law and Hegemony: A Reconfiguration,* 17 Cambridge Rev. of Int'l Affairs 197 (2004).

[20] After Hobbes and Spinoza paved the way for a human analogy, Pufendorf ascribed an intellect to the state and created anthropomorphic vocabularies and images about the main institution of international law, i.e., the state. Such anthropomorphism was later taken over by Vattel – not without adjustment – and subsequently translated itself in the classical positivist doctrine of fundamental rights of states which contributed to the consolidation of modern international law in the nineteenth century. On this point, *see* Michael Nutkiewicz, Samuel Pufendorf, *Obligation as the Basis of the State,* 21 J. of the Hist. of Phil. 15 (1983); Fiammetta Palladini, *Pufendorf Disciple of Hobbes: The Nature of Man and the State of Nature: The Doctrine of socialitas,* 34 History of Eur. Ideas 26 (2008). For a criticism of the analogy, *see* Edwin De Witt Dickinson, *The Analogy Between Natural Persons and International Persons in the Law of Nations,* 26 Yale L.J. 564 (1917). See the discussion of this analogy in J. d'Aspremont, *The Doctrine of Fundamental Rights of States and Anthropomorphic Thinking in International Law,* 4 Cambridge J. of Int'l and Comparative L. (2015) (Forthcoming) or T. Carty, THE DECAY OF INTERNATIONAL LAW 44–6 (1986).

[21] M. Koskenniemi, FROM APOLOGY TO UTOPIA – THE STRUCTURE OF INTERNATIONAL LEGAL ARGUMENT 106 (2006).

[22] *See* J. d'Aspremont, *The Professionalization of International Law, in* INTERNATIONAL LAW AS A PROFESSION 19 (J. d'Aspremont et al. eds., 2017).

[23] D. Kennedy, *The Disciplines of International Law and Policy,* 12 Leiden J. of Int'l L. 9 (1999); D. Kennedy, *Tom Franck and the Manhattan School,* 35 N.Y.U. J Int'l L. & Pol. 397–435 (2003); M. Koskenniemi, FROM APOLOGY TO UTOPIA – THE STRUCTURE OF

instrumentality of formalism in the project of a displacement of politics by international law.[24] With modern international law, one witnessed a growing sophistication of the resort to legal forms and their constraining effects on the generation of authority and bindingness by virtue of the development of systematised sets of modes of legal arguments packaged into a few fundamental formal doctrines, like sources or responsibility. This sophistication of the resort to legal forms since the rise of modern international law calls for a few observations with a view to sketching out the two main approaches to formalism in contemporary international legal thought and practice.

Since the inception of modern international law, formalism can generically be understood as the acknowledgement of the constraining role of legal forms – that is, some pre-agreed formal signals – in legal argumentation, and their correlative contribution to the generation of pervasive authority (or bindingness) of legal arguments. In this generic sense, formalism is thus intrinsically associated with two inseparable ideas: constraint and authority. Indeed it is the constraining effect of legal forms on decisional opportunities that allows the production of authority (or bindingness), for legal forms curtail substantively (or morally) motivated and content-dependent decision-making processes.[25]

Needless to say, such an elementary and generic understanding of formalism accommodates numerous variants.[26] Most of them pertain to the constraining role of legal forms in the determination of the *content* of rules in authoritative decision-making processes.[27] This means that

INTERNATIONAL LEGAL ARGUMENT 158 (2006); M. Koskenniemi, *The Politics of International Law*, 1 Eur. J. of Int'l Law 4, 5–7 (1990). E. Jouannet, *A Critical Introduction, in* M. Koskenniemi, THE POLITICS OF INTERNATIONAL LAW 15 (2011); Olivier Corten, LE DISCOURS DU DROIT INTERNATIONAL. POUR UN POSITIVISME CRITIQUE 45–67 (2009).

[24] For Jochen von Bernstorff, the idea of 'more international law is more progress' culminated in the late nineteenth century and beginning of the twentieth century. *See* J. von Bernstorff, *International Legal Scholarship as a Cooling Medium in International Law and Politics*, 25 Eur. J. of Int'l L. 977 (2014), esp. 984–6.

[25] For some various associations between formalism and the idea of constraint, *see* F. Schauer, THINKING AS A LAWYER (2009), at 30. *See also* the variants of formalism discussed (and critiqued) by R. Unger, *The Critical Legal Studies Movement*, 96 Harv. L. Rev. 561, 563–76 (1983).

[26] On the many 'manifestations' of formalism pervading the phenomenon of law, *see* Frederick Schauer, *Formalism*, 97 Yale L. J 509, 510 (1988). *See also* the taxonomy offered by Duncan Kennedy, *Legal Formalism*, ENCYCLOPAEDIA OF THE SOCIAL & BEHAVIORAL SCIENCES, vol. 13, 634 (2001). *See also* the forms of formalism discussed by Richard Pildes, *Forms of Formalism*, 66 U. Chi. L. Rev. 607 (1999); *see also* R. Summers, *How Law Is Formal and Why It Matters*, 82 Cornell Int'l L.J. 1165 (1997), esp. 1180–1.

[27] On this association, *see* D. Patterson, LAW AND TRUTH (1996), at 26. *See also* the remarks of O. Corten, MÉTHODOLOGIE DU DROIT INTERNATIONAL PUBLIC (2009) at 57 et seq.

formalism is most commonly associated with constraining the scope of law appliers when they extract the content of a rule which they apply to the specific set of facts falling within their jurisdiction. In that sense, formalism is most commonly construed as conveying a hermeneutic theory about content-determination that is content-independent.[28] This is what is called *content-determination formalism*.

The most extreme version of content-determination formalism proposes to infer the constraint of legal forms from some sort of immanent rationality according to which law comes with internal intelligibility. It is premised on the idea that the content of rules can sustain itself from within in a non-instrumental way.[29] This radical version of formalism presupposes meaning-based gaplessness.[30] Such an extreme type of content-determination formalism proved one of the main targets of rule-scepticism and legal realism,[31] which construe law-application as totally indeterminate and equate law with law-application.[32] This type of formalism is sometimes called 'old formalism'.[33] The rationale of such formalism usually is found in the predictability supposedly provided by legal forms to the behaviour of

---

[28] It must be acknowledged that the notion of content-independency is most of the time discussed in connection with authority of law. *See* F. Schauer, THINKING AS A LAWYER (2009), at 62. *See also* F Schauer, *The Questions of Authority*, 81 Ga. L. Rev. 95 (1992).

[29] E. J. Weinrib, *On the Immanent Rationality of Law*, 97 Yale L. J. 949 (1988) (who argues that formalism postulates a non-instrumental and internal intelligibility of law). For a specific criticism of Weinrib's approach for trying to transpose his well-known tort theory into a full-blown theory of law, *see* S. Perry, *Professor Weinrib Formalism: The Not-So-Empty Sepulchre*, 16 Harv. J.L. & Pub. Pol'y 597 (1993).

[30] On the notion of meaning-based gaplessness, *see* Duncan Kennedy, *Legal Formalism, in* ENCY. OF THE SOCIAL & BEHAVIORAL SCIENCES, 86,35 (Vol. 13, 2001). On the completeness presupposed by formalism, *see* Richard Pildes, *Forms of Formalism*, 66 U. Chi. L. Rev. 607, 608 (1999). *See also* D. Patterson, LAW AND TRUTH 22 (1996).

[31] It is important to note that rule-skepticism is a much broader phenomenon than the move away from legal forms. For an understanding of rule-skepticism as a rebellion against the conception of law as a system of rules, *see* G. Verdirame, *The Divided West*, 18 Eur. J. of Int'l L. 553, 564–7 (2007) (also arguing that rule-skepticism in American international legal scholarship is also a rather recent phenomenon). *See* the famous plea against the American variant of rule-skepticism by Herbert Hart, *American Jurisprudence Through English Eyes: The Nightmare and the Noble Dream*, 11 Ga. L. Rev. 969 (1977).

[32] Such a binary understanding of formalism is found in the *Concept of Law*. Hart construes formalism and rule-scepticism as the 'Scylla and Charybdis of justice theory' and rejects both of them. *See* THE CONCEPT OF LAW 124–54 (2nd ed., 1997). *See also* the remarks of Judge Ad Hoc Sur in his separate opinion appended to the Order of 28 May 2009 in ICJ, Questions relating to the Obligation to Prosecute or Extradite (Belgium v. Senegal), Rec. 2009, available at www.icj-cij.org.

[33] G. Postema, LEGAL PHILOSOPHY IN THE TWENTIETH CENTURY: THE COMMON LAW WORLD 389 (2001).

law-applying authorities and the enhanced legitimacy of their decisions.[34] The idea of internal intelligibility – which is said to require an internal point of view[35] – has sometimes been nuanced as to accommodate zones of penumbra where discretion is unconstrained.[36] Some more subtle understandings of content-determination formalism locates the constraining role of legal forms, not in an idealist or immanent rationality, but in linguistic limitations on the power of a law applier,[37] meant to create a-contextual rigidity in legal argumentation.[38] In that sense, formalism is very much associated with legal reasoning deploying itself content-independently.[39] Such understandings have sometimes been called 'neo-formalist'.[40]

It must be made clear that the abovementioned variants of formalism are not only variants of hermeneutic theories of content-determination. Formalism has also been located in the ascertaining role of legal forms in processes whereby legal rules are identified as legal rules in a content-independent way.[41] This is the other main dimension of formalism in international legal thought and practice. In this other sense, formalism is associated with law-identification processes and principally with the doctrine of sources. This type of formalism has also been occasionally dubbed 'neo-formalism'.[42] It is what is called here *law-ascertainment formalism*.

It is against the backdrop of these various understandings of formalism that the discussion continues by questioning the common narrative according to which European international lawyers have perpetuated the centrality of

---

[34] *See* E. J. Weinrib, *Legal Formalism: On the Immanent Rationality of Law*, 97 Yale L.J. 949 1988); S. V. Scott, *International Law as Ideology: Theorizing the Relationship between International Law and International Politics*, 5 E.J.I.L. 313 (1994), esp. 322. *See also* the remarks of M. Koskenniemi, *What Is International Law For?*, in INTERNATIONAL LAW, 57, at 69 (M. Evans ed., 2nd ed., 2006).

[35] E. J. Weinrib, *On the Immanent Rationality of Law*, 97 Yale L.J. 949, 952 (1988).

[36] *See e.g.* Hart or Kelsen.

[37] F. Schauer, *Formalism*, 97 Yale L.J. 509 (1988).

[38] F. Schauer, *Formalism*, 97 Yale L.J. 509, 535 (1988).

[39] Some of the proponents of such forms of formalism are well aware that legal forms serve as conscious barrier to 'optimally sensitive decision-making' and condemns law-application to 'mediocrity' by 'mandating the inaccessibility of excellence'. For them, formalism is only a descriptive category, for it is undisputed that law-application would be made if the law applier was not constrained by legal forms. *See* F. Schauer, THINKING AS A LAWYER (2009), at 31; F. Schauer, *Formalism*, 97 Yale L.J. 509, 539 (1988).

[40] G. Postema, LEGAL PHILOSOPHY IN THE TWENTIETH CENTURY: THE COMMON LAW WORLD 389 (2001).

[41] J. d'Aspremont, FORMALISM AND THE SOURCES OF INTERNATIONAL LAW (2011).

[42] Sahib Singh, *International Law as a Technical Discipline: Critical Perspectives on the Narrative Structure of a Theory* (May 26, 2013), Appendix 2 in J. d'Aspremont, FORMALISM AND THE SOURCES OF INTERNATIONAL LAW 236 (2013).

formalism inherited from the liberal doctrine of politics, in contrast to American international lawyers who have developed an anti-formalist attitude towards international law.

1.2 THE EAST ATLANTIC TALE: THE EUROPEAN REVERENCE OF LEGAL FORMS

One facet of the common narrative under discussion here posits that European international lawyers revere formalism and many of its variants. According to this image, European international lawyers are represented as perpetuating the centrality of legal forms.[43] Certainly, this side of the narrative is not entirely groundless. Europeans bespeak a stronger attachment to formalistic modes of reasoning. Indeed, it seems conspicuous that Europeans – for good or bad reasons – make formal sources a linchpin of law-ascertainment,[44] formal techniques of interpretation a key in content-determination[45] and formal responsibility a kingpin of the apportionment of liability in international law.[46] Europeans are similarly and correspondingly known for their aversion to deformalisation. For them, deformalisation should be feared for threatening the very existence of law,[47] for allowing 'the increasing management of the world's affairs by flexible and informal, non-territorial networks within which decisions can be made rapidly and effectively'[48] as well as for the related 'process whereby the law retreat solely to the provision of procedures or broadly formulated directives by experts and decision-makers for the purpose of administering international problems by means of functionally effective solutions and "balancing

---

[43] This often manifests itself in the image – very common in the United States, that Europeans are 'imprisoned in an inveterate and somewhat dull positivism'. *See* G. Verdirame, *'The Divided West': International Lawyers in Europe and America*, 18 Eur. J. Int'l L. 553, 554 (2007).

[44] J. d'Aspremont, *The European Tradition of the Sources of International Law, in* UNITY AND DIVERSITY OF INTERNATIONAL LAW, ESSAYS IN HONOUR OF PROFESSOR PIERRE-MARIE DUPUY (Denis Alland, Vincent Chetail, Olivier de Frouville & Jorge E. Viñuales eds., 2014).

[45] *See* the works cited by M. Waibel, *Demystifying the Art of Interpretation*, 22 Eur. J. Int'l L. 571 (2011). *See also* the works cited by Andrea Bianchi, *The Game of Interpretation in International Law, in* INTERPRETATION IN INTERNATIONAL LAW (A. Bianchi, D. Peat & M. Windsor eds., 2014).

[46] *See* the remarks of A. Nollkaemper, *Power and Responsibility, in* A. Di Stefano, UN DIRITTO SENZA TERRA? FUNZIONI E LIMITI DEL PRINCIPIO DI TERRITORIALITÀ NEL DIRITTO INTERNAZIONALE E DELL'UNIONE EUROPEA (2015).

[47] J. Crawford. *International Law as a Discipline and Profession*, 106 Proceedings of the Am. Society of Int'l L. 471, 486 (2012).

[48] M. Koskenniemi, *Global Governance and Public International Law*, 37 Kritische Justiz, 241, 243 (2004).

interests"'.[49] In the same vein, it seems that for Europeans the move away from formalism brings about a dangerous loss of accountability[50] while also frustrating the distinction between law and non-law.[51]

Whilst the attachment to legal forms by European international lawyers cannot be entirely denied, especially when it comes to uphold the autonomy of international law, this narrative fails to account for the complexity of European engagement with legal forms. Indeed, it seems that Europeans have been critical of the cost of formalism and have continuously sought to recalibrate the role of legal forms. It is no coincidence in this respect that Europe has been the cradle of several intellectual projects calling for a rejuvenation of formalism and what we do with legal forms. The best example of this is probably found in Martti Koskenniemi's plea for a 'culture of formalism'[52] – a reinvention of formalism which he has however never fully developed.[53] Several other endeavours to reinvent formalism with some self-declared self-reflexivity have been witnessed.[54] Among them, international

[49] M. Koskenniemi, *Constitutionalism as Mindset: Reflections on Kantian Themes About International Law and Globalization* 8 Theoretical Inquiries of Law 9, 13 (2007). NB. The characterisation of Koskenniemi's concept of deformalisation, as well as the quotes by Koskenniemi, are derived from J. G. Van Mulligen, *Global Constitutionalism and the Objective Purport of the International Legal Order* 24(02) Leiden J. Int'l L. 277, 287 (2011).

[50] Jan Klabbers, *Institutional Ambivalence by Design: Soft Organizations in International Law* 70 (3) Nordic J. of International Law 403, 420 (2001).

[51] J. d'Aspremont, FORMALISM AND THE SOURCES OF INTERNATIONAL LAW: A THEORY OF THE ASCERTAINMENT OF LEGAL RULES (2011); J. d'Aspremont. *The Politics of Deformalization in International Law*, 3 Goettingen J. Int'l L. 503 (2011).

[52] *See* the famous plea of M. Koskenniemi for a culture of formalism. *See* M. Koskenniemi, THE GENTLE CIVILIZER OF NATIONS: THE RISE AND FALL OF INTERNATIONAL LAW 1870–1960, 502 (2002). M. Koskenniemi, *What Is International Law For?*, in INTERNATIONAL LAW 57, 69–70 (M. Evans ed., 2nd ed., 2006). *See also* M. Koskenniemi, Carl Schmitt, *Hans Morgenthau and the Image of Law in International Relations*, in THE ROLE OF LAW IN INTERNATIONAL POLITICS: ESSAYS IN INTERNATIONAL RELATIONS AND INTERNATIONAL LAW 17, 32–3 (M. Byers ed., 2000). It is well-known that the notion has proved semantically instable and has generated a lot of diverging interpretations. Among others, *see* E. Jouannet, *Présentation critique*, in LA POLITIQUE DU DROIT INTERNATIONAL 32–3 (M. Koskenniemi ed., 2007). *See also* Ignacio de la Rasilla del Moral, *Martti Koskenniemi and the Spirit of the Beehive in International Law*, 10 Global Jurist (2010); J. von Bernstorff, *Sisyphus Was an International Lawyer. On Martti Koskenniemi's, "From Apologia to Utopia" and the Place of Law in International Politics*, 7 Ger. L.J. 1015, 1029–31 (2006); J. A. Beckett, *Rebel Without a Cause, Martti Koskenniemi and the Critical Legal Project*, 7 Ger. L. Rev. 1045 (2006); *See also* the book review of Martti Koskenniemi, THE GENTLE CIVILIZER OF NATIONS: THE RISE AND FALL OF INTERNATIONAL LAW 1870–1960 by Nicholas Tsagourias, 16 Leiden J. International Int'l L. 397, 398–9 (2003).

[53] For a recent re-evaluation of the work of Martti Koskenniemi, *see* J. d'Aspremont, *Martti Koskenniemi, the Mainstream, and Self-Reflectivity*, 29 Leiden J. Int'l L. 625 (2016).

[54] For another attempt, *see* J. d'Aspremont, FORMALISM AND THE SOURCES OF INTERNATIONAL LAW (2011).

constitutionalism – which primarily finds its roots in European legal thought – stands out and can be construed as an attempt to rethink the role of legal forms.[55] In fact, international constitutionalism denotes a dramatic ambiguity towards legal forms, thereby showing that the European engagement with legal forms is much more subtle than the image conveyed by the common narrative discussed here. The following paragraphs focus on international constitutionalism to shed light on the complexity – and the paradoxes – of the European attachment to legal forms.

It is submitted here that the European project of international constitutionalism is riven by a foundational tension, namely the need to preserve some minimal formalism in constitutionalist patterns of argument, structures of thought or conceptual frameworks while simultaneously keeping legal forms at bay in order to realise the normative agenda of international constitutionalism.[56]

On the one hand, constitutionalist scholars continue to adhere to a more or less formal understanding of the sources of international law and the law-ascertainment mechanisms that come with it.[57] Indeed, constitutionalist scholars continue to uphold formal mechanisms of law-identification to preserve the possibility of a distinction between law and non-law which they see as being as indispensable for the authority of law, the viability of the legal system as well as the rule of law without which their agenda could not be realized.[58] The indispensable role of legal forms also explains why constitutionalists loath the 'deformalisation' of international law,[59] including the

---

[55] On this aspect of constitutionalism, see generally J. d'Aspremont, *International Legal Constitutionalism, Legal Forms, and the Need for Villains*, in HANDBOOK ON GLOBAL CONSTITUTIONALISM (A. Lang & A. Weiner eds., 2017).

[56] Such tensions are sometimes acknowledged by international constitutionalists themselves. See B. Fassbender, *The Meaning of International Constitutional Law*, in TRANSNATIONAL CONSTITUTIONALISM: INTERNATIONAL AND EUROPEAN PERSPECTIVES 307, 320 (N. Tsagourias ed., 2007).

[57] In the same sense, see W. Werner, *The Never-ending Closure: Constitutionalism and International Law*, in TRANSNATIONAL CONSTITUTIONALISM: INTERNATIONAL AND EUROPEAN PERSPECTIVES 329, 330 (N. Tsagourias ed., 2007). For J. Klabbers, much of the debate on constitutionalism in international law can be seen as a debate on sources in disguise. See J. Klabbers, *Constitutionalism and the Making of International Law*, 5 NoFo 84, 88 (2008). See also the remarks of S. R. Ratner, *From Enlightened Positivism to Cosmopolitan Justice: Obstacles and Opportunities*, in FROM BILATERALISM TO COMMUNITY INTEREST: ESSAYS IN HONOUR OF JUDGE BRUNO SIMMA 2 (2011).

[58] C. Tomuschat, *General Course on Public International law*, 281 Collected Courses 9–438, 26 (1999).

[59] A. Peters, *The Merits of Global Constitutionalism*, 16 Ind. J. Global Legal Stud. 397, at 409 (2009). On the notion of deformalisation and its various manifestations, see J. d'Aspremont, *The Politics of Deformalization in International Law* (October 12, 2011), Goettingen J. of Int'l L. 503 (Vol. 3, No. 2 2011).

'softening' of international law.[60] For constitutionalists, legal forms are supposed to bring about legitimacy[61] and credibility[62] to those patterns of argument, structures of thought or conceptual frameworks promoted by constitutionalist thinking. Legal forms are also meant to endow constitutionalist lexicon with some sort of constraining power[63], for, short of legal forms, states' autonomy would be left intact.[64] Without formalism, international constitutionalism 'remains ultimately incoherent and, what is worse, runs the risk of becoming a fig leaf for hegemonic exercises of power cross-dressed in a mantle of universal values'.[65]

On the other hand – and showing the intricacy of European engagement with legal forms – constitutionalists simultaneously denote strong inclination to depart from such formal constrains when necessary to realise their normative agenda. Indeed, constitutionalist patterns of argument, structures of thought or conceptual frameworks are frequently non-formalistic and purely content-dependent.[66] Although the traditional kinship between formalism and voluntarism, as well as state-centrism, is far from being self-evident,[67] constitutionalist thinkers deem a departure from legal forms to play down the allegedly dominant state-centrism in international law or seek to undo the role of consent in constitutionalist patterns of argument, structures of thought and conceptual frameworks.[68] This move away from legal forms in international

---

[60] A. Peters, *Compensatory Constitutionalism: The Function and Potential of Fundamental International Norms and Structures*, 19 Leiden J. Int'l L. 579, 603 (2006).

[61] A. Peters, *The Merits of Global Constitutionalism*, 16 Ind. J. Global Legal Stud. 397, at 409 (2009).

[62] *See e.g.* C. Tomuschat, *International Law: Ensuring the Survival of Mankind on the Eve of a New Century: General Course on Public International Law*, 281 Collected Course 26 (1999). *See* the remarks J. Klabbers, *International Legal Positivism and Constitutionalism, in* INTERNATIONAL LEGAL POSITIVISM IN A POSTMODERN WORLD 264, 285 (J. Kammerhofer and J. d'Aspremont eds., 2014).

[63] C. Schwöbel, *The Appeal of the Project of Global Constitutionalism to Public International Lawyers*, 13 Ger. Law J 1, at 8 (2012).

[64] A. Peters, *Compensatory Constitutionalism: The Function and Potential of Fundamental International Norms and Structures*, 19 Leiden J. Int'l L. 579, 603 (2006).

[65] J. Klabbers, *International Legal Positivism and Constitutionalism, in* INTERNATIONAL LEGAL POSITIVISM IN A POSTMODERN WORLD 264, 290 (J. Kammerhofer and J. d'Aspremont eds., 2014).

[66] A. Peters, *The Merits of Global Constitutionalism*, 16 Ind. J. Global Legal Stud. 397, at 406 (2009).

[67] *See* the remarks of J. d'Aspremont and J. Kammerhofer, *The Future of International Legal Positivism, in* INTERNATIONAL LEGAL POSITIVISM IN A POSTMODERN WORLD 1 (J. d'Aspremont and J. Kammerhofer eds., 2014).

[68] *See e.g.* C. Walter, *International Law in a Process of Constitutionalization, in* NEW PERSPECTIVES ON THE DIVIDE BETWEEN NATIONAL AND INTERNATIONAL LAW 191 (Nollkaemper and J. E. Nijman eds., 2007).

constitutionalism is certainly not surprising. It is not difficult to see the extent to which the attachment to legal forms can simultaneously lay down lethal constraints to the project of international constitutionalism. Indeed, in the eyes of constitutionalists, legal forms can, at times, dangerously frustrate the agenda of international constitutionalism, and especially the substantive unity, the demotion of consent and what they call the legal control of politics.[69] A move away from legal forms is also necessary to allow international constitutionalism to swallow the 'transnational' and 'informal'[70] – which could not be apprehended through legal forms – and subject them to its constitutional structures and its global values.[71]

With a focus on international constitutionalism, the foregoing demonstrates the fundamental ambivalence that permeates international constitutionalism when it comes to the role of legal forms and, more generally, the complexity of European international lawyers' engagement with formalism.[72] This helps faults the narrative whereby Europeans are portrayed as unqualified formalists. The following section turns the attention to the other side of the story, namely the image of an American international legal scholarship as being dominantly anti-formalist.

1.3 THE WEST ATLANTIC TALE: THE AMERICAN REBELLION AGAINST FORMALISM

According to this side of the narrative, formalism – especially the role of legal forms in hermeneutics theories[73] – has long been discredited in American legal thought. The story teaches us that, after a passionate honeymoon,[74]

---

[69] See e.g. B. Fassbender, *The Meaning of International Constitutional Law, in* TRANSNATIONAL CONSTITUTIONALISM: INTERNATIONAL AND EUROPEAN PERSPECTIVES 307, 320 (N. Tsagourias ed., 2007). J. Klabbers, *International Legal Positivism and Constitutionalism, in* INTERNATIONAL LEGAL POSITIVISM IN A POSTMODERN WORLD 264, 285 (J. Kammerhofer and J. d'Aspremont eds., 2014).

[70] Erika de Wet, *The Constitutionalisation of Public International Law, in* THE OXFORD HANDBOOK OF COMPARATIVE CONSTITUTIONAL LAW 1209, 1222 (Michel Rosenfeld and Andras Sajo eds., 2012).

[71] It is interesting to note that the exact same move is witnessed in Global Administrative Law. J. d'Aspremont, *Droit Administratif Global et Droit International (Global Administrative Law and International Law), in* LE DROIT ADMINISTRATIF GLOBAL (C. Bories ed., 2012.).

[72] Klabbers prefers to speak of a 'dilemma'. *See* J. Klabbers, *International Legal Positivism and Constitutionalism, in* INTERNATIONAL LEGAL POSITIVISM IN A POSTMODERN WORLD 262, 285 (J. Kammerhofer and J. d'Aspremont eds., 2014).

[73] For an overview of those criticisms, *see* F. Schauer, THINKING AS A LAWYER, at 30.

[74] For a detailed account of that honeymoon, *see* Mark Janis, THE AMERICAN TRADITION OF INTERNATIONAL LAW. GREAT EXPECTATIONS 1789–1914 117 (2004).

contestation rose with Legal Realism[75] and was made even more compelling, several decades later, by scholars affiliated with Critical Legal Studies.[76] This American aversion for formal modes of legal reasoning is said to have made its way into American international legal thought,[77] leading American international lawyers to demote formalism to irrelevance or described as dangerously hegemonic and ideological.[78] The rebellion against formalism in American international legal thought is often epitomised by the success of the famous New Haven school of international law, which is said to have vindicated '*process*' over 'rules'.[79]

It is noteworthy that New Haven never enjoyed a monopoly of this self-declared anti-formalist ethos of American international lawyers.[80] This alleged abhorrence of formalism (and the discredit in which the latter was plunged) manifests itself in extremely diverse ways in American international legal thought. Mention can be made of the rise of 'deformalization'[81] and the resort to non-formal law-ascertainment criteria (e.g. the ascertainment of customary law based on ethical principles),[82] the success of effect- and impact-based

---

[75] O. W. Homes, *The Path to Law*, 10 Harv. L. Rev. 457 (1897); R. Pound, *Do We Need a Philosophy of Law*, 5 College L. Rev. 339 (1905); R. Pound, *Common Law and Legislation*, 21 Harv. L. Rev. 383 (1908): R. Pound, *The Theory of Judicial Decisions*, 36 Harv. L. Rev. 802 (1923).

[76] R. Unger, *The Critical Legal Studies Movement*, 96 Harv. L. Rev. 561, 571 (1983); R. Unger, THE CRITICAL LEGAL STUDIES MOVEMENTS 1–2 (1986); David Kennedy, *Legal Formality*, 2 J. of Leg. Stud. 351 (1973).

[77] For a discussion of American scepticism from a comparative perspective, *see* Richard H. Pildes, *Conflicts between American and European Views of Law: The Dark Side of Legalism*, 44 Va. J. Int'l L. 145, 148 (2003).

[78] *See* E. Jouannet, *French and American Perspectives on International Law*, 58 Me. L. Rev. 15 (2006).

[79] In the same vein, *see* G. J. H. Van Hoof, RETHINKING THE SOURCES OF INTERNATIONAL LAW 283 (1983). *See also* one of the grounds of the criticisms of F. Kratochwil, RULES NORMS AND DECISIONS: ON THE CONDITIONS OF PRACTICAL AND LEGAL REASONING IN INTERNATIONAL RELATIONS AND DOMESTIC AFFAIRS 194 (1989). *See also* J. d'Aspremont, *The Politics of Deformalization in International Law*, 3 Goettingen J. Int'l L. 503, at 508–10 (2011). Please note that a process-based representation of law only generates deformalisation to the extent of the accompanying rejection of formal criteria that distinguish between law and non-law or the total rejection of the necessity to ascertain legal rules, as has been advocated by some scholars affiliated with the New Haven Law School.

[80] It could be said that New Haven enjoyed a monopoly on rule-skepticism, which is a broader phenomenon than the move away from formalism. *See* G. Verdirame, '*The Divided West*': *International Lawyers in Europe and America*, 18 Eur. J. Int'l L. 553, 566–7 (2007).

[81] *See generally* J. d'Aspremont, *The Politics of Deformalization in International Law*, 3 Goettingen J. Int'l L. 503, 532–3 (2011).

[82] B. Lepard, CUSTOMARY INTERNATIONAL LAW: A NEW THEORY WITH PRACTICAL APPLICATIONS (2010).

International Lawyers and Legal Forms

approaches to law-ascertainment,[83]and the increasing importance attached to lawmaking output by *informal networks*.[84] The multiplication of attempts to reconstruct, challenge and reform international law from the vantage point of legitimacy[85] which have usually been accompanied by the claim that consent cannot perform any legitimising function can similarly be construed as a move against formalism.[86] Indeed, this turn to legitimacy[87] supposedly 'releases us from law's binary bind'[88] and it becomes possible to move from institutions to regimes, from rules to regulation, from government to governance, from responsibility to compliance, from legality to legitimacy, from legal expertise to international relations expertise.[89]

According to the same narrative, the disrepute of formalism can equally be witnessed in many of the leading scholarly projects in which international legal scholars engage today. This is the case, for instance, in the alleged turn to

[83] J. E. Alvarez, INTERNATIONAL ORGANIZATIONS AS LAW-MAKERS (2005); J. Brunnée and S. J. Toope, *International Law and Constructivism, Elements of an International Theory of International Law*, 39 Colum. J. Transnat'l L. 19, 65 (2000–1). These effect-based approaches must be distinguished from the subtle conception defended by Kratochwil based on the *principled rule-application* of a norm which refers to the explicitness and contextual variation in the reasoning process and the application of rules in 'like' situations in the future. *See* F. Kratochwil, RULES NORMS AND DECISIONS: ON THE CONDITIONS OF PRACTICAL AND LEGAL REASONING IN INTERNATIONAL RELATIONS AND DOMESTIC AFFAIRS 206 (1989). *See also* F. Kratochwil, *Legal Theory and International Law*, *in* ROUTLEDGE HANDBOOK OF INTERNATIONAL LAW 1, 58 (D. Amstrong ed., 2009).

[84] Anne-Marie Slaughter, *The Real New World Order*, 76 Foreign Affairs 183 (1997); David Zaring, *Informal Procedure, Hard and Soft, in International Administration*, 5 Chi. J. Int'l L. 547 (2005); Benedict Kingsbury, *Sovereignty and Equality*, 9 Eur. J. Int'l L. 611 (1998).

[85] For some illustrations of this common account of the rise of legitimacy in international legal studies, *see* John Tasioulas, *The Legitimacy of International Law*, *in* THE PHILOSOPHY OF INTERNATIONAL LAW, 97 (Samantha Besson and John Tasioulas eds., 2010); C. A. Thomas, *The Concept of Legitimacy and International Law*, LSE Law, Society and Economy Working Papers 12/2013 (also published as C. A. Thomas, *The Use and Abuse of Legitimacy in International Law*, Oxford J. of Legal Studies 1–30 (2014); R. Wolfrum, *Legitimacy in International Law from a Legal Perspective*, *in* LEGITIMACY IN INTERNATIONAL LAW 1 (R Wolfrum and V. Roben eds., 2008); Hilary Charlesworth, *Conclusions*, *in* THE LEGITIMACIES OF INTERNATIONAL LAW 389. For a discussion of some of the driving forces behind the rise of legitimacy as a central topic of scholarly study, *see* Mattias Kumm, *The Legitimacy of International Law. A Constitutionalist Framework of Analysis*, 15 E. J.I.L. 907 (2004).

[86] R. Wolfrum, *Legitimacy in International Law from a Legal Perspective*, *in* LEGITIMACY IN INTERNATIONAL LAW 1, 7–19 (R. Wolfrum and V. Roben eds., 2008; Allen Buchanan, *The Legitimacy of International Law*, *in* BESSON & TASIOULAS 79, 90–4.

[87] T. Franck, THE POWER OF LEGITIMACY AMONG NATIONS at 27 (1990).

[88] T. Franck, THE POWER OF LEGITIMACY AMONG NATIONS at 36 (1990).

[89] J. d'Aspremont. *The Politics of Deformalization in International Law*, 3 Goettingen J. Int'l L. 503, 510 (2011). The above typology of the broad, inclusive concept of deformalisation derives from the same article at 508–10.

empiricism,[90] inquiries into the means to ensure accountability in the exercises of power outside traditional legal categories,[91] the new modelling of international authority and the structure of global governance,[92] the quest for sociological insights about the functioning of international law,[93] the studies of expert-ruling and expert-knowledge,[94] or the potential transformation of global and national regulations through international and regional agreements.[95] In shifting their attention to these new objects of investigation, and irrespective of their newly acquired theoretical,[96]

---

[90] *See* Gregory Shaffer and Tom Ginsburg, *The Empirical Turn in International Legal Scholarship*, 106 Am. J. Int'l L. 1 (2012). For an illustration, *see* Pierre-Hugues Verdier and Erik Voeten, *How Does Customary International Law Change? The Case of State Immunity*, 59 International Studies Quarterly 209 (2015). *See also* Jakob v. H. Holtermann and Mikael Rask Madsen, *Toleration, Synthesis or Replacement? The 'Empirical Turn' and Its Consequences for the Science of International Law*, 29 Leiden J. Int'l L. (2016).

　　The turn to empirical studies of international law is not completely unprecedented. *See e.g.* the work of the New Haven School and in particular that of Myres McDougal, *Law and Power*, 46 Am. J. Int'l L. 102 (1952). *See also* the work of the legal process school as is illustrated by Abram Chayes and Antonia Handler Chayes, THE NEW SOVEREIGNTY: COMPLIANCE WITH INTERNATIONAL. REGULATORY AGREEMENTS (1995). For a claim about the virtuosity of empirical sensitivity, *see* J. Vinuales, *On Legal Inquiry*, in UNITY AND DIVERSITY OF INTERNATIONAL LAW – ESSAYS IN HONOUR OF PROFESSOR PIERRE-MARIE DUPUY 45 – 75, at 72 –5 (D. Alland, V. Chetail, O. de Frouville and J. Vinuales eds., 2014).

[91] *See e.g.* the studies on Global Administrative Law by B. Kingsbury, N. Krisch and R. Steward, *The Emergence of Global Administrative Law*, 68 Law and Contemporary Problems 3 & 4, 15–61, 29 (2005); C. Harlow, *Global Administrative Law: The Quest for Principles and Values*, 17 Eur. J. Int'l L. 1, 187 (2006); *See also* the studies on the Exercise of International Public Authority by A. von Bogdandy, P. Dann and M. Goldmann, *Developing the Publicness of Public International Law: Towards a Legal Framework for Global Governance Activities*, 9 Ger. L. J. 1375 (2008); M. Goldmann, *Inside Relative Normativity: From Sources to Standards Instruments for the Exercise of International Public Authority*, 9 Ger. Law J. 1865 (2008). *See generally* the remarks of D. Kennedy, *The Mystery of Global Governance*, 34 Ohio N.U. L. Rev. 827 (2008).

[92] N. Krisch, BEYOND CONSTITUTIONALISM: THE PLURALISTIC STRUCTURE OF POSTNATIONAL LAW (2010); N. Krisch, *Subsidiarity in Global Governance*, 79 Law and Contemporary Problems (2016); *see also* E. Benvenisti, THE LAW OF GLOBAL GOVERNANCE (2014); E. Benvenisti and G. W. Downs, *The Empire's New Clothes: Political Economy and the Fragmentation of International Law*, 60Stan. L. Rev. 595 (2007).

[93] Moshe Hirsch, INVITATION TO THE SOCIOLOGY OF INTERNATIONAL LAW (2015). *See also* J. d'Aspremont, André Nollkaemper and Tarcisio Gazzini, INTERNATIONAL LAW AS PROFESSION (2016).

[94] *See e.g.* David Kennedy, A WORLD OF STRUGGLE: HOW POWER, LAW, AND EXPERTISE SHAPE GLOBAL POLITICAL ECONOMY (2016); M. Koskenniemi, *The Politics of International Law – 20 Years Later*, 20 Eur. J. Int'l L. 7 (2009).

[95] *See generally* www.iilj.org/research/MegaReg.asp.

[96] See some recent and unprecedented collections of essays on the theory of international law, *see* Alexander Orakhelashvili, RESEARCH HANDBOOK ON THE THEORY AND HISTORY OF INTERNATIONAL LAW (2013); THE OXFORD HANDBOOK OF THE THEORY OF INTERNATIONAL LAW (A. Orford and F. Hoffmann eds., 2016); FUNDAMENTAL CONCEPTS FOR INTERNATIONAL LAW (J. d'Aspremont and S. Singh eds., 2017).

historical[97] and multidisciplinary[98] appetites, international legal scholars could be seen as breaking away from the centrality of legal forms inherited from the Enlightenment.

Yet, this anti-formalist narrative provides a very distorted image of the role and place of formalism in international American legal thought and practice. Indeed, despite the common self-representation of American scholarship as having distanced itself from formal modes of reasoning, it is possible to project a very different image of the American tradition of international law. According to this alternative image, the American tradition of international law comes to be understood as being in a constant quest, not to repudiate formalism, but to reinvent it. Indeed, legal forms have continued to occupy a very central role in the descriptive and analytical categories of most scholarly enterprises designed by American international lawyers. For instance, reconstructions of international law around the paradigm of legitimacy have continued to rest on mechanisms of 'symbolic validation', which can be read as the perpetuation of formalism in legal reasoning.[99] Likewise, the role of 'authority signals' in the New Haven process-based approach to international law, by virtue of its emphasis on 'authority signals' can also be construed as perpetuating, albeit in a covert fashion, the resort to formal modes of reasoning, thereby seriously qualifying the deformalisation traditionally associated with process-based approaches like New Haven.[100] By the same token, it can be contended that the rise of the so-called new legal realism in American legal thought has not necessarily contradicted the need for formal modes of reasoning,

---

[97] On the turn to history in contemporary international legal scholarship *see* M. Craven, *Theorizing the Turn to History in International Law, in* THE OXFORD HANDBOOK OF THE THEORY OF INTERNATIONAL LAW 21–37 (A. Orford and F. Hoffmann eds., 2016); *see also* G. Galindo, *Martti Koskenniemi and the Historiographical Turn in International Law*, 16 Eur. J. Int'l L. 539 (2005).

[98] *See e.g.* INTERDISCIPLINARY PERSPECTIVES ON INTERNATIONAL LAW AND INTERNATIONAL RELATIONS – THE STATE OF THE ART (Jeffrey L. Dunoff and Mark A. Pollack eds., 2013).

[99] It is noteworthy Franck, because he still insisted in need for symbolic validation may seem more formalist than those who succeeded him and which he contributed to engender. T. Franck, THE POWER OF LEGITIMACY AMONG NATIONS at 92 (1990).

[100] W. M. Reisman, *International Lawmaking: A Process of Communication*, 75 Am. Society Int'l L. Proceedings 101, 110 (1981) (where he emphasises the need for authority signals which can be formal). On the idea that New Haven did not shed formalism but reinvented it through a form of policy conceptualism, see the remarks of H. Saberi, *Yale's Policy Science and International Law. Between Legal Formalism and Policy Conceptualism, in* THE OXFORD HANDBOOK OF THE THEORY OF INTERNATIONAL LAW 427 (A. Orford and F. Hoffmann eds., 2016).

especially with respect to law-ascertainment.[101] Mention can similarly be made of some of the most reformist approaches to the classical sources of international law, which have not done away with the formal modes of legal reasoning traditionally associated with the sources of international law and which have continued to articulate legal claims around a series of pre-existing formal signals[102] Eventually, and provided that an American pedigree can be awarded to Global Administrative Law – and all the other 'managerialists'[103] – it is noteworthy that studies that embrace the paradigms of Global Administrative Law rest on a dialectical approach which oscillates between a deformalisation of its object of study (namely the exercise of public authority at the international level) and a (re-)formalisation of principles of accountability, participations and transparency.[104]

These few examples suffice to show that the limits of the common portrayal of American international lawyers as anti-formalist and demonstrate that formalism – and the resort to legal forms – have not evaporated in American international legal thought. On the contrary, the reinvention of formalism in more covert variants in American international legal thought has made formalism more present, if not more pivotal than ever. This helps us challenge the traditional and popular narrative whereby American are said to be anti-formalists.

1.4 CONCLUDING REMARKS: ARE WE ALL FORMALISTS?

The preceding sections have taken issue with the common narrative that pits the European formalists against the American anti-formalists. They have

---

[101] *See generally* G. Shaffer, *A New Legal Realism: Method in International Economic Law Scholarship, in* INTERNATIONAL ECONOMIC LAW – THE STATE AND FUTURE OF THE DISCIPLINE 29 (C. B. Picker, I. Bunn and D. Arner eds., 2008); H. Erlanger, B. Garth, J. Larson, E. Mertz, V. Nourse and D. Wilkins, *New Legal Realism Symposium: Is It Time for a New Legal Realism?* 2 Wisconsin Law Review 335 (2005); S. Macaulay, *The New Versus the Old Legal Realism: Things Ain't What They Used to Be*, 2005 Wis. L. Rev. 365, 375 (2005); V. Nourse and G. Shaffer, *Varieties of New Legal Realism: Can A New World Order Prompt A New Legal Theory*, 95 Cornell Int'l L.J. 61 (2009).

[102] *See e.g.* Harlan Cohen, *Finding International Law, Part II: Our Fragmenting Legal Community*, 44 N.Y.U. J. Int'l L. & Pol. 1049 (2012) esp. at 1063. Comp. with M. Goldmann, *We Need to Cut off the Head of the King: Past, Present, and Future Approaches to International Soft Law*, 25 L.J.I.L. 335 (2012).

[103] The term comes from M. Koskenniemi, *The Politics of International Law – 20 Years Later*, 20 E.J.I.L. 7–19 (2009).

[104] *See* J. d'Aspremont, Droit Administratif Global et Droit International (Global Administrative Law and International Law), in LE DROIT ADMINISTRATIF GLOBAL (C. Bories ed., 2012).

demonstrated that such a narrative, whilst undoubtedly popular, is deceptive. These observations have simultaneously shown, I trust, the complexity of the engagement of Europeans and Americans with formalism and the extent to which international lawyers on both sides of the Atlantic are geared towards the reinvention of formalism, and not is veneration or repudiation.[105] Does this mean that European and American international lawyers are all formalists and have been so since the inception of modern international law?[106] My answer is 'unsurprisingly yes!', for engagement with formalism is a common denominator of the European and American traditions of international law. In that sense, it can be contended that, notwithstanding variations in their engagement with legal forms and in the agendas behind their respect projects of renewal, formalism unites rather than distinguishes European and American international lawyers.

The claim that Europeans and Americans share some common engagement with formalism – and thus the corresponding idea that 'we are all formalists' – will probably not be received with much enthusiasm by European and American international lawyers as they relish their simplistic narratives and self-professed dividing lines. The claim developed here could even be found insolent and disrespectful. This is not only because this claim entails that, by adhering to some formalism of sort, both Europeans and Americans reproduce all the problems that come with formalism, and especially the obfuscation of politics and hegemonism as well as the fake determinacy of patterns of argument, structures of thought or conceptual frameworks. The claim made in this chapter – and thus the challenge of one of international lawyers most simplistic self-representation – can also prove vexing because formalism certainly counts as one of the 'villains'[107] of international legal thought nowadays. Indeed, formalism has long joined natural law, voluntarism, consensualism, legal positivism and others – which are often all conflated under the bogey of 'Westphalia'[108] – as those ideas *against* which

---

[105] For a similar argument, *see* Umut Özsu, *Legal Form, in* Concepts for International Law (J. d'Aspremont and S. Singh eds., 2019).

[106] This echoes the famous question: 'are we all legal realists?' *See* Harlan Cohen, Chapter 2 in this volume. *See also* Gregory S. Alexander, *Comparing the Two Legal Realisms American and Scandinavian*, 50 Am. J. Comp. L. 131, 131 (2002); Brian Leiter, *Rethinking Legal Realism: Toward a Naturalized Jurisprudence*, 76 Tex. L. Rev. 267, 267–8 (1997); Joseph William Singer, *Legal Realism Now*, 76 Cal. L. Rev. 465, 467 (1988).

[107] I have used this expression elsewhere. *See* J. d'Aspremont, *International Legal Constitutionalism, Legal Forms, and the Need for Villains, in* Handbook on Global Constitutionalism (A. Lang and A. Weiner eds., 2017).

[108] On the idea that Westphalia constitute a myth, *see* Andreas Osiander, *Sovereignty, International Relations, and the Westphalian Myth*, 55 Int'l Org. 251 (2001). *See also* Pärtel

the profession must define itself and its ideals.[109] It can prove vexing for international lawyers to realise that, after all, they are doing just what they deny to do.

That said, it is important to highlight that the discussion conducted here should certainly not be read as a call for a catharsis and a generalised acknowledgement by international lawyers that they are and remain formalists. If international lawyers want to live in denial of their abiding engagement with formalism, so be it. In the end, it may be that international lawyers need simplistic self-representations to avoid that their craft implodes under the weight of the contradictions of their discourses.

Piirimäe, *The Westphalian Myth and the Idea of External Sovereignty, in* SOVEREIGNTY IN FRAGMENTS 64–80 (Q. Skinner and M. Koskenniemi eds., 2010).

[109] On the idea that formalism has a bad connotation, *see* D. Bederman, THE SPIRIT OF INTERNATIONAL LAW at 163 and 171 (2002).

2

Are We (Americans) All International Legal Realists Now?

Harlan Grant Cohen[*]

2.1 INTRODUCTION

"You're such an American legal realist," retorted the German-trained JSD student in my international law class. Although I probably would not disagree (except maybe with the "such"), that was the first time the term had been thrown at me so dismissively. The back-and-forth was in good fun – my response was that he was such a German positivist (which he seemed to accept) – and became a running theme for the rest of the course, a useful vehicle to explore the whole class's unspoken biases about the nature and function of international law and to reflect on how acknowledging those assumptions might unveil aspects of areas of international law we might otherwise have missed.

I am far from the first American-trained international lawyer or international law scholar to be branded a legal realist. While not all American-trained international lawyers would accept the label, many non-Americans have been quite ready to group them in that way.[1] This chapter takes this claim seriously and explores the ways in which American international law may in fact be tinged with legal realism. If American international law scholarship is in fact legal realist in its orientation, what does that mean? Where does that orientation come from, and what do those origin stories mean for current international law work? Are there common realist-inspired approaches within the varied schools of American international law scholarship? Does wielding

---

[*] Gabriel M. Wilner/UGA Foundation Professor in International Law, University of Georgia School of Law. Thank you to Victoria Barker for her research assistance.

[1] *See, e.g.,* Emmanuelle Jouannet, *French and American Perspectives on International Law: Legal Cultures and International Law,* 58 ME. L. REV. 292 (2006); Martti Koskenniemi, *Letter to the Editors of the Symposium,* 93 AM. J. INT'L L. 351 (1999) ("European rule-positivism might seem hopelessly old-fashioned in front of a postrealist American audience – while informal American arguments about policy goals or economic efficiency associate with European experience in bureaucratic authoritarianism.").

those approaches produce distinctly American views on international law doctrine, its operation, or its function? And if American international law scholarship and practice is, in these ways, somewhat distinct, what does it mean for the broader, global project of international law?

This chapter explores how a number of intellectual trends – American jurisprudential legal realism, post–World War II international relations scholarship, utopian strands in American foreign policy thinking, and US-specific foreign relations law – converged to bring a series of specific methods or attitudes to the forefront in American approaches to international law. Perhaps provocatively, this chapter argues that all the major schools of American international law – New Haven, International Legal Process, Transnational Legal Process, Law and Economics, International Relations and International Law, and others – have picked up these methods, attitudes, or approaches – enough to warrant labeling all of them as essentially "legal realist."

This is a self-consciously reductivist project. Not all American international law scholars would subscribe to these descriptions of their work. At the same time, many of the approaches identified as "legal realist" are pitched at a high enough level of abstraction that they might be shared by many international law scholars and practitioners, trained inside and outside the United States. And of course, the influences on any specific American international lawyer are wide-ranging and idiosyncratic. The point of this exercise though is to explore features that may be common among American international lawyers and how those common features may impact the study and practice of international law more broadly. A different study could easily and fruitfully focus on the features and intellectual backstories that bind American and European scholars together into a single community.[2]

2.2 WHAT IS LEGAL REALISM?

"American" legal realism is a jurisprudential movement or orientation that, originating in the late-nineteenth century, came to prominence in the first half of the twentieth century.[3] Many cite Oliver Wendell Holmes as the most influential early legal realist thinker. Other prominent legal realists included Roscoe Pound, Jerome Frank, Felix Cohen, Benjamin Cardozo, and Karl

---

[2] See Jean D'Aspremont, Chapter 1 in this volume.

[3] American Legal Realism did have European progenitors and counterparts, in particular, the legal historicism of Henry Maine and Friedrich von Savigny and the legal pluralism of Eugen Ehrlich.

Llewellyn.[4] As a movement defined largely in terms of what it was against,[5] namely Classical Legal Thought and the political conservatism it had supported, legal realism can be difficult to define with precision. Prominent legal realists disagreed with each other on many things, and who actually deserves the moniker of "legal realist" can be subject to debate. As Karl Llewellyn once famously observed, legal realism might best be conceived as a "movement in thought and work about law" rather than a "school."[6]

That said, some key attributes or orientations can be distilled from the movement. Legal realists rejected what they saw as the two main tenets of Legal Classicism: formalism and autonomy. Thus they rejected the idea that legal questions could be definitively answered solely through the application of legal logic and doctrine, something legal realists referred to as mechanical jurisprudence, legal fundamentalism, or "rule-fetichism."[7] They also rejected the idea that law was completely autonomous from morality and politics. Instead, legal realists sought to understand law as a product of a particular time and place, a reflection of a society's culture, politics, and power balances that operated to both enable and constrain those forces. Legal realists were thus empirically minded, interested in both how laws developed and operated and the actual results of particular rules. This required understanding law within its context – law in society – and encouraged an orientation away from doctrine and towards process and practice. Given their rejection of the autonomy principle, it also encouraged legal realists to think in terms of "who decides," and to focus on questions of institutional choice (e.g., Congress versus courts, federal versus state). Legal realists were legal instrumentalists, viewing laws as means to achieving particular ends. Far from eschewing normative questions about law's proper purpose, legal realism encouraged or even required them. Legal questions could not be answered without some notion of the ultimate goal. And legal realists were pragmatists, interested in questions about how laws could best be developed, shaped, and reshaped to achieve various goals. Thus, in summary, legal realism might be defined by (1) empiricism, (2) an orientation towards process, practice, and institutional

---

[4] *See, e.g.,* Brian Z. Tamanaha, *Legal Realism in Context,* in THE NEW LEGAL REALISM: TRANSLATING LAW-AND-SOCIETY FOR TODAY'S LEGAL PRACTICE at 147 (Elizabeth Mertz, et al. 2016).

[5] *See, e.g.,* Stewart MaCauley, *The New Versus the Old Legal Realism: "Things Ain't What They Used to Be,"* 2005 WISC. L. REV. 365, 369 (2005).

[6] Karl Llewellyn, *Some Realism about Realism: Responding to Dean Pound,* 44 HARV. L. REV. 1222 (1931).

[7] JEROME FRANK, LAW AND THE MODERN MIND 295 (1930).

choice rather than doctrine, (3) antiformalism, (4) instrumentalism, and (5) pragmatism.[8]

A wide range of schools of American legal thought drew from legal realism (sometimes taking it in opposing directions), including the Legal Process School of Hart and Sacks,[9] Law and Society, Critical Legal Studies, and Law and Economics.[10] Each drew upon various aspects of the approaches emphasized by legal realism.

This chapter argues that the varied schools of modern American international law also instantiate the key characteristics of legal realism. Some schools like the Policy Science School of Myres McDougal and Harold Lasswell and its progeny the New Haven School and "New" New Haven School (or Transnational Legal Process) are direct, explicit descendants of the legal realists. Others have their origins in other intellectual streams, like American International Relations scholarship. Over time, however, the various strands have converged and have become mutually reinforcing. International relations scholarship has been refracted through legal realism; American international law scholarship has borrowed from constitutional law scholarship already suffused with realism.

2.3 WHERE DOES AMERICAN INTERNATIONAL LEGAL REALISM COME FROM?

As explained above, American jurisprudential legal realism is only one strand supporting the legal realism exhibited in the various schools of American international law. The influence of international relations scholarship and, in particular, International Relations Realism, utopian strands within American foreign policy thinking, and the unique relationship in the United States between international law and US law of foreign relations have also contributed to the legal realism apparent in American approaches to international law.

2.3.1 *Domestic American Legal Realism*

American jurisprudential legal realism is, of course, the most obvious source of the legal realism in American international law. McDougal and

---

[8] *See, e.g.*, Tamanaha, *supra* note 4, at 147.
[9] *See* HENRY M. HART, JR. & ALBERT M. SACKS, THE LEGAL PROCESS: BASIC PROBLEMS IN THE MAKING AND APPLICATION OF LAW (1958).
[10] For a sampling of American international law schools, *see* Steven R. Ratner & Ann-Marie Slaughter, *Symposium on Method in International Law*, 93 AM. J. INT'L L. 291, 293–94 (1999).

Lasswell specifically built upon legal realism in developing the sociological approach of the Policy Science School, which eventually developed into the New Haven School.[11] Directing American legal realism's skepticism of formalism at international law, McDougal and Lasswell rejected the prevailing picture of international law as a body of rules and doctrines. Picking up on legal realist themes, McDougal and Lasswell explained their approach was "a functional critique of international law in terms of social ends … that shall conceive of legal order as *process* and not as a condition."[12] Together with Michael Reisman, they argued that international law should best be seen as a constantly evolving process of "authoritative decisionmaking," one "whose goal is world public order of human dignity, designed to serve particular ends and values by establishing regimes of effective control."[13]

The International Legal Process School developed by Abram Chayes, Thomas Ehrlich, and Andreas Lowenfeld at Harvard,[14] and later refined by Henry Steiner, Detlev Vagts, and Harold Koh,[15] drew upon the Legal Process materials of Henry Hart and Albert Sacks.[16] Their work was echoed at Columbia, where Louis Henkin and Oscar Schacter (a one-time colleague of Lasswell and McDougal)[17] developed their own version of the Legal Process approach.[18] While the Legal Process approach is often seen as a response to

---

[11] For an extended discussion of McDougal and Lasswell's origins in and departures from America legal realism, *see* NEIL DUXBURY, PATTERNS OF AMERICAN JURISPRUDENCE 161–203 (1995).

[12] MYRES MCDOUGAL, INTERNATIONAL LAW, POWER AND POLICY: A CONTEMPORARY CONCEPTION 137 (1954) (emphasis added) (*quoting* ROSCOE POUND, PHILOSOPHICAL THEORY AND INTERNATIONAL LAW).

[13] Harold Hongju Koh, *Why Do Nations Obey International Law*, 106 YALE L.J. 2599, 2618 (1996).

[14] ABRAM CHAYES, THOMAS EHRLICH, & ANDREAS F. LOWENFELD, INTERNATIONAL LEGAL PROCESS (1968).

[15] HENRY J. STEINER, DETLEV F. VAGTS, & HAROLD HONGJU KOH, TRANSNATIONAL LEGAL PROBLEMS (4th ed. 1994).

[16] *See* HART & SACKS, *supra* note 9.

[17] Harold Koh notes that "Although he later broke from the New Haven School, Oscar Schachter, who would become famous at Columbia Law School, co taught the course in World Public Order at Yale Law School with McDougal and Lasswell from 1955 to 1970." Harold Hongju Koh, *Is There a "New" New Haven School?*, 32 YALE J. INT'L L. 559, 561 (2007).

[18] *See* Koh, *supra* note 13, at 2621 (identifying Henkin with the Legal Process school); MARTTI KOSKENNIEMI, THE GENTLE CIVILIZER OF NATIONS: THE RISE AND FALL OF INTERNATIONAL LAW 1870–1960 477–78 (2001) (explaining that the "Columbia scholars" "sometimes articulated their theoretical views in terms of the (American) 'legal process' school that had been the leading successor to legal realism in the 1950s and had accepted much of the realists' emphasis on discretion but sought control by focusing on negotiating behavior, competence, and restraint inside formal and informal institutions").

Legal Realism, it is in many ways an extension of it, shifting the focus away from doctrine towards agreed upon processes and questions of comparative institutional competence.[19] Legal Process "solves" the indeterminacy of legal rules identified by Legal Realists by embedding them within "principled" legal process. International Legal Process extends that orientation to rise above arguments about international law's indeterminacy.[20] The commonality between the two, sometimes warring, schools is underscored in the Transnational Legal Process of Harold Koh, which explicitly claims both International Legal Process and the New Haven School as intellectual forebears.[21]

But other, seemingly more distant American schools of international trace their origins to American legal realism as well. Both Law and Society[22] and Law and Economics[23] have origins in legal realism's anti-formalism, pragmatism, functionalism, and focus on social science. When scholars like Gregory Shaffer[24] or Jack Goldsmith and Eric Posner[25] extend Law and Society or Law and Economics, respectively, to international law, they bring with them the inherited assumptions of American legal realism.

[19] See generally Charles Barzun, The Forgotten Foundations of Hart & Sacks, 99 VA. L. REV. 1 (2013) (describing Hart & Sacks' intellectual relationship to the Legal Realists); see also DUXBURY, supra note 11, 205–99. As Martti Koskenniemi observes, "The one theme that connected the different strands of US international law scholarship after the realist challenge was its deformalized concept of law. Whatever political differences there were between McDougal and the Columbia scholars, they agreed that international law was not merely formal diplomacy or cases from the International Court of Justice but that – if it were to be relevant – it had to be conceived in terms of broader political processes or techniques that aimed towards policy 'objectives.' A relevant law would be enmeshed in the social context and studied through the best techniques of neighboring disciplines." Koskenniemi, supra note 18, at 479. Dan Bodansky notes the legal realist assumptions underlying the work of Chayes, Schacter, and Henkin in Daniel Bodansky, Legal Realism and Its Discontents, 28 LEIDEN J. INT'L L. 267, 277 (2015).

[20] As Koskenniemi explains, the legal process school "accepted much of the realists' emphasis on discretion but sought control by focusing on negotiating behavior, competence, and restraint inside formal institutions." Koskenniemi, supra note 18, at 477–78.

[21] See Koh, supra note 17; Koh, supra note 13.

[22] BRIAN Z. TAMANAHA, LAW AS A MEANS TO AN END 123 (2006). See also Victoria Nourse & Gregory Shaffer, Varieties of New Legal Realism: Can a New World Order Prompt a New Legal Theory?, 95 CORNELL L. REV. 61 (2009).

[23] Thomas W. Merrill & Henry E. Smith, What Happened to Property in Law and Economics?, 111 YALE L.J. 357, 366 (2001); Joseph William Singer, Legal Realism Now, 76 CAL. L. REV. 465, 513–16 (1988).

[24] TRANSNATIONAL LEGAL ORDERS (Terence C. Halliday & Gregory Shaffer, eds., 2015).

[25] JACK L. GOLDSMITH & ERIC A. POSNER, THE LIMITS OF INTERNATIONAL LAW (2005).

2.3.2 *The Realist Turn in American International Relations Post–World War II*

The other obvious source of this legal realism is a different type of realism: International Relations Realism. The post-war shift towards Realism in international relations theory has been well-documented. E. H. Carr[26] and George F. Kennan famously blamed World War II on "the legalistic-moralistic approach to international problems,"[27] and the binary power politics of the Cold War seemed to leave little space for law. Exemplified by the work of Hans Morgenthau,[28] Realism focused on states' material interests in international relations, viewing structures and rules as instantiations of power relations. International law and "institutions" were epiphenomenal, representations of the power relations at a particular time.

Some international law scholars felt the need to respond. The work of international legal process scholars like Chayes[29] and Henkin[30] was as much a response to international relations realism as it was an outgrowth domestic legal process approaches. For the most part though, International Relations Realism drove a wedge between the fields of international relations and international law. Scholars in the two fields would spend decades talking past each other.[31]

Within international relations theory though, the effects of Realism's rise were profound. The long post-war dominance of Realism meant that much of international relations scholarship has developed as a response to it, taking on Realism's basic assumptions even while questioning Realism's outlook. In so doing, international relations scholarship ended up mirroring many of the attitudes emblematic of legal realism, including its antiformalism, its pragmatism, its instrumentalism, and its focus on interests, power, and process. The Rationalist Institutionalism spearheaded by Robert Keohane argued that cooperation and law could emerge out of rational state interest, that law and institutions could be understood as means to expand the payoffs for cooperating states, as pragmatic tools to achieve their ends.[32] Studies of institutional

---

[26] EDWARD H. CARR, THE TWENTY-YEARS' CRISIS: 1919–1939 (1964).
[27] GEORGE F. KENNAN, AMERICAN DIPLOMACY: 1900 1950 (1951).
[28] HANS MORGENTHAU, POLITICS AMONG NATIONS (1948).
[29] Mary Ellen O'Connell, *New International Legal Process*, 93 AM. J. INT'L L. 334, 336–37 (1999).
[30] MARY ELLEN O'CONNELL, THE POWER & PURPOSE OF INTERNATIONAL LAW 71, 75 (2008).
[31] *See, e.g.*, Oona A. Hathaway & Harold Hongju Koh, FOUNDATIONS OF INTERNATIONAL LAW AND POLITICS iii (2005); Kenneth W. Abbott, *Modern International Relations Theory: A Prospectus for International Lawyers*, 14 YALE J. INT'L L. 335, 337–38 (1989).
[32] ROBERT KEOHANE, AFTER HEGEMONY (1984).

and treaty rational design in both political science and law draw from these same assumptions to derive empirically testable hypotheses about the "best" legal rules to achieve states' instrumental ends.[33] Liberal International Theory also assumes international law's instrumentalism, but shifts the focus from the interstate arena to the intrastate one, focusing on how domestic politics and interests are instantiated in international law rules: Joining the European Convention on Human Rights, Andrew Moravcsik explains, serves the instrumental goals of the ruling liberal parties of post-war France.[34] Even Constructivism has realist strains, focusing on law as a product of social context, practice, and discourse – in this case, among states and state actors.

As international relations and international law scholars renewed their contacts over the past two decades, these common themes served as a bridge between fields. Scholars on both sides recognized common attitudes that made them fellow travelers in the study of international governance.[35] And as legal scholars adopted the tools and approaches of these international relations schools, they refracted them through their training on legal realism, law and society, law and economics, or New Haven Policy Science.[36] International relations theory thus strengthened existing tendencies in the American international law academy toward legal realism. In the hands of lawyers, these international relations schools are incorporated into the jurisprudential schools of the legal academy, merging into new forms of international legal realism.

2.3.3 *Utopian Notions of American Mission*

In an earlier essay,[37] I argued that historical American views of international law have been shaped by idealist visions of American mission. I argued that deep strains of American political and foreign policy thinking instantiated an understanding of American liberal constitutionalism as a utopian worldview,

---

[33] *See, e.g.*, Barbara Koremenos, Charles Lipson & Duncan Snidal, *The Rational Design of International Institutions*, 55 INT'L ORG. 761 (2001).

[34] Andrew Moravcsik, *The Origins of Human Rights Regimes: Democratic Delegation in Postwar Europe*, 54 INT'L ORG.217 (2000).

[35] It is notable that the work of H. L. A. Hart, a favorite non-American thinker in the international legal process school, *see* O'CONNELL, *supra* note 30, at 72–74, becomes a foundation for international relations work on rational institutional design. *See* Korememos, et al., *supra* note 33.

[36] Oscar Schachter, *McDougal's Jurisprudence: Utility, Influence, Controversy*, 79 AM. SOC'Y INT'L L. PROC. 266, 272–73 (1987) (remarks reported by Paula Wolff).

[37] Harlan Grant Cohen, *The American Challenge to International Law: A Tentative Framework for Debate*, 28 YALE J. INT'L L.551 (2003).

an achievement that should protected against outside influence but also spread to the rest of the world. American interventionism and isolationism have actually pivoted on these two; depending on the US's position in the world, protecting the revolution or spreading it might become paramount. I argued in that essay that seemingly hypocritical positions of the United States on international law could actually be understood a part of an American understanding of international law that incorporated that vision.

It might seem paradoxical to suggest that this kind of moral idealism could be a source of American legal realism. But, in differentiating international justice from formal international law, American liberal-constitutionalist utopianism seems to have done exactly that – transforming international law into mere tools to protect American interests and spread American views of global justice. Seeing this strand of thinking in the merger of Realism and neoconservativism is easy, but the influence of this strand of foreign policy thinking on American international legal realism is perhaps most visible in the New Haven School's focus on World Public Order.[38] For McDougal, Lasswell, and Reisman, the goal of international policy science was a world order based on shared values and human dignity. But to the New Haven school's many critics, those values looked suspiciously American and policy science like "a smoke screen for a defense of American foreign policy."[39] Oscar Schacter famously took the school to task for "the tendency ... to apply their theory in a highly selective manner to override the constraints of law in favor of the 'higher ends' sought by present U.S. policy."[40] In fact, it was the close connection between the New Haven School and "American" notions of global justice that critics most opposed.[41] The influence is also visible in Louis Henkin's influential human rights casebook, which began with the Anglo-American rights tradition, the Magna Carta, and the American Declaration of Independence.[42]

2.3.4 *Interaction with US Foreign Affairs Law*

A third stream of support for American International Legal Realism is American international law's interaction with a related but different field:

---

[38] DUXBURY, *supra* note 11, at 196–97.
[39] Koskenniemi, *supra* note 18, at 476.
[40] "Their strong patriotic attachment to U.S. institutions and their concern over 'totalitarian' dangers are understandable reasons for their political views. But the selective application of their jurisprudential theory in emphasizing certain policy objectives as fundamental goals and minimizing others has thrown a sharp light on the dangers of policy-oriented jurisprudence."
[41] O'CONNELL, *supra* note 30, at 70.
[42] HUMAN RIGHTS 16–31 (Louis Henkin, et. al., eds., 1999).

Foreign Relations Law of the United States. In part because of the structure of the US constitution, questions in the United States about international law usually involve two different lines of inquiry: one, the relevant rules of international law, and two, the relevant constitutional and statutory laws defining the impact of international law for the United States. Because of the importance of separation of powers thinking to constitutional foreign affairs questions, international legal questions often boil down to an institutional question of who (Congress, the President, the courts, states, private plaintiffs) should decide for American law.[43]

US Foreign Relations Law and American International Law have interacted in a variety of different ways over the years. For much of the twentieth century, foreign affairs law actually became the domain of international law rather than constitutional law.[44] That balance has shifted over the past three decades.[45] There is now a robust dialogue between constitutional and international legal scholars on both sides of these issues. More importantly, many American international law scholars have spent time in the US Government, particularly as lawyers at the Department of State. This experience dealing directly with both internal separation of powers debates and international law questions can only have strengthened the interrelationship between these two lines of inquiry.

US Foreign Relations Law has been particularly influenced by legal realism, focusing less on doctrine than on institutional analysis, asking big normative questions about what the laws are for, and applying a type of pragmatism to problem-solving[46] exemplified by Justice Jackson's famous concurrence in *Youngtown*.[47] Forced to judge President Truman's attempt to nationalize

---

[43] *See, e.g.*, Michael D. Ramsey, *Review Essay: Textbook Revisionism*, 43 Va. J. Int'l L. 1111, 1114 (2003) (Foreign Relations law "is about how various parts of the U.S. government relate to each other, and to persons within the United States, in the formulation and execution of U.S. foreign relations.").

[44] As Peter Spiro explained, "Many of the most celebrated American international law academics of the post-World War II era made their names in the legal academy with scholarship on the domestic law of foreign relations, with its familiar constitutional controversies." Peter J. Spiro, *Globalization, International Law, and the Academy*, 32 N.Y.U. J. Int'l L. & Pol. 567, 577 (2000) (specifically mentioning, McDougal, Henkin, and Thomas Franck).

[45] G. Edward White, *Observations on the Turning of Foreign Affairs Jurisprudence*, 70 U. Colo. L. Rev. 1109 (1999).

[46] *See* Ramsey, *supra* note 43, at 1116 ("Until recently, foreign relations law, although primarily concerning the U.S. Constitution, was viewed somewhat differently from ordinary constitutional law. Constitutional text, structure and history played much less of a role in addressing modern foreign affairs controversies than might be expected. Instead, the leading emphasis might be broadly characterized as functionality.").

[47] Youngstown Sheet & Tube Co. v. Sawyer, 343 U.S. 579, 637 (1952) (Jackson, J., concurring). *See also* Stephen Vladeck, *Foreign Affairs Originalism in* Youngstown's *Shadow*, 53 St. Louis U. L.J. 29 (2008).

steel mills during the Korean War, Justice Jackson described three categories of Presidential action: (1) those backed by Congress's explicit or implicit approval, (2) those taken in the face of Congressional silence, and (3) those taken in the face of contrary Congressional action. Presidential acts in the first category are on the strongest constitutional footing; those in the third are most constitutionally suspect. This highly functional approach has dominated separation-of-powers questions over the past few decades.

The interaction between US Foreign Relations Law and American international law seems likely to have had an influence on the thinking of American international lawyers and law scholars, helping frame the sorts of questions they ask. Many American scholars of international law are also scholars of foreign relations law; even more pay close attention to Foreign Relations Law developments. We can only speculate, but the focus on international institutional choice that has become so common in the international law literature could easily have borrowed from constitutional foreign affairs. Certainly, there are innumerable articles that argue for applying political economy insights from American constitutional law to the understand international law.[48]

2.4 WHAT INTERNATIONAL LEGAL REALISM MEANS

So what does a legal realist orientation mean for American international law? Legal realism's five features – (1) empiricism, (2) an orientation towards process, practice, and institutional choice rather than doctrine, (3) antiformalism, (4) instrumentalism, and (5) pragmatism – play out in specific ways with regard to international law. These five features are visible in four trends in American approaches to international law: (1) a focus on norms rather than rules, (2) a focus on process rather than doctrine, (3) a focus on institutions and power rather than substantive rules, and (4) an emphasis on pragmatism and practicality.

2.4.1 *A Focus on Norms Rather than Rules*

European international law scholars often complain that Americans seems maddeningly (to Europeans) uninterested in the actual requirements of

---

[48] *See, e.g.*, Curtis A. Bradley & Jean Galbraith, *Presidential War Powers as an Interactive Dynamic: International Law, Domestic Law, and Practice-Based Legal Change*, 91 N.Y.U. L. REV. 689 (2016); Timothy L. Meyer, *From Contract to Legislation: The Logic of Modern International Lawmaking*, 14 CHI. J. INT'L L. 559 (2014) (applying lessons about voting in Congress).

international law doctrine. Whether this critique is fair or not, American international law scholarship does often express a pragmatism about legal rules that emphasizes achieving norms over rules, function over form. Exemplifying American legal realism's antiformalism, instrumentalism, and pragmatism, American international law scholars often focus on "norm diffusion" rather than "rule application."[49] Translating international law rules for local contexts and hybridizing international law rules with domestic law ones doesn't dilute pure international law rules, but instead spreads the underlying norms. Pluralism is a positive value.[50]

Harold Koh's Transnational Legal Process exemplifies this sort of thinking. By focusing on how legal norms are transferred to and translated by domestic actors and institutions, the model and its varied proponents accept a certain amount of variability in how international law is actually implemented.[51] Human rights rules, for example, may take somewhat different forms depending on the particular domestic legal system. Those varieties of form are inconsequential so long as the basic norm underlying the international law rule is achieved.[52]

The focus on norms rather than rules is also evident in a pragmatic approach to bindingness.[53] "Hard" law is merely one option for achieving

---

[49] Christopher J. Borgen, *Transnational Tribunals and the Transmission of Norms: The Hegemony of Process*, 39 GEO. WASH. INT'L L. REV. 685 (2007); C. Cora True-Frost, *The Security Council and Norm Consumption*, 40 N.Y.U. J. INT'L L. & POL. 115 (2007); Galit A. Sarfaty, *International Norm Diffusion in the Pimicikamak Cree Nation: A Model of Legal Mediation*, 48 HARV. INT'L L.J. 441 (2007); Harold Hongju Koh, *Transnational Legal Process*, 75 NEB. L. REV. 181 (1996).

[50] Paul Schiff Berman, *From International Law to Law and Globalization*, 43 COLUM. J. TRANSNAT'L L. 485 (2005).

[51] Harold Hongju Koh, *Bringing International Law Home*, 35 HOUSTON L. REV. 623 (1998). Not surprisingly, many have noted a form of pluralism embedded in both transnational legal process and New Haven School scholarship; *See, e.g.*, Paul Schiff Berman, *A Pluralist Approach to International Law*, 32 YALE J. INT'L L. 301 (2007); Janet Koven Levitt, *Bottom-up International Lawmaking: A Perspective from the New Haven School of International Law*, 32 YALE J. INT'L L. 393, 395 (2007) (describing pluralism as "New Haven School-esque"); Hari M. Osofsky, *Climate Change Litigation as Pluralist Legal Dialogue?*, 26 STAN. ENVTL. L. J. 181, 185 (2007) (associating global legal pluralism with New Haven school).

[52] *See, e.g.*, Alexander K. A. Greenawalt, *The Pluralism of International Criminal Law*, 86 IND. L.J. 1063 (2011); Laura A. Dickinson, *The Promise of Hybrid International Courts*, 97 AM. J. INT'L L. 295 (2003) (extolling the norm diffusion benefits of mixing notions of international and domestic justice).

[53] Ugo Mattei, *A Theory of Imperial Law: A Study on U.S. Hegemony and the Latin Resistance*, 10 IND. J. GLOBAL LEGAL STUD. 383, 430 (2003) (describing soft law as "an American metaphor").

normative goals. How hard or soft to make a legal rule is a function of pragmatic considerations of effectiveness and desirability.[54]

2.4.2 A Focus on Process Rather than Doctrine

Transnational Legal Process highlights another key and common attribute of American International Legal Realism: the focus on process. This is, of course, a key attribute of the International Legal Process School and the Managerial School later developed by one of International Legal Process's founders, Abram Chayes along with Antonia Chayes.[55] It is also a focus, of course, of Transnational Legal Process. But process is also key to rationalist and rational design literatures, which focus on *how* states achieve various goals in different negotiating environments and liberal international theory and its focus on domestic political process. And constructivist literature often focuses on the communities who practice within international law, exploring the norms they develop to guide their discussions and debates.[56] Jeffrey Dunoff, Steven Ratner, and David Wippman explain in their international law coursebook, International Law: Norms, Actors, Process: A Problem-Oriented Approach, one of the most popular international law teaching texts in the United States, that their book is "designed to convey to students a keen sense of the process for the making, interpretation, and application of international legal norms, rather than focusing on law as a set of detailed rules or doctrines."[57]

---

54 Gregory C. Shaffer, *Hard vs. Soft Law: Alternatives, Complements and Antagonists in International Governance*, 94 MINN. L. REV. 706 (2010); Kenneth W. Abbott & Duncan Snidal, *Hard and Soft Law in International Governance*, 54 INT'L ORG. 421 (2000).

55 ABRAM CHAYES & ANTONIA HANDLER CHAYES, THE NEW SOVEREIGNTY: COMPLIANCE WITH INTERNATIONAL REGULATORY AGREEMENTS (2006).

56 EMANUEL ADLER, COMMUNITARIAN INTERNATIONAL RELATIONS: THE EPISTEMIC FOUNDATIONS OF INTERNATIONAL RELATIONS (2005); John Gerard Ruggie, *The New Institutionalism in International Relations*, in CONSTRUCTING THE WORLD POLITY 45, 55 (1998), Emanuel Adler & Peter M. Haas, *Conclusion: Epistemic Communities, World Order, and the Creation of a Reflective Research Program*, 46 INT'L ORG. 367 (1992), Emanuel Adler, *The Emergence of Cooperation: National Epistemic Communities and the International Evolution of Nuclear Arms Control*, 46 INT'L ORG. 101 (1992); Peter M. Haas, *Introduction: Epistemic Communities and International Policy Coordination*, 46 INT'L ORG. 1 (1992). *See also* JUTTA BRUNNÉE & STEPHEN J. TOOPE, LEGITIMACY AND LEGALITY IN INTERNATIONAL LAW: AN INTERACTIONAL ACCOUNT 13–16, 28 (2010) (developing an "interactional" account of international law).

57 INTERNATIONAL LAW: NORMS, ACTORS, PROCESS: A PROBLEM-ORIENTED APPROACH xxiii (Jeffrey Dunoff, Steven Ratner, & David Wippman, eds., 4th ed., 2015).

2.4.3 *A Focus on Institutions and Power over Substantive Rules*

Exhibiting the empiricism, orientation towards process, practice, and anti-formalism associated with American legal realism, these various different schools also share a focus on finding and describing the *actual* sources of authority in international law. This may mean looking for the rules of road rather than the formal rules, as Michael Reisman once explained.[58] More generally though, it leads to an emphasis on institutional analysis.[59] Who makes the rules of international law? How are negotiations structured by international's spoken and unspoken rules?[60] How do different voting structures in international regimes and organizations allocate power over rulemaking?[61] How do or should various regimes balance the needs of parties for exit and/or voice?[62] How much authority is or should be delegated to tribunals to resolve disputes or develop the law? Are international organizations or courts best seen as agents or trustees?[63] These sorts of questions animate the law and economics, rational design, and managerialist literature, but are also prevalent in New Haven and International Legal Process schools' work.

2.4.4 *Pragmatism and Practicability As a Starting Point*

A fourth way legal realism plays into American international law is its orientation towards pragmatism.[64] This international pragmatism can take

---

[58] MICHAEL REISMAN, FOLD LIES: BRIBERY, CRUSADES, AND REFORMS 15–36 (1979); Daniel Bodansky, *Prologue to a Theory of Non-Treaty Norms, in* LOOKING TO THE FUTURE: ESSAYS ON INTERNATIONAL LAW IN HONOR OF W. MICHAEL REISMAN 119 (Mahnoush H. Arsanjani et al., eds., 2011).

[59] *See, e.g.,* Gregory Shaffer, A *Structural Approach to WTO Jurisprudence: Why Institutional Choice Lies at the Center of the GMO Case,* 41 NYU J. INT'L L. & POL. 1 (2008); Gregory Shaffer & Joel Trachtman, *Interpretation and Institutional Choice at the WTO,* 52 VIRGINIA J. INT'L L. 103 (2011).

[60] Kal Raustiala, *Form and Substance in International Agreements,* 99 AM. J. INT'L L. 581 (2005); Timothy L. Meyer, *Codifying Custom,* 160 U. PA. L. REV. 995 (2012).

[61] *See* Meyer, *supra* note 48; Andrew Guzman, *International Organizations and the Frankenstein Problem,* 24 EUR. J. INT'L L. 999 (2013); Jacob Katz Cogan, *Competition and Control in International Adjudication,* 48 VA. J. INT'L L. 411 (2008).

[62] Jacob Katz Cogan, *Representation and Power in International Organization: The Operational Constitution and Its Critics,* 103 AM. J. INT'L L. 209 (2009); Laurence Helfer, *Exiting Treaties,* 91 VA. L. REV. 1579 (2005); Alan O. Sykes, *Protection as a "Safeguard": A Positive Analysis of the GATT "Escape Clause" with Normative Speculations,* 58 U. CHI. L. REV. 255 (1991).

[63] Karen J. Alter, *Agents or Trustees? International Courts in their Political Context,* 14 EUR. J. INT'L REL. 33 (2008); Laurence Helfer & Timothy Meyer, *The Evolution of Codification, in* CUSTOM'S FUTURE (Curtis Bradley ed., 2015) (looking at the ILC).

[64] Guglielmo Verdirame, *"The Divided West": International Lawyers in Europe And America,* 18 EUR. J. INT'L L. 553, 558–60 (2007).

various forms. One form is a focus on effectiveness and an attendant interest in social scientific methods.[65] This form draws not only from legal realism's pragmatism, but from its empirical orientation. Describing a new "empirical turn" in international law scholarship that echoes work of the New Haven and International Legal Process schools, Tom Ginsburg and Gregory Shaffer explain that "[w]hat matters now is the study of the conditions under which international law is formed and has effects."[66] Ginsburg and Shaffer continue to survey the wide range of social science methods now applied to international legal questions.

A second form that also captures legal realism's empiricism, antiformalism, and instrumentalism is a willingness to look for solutions than transcend formal rules and sources of international law. This could be seen in Philip Jessup's marketing of the term "transnational law,"[67] and in the Transnational Legal Problems Casebook developed by Henry Steiner, Detlev Vagts, and Harold Koh.[68] It is visible in the Global Administrative Law project developed at NYU by Richard Stewart and Benedict Kingsbury that looks for administrative law rules and processes in public-private and private regimes like the International Organization for Standardization (ISO) that international law may not actually govern.[69]

A third form that marries pragmatism with empiricism and instrumentalism is visible in discussions of legitimacy and international law. American international law scholarship often seems more interested in what Dan Bodansky calls "sociological" rather than "normative" legitimacy,[70] focused first and foremost on what international actors *perceive* to be legitimate or could be persuaded to see as legitimate. Legitimacy derived from technical expertise or from positive outcomes is widely seen as an

---

[65] *Id.* at 556 ("Much contemporary American scholarship on international law, regardless of its political orientation, makes extensive use of scientific and empirical methods."); *See also* Gregory Shaffer, *The New Legal Realist Approach to International Law*, 28 Leiden J. Int'l L. 189 (2015) (promoting an approach to international law that is "both empirical and problem-centered").

[66] Gregory Shaffer & Tom Ginsburg, *The Empirical Turn in International Legal Scholarship*, 106 Am. J. Int'l L. 1 (2012).

[67] Philip Jessup, Transnational Law 2 (1956).

[68] *See* Steiner, et al., *supra* note 15.

[69] Benedict Kingsbury et al., *Foreword: Global Governance as Administration — National and Transnational Approaches to Global Administrative Law*, 68 Law & Contemp. Probs. 1 (2005).

[70] Daniel Bodansky, *The Legitimacy of International Governance: A Coming Challenge for International Environmental Law?*, 93 Am. J. Int'l L. 596 (1999).

effective substitute for democracy or values-based sources of legitimacy in international institutions.[71]

Finally, this pragmatism seems to be a starting point on many American discussions of international law doctrine. From this perspective, any reasonable interpretation of international law's requirements must take into account practical realities, must accord with the actual practice of international actors.[72] This is particularly noticeable in debates over the law of armed conflict and international humanitarian law.[73] It can be seen in discussion of specific IHL rules on targeting or detention, as well as broader questions like the right of self-defense against non-state actors. Whereas some might derive the rules in these areas first from formal sources, there seems to be an American tendency to start from world realities and the actual practice of states. A purported rule that flies completely in the face of what states actually do is unlikely under this view to be right.

2.5 REALISM REALITY CHECK?

These four trends inspired by or consistent with legal realism – (1) an orientation towards norms rather than rules, (2) a focus on process rather than doctrine, (3) a focus on institutions and power over substantive rules, and (4) a commitment to pragmatism and practicality – are visible across American approaches to international law. In fact, despite their differences and disagreements, all the major schools of American international law – New Haven, International Legal Process, Liberal International Law, New New Haven or Transnational Legal Process, Global Administrative Law, Empirical Legal Studies, Rational Choice and Rational Design, and Law Economics – embody commitments to these themes. Recognizing these common threads, allows us to better understand the relationship between these schools – what they share in common and how they differ.

---

[71] Joseph S. Nye, Jr., *Globalization's Democratic Deficit*, FOREIGN AFFAIRS 80, 4 (July–August 2001), at 121–25; Robert Keohane, Stephen Macedo & Andrew Moravscik, *Democracy Enhancing Multilateralism*, 63 INT. ORG. 1 (2009).

[72] Emmanuelle Jouannet, *French and American Perspectives on International Law: Legal Cultures and International Law*, 58 ME. L. REV. 292, 313 (2006) ("Americans prioritize practice itself in a very flexible manner. Similarly, Americans prioritize all types of actions and behaviors, if they are those of 'major states,' because their realist and policy-oriented perspective leads them to consider such actions and behaviors as decisive.").

[73] Oliver Corten, *The Controversies Over the Customary Prohibition on the Use of Force: A Methodological Debate*, 16 EUR. J. INT'L L. 803 (2006).

Are We (Americans) All International Legal Realists Now? 49

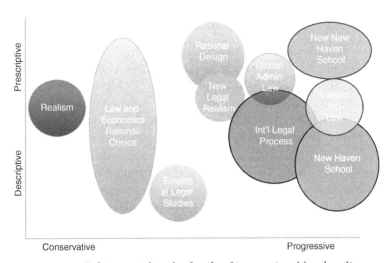

FIGURE 2.1 Relations within the family of international legal realisms

Figure 2.1 is meant to be suggestive of how we might understand the relationship between these schools. Other American approaches could easily be added. The vertical axis measures the extent to which work within a particular school uses its realism to describe existing international law or to move international law in a particular direction. The horizontal axis describes the school's relationship to status quo. Schools on the "conservative" side of the graph are less interested in shaping normative outcomes than schools on the "progressive" one. The size of the circles or ovals around particular schools reflects the amount of variation with the school. Whereas some Law and Economics scholars like Andrew Guzman or Joel Trachtman are primarily concerned with describing "how international law works,"[74] others like Eric Posner and Jack Goldsmith give Law and Economics normative force, providing tools to see the "limits of international law."[75]

This figure also suggests what might lie beyond this graph. Understanding American international legal realism as a function of the four trends described above allows us to distinguish these schools from other approaches, highlighting biases and blind spots they share that might be obscured in the constant bickering over those views that they do not.

---

[74] See ANDREW T. GUZMAN, HOW INTERNATIONAL LAW WORKS: A RATIONAL CHOICE THEORY (2007).
[75] See GOLDSMITH & POSNER, *supra* note 25.

2.6 BEYOND ARMCHAIR INTELLECTUAL HISTORY?

But if American international law is suffused with legal realism, does it matter? Is that fact relevant or interesting beyond the realm of armchair intellectual history? Is it even a uniquely American phenomenon? American legal realism has always had counterparts in other parts of the world, and one could question whether the thick lines between realism and positivism look much thinner and more porous in actual practice.[76]

One question one could ask is how this American international legal realism interacts with the increased and increasing professionalization of international legal practice. On the one hand, professionalization has undoubtedly helped to deepen some of these tendencies towards legal realism by deepening the relationship between American international lawyers and American lawyers more generally. International law, whether in terms of diplomacy, armed conflict, trade, or investment is no longer the exclusive domain of lawyer-statesmen like Elihu Root or Pierre Lalive,[77] but is practiced by a broad cadres of professional lawyers trained next to future domestic litigators and transactional attorneys who, we have been taught, are all legal realists now.[78]

On the other hand though, professionalization should create countervailing pressures away from legal realism and towards positivism. International legal practice is now much broader, denser, and more common. It is, in a sense, increasingly ordinary. The focus on the everyday negotiation of deals and resolution of disputes may make functionalist theorizing far less useful than a positivist orientation towards finding formal doctrinal answers. The broad, global professionalization of the practice also means that American international lawyers are in increasingly dense practice with their foreign counterparts. While those interactions might work to spread American legal realism abroad (compare, for example, claims in arbitration that Americans have brought with them "a common law adversarial style"),[79] they are also likely

---

[76] *See* D'Aspremont, Chapter 1 in this volume.

[77] *See* Bryant Garth & Yves Dezalay, Dealing in Virtue: International Commercial Arbitration and the Construction of a Transnational Legal Order (1996); Sergio Puig, *Social Capital in the Arbitration Market*, 25 E.J.I.L. 387, 392 (2014).

[78] Gary Peller, *The Metaphysics of American Law*, 73 Calif. L. Rev. 1151, 1152 (1985) (asserting that "we are all [legal] realists now"). *See also* Jason Webb Yackee, *Controlling the International Investment Law Agency*, 53 Harv. Int'l L.J. 391, 410 n.90 (2012) (describing this as a cliché).

[79] Roger P. Alford, *The American Influence on International Arbitration*, 19 Ohio St. J. on Disp. Resol. 69, 82–87 (2003).

to grind away any differences in approaches to international law, as all parties work towards shared understandings of the rules of the game. And while the regular interactions between lawyers and policymakers might be a pressure towards legal realism – attorney advisors may want to give legal advice that speaks to the types of pragmatic concerns policymakers are likely to raise – the increased distance between the two roles forced by specialization may have opposite effects. To the extent lawyers are increasingly cast as foils to policymakers, entrusted to speak law to power, one might expect those lawyers to see their roles as different from policymakers and to develop a more positivist ethos to contrast with the realism of their clients.[80]

Whether it continues or not, American international legal realism is of some interest for those working on the (re)emerging idea of comparative international law, currently being explored by Anthea Roberts, Mila Versteeg, Paul Stephan, Pierre-Hugues Verdier, and their collaborators, among other.[81] These projects seek to take seriously the possibility that far from being universal, understandings of international law and how it works may actually be national and parochial. It seeks to understand where those differences in views of international law come from and how they may play out in arguments over international law rules. For some, this may carry an air of the clash of civilizations, reframing states' appeals to international law as nothing more than extensions of their own values and political interests. Some may be tempted to view Russian, Chinese, or American views of international law in that way.[82] Differences in views on international law become pathways for studying states' particular understandings of their roles in the world.

A more sociological approach though would take the opposite perspective, using these national differences as a way to understand debates between states over different rules of international law, helping to identify which arguments are simply over doctrine and which run deeper, to divergent views on international law more broadly, different views on where international law comes

---

[80] Martti Koskenniemi, *Constitutionalism as Mindset: Reflections on Kantian Themes About International Law and Globalization*, 8 Theoretical Inquiries in L. 9 (2007); Koskenniemi, *supra* note 18, at 500. *See also* William H. Taft IV, A View from the Top: *American Perspectives on International Law After the Cold War*, 31 Yale J. Int'l L. 503, 510 (2006) (arguing that government lawyers should give legal advice and leave policymaking to policymakers).

[81] Anthea Roberts, Paul B. Stephan, Pierre-Hugues Verdier, & Mila Versteeg, *Comparative International Law: Framing the Field*, 109 Am. J. Int'l L. 467 (2015).

[82] William W. Burke-White, *Power Shifts in International Law: Structural Realignment and Substantive Pluralism*, 56 Harv. Int'l L.J. 1 (2015); *see also* Anu Bradford & Eric A. Posner, *Universal Unilateralism in International Law*, 52 Harv. Int'l L.J. 1 (2011).

from, the sources of legitimacy and authority.[83] Properly diagnosing the underlying cause of disputes should allow for crisper, more realistic arguments and should help in identifying which arguments over international law might be resolved by continued debate over the rules and which may remain essentially unresolvable.

[83] See Harlan Grant Cohen, *Theorizing Precedent in International Law*, in INTERPRETATION IN INTERNATIONAL LAW (Andrea Bianchi, Daniel Peat, & Matthew Windsor, eds., 2015); Harlan Grant Cohen, *Finding International Law, Part II: Our Fragmenting Legal Community*, 44 NYU J. INT'L L. & POL. 1049 (2012).

3

Are Liberal Internationalists Still Liberal?

Guglielmo Verdirame

3.1 INTRODUCTION

Sovereignty has become a toxic word. It is nowadays associated with populists in Europe, with Trumpists in America, and with enemies of a rule-based world order and of internationalist progressive politics in general. In some languages, new words (*souverainisme/sovranismo*, *souverainiste/sovranista*) have entered the political vocabulary to describe those who defend sovereignty, normally with a pejorative connotation. Until only thirty years ago, sovereignty would not have come with such negative baggage, particularly when associated with the people. What explains such a remarkable change? When did sovereignty become toxic, and why? And what does this tell us about modern-day internationalism?

International lawyers traditionally think of sovereignty as *state* sovereignty. With self-determination however, a different tradition of sovereignty, centred on the people rather than the state, became part of international law.[1] Self-determination, that is the pursuit of collective political liberty and self-government, was the driving idea behind the national liberation struggles in Europe against the Ottoman and Hapsburg Empires in the nineteenth and early twentieth centuries.[2] President Wilson placed it at the heart of the post–World War I settlement. The UN Charter went further enshrining it in Article 1 as a core principle of the United Nations.

Although uncertainty on its exact legal scope persisted until decolonisation in the 1950s and 1960s, self-determination became established as a fundamental principle of international law, and as the right of every people,

---

[1] Guglielmo Verdirame, 'Sovereignty', in Jean D'Aspremont and Sahib Singh (eds.), *Concepts of International Law: Contributions to Disciplinary Thought* (Cheltenham: Edward Elgar Publishing Limited, 2019), chapter 54.

[2] Richard J. Evans, *The Pursuit of Power* (New York: Viking, 2016), p. 583 and p. 673.

53

in the words of the International Bill of Rights, to 'freely determine their political status and freely pursue their economic, social and cultural development'.[3] True, neither the Charter nor the legal developments that accompanied the process of decolonisation elevated self-determination to a principle of *democratic* self-government. Nonetheless, it is fair to say that, through self-determination, the idea of popular sovereignty has flowed through the veins of international law for over a century now and gained an important, if still incomplete, measure of recognition.

Contrary to a widespread perception, the world order created by the UN Charter was not premised on the rejection of sovereignty. It was fundamentally, and in some ways more purposefully than before, *souverainiste* – not in the sense that it admitted of no higher authority than the sovereign state, for such extreme *souverainisme* would have been not only inconsistent with the Charter, but also impossible to reconcile with any kind of international law. Rather, the idea underlying the Charter was one of state sovereignty constrained by international law and also deepened by a sense of purpose, namely the flourishing of human communities through the advancement of self-government and human rights. Sovereignty thus conceived was meant to provide support and legitimacy to the new world order.

This understanding of sovereignty was not contradicted by the curtailment of certain aspects of state sovereignty under the Charter. Most crucially, sovereign states lost the legal power, if they ever had it, to wage aggressive war. The post-war constitutions of the defeated Axis powers – Germany, Japan and Italy – mirrored this understanding of sovereignty at the heart of the new liberal order, as they provided both for the renunciation of war as an instrument of state policy and for popular sovereignty as the foundation of the new constitutional orders.[4]

With the fall of the Berlin Wall, many predicted that international law would take a democratic turn,[5] and complete the transformation that had begun with the UN Charter. There was probably no better moment for

---

[3] The International Bill of Human Rights, The International Covenant on Economic, Social and Cultural Rights, New York, 16 December 1966, in force 23 March 1976, 2200 A (XXI), Part 1, Article 1.

[4] Article 1 of the Constitution of the Italian Republic, 27 December 1947; Article 2 of the Constitution of the IVe French Republic, 13 October 1946; Article 3 of the Constitution of the V French Republic, 4 October 1958; Article 20(2) of the Basic Law for the Federal Republic of Germany, 23 May 1949, amended 28 March 2019.

[5] The most influential and lasting work from that period to make such prediction is Francis Fukuyama , *The End of History and the Last Man* (New York: Free Press, 1992). In the field of international law, a similar view is adopted in Thomas Franck, 'The Emerging Right to Democratic Governance', (1992) 86 *American Journal of International Law* 46–91.

international law to embrace the democratic ideal, and the principle of self-determination would have been the obvious vehicle for this change. Yet, democracy does not seem to have made much progress as a principle of international law since 1989. Arguments based on purposive and evolutive interpretations of self-determination and human rights can be made in support of it now as in 1989; and they would be met with similar objections today as then. There has been no radical change, in other words, whether through treaty or custom, that would allow us to say that a democratic principle has crystallised in international law, let alone become a central part of it. Why did the 1989 promises of a democratic turn in international law fail to bear fruit?

The answer cannot be found in the fact that democracies no longer dominate international affairs. It is true that the rise of China has resulted in a momentous shift in political and economic power from democracies to autocracies, and there is much merit in the notion, advanced by scholars like Tom Ginsburg, that we may be at the beginning of a paradigm of 'authoritarian international law'.[6] But these are recent developments. For at least two decades after the fall of the Berlin Wall, democracies had the upper hand and dominated the development of international law. They had the opportunity to effect change – as they did successfully in a number of other areas. So why did they fail to advance the democratic principle in international law?

The answer may lie in the transformation of liberal internationalism over the last decades. Before authoritarian international law was even on the horizon, liberal internationalism had been reshaped by two powerful forces: one ideological (supranationalism), and the other socio-economic (globalisation). Each of these forces stymied the democratic transformation of international law, and changed the concept of the liberal international order in the minds of liberal internationalists.

To appreciate this change, we must recall that the liberal tradition has a complex relationship with democracy. Beginning in the nineteenth century and then continuing in the twentieth, liberalism however became progressively democratised.[7] Thinkers like Benjamin Constant and Alexis de Tocqueville exemplify liberalism's embrace of democracy – admittedly more cautious and qualified for some than others – and the hope that liberty could coexist with democratic representative government.

Others were more cautious, see James Crawford, *International Law as an Open System* (London: Cameron May, 2002), p. 50, first published British Year Book 1994.

[6] See Tom Ginsburg, *Lauterpacht Lectures* (Cambridge, 2019), https://upload.sms.csx.cam.ac.uk/media/2939251.

[7] On this point see Norberto Bobbio, *Teoria Generale della Politica* (Rome: Einaudi, 1999), p. 219ff.

But the ideal of democratic self-government is at best marginal, at worst antithetical, to modern-day internationalism as reshaped by the forces of supranationalism and globalisation. The tension between liberalism and democracy, which the liberal tradition had all but overcome, has now resurfaced.

The world order propounded by modern-day internationalists – as opposed to post-war liberal internationalists – embodies the vision of a pervasive system of global rules, courts and institutions, as well as transnational networks of regulators and administrators, that has as its principal *raison d'être* the efficient management of globalisation. Self-government plays a marginal role in this vision. Indeed, there is perhaps no better indicator of the differences between the liberal internationalism that underpinned the UN Charter and modern-day internationalism than what happened to the idea of self-government, which would have been regarded as central to any progressive political agenda until a few decades ago, but is now looked at with suspicion or, at best, with indifference among internationalists. Liberals of only one or two generations ago would have been horrified at the prospect of a populist right, rather than the liberal centre or the progressive left, becoming the natural political home for claims to popular sovereignty. Yet, this is what happened over the last two decades.

Modern-day internationalism differs from traditional liberal traditionalism also because of its deep-seated Whig-historicist belief in the inevitable demise of sovereignty and the conviction that such demise is necessary to the progress of humanity. Many international lawyers today are so committed to these assumptions and beliefs that they no longer seem to appreciate the difference between the values of the UN Charter and the values of what is somewhat loosely described as the 'liberal cosmopolitan project'.[8] They seem to assume that the architects of the UN Charter and the Universal Declaration of Human Rights were cosmopolitans favouring the rise of world government. This is a gross historical, political and ultimately moral error.

To understand the profound transformation of liberal internationalism in the last decades we must explore the role of two key forces that have reshaped it which are, as mentioned, supranationalism and globalisation. But before doing that, let us begin with some observations on the concept of sovereignty and, in particular, on the relationship between state sovereignty and popular sovereignty.

---

[8] Douglas Guilfoyle, 'The Future of International Law in an Authoritarian World' (2019) *EJIL Talk*.

3.2 SOVEREIGN STATES AND SOVEREIGN PEOPLES

The conventional account is that the idea of absolute sovereignty, 'Westphalian sovereignty' as it is normally called, remained almost unchallenged until the end of World War II, when it began to be steadily eroded through the top-down intervention of international law. But, for all its ubiquity, this account must be taken with more than a pinch of salt.

To begin with, it bears little relation to the content of the Treaties of Westphalia which included 'provisions to circumscribe and restrain the Princes' formerly absolute authority over the religious sphere'.[9] Indeed – as Brendan Simms observes – 'the whole purpose of the treaty was to guard against German princes exercising an untrammelled sovereignty which might jeopardise the confessional peace of the Empire and thus the whole European balance'.[10] Far from enshrining an absolutist idea of state sovereignty – argues Simms – 'the Westphalian treaties were nothing less than a charter for intervention'.[11]

In addition, the myth of a Westphalian era of absolutist sovereignty ignores the role that representative institutions had played in Western political history for centuries before. What is indeed surprising about the evolution of political institutions in Europe is not that absolutism prevailed in certain periods but that, when it did, it seldom, if ever, went unchallenged for long. It was the Church after all that laid the groundwork for challenges to absolutism by articulating, within barely a generation from the fall of the Western Empire, a dualist conception of authority reflecting the distinction between the spiritual and temporal spheres.[12]

A defining moment in the history of political institutions in Europe was the conflict between the Empire and the Italian city states in the eleventh century. At its heart was the clash between the Empire's claims to final authority (*imperium*) and the city states' claims to self-government (*libertas*). As Quentin Skinner explains, initially the Italian city states 'had no means of investing [their assertions of libertas] with any legal force',[13] because of the position of ultimate authority over the world (*dominus mundi*) which Roman law ascribed to the Emperor. But an 'alteration of perspective' in favour of the

---

[9] Stéphane Beaulac, 'The Westphalian Legal Orthodoxy - Myth or Reality?' (2000) 2 *Journal of the History of International Law*, 148–77 at 164.

[10] Brendan Simms, *Europe: The Struggle for Supremacy, 1453 to the Present* (New York: Basic Books, 2013), p. 38

[11] Ibid., p. 39.

[12] Verdirame, 'Sovereignty', pp. 827–30.

[13] Quentin Skinner, *The Foundations of Modern Political Thought* (Cambridge: Cambridge University Press, 1978), vol. I, p. 7.

claims of the city states took place in the eleventh to twelfth centuries, enabled by the work of Bologna jurist Bartolus of Saxoferrato, which led to the rise of 'the distinctively modern concept of a plurality of sovereign political authorities, each separate from one another as well as independent of the Empire'.[14] It also led to the emergence of a dialectics between authority/*imperium* and self-government/*libertas* which the dual ascription of sovereignty to states and peoples still reflects.

By 1450, representative institutions in Europe included 'the English, Irish and Scottish Parliaments, the States General of the Low Countries, the Estates General of France, the Cortes of Castile, the Hungarian, Polish and Swedish Diets, and the German Reichstag',[15] as well as various representative bodies in Italian city states although by the middle of the fifteenth century those city states were well down the path of becoming principates.

In its struggle with the Crown in the seventeenth century, the English parliament justified its greater authority on the basis that it – not the monarch – represented the people. It is true that, as observed by Edmund Morgan in his history of the idea of popular sovereignty, 'the first formulations of popular sovereignty in England, from which it never quite escaped, elevated the people to the supreme power by elevating their elected representatives'.[16] But contrary to a view often heard in Britain since the Brexit referendum,[17] popular sovereignty is not a novel idea in British constitutional history: since at least the seventeenth century the authority of the House of Commons has been understood to rest on it.

Late medieval and early modern representative institutions were fuelled by a powerful sense of self-government, but were not yet democratic in the modern sense as they were not based on universal suffrage. Once the conviction that the right to rule belongs to the people took root, all that stood in the way of democracy was inequality of status. It was no small obstacle but one that would be slowly overcome. The revolutionary belief in the moral equality of human beings – as Larry Siedentop's magisterial account shows –[18] took centuries to establish itself, but it succeeded in transforming social life and institutions across the West and beyond.

---

[14] Ibid., p. 9.
[15] Simms, *Europe: The Struggle for Supremacy*, p. 1.
[16] Edmund S. Morgan, *Inventing the People: The Rise of Popular Sovereignty in England and America* (New York: W. W. Norton and Company, 1988), p. 58.
[17] Vernon Bogdanor, 'After the Referendum, the People, Not Parliament, Are Sovereign', *Financial Times*, 9 December 2016.
[18] Larry Siedentop, *Inventing the Individual: The Origins of Western Liberalism* (Cambridge, MA: Harvard University Press, 2014).

Notwithstanding the complexity and variety of the history of the idea of sovereignty, it is true that in international law sovereignty meant essentially state sovereignty until self-determination entered the scene. Then, the twofold dimension of *imperium* and *libertas* began to define the concept of sovereignty in international law too. How does international law manage this tension between the people and the constituted authority?

Two areas where this tension manifests itself are secession and resistance. In a state-*souverainiste* perspective, there would be no room for either. By contrast, the principle of popular sovereignty requires some accommodation in favour of a right to secede, albeit qualified, from an existing state as well as of a right to resist the constituted authority in certain circumstances.

Unsurprisingly, states have been reluctant to recognise either of these claims as international legal rights.[19] There is still no basis in international law to argue for a general right of secession. As for resistance, the Universal Declaration on Human Rights states in the Preamble that '[i]t is essential, if man is not to be compelled to have recourse, as a last resort, to rebellion against tyranny and oppression, that human rights should be protected by the rule of law', but this amounts to a recognition of resistance as a social fact rather than a legal right. The point is that both secession and resistance threaten the constituted authority and clash with a state's interest in self-preservation. Resistance does so less acutely perhaps, as it can in principle be directed at the government rather than the state itself, while secession by definition entails an attack on the authority of the state.

In spite of these conceptual and practical difficulties, international law has been able to accommodate both the enduring idea that sovereignty vests in the state and the more recent notion that peoples have the right to govern themselves. Important differences persist between the position in the constitutional law of democratic states and in international law. In particular, although it is seldom denied these days that the principle of self-determination has an internal dimension in addition to its external one, international law does not assimilate that internal dimension to a right of democratic self-government.

Having outlined the conceptual distinction between state and popular sovereignty, the relationship between the two, and the role of each in

---

[19] They have also been reluctant to give them wide constitutional recognition. Constitutions providing for either a right to secede or a right to resist are in fact rare. See: Article 39 of the Ethiopian Constitution 8 December 1994; US Declaration of Independence 4 July 1776, para. 2. See Tom Ginsburg, Daniel Lansberg-Rodriguez & Mila Versteeg, 'When to Overthrow Your Government: The Right to Resist in the World's Constitutions' (2013) 60 *UCLA Law Review* 1184.

60   *Guglielmo Verdirame*

international law, let us now return to the question posed in the introduction: why did the democratic transformation of international law foreseen by many after the Cold War fail to materialise? In the search for an explanation, let us begin to consider the impact of supranationalism – an ideology that, even before the end of the Cold War, had begun to redefine liberal internationalism.

3.3 SUPRANATIONALISM

The origins of modern supranationalism lie in a mindset that first emerged in Europe after World War I and took root in the aftermath of World War II. For nineteenth-century liberals, like Alexander Herzen or Giuseppe Mazzini,[20] there was no contradiction between liberal nationalism and cosmopolitan peace; on the contrary, they considered the former necessary to the attainment of the latter. They regarded tyranny and absolutism as the main causes of war; in a world of free self-governing nations, peaceful coexistence between states would become the norm.

In the aftermath of the two global conflicts of the twentieth century, a different view emerged in Europe. Its main tenets were that the nineteenth-century liberal nation state, as the experience of France but especially Italy and Germany had shown, was unstable and fragile; that liberal patriotism over time degenerates into nationalism; and that international peace cannot be secured within a framework of nation states. According to this view, in other words, the problem was the state itself.[21] The project of European integration drew moral and political legitimacy from these growing anti-national and anti-statist sentiments.

With distrust of the sovereign nation state came also 'distrust of unrestrained popular sovereignty'.[22] It would be simplistic however to think of post-war Europe as defined entirely by this dual distrust of sovereign states and sovereign peoples. The picture is complicated by the fact that the idea of popular sovereignty was at the same time reinvigorated by the experience of the war and partisan resistance; and – as we have seen – popular sovereignty featured prominently in post-war constitutions. Anti-statist beliefs and values thus grew

---

[20] Giuseppe Mazzini, *A Cosmopolitanism of Nations: Giuseppe Mazzini's Writings on Democracy, Nation Building, and International Relations*, Stefano Recchia and Nadia Urbinati (eds.), Stefano Recchia (trans.) (Princeton: Princeton University Press, 2009), pp. 53–4.

[21] Ernst Cassirer, *The Myth of the State* (Yale: Yale University Press, 1946), p. 3.

[22] Jan-Werner Müller, *What Is Populism?* (Philadelphia: University of Pennsylvania Press, 2016), p. 95.

alongside the more traditional liberal belief in national self-government under the rule of law. It took a while before anti-statist internationalist liberalism and democratic liberalism clashed.

To understand supranationalism, it is important to appreciate a wider transformation in Western liberal thought that began in the twentieth century: the drift to technocracy. Nineteenth-century liberals in Europe had relied on the aristocracy as a check-and-balance on democracy to guard against the risk of democracy degenerating into populism. As Tocqueville understood, the genius of American liberalism was to protect liberty from the dangers of democratic rule in a society without a natural aristocracy through the Constitution. But in the second half of the twentieth century, government of the people, by the people, for the people began to be seen with growing apprehension, and constitutionalism as an inadequate bridle on the expanding power of the masses. A 'revolt of the elites', to use Christopher Lasch's provocative expression, mounted. Democracy had to be rethought – a process best illustrated by the work of the American sociologist Walter Lippmann. For Lippmann '[d]emocracy did not require that the people literally govern themselves. The public's stake in government was strictly procedural. The public interest did not extend to the substance of decision making'.[23] When it came to questions of substance, decisions should be left to 'knowledgeable administrators whose access to reliable information immunised them against the emotional symbols and stereotypes that dominated public debates'.[24]

Technocracy shaped European supranationalism particularly through the figure of Jean Monnet. The founding father of the European project exemplified distrust of both popular and state sovereignty, which he sought to replace with a 'souveraineté élitaire/européenne'.[25] This was not a return to the nineteenth-century order based on European royalty and aristocracy. What defined this new elite was not blood but knowledge, as well as shared values such as the rejection of nationhood and a commitment to supranationalism. For Monnet the creation of this supranational elite-based order was Europe's new *mission civilisatrice* which would spread to the rest of the world freeing it from the dangers of nationalism and conflict.[26] This vision of a 'Europe of Offices', to use Luuk van Middelaar's phrase, was not the only on that shaped the European project – the 'Europe of States' and the 'Europe of Citizens' played

---

[23] Christopher Lasch, *The Revolt of the Elites and the Betrayal of Democracy* (New York: W. W. Norton and Company, 1995), p. 168.

[24] Ibid., p. 168.

[25] Marc Joly, *L'Europe de Jean Monnet* (Paris: CNRS, 2007), pp. 160–1.

[26] Ibid., p. 121.

a role too.[27] But it is the 'Europe of Offices', the idea of a supranational technocratic elite in charge of the substance of decision-making, that was most distinctive. The principles of supremacy and direct effect of EU law are all but impossible to conceive without it.

It is difficult for this elitist, technocratic and supranationalist vision to coexist with self-government other than in a merely procedural sense as advocated by Lippman. As European supranationalists became ever more committed ideologically to the demise of the nation state in Europe, the tension between supranationalism and self-government has become an almost insoluble contradiction.

Outside Europe however support for supranationalism remains scant. Emerging powers, China in particular, not only reject it but often appear to be driven by a crude *souverainisme* with which international law, let alone supranational law, is barely compatible. Countries that have not yet had their *Alabama* moment and resist binding international dispute settlement are not going to embrace supranationalism any time soon.

Supranationalism faces resistance in the USA too. Trump administration aside, a supranationalist international law would be hard to reconcile with American liberal constitutionalism. This deeper commitment to liberal constitutionalism may be one, albeit surely not the only, reason for the distinct approach to international law in American academia.[28] This is illustrated not only by the fierce critiques of global legalism[29] which are almost non-existent in European academia, both also by the apprehension with which both the left and the right of American legal academia view investor-state dispute settlement – a project which is not even supranationalist in nature.[30]

Last but not least, and contrary to Monnet's predictions, resistance to a supranationalist transformation of international law may also come from the very place where supranationalism began: the European Union. There is indeed no sign of the European Union being willing to subject itself

---

[27] Luuk Van Middelaar, *The Passage to Europe: How a Continent Became a Union* (Yale: Yale University Press, 2013), p. 2.

[28] See Anthea Roberts, *Is International Law International?* (Oxford: Oxford University Press, 2017).

[29] See Eric Posner, *The Perils of Global Legalism* (Chicago: University of Chicago Press, 2009), p. xi, but see also earlier works by the scholars called 'New Sovereigntists', e.g. Jeremy A. Rabkin, *Why Sovereignty Matters* (Washington DC: The AEI Press, 1998), p. 2.

[30] Laurence H. Tribe, Joseph Stiglitz, Jeffrey D. Sachs and others, 'Letter Urging Congress to Reject the TPP and Other Prospective Deals that Include Investor-State Dispute Settlement (ISDS)', 7 September 2016; *The Economist*, 'The Arbitration Game', 11 October 2014; Wayne David, 'Is TTIP a Threat or an Opportunity?', *New Statesman*, 5 May 2016, www.newstatesman.com/politics/staggers/2016/05/ttip-threat-or-opportunity.

unconditionally to a higher authority, and to accept an upwards extension of the same principle it applies to its member states. When it has been confronted with an international law-based claim of supremacy, the EU has often responded by defending the autonomy and primacy of its own legal order.[31] If supranationalism in Europe was supposed to be the first step towards a Platonic cosmopolis of administrators and judges, the EU itself may be on course to proving this Whiggish prediction wrong.

In fact, the risk is that the EU may end up looking more and more like a state. Or worse: like an empire. Faced with the deep crisis of legitimacy that followed the rejection of the Constitutional Treaty and with the euro crisis, European supranationalism appears to be abandoning any attempt to define itself as an alternative to statehood. Its advocates now speak openly of 'European sovereignty',[32] a self-defeating notion for supranationalism in that it accepts the inescapability of sovereignty and transforms supranationalism into just a state-building project on a continental scale aimed, as its critics throughout argued, at the suppression of existing statehood and its replacement with another one. Some – including those who claim to be motivated by a desire to reform the EU and make it more legitimate –[33] even speak of the need for a European Empire, lending support to those who throughout sensed the ghost of empire lurching behind the European project.

Disconcertingly, these problems and contradictions are barely acknowledged by supranationalism's staunchest supporters. A recent BBC Radio 4 documentary, entitled 'The Dream of World Government' presented by David Miliband, the former UK Foreign Secretary,[34] illustrates the depth of

---

[31] See, in this respect, the *Kadi* and *Achmea* litigations: Cases C-402/05 P & 415/05 P, *Yassin Abdullah Kadi and Al Barakaat International Foundation v. Council and Commission of the European Union* [2008] ECR I-6351 ('*Kadi I*'); Cases C-584/10 P, C-593/10 P and C-595/10 P, *European Commission et al v. Yassin Abdullah Kadi*, [2013] ('*Kadi II*'); Case C-284/16, *Slovak Republic v. Achmea BV*, [2018].

[32] See for example the 'European sovereignty' web pages from one of Europe's leading foreign policy think-tanks at www.ecfr.eu/europeanpower/european_sovereignty. Various pro-EU politicians are now also more openly calling for the creation of a European State, e.g. Italian Prime Minister Matteo Renzi (Martin Banks, 'Italy to push for "United States of Europe" When It Holds the EU Presidency', *The Telegraph*, 22 June 2014, www .telegraph.co.uk/news/worldnews/europe/eu/10918134/Italy-to-push-for-United-States-of-Euro pewhen-it-holds-the-EU-presidency.html); or Martin Schulz, former leader of the SDP in Germany and former President of the European Parliament (Philip Oltermann, 'Martin Schulz Wants "United States of Europe" within Eight Years', *The Guardian*, 7 December 2017, www.theguardian.com/world/2017/dec/07/martin-schulz-united-states-of-europe-germany-sdp).

[33] Victor Mallet, 'Le Maire Calls for "New Empire" to Save EU from Rival Powers', *Financial Times*, 2 April 2019.

[34] David Miliband, 'The Dream of World Government' on Radio 4, 8 September 2018.

the belief in Europe's post-war *mission civilisatrice* among that generation of European liberal and progressive intellectuals and politicians. But it also revealed profound cultural and political misunderstandings, ignoring swathes of liberal political philosophy – from Kant to Rawls – that have been sceptical about the idea of world government. These philosophical blind spots become political ones: as in the Milliband documentary, anyone who expresses concerns or reservations about world government is quickly caricatured as Trumpian or worse.

Supranationalism goes a long way towards explaining why the democratic revolutions of 1989 did not lead to a democratic revolution in international law. By embracing supranationalism and a crude and unreflective cosmopolitanism, the current generation of liberal internationalists seems to have lost interest, and perhaps faith too, in democracy. Against this intellectual and political background – defined by distrust of sovereign states and sovereign peoples, and a chiliastic faith in a world government run by lawyers and administrators – another momentous transformation was taking place: the globalisation of the markets.

3.4 GLOBALISATION AND THE CRISIS OF DEMOCRACY

The expectation that democracy would spread after the fall of the Berlin Wall was accompanied by a sense that a new era of individualism had begun. In international law, this intellectual mood found its best expression in Thomas Franck's last book,[35] with the prediction that renewed confidence about freedom and choice would empower individuals, and this sense of individual empowerment would reshape international law.

Thirty years on after the fall of the Berlin Wall however, the prevalent sense is quite different. Far from being empowered, the individual appears to be *disempowered* as a result of social and technological changes that threaten the very notion of personal autonomy. Financial transactions are decided by algorithms operating at speeds well beyond the computing capacity of the human brain. Individuals are being harvested for data ranging from their consumer preferences to their DNA so that their choices can be manipulated – a new global system of behaviour modification which Shoshana Zuboff describes as 'surveillance capitalism'.[36] Rather than resist these trends, liberals

---

[35] Thomas Franck, *The Empowered Self: Law and Society in the Age of Individualism* (Oxford: Oxford University Press), p. 1.

[36] Shoshana Zuboff, *The Age of Surveillance Capitalism: The Fight for a Human Future at the New Frontier of Power* (New York: Public Affairs, Hachette Book Group, 2019), p. 8.

and progressives have sometimes merrily gone along with them, promoting – for example – 'nudge' as a way of redirecting the behaviour of individuals towards socially more useful goals.[37] The fact that we speak more often of human, social (and even state) 'behaviour' rather than 'action' is itself revealing of a change in assumptions: while the term 'action' seems to indicate a preceding deliberation and choice, 'behaviour' does not.

While the disempowerment of the individual is a fairly recent development, it is now intertwined with a crisis of democratic legitimacy that began before. Writing in the early 1980s – and thus before both the wave of post–Cold War globalisation in the 1990s and the rise of surveillance capitalism in the 2010s – the Italian political philosopher, Norberto Bobbio, argued that mature democracies were failing to deliver the key promises of democracy,[38] such as taming the influence of oligarchies, widening access to deliberation, and making power less opaque. Around the same time, Jürgen Habermas published his famous analysis of the legitimation crisis of late-capitalism where he reached similar conclusions to Bobbio's.[39]

The globalisation of the market has made democracy's unfulfilled promises even more difficult to deliver. If national oligarchies proved surprisingly resistant to national democratic control, transnational ones are almost entirely impervious to it; at the same time power has become more opaque and out of reach as a result of the expansion of transnational networks of regulators, policymakers and experts tasked with the administration of the global markets; these transnational deliberative spheres are, in turn, more exclusive and removed from ordinary people than democratic deliberative spheres at the national level. Even more fundamentally, globalisation has weakened the state's ability to exercise core functions on which its political legitimacy depends, namely the regulation of the market and the pursuit of socio-economic change.

In Europe, supranationalism adds a new dimension to the legitimation crisis first diagnosed by Bobbio and Habermas. EU law-making illustrates both the continuing influence of oligarchy and the opacity of power. Central to the EU

---

[37] Richard H. Thaler and Cass R. Sunstein, *Nudge: Improving Decisions about Health, Wealth and Happiness* (New York: Penguin Books, 2009), p. 6.

[38] Norberto Bobbio, *Il Futuro della Democrazia* (Rome: Einaudi, 1984).

[39] Jürgen Habermas, *Legitimationsprobleme im Spätkapitalismus* (Frankfurt am Main: Suhrkamp Verlag, 1973). For the English edition see Jürgen Habermas, *Legitimation Crisis* trans. Thomas McCarthy (Boston: Beacon Press, 1975), p. 41, p. 95. For a discussion of the relevance of Habermas's thesis to the current phase of globalised capitalism, see Nancy Fraser, 'Legitimation Crisis? On the Political Contradictions of Financialized Capitalism' (2015) 2 *Critical Historical Studies* 157–89.

66   *Guglielmo Verdirame*

ordinary lawmaking process are trilogues, behind-closed-doors informal meetings between representatives of EU institutions. As the authors of a leading textbook on EU law explain, the Commission is the 'big winner' of the trilogue system, while formal procedures 'do no more than rubber stamp prior agreements'. Their concluding assessment ought to be damning:

> Only very well connected actors have the opportunity to lobby these informal processes because only they can know where they are taking place or who is important within them. Furthermore, only they will have the resources to arbitrage between these centres of powers, lobbying both central protagonists in the trilogue and other important actors in the Council, the Parliament and the Commission.[40]

The influence of powerful lobbies is a problem in domestic lawmaking too. But EU lawmaking maximises that influence, and the checks and balances it offers are very limited. Fixing any of these problems does not appear to be a priority for supranationalists. Following the damning assessment reproduced above, the authors of the textbook justify the European Parliament's reluctance to confront the Commission with the gleeful comment that 'imperfect EU legislation is better than no legislation'.

Notwithstanding Bobbio's and Habermas's early warnings, the mainstream political debate, on the left as well as the right, paid little attention to the relationship between globalisation and the crisis in democratic legitimacy until recently. The anti-globalisation movement of the late 1990s was generally regarded as a marginal phenomenon politically, and the expression of a radical left which had some following in metropolitan areas and among students, but never came close to becoming a mass movement or even to having much impact on mainstream liberal and progressive politics. The Clinton-Blair centre-left, which embodied the predominant mindset of liberal progressives in the West in the two decades from the fall of the Berlin Wall to the financial crisis, never took the anti-globalisation critique seriously. This disconnect between radical left critiques and centre-left politics may explain why, in the end, it was the political right, whose intellectual contribution to the critique of globalisation had been modest, that managed to benefit politically from the backlash against globalisation.

But what is the solution to the crisis of democracy which globalisation has deepened? Dani Rodrik argues that we are faced with a trilemma, involving

---

[40] Giorgio Monti, Gareth Davies and Damian Chalmers, *European Union Law* (2014, 3rd ed.), p. 123.

a choice between three goods: globalisation, the state and democracy.[41] The problem, he argues, is that they cannot all be secured at the same time. At most we can attain two. If Rodrik is right, democracy on a national scale cannot survive in a hyperglobalised world where national institutions lose the power to regulate the market, and thus the only options for those who value self-government are global democracy or less globalisation. Let's consider them in turn.

Global democracy would have to be invented anew, for the only form of a democracy we know is state-based. The biggest problem with global democracy is not however that it has not happened in practice before. If the fact that something has not been done before were to be regarded as an insuperable practical limit, as Kant noted in his famous essay *On the Common Saying*,[42] we would have never had any progress. The problem with global democracy is, rather, that we do not even have a theory on how it could work.

Thomas Christiano identifies the 'weakness of global civil society' as a key obstacle to global democracy.[43] It may be tempting to rebut that weaknesses of global civil society are destined to improve with the help of new technologies and social media creating a transnational and even global civil sphere. Some of these hopes may be justified, but we should not think of 'civil society' in the narrow sense in which the term is used these days, that is, essentially as a synonym for 'NGOs'. In political theory, from Tocqueville to Gramsci, civil society is a more complex concept, encompassing all forms of associative life in the social, cultural, religious or educational spheres. It may be the case that, for example, climate change activists coordinating across borders are an expression of global civil society, but this is not unprecedented: the Communist International or religious movements also transcended borders, and probably involved even greater proportions of the population at their respective time. But the associative forms that matter to the lives of the vast majority of people today remain local or national.

Nevertheless, even if weaknesses in global civil society could improve over time, other problems may prove more intractable. First, there is the issue of identity. Perhaps the clearest expression of a self-governing will is the

---

[41] Dani Rodrik, *The Globalisation Paradox: Why Global Markets, States and Democracy Can't Coexist* (Oxford: Oxford University Press, 2011), pp. 184–206.

[42] Immanuel Kant, 'On the Common Saying: "This May Be True in Theory But It Does Not Apply in Practice"' in M. J. Gregor (ed.), *The Cambridge Edition: Practical Philosophy* (Cambridge: Cambridge University Press, 1999) pp. 273–310.

[43] See, for example, Thomas Christiano, 'Democratic Legitimacy and International Institutions' in Samantha Besson and John Tasioulas (eds.), *The Philosophy of International Law* (Oxford: Oxford University Press, 2010), p. 119 and p. 137.

preference to be ruled by one's own people rather than foreigners. If you ask Italians whether German politicians are better than Italian politicians, a large majority will probably answer affirmatively. But if you then ask them whether they would be happy for Germans to run the Italian government, very few would agree.

Not wanting to be governed by foreigners is not an expression of narrow-minded nationalism. It is a reflection of important moral ideas of self-respect and self-ownership, which apply to political communities as they do to individuals. We prefer to be governed by our own incompetent rulers rather than by more competent foreigners for the same reason why, as individuals, we value taking decisions for ourselves rather than letting others, even if better informed, decide for us. The rejection of foreign rule is the force that wore out empires in the nineteenth and twentieth centuries, and it is difficult to see how global democracy could ever respond to this deep-felt need for identity, belonging and ultimately self-ownership.

The other problem with global democracy is size, understood in terms of both population and space. Insofar as India can be regarded as a democratic success, it is perhaps true that democracy has been proven achievable on a very large scale. In the Indian case, as in the US one, federalism is the key to such success. But the leap from subcontinental democracy to global democracy is huge.

Size is the main reason why, contrary to the common mischaracterisation of Kant as a cosmopolitan, Kant actually rejected cosmopolitanism. In a key passage in his *Essay on Perpetual Peace* he wrote:

> The idea of the right of nations presupposes the separation of many neighbouring states independent of one another; and though such a condition is of itself a condition of war (unless a federative union of them prevents the outbreak of hostilities), this is nevertheless better, in accordance with the idea of reason, than the fusion of them by one power overgrowing the rest and passing into a universal monarchy, since as the range of government expands laws progressively lose their vigour, and a soulless despotism, after it has destroyed the seed of good, finally deteriorates into anarchy.[44]

A future generation of liberal thinkers may be able to find a solution to the problem identified by Kant that world government will descend into soulless despotism. The current one, for all its internationalist flair and 'citizen of the world' rhetoric, has performed remarkably poorly. Modern-day

---

[44] I. Kant, 'Toward Perpetual Peace' in M. J. Gregor (ed.), *The Cambridge Edition of the Works of Immanuel Kant in Translation: Practical Philosophy* (Cambridge University Press, 1999), pp. 311–51 at 336.

internationalists in fields like law or political science may often identify as cosmopolitan but have produced no serious breakthrough in cosmopolitan political and legal theory. 'Global democracy' is not even a theory of which it might be said that it does not work in practice – it is still waiting to be theorised.

If the prospects for global democracy are so dim, and assuming Rodrik is right about his trilemma, the only way to preserve democracy is putting the brakes on globalisation and on the expansion of technocracy. A typical riposte to this suggestion is that globalisation is inevitable. TINA ('there is no alternative') has been 'the pensée unique of both the centre left and the centre right' for the last three decades now,[45] with those who contest this pensée unique, whether from the right or the left, dismissed as populists.

Interestingly however, at the time of writing this contribution (end of 2019), in Europe it is the centre-left that seems more dogmatically committed to TINA than the centre-right. It is true that subjecting the unelected power of transnational and international institutions may be more challenging than doing the same, as some are now proposing,[46] with national ones like central banks. The latter is a matter of domestic law and politics, while the former is difficult, perhaps impossible, to achieve without international cooperation. As Rodrik reminds us, both the gold standards and the Bretton Woods arrangements were a compromise between trade and national sovereignty. And there is no reason in principle why a new compromise could not be struck with a view to protecting national decision-making. As long as anyone who raises these concerns is dismissed, demonised even, as a populist or a *souverainiste* by the mainstream of modern-day liberal internationalism, it will be difficult to make any progress.

3.5 CONCLUSION: AUTOCRATIC INTERNATIONAL LAW VERSUS TECHNOCRATIC INTERNATIONAL LAW?

The conventional account among liberal internationalists is that the rules-based order is threatened both by populists in Europe and North-America and by autocratic powers like Russia and China. But this account misses out on a different threat, and one that is perhaps genuinely existential: the transformation of liberal internationalism into *il*liberal internationalism. I have sought

---

[45] W. Streeck, 'The Return of the Repressed', 104 *New Left Review* March/April 2017, p. 6.
[46] Paul Tucker, *Unelected Power: The Quest for Legitimacy in Central Banking and the Regulatory State* (Princeton, NJ: Princeton University Press) 2018.

to explain the reasons for this transformation in this chapter. By way of conclusion, I will illustrate it with two anecdotes.

The first one is from a recent academic conference where an American international law scholar and practitioner who perhaps more than anyone of his generation embodies the centre-left's unquestioning support for globalisation typical of the Blair-Clinton years presented a paper on transnational governance. 'Where does self-government fit in your theory of transnational governance?' he was asked at the end of his presentation. 'I have nothing against self-government' his answer began. It is a comment that captures the transformation of liberal internationalism that I have examined.

Unlike their counterparts of forty or fifty years ago, modern-day liberal internationalists are unwilling, and perhaps even unable, to make the case for self-government. It is not only a Lincoln or a Mazzini who would have been horrified at such rejection of self-government, or at best timidity in supporting it; the Roosevelts or the Attlees would have reacted similarly too. The problem may not be that the masses in the West are deserting democratic liberalism and falling for the temptations of populism and even authoritarianism as they did in the first half of the last century. The problem also lies with liberal elites abandoning the idea of self-government as a fundamental political and moral value and as the foundation of a liberal international order.

The second illustration is a speech by the former President of the European Parliament, Guy Verhofstadt, at the annual conference of the UK Liberal Democrats – the most pro-EU and internationalist party in Britain and putative heir to the Whig tradition.[47] Arguably one of Europe's leading liberal politician, Mr Verhofstadt opined that 'the world order of tomorrow is not a world order based on nation states or countries; it is a world order that is based on Empires'. Men and women who style themselves as liberals, democrats and internationalists applauded. Something sinister is going on. Anyone making the case for a world order based on empires would have been laughed off stage or booed at the conference of any European centre-left party in the 1960s or 1970s. Has the world really changed so fundamentally that liberals now want to build empires? And, even it has, isn't it too soon to give up on self-government?

Modern-day liberal internationalism may still be animated by a genuine concern for values that liberals share – such as human rights – but commitment to political liberty and self-government has been waning to say the least. With no serious democratic alternative to national democracy having been

---

[47] See www.youtube.com/watch?v=8v3xruukans.

even theorised, internationalism risks becoming an illiberal credo. For the vision of a platonic cosmopolis with judges and knowledge administrators in charge of supranational adjudication and administration, is not a liberal vision. It is a deeply illiberal one.

The clash between liberal internationalism and authoritarian international law does not capture these developments. Authoritarian international law is certainly a threat to a liberal world order, but the threat within 'liberal internationalism' is more pressing, and perhaps even more momentous for it creates a moral and political confusion about liberalism from which it will be difficult to recover. In a clash between faux liberals and real authoritarians, there will be no one making the case for a liberal world order founded on the values of self-government and political liberty.

The alternative is not a return to a romanticised world of self-governing political communities in peaceful coexistence with one another. Quite aside from the fact that that world never existed, there is no running away from the fact that the practice of self-government faces phenomenal challenges in the modern world. But the biggest challenge may come from the disavowal of the idea of self-government by modern-day 'liberal' internationalists. Public argument about Brexit in the UK in 2016–19 revealed the extent of this disavowal. 'Liberal' internationalists pooh-poohed arguments about sovereignty and democratic control as passé and nostalgic at best, as an expression of nationalism or racism at worst. But if, as was claimed repeatedly, the world's fifth largest economy cannot afford self-government, does it not mean that this great progressive democratic idea is essentially defunct? And when did it die and who killed it? Has the people's right to freely pursue their economic, social and cultural development, which the International Covenant on Civil and Political Rights solemnly declares, become an impossibility? Or, worse, was it always a lie?

Faced with the referendum result, in an attempt to undermine its legitimacy, some 'liberal' internationalists resorted to views that would have been regarded as abhorrent by liberals until a generation or two ago; some voters should be allowed to cast two votes;[48] universal suffrage should be dismantled and replaced with a system where educated people have more of a say;[49] and a host of gleeful comments about the imminent death of elderly voters among

---

[48] Nick Clegg argued for a second referendum on UK membership of the EU and suggested that '[w]e should give every youngster under 30 a weighted vote of twice the value of everybody else', www.dailymail.co.uk/news/article-4697984/Let-s-second-Brexit-referendum-says-Nick-Clegg.html.

[49] This argument has been advanced by A. C. Grayling in his post-Brexit pamphlet *Democracy and Its Crisis* (2018). See Giles Fraser's critical comment on these views in: www.theguardian.

whom support for leave had been higher.[50] These were not just the views of eccentrics on twitter. They were those of a former deputy PM and leader of a party that claims to be the heir to that Whig tradition that fought for equal and universal suffrage; from a professor of philosophy who is a professed champion of liberalism and human rights; and from one of the Britain's most renowned writers. If liberalism survives this self-destructive moment, future liberals will look back with a mixture of amusement and horror to the illiberalism of our generation of 'liberal' internationalists.

com/commentisfree/belief/2017/sep/21/the-wrong-sort-of-voter-theres-no-such-thing-ac-grayling.

[50] See Ian McEwan's comments at a Brexit conference in London, www.theguardian.com/politics/2017/may/12/15m-oldsters-in-their-graves-could-swing-second-eu-vote-says-ian-mcewan.

4

The New, New Sovereigntism, or How the European Union Became Disenchanted with International Law and Defiantly Protective of Its Domestic Legal Order

Mark A. Pollack[*]

Europe as a political entity will either be united, or will not be at all. Only a united Europe can be a sovereign Europe in relation to the rest of the world. And only a sovereign Europe guarantees independence for its nations, guarantees freedom for its citizens.

– Donald Tusk[1]

Within the West, the United States of America (USA) and the European Union (EU) are often depicted as being divided in their attitudes towards international law, with a "Normative Power Europe" embracing the rule of international law while an exceptionalist and "New Sovereigntist" USA opposes any incursion of international law into the US legal order. More specifically, the new sovereigntist critique of international law, which comes primarily from the American right, can be broken down into three essential claims: first, that international legal processes are procedurally flawed, and inferior to the US democratic, constitutional system of making and interpreting law; second, that international legal norms and rules are also substantively flawed, in conflict (or at least tension) with core US values; and third, that US sovereignty and the US domestic legal order must be protected – often defiantly so – against international law, through means such as non-ratification of, reservations to, and non-self-executing status of treaties, as

---

[*] This chapter builds from a paper prepared for presentation at the International Studies Association Annual Conference, Baltimore, 22–25 February 2017. The author is grateful to Janina Dill, Jeff Dunoff, Chiara Giorgetti, Monika Heupel, Christian Kreuder-Sonne, Guglielmo Verdirame, and Michael Zürn for comments on earlier drafts of this chapter.

[1] Donald Tusk, *Speech by President Donald Tusk at the Ceremony of the 60th Anniversary of the Treaties of Rome* (25 March 2017), www.consilium.europa.eu/en/press/press-releases/2017/03/2 5-tusk-ceremony-rome-speech/.

74   *Mark A. Pollack*

well as refusal by Congress and the courts to give direct effect to international treaties, custom and judicial decisions in the US legal order.

In this chapter, I question this transatlantic dichotomy, documenting the rise of what one might call a "new, new sovereigntism" emanating from Europe. Contrary to what one might expect, I do not locate this new European sovereigntism on the far right. To be sure, nationalist far-right parties are resurgent across Europe, deeply attached to traditional state sovereignty, and overtly hostile to the EU's intrusions on the nation-state.[2] By and large, however, far-right parties and movements in Europe have concentrated their fire on the EU, and largely ignored the more distant body of public international law. The new sovereigntism that I trace in this chapter, rather, has arisen among *pro-European* parties and movements, and primarily on the left and center-left of the political spectrum, seeking to defend *EU* laws and the autonomy of *EU* legal order against the intrusions of a growing body of public international law to which they object.

In parallel to American sovereigntism, I argue, the new European sovereigntism makes three essential claims: first, that international lawmaking and interpretive processes are procedurally flawed, in the sense of being secretive and dominated by the USA and by corporate influence; second, that at least some international rules and norms are illiberal in their substantive content, conflicting with and threatening to destroy core principles of European fundamental rights and social and environmental regulations; and third, that the European legal order must be defiantly protected against the intrusion of illiberal international legal influences. Put simply, the European left has discovered the importance of protecting EU laws, values and legal autonomy against what is perceived to be a procedurally flawed and substantively objectionable body of international law. We see this phenomenon also in the domestic politics of individual European states, but it is most clearly manifest at the level of the EU, the institutions of which provide opponents of international law with multiple veto points through which to block the adoption of, consent to, compliance with, and internalization of international rules and norms.

Empirically, the chapter explores the rise of this new, European version of sovereigntism by tracing European responses to three recent developments in international law: (1) the Anti-Counterfeiting Trade Agreement (ACTA), which was rejected by EU institutions for failing to protect the rights of EU citizens; (2) the proposed Transatlantic Trade and Investment Partnership (TTIP) with the USA and the Comprehensive Economic and Trade

---

[2] *See, e.g.,* CAS MUDDE, POPULIST RADICAL RIGHT PARTIES IN EUROPE (2007).

Agreement (CETA) with Canada, both of which have been denounced by political leaders and civil society for their secrecy as well as for alleged corporate domination of investor-state dispute settlement (ISDS); and (3) the Union's long-running rejection of, and defiant noncompliance with, the World Trade Organization (WTO) rulings on hormone-treated beef and genetically modified (GM) foods, which the EU found to be inconsistent with the Union's precautionary principle as well as the will of the people.

As we shall see, the new European sovereigntism is not identical to its American cousin: coming primarily from the left and center rather than the right, the new European variant objects to different features and fields of international law, seeks to defend different bodies of domestic law, and for the most part engages with the international legal order more constructively than American sovereigntism. The point of this chapter, therefore, is not to equate the American and European versions of sovereigntism from a normative or political perspective, but rather to note that we are witnessing the emergence of a genuinely new phenomenon: for decades, Europe has been characterized by a mainstream, consensual and almost uncritical enthusiasm for international law, seen as legitimate in process as well as in content, and welcome in the EU legal order. I argue, however, that contemporary Europe, particularly on the left, has lost this uncritical acceptance of international law, replaced with a growing conviction that at least some parts of international law are objectionable both in process and in substance, and that domestic European rules and values must be defended against it. Proponents of international law, and those who would advocate its progressive development, ignore the rise of this new European skepticism at their peril.

4.1 THE ARGUMENT

Over the past several decades, it has become commonplace in both scholarly and political circles to contrast the positions of the USA and the European Union EU toward the rule of international law.[3] Especially during the years after the September 11, 2001 terrorist attacks, critics argued that the USA had abandoned its post war role as the champion of the international legal order, being instead characterized at best by ambivalence toward legal constraints, and at worst as a "rogue nation."[4] By contrast, the EU has been seen as

---

[3] For an excellent discussion of transatlantic disagreements among legal scholars as well as political actors, see Guglielmo Verdirame, "The Divided West": International Lawyers in Europe and America, 18 EUR. J. OF INT'L L 553 (2007).

[4] See, e.g., Peter J. Spiro, The New Sovereigntists: American Exceptionalism and Its False Prophets, 79 FOREIGN AFF. 9 (2000); Harold Hongju Koh, On American Exceptionalism, 55

inherently committed to the rule of law and a strong international legal order.[5] This stark contrast has, in recent years, taken on the status of conventional wisdom, among both liberal European scholars, who present the rule of law as a cornerstone of the nascent EU foreign policy,[6] and American neoconservative commentators, who proudly defend US defiance of international law they see as illegitimate.[7]

This strong transatlantic contrast in US and EU attitudes towards international law is certainly overdrawn. In a recent, collective project on US and EU support for international law, I have argued that one can and should disaggregate the overly broad notion of "support" into four dimensions or stages – from *leadership* in the negotiation of international agreements, through *consent* to those agreements, *compliance* with legal obligations and *internalization* of international law into the domestic legal order.[8] Disaggregating support in this manner, we see a much more complex picture, with considerable variation within as well as across the USA and the EU, across dimensions, among issue-areas, and over time. The USA, for example, has indeed demonstrated considerable reluctance to commit itself to multilateral agreements though Congressional ratification, and also to internalize international law in the domestic legal order, both of which lend support to the "new sovereigntist" image of America. Yet the USA has played an important (if inconsistent) leadership role in the creation of the international legal order, and its record of compliance with international law remains strong in many areas. Empirical examination of the EU's engagement with the international legal order reveals a similarly nuanced story. On the one hand,

---

STAN. L. REV. 1479 (2003); JOHN F. MURPHY, THE UNITED STATES AND THE RULE OF LAW IN INTERNATIONAL AFFAIRS (2004); CLYDE V. PRESTOWITZ, ROGUE NATION: AMERICAN UNILATERALISM AND THE FAILURE OF GOOD INTENTIONS (2004); PHILIPPE SANDS, LAWLESS WORLD: THE WHISTLE-BLOWING ACCOUNT OF HOW BUSH AND BLAIR ARE TAKING THE LAW INTO THEIR OWN HANDS (2006); and JENS DAVID OHLIN, THE ASSAULT ON INTERNATIONAL LAW (2015).

[5] *See, e.g.,* Ian Manners, *Normative Power Europe: A Contradiction in Terms?*, 40 J. OF COMMON MKT. STUD. 235 (2002); Liesbeth Aggestam, *Introduction: Ethical Power Europe?*, 84 INT'L AFF. 1 (2008); and Verdirame, *supra* note 3, at 576, ("Invoking a rule of international law carries, ipso facto, some weight in Europe, the normativity of international law being psychologically and politically widely accepted").

[6] *See, e.g.,* Ian Manners, *The Normative Ethics of the European Union*, 84 INT'L AFF. 45 (2008).

[7] JACK L. GOLDSMITH & ERIC A. POSNER, THE LIMITS OF INTERNATIONAL LAW (2005); and ERIC A. POSNER, THE PERILS OF GLOBAL LEGALISM (2009).

[8] The discussion in this and the previous paragraph draws on Mark A. Pollack, *Who Supports International Law, and Why? The United States, the European Union, and the International Legal Order*, 13 INT'L J. CONST. L. 873 (2015) (introducing a symposium of six articles, with case studies on international human rights law, trade law, criminal law, environmental law and the reception of international law in US and EU courts, respectively).

The New, New Sovereigntism 77

European countries and the EU itself appear substantially more ready to consent to international legal agreements (at least until very recently), and Europe also has a strong record of compliance in most areas of international law. On the other hand, EU leadership has been selective both across issue areas and over time, and there is reason to question the image of the EU as open to internalization of international law, given evidence that European courts have increasingly sought to protect the autonomy of the EU legal order.

My aim in this chapter is not to attack, much less to debunk, the conventional dichotomy between a scofflaw America one the one hand and an international law-loving Europe on the other. The aim of this chapter, rather, is to suggest that European attitudes towards international law may be *changing*, and that the EU is developing a European variant of the American new sovereigntism, in which a growing number of critics – concentrated primarily, though not only, among the pro-European left and center-left – have raised fundamental procedural and substantive objections to international rules and norms, which they depict as hostile to European laws and values, and against which they champion a defiant resistance. In a growing number of areas of international law, including international trade, economic regulation, food safety, data privacy, and national security, the European center-left has moved towards a sharply critical view of international law, alternatively resisting consent to unwelcome agreements,[9] compliance with unwelcome international judicial decisions,[10] and internalization of international laws perceived to be in tension with domestic EU rules and rights.[11] These changing attitudes towards international law, in turn, have been magnified and translated into policy outcomes through the EU's "hyper-consensus" political institutions, which create multiple veto points allowing critics of international law to block EU consent to, compliance with, and internalization of a growing

---

[9] Examples include the ACTA, TTIP and CETA cases discussed below, as well as several bilateral agreements with the United States dealing with the sharing of Passenger Name Recognition flight information and SWIFT banking data. On the latter two cases, *see, e.g.,* Jörg Monar, *The Rejection of the EU-US SWIFT Interim Agreement by the European Parliament: A Historic Vote and Its Implications*, 15 Eur. Foreign Aff. Rev. 143 (2010); and Katharina Meissner, *Democratizing EU External Relations: The European Parliament's Informal Role in SWIFT, ACTA, and TTIP*, 21 Eur. Foreign Aff. Rev. 269 (2016)

[10] *See, e.g.,* the beef-hormones and GM foods cases discussed below, as well as the discussions of EU "obstructionism" and occasional noncompliance in international trade law, in Christina L. Davis, *A Conflict of Institutions? The EU and GATT/WTO Dispute Adjudication, Department of Politics*, Princeton University, March 12, 2007; and Jappe Eckhardt & Manfred Elsig, *Support for International Trade Law: The US and the EU Compared*, 13 Int'l J. Const. L. 966 (2015).

[11] Gráinne de Búrca, *Internalization of International Law by the CJEU and the US Supreme Court*, 13 Int'l J. Const. L. 987 (2015).

Mark A. Pollack

number of areas of international law. Let us consider each of these two factors – changing European attitudes and EU institutions – in turn.

4.1.1 *The New, New Sovereigntism in Europe, in Three Theses*

As noted above, the new sovereigntist critique of international law in the United States can be summarized in three essential claims: that international legal processes are procedurally flawed and inferior to the US democratic, constitutional system of making and interpreting law; that international legal norms and rules are substantively flawed, in conflict with core US values; and that the US domestic legal order must therefore be protected against international law. In this section, I briefly unpack each of these three claims, and argue that a parallel set of claims is emerging in Europe. To be clear, I do not argue that these claims are substantively identical, for they are not: indeed, the "new, new sovereigntism" in today's EU emerges primarily (though not only) from the left and center-left rather than the right; it seeks to protect a different set of domestic values (centered around European conceptions of fundamental rights and the "European social model"); and it objects to different features and bodies of international law. Structurally, however, the two sovereigntisms share a similar architecture.

First, at the most general level, the new sovereigntism on both continents manifests as a normative critique of international legal *processes*, which are depicted as inferior to domestic constitutional practices of democratic lawmaking (in the legislative function) and legal due process (in the executive and judicial functions). In the USA, we see a widespread view on the conservative right that international legal processes are illegitimate, seeking to replace US constitutional procedures for making, executing and interpreting the law with flawed international processes in which multilateral treaty-making (at the United Nations in particular) is driven by coalitions of illiberal states using their numbers to ride roughshod over the minority of liberal democracies, while international legal interpretation and adjudication is undertaken by unaccountable, low-quality or biased international adjudicators, with insufficient due process accorded to either state or (in the case of international criminal law) individual defendants. It is, in part, views such as these that explain domestic US opposition to the workings of UN human rights treaty bodies, interstate courts such as the International Court of Justice and the International Tribunal on the Law of the Sea, and the International Criminal Court. In Europe, we see a variant of this procedural argument emerging from the center-left. Like their American counterparts, European sovereigntists see international legal processes as flawed, threatening to replace democratically legitimate domestic decisions with normatively inferior international processes, but the specific criticisms are different. In the European critique, many international legal decisions, in areas ranging from international trade to international security, are taken in secret by executives of states, with inadequate or nonexistent supervision by democratically elected legislatures. These secret negotiations, moreover, disproportionally benefit great powers, most notably the United States, as well as the multinational corporations that enjoy privileged access to them. Moving from lawmaking to adjudication, and continuing the focus on secrecy and corporate power, European sovereigntists focus their procedural skepticism on the arbitral procedures of investor-state dispute settlement, which gives corporate investors a privileged right to challenge the economic policies and regulations of sovereign states before secretive arbitral tribunals.

Second, sovereigntists in Europe and the USA both stand opposed to the *substance* of many international rules and norms, which are held to contradict deeply held domestic values and/or violate fundamental rights. On the American right, the argument is that, in part because the making and interpretation of international law has been captured by illiberal and undemocratic governments, the substance of international rules is foreign to US constitutional and legal traditions, and/or harms US national interests. These substantive concerns are arguably at the heart of sovereigntist opposition to UN human rights law (which is seen to be foreign to either the US constitutional order or the Judeo-Christian tradition), environmental law (seen as imposing an unfair burden on the USA or constraining US economic growth), as well as the law of the sea, humanitarian law and criminal law. European sovereigntists similarly find substantively objectionable provisions in international law, although again the specific complaints are different. As we shall see, Europeans express an increasingly common belief that, because so much of international law has been captured by the USA and multinational corporations, much of contemporary international law represents a neoliberal assault on the social regulations and fundamental rights that together form Europe's *acquis social*.

Finally, following from these first two elements, the third common element is a commitment to protecting domestic (national or European) sovereignty against the encroachment of flawed international rules and processes, by (1) blocking agreement on or consent to objectionable international legal agreements, or, if such obstruction is impossible, then (2) blocking compliance with or internalization of international rules in the domestic legal order. Indeed, the most visible hallmark of the new sovereigntism is not just defiance, but proud defiance, of international legal rules and processes, coupled with

80   Mark A. Pollack

a zealous effort to protect valued domestic rules and processes from their baleful effects. In the USA, conservatives defiantly and successfully block ratification of unwelcome treaties in areas as diverse as human rights, environment, law of the sea, criminal law and arms control, among others. In Congress, mostly conservative majorities ensure that many of the treaties that *are* ratified are declared non-self-executing, and/or the subject of extensive reservations. And in US courts, conservative judicial majorities frequently decline to give direct effect to international treaties and international judicial decisions. In Europe, the defiant protection of national sovereignty comes primarily from the left, seeking to protect fundamental rights and economic and social regulations from the economically liberalizing or securitizing influences of international law. Here, we find socialists, liberals and Greens (among others) defiantly opposing conclusion of TTIP, and blocking European ratification of treaties like ACTA and CETA on the grounds that they would violate the rights of European citizens. Where critics of international law fail to block the initial adoption of international legal obligations, as with the WTO and its attendant technical agreements, they may seek to obstruct compliance with unwelcome judicial rulings, as in the US/EU disputes over hormone-treated beef and genetically modified foods. Notwithstanding the long tradition of presenting the EU as valuing international law independent of content, a growing number of EU citizens and legislators now view at least some areas of international law as threatening, and to be resisted rather than welcomed.

In sum, while the American and European versions of sovereigntism may seem like opposites – coming from different ends of the political spectrum, objecting to different features of international law and seeking to protect different elements of their own domestic legal orders – they are nevertheless structurally quite similar, combining procedural and substantive critiques of international law with a determined effort to cordon off and protect the autonomy of their domestic legal orders.

4.1.2 *The Aggravating Effect of Institutions: the EU As a Separation of Powers System with Multiple Veto Points*

The emergence of a European legal sovereigntism is primarily the result of changes in European attitudes towards international law and the need to protect domestic (national or EU) sovereignty against it. As in the USA, however, attitudes are only part of the story, because in both polities, *decentralized, separation-of-powers political institutions create multiple veto points, amplifying the influence of critics of international law.*

In principle, a huge variety of legal and constitutional features – including not least broad differences in regime type between democratic and authoritarian regimes, or legal differences between monist and dualist legal systems – might influence the approach of a given state to international law. For our purposes here, however, the most significant feature of both EU and US institutions has to do with the horizontal and vertical separation of powers, and the multiplication of veto points that allow domestic actors in both settings to block or challenge the consent to, compliance with and internalization of international law.[12] More precisely, the EU, like the USA, is characterized by both a horizontal separation of powers among the legislative, executive and judicial branches of the EU government, and a vertical separation of powers between the EU and its constituent member states. Both of these separations of powers, and the resulting multiplication of veto players, complicate the ability of the EU, like the USA, to commit to international legal agreements *ex ante*, and to comply with and internalize those agreements *ex post*. Let us consider each separation of powers in turn.

The horizontal separation of powers in the USA divides governmental authority among an executive branch that negotiates and executes international legal agreements, a legislative branch whose consent is required for ratification of most international treaties, and a judicial branch that interprets those treaties and facilitates or blocks their internalization in the domestic legal order. The result of that separation of powers for US engagement with international law is well known, perhaps most strikingly with respect to challenge of treaty ratification. Not only does the two-thirds majority requirement in the US Senate necessitate in most cases a bipartisan majority to ratify any proposed treaty, but the structure of the Senate also results in the overrepresentation of the less populous states, such that Senators representing only 17 percent of the US population are in theory capable of rejecting any international treaty.[13] Furthermore, the US presidential system, by contrast with the parliamentary systems characteristic of nearly all European countries, includes within it the prospect of divided government, in which a President is often faced with the prospect of sending a treaty to a Senate with a majority (or a blocking minority) from the opposition party. Taken together, these

[12] On the EU as system characterized by a vertical and horizontal separation of powers, *see* Mark A. Pollack, *Theorizing EU Policy-Making*, in POLICY-MAKING IN THE EUROPEAN UNION (Helen Wallace, Mark A. Pollack, Christilla Roederer-Rynning, & Alasdair Young, eds., 2020). On the significance of veto points and veto players, *see* GEORGE TSEBELIS, VETO PLAYERS: HOW POLITICAL INSTITUTIONS WORK (2002).

[13] Oona Hathaway, *Treaties' End: The Past, Present, and Future of International Lawmaking in the United States*, 117 YALE L. J. 1236, 1271 (2008).

institutional rules privilege status-quo interests seeking to block the ratification of treaties to which they are opposed, and no doubt help to explain the extremely large backlog of treaties signed by the President but not subsequently approved by the Senate – a classic case of what Robert Putnam has called "involuntary defection" from international agreements as a result of failed ratification.[14]

Although the majority of European states are characterized by parliamentary systems with relatively few veto players, the EU itself strongly resembles the USA as a separation-of-powers system, with independent and powerful executive, legislative and judicial branches of government. In the EU, the Brussels-based Commission acts as the core executive, while the legislative function is shared by the intergovernmental Council of Ministers and by the directly elected European Parliament (EP), and the Court of Justice of the European Union (CJEU) acts as the independent and powerful judicial branch. Taken together, these institutions create multiple veto points and veto players, and make the Union a "hyper-consensus polity" requiring broad agreement to enact domestic and international policies and allowing multiple actors to block any unwelcome initiatives.[15]

This hyper-consensus nature of EU institutions has been studied most prominently in domestic EU rulemaking, but it is increasingly manifest in EU foreign relations as well. Under the terms of the 2009 Treaty of Lisbon, the Union as such is empowered to negotiate and act as a party to international treaties within its areas of competence (most notably trade), subject to ratification by both the Council of Ministers and the European Parliament. Indeed, it appears that the recent empowerment of the Parliament to consent to international agreements has resulted in a modest "ratification problem" for the Union, manifested in the Parliament's rejection of agreements such as the US/EU agreement on the sharing of banking data,[16] another bilateral

---

[14] Robert D. Putnam, *Diplomacy and Domestic Politics: The Logic of Two-Level Games*, 42 INT'L ORG. 427, 438 (1988) ("The possibility of failed ratification suggests that game theoretical analyses should distinguish between *voluntary* and *involuntary defection*. Voluntary defection refers to reneging by a rational egoist in the absence of enforceable contracts-the much-analyzed problem posed, for example, in the prisoner's dilemma and other dilemmas of collective action. Involuntary defection instead reflects the behavior of an agent who is unable to deliver on a promise because of failed ratification").

[15] On the EU as a "hyper-consensus polity," *see* SIMON HIX, THE EU AS A POLITICAL SYSTEM (2008).

[16] Stanley Pignal, *European Parliament Rejects US Data Swap Deal*, FT.COM, Feb. 11, 2010, https://proxy.library.upenn.edu/login?url=https://proxy.library.upenn.edu:2072/docview/2293 20051?accountid=14707.

agreement with Morocco over fisheries,[17] and the multilateral ACTA (discussed in Section 4.2). In this sense, the empowerment of the EP, which has been rightly presented as a victory for democratic accountability in the Union,[18] has also increased the incidence and the future likelihood of involuntary defection. Much the same is true of the CJEU, which is entrusted with ensuring that EU foreign policy conforms to the requirements of the Treaties, and which in that context has denied direct effect to WTO law in the EU legal order,[19] nullified the application of UN Security Council Resolutions in the EU,[20] and blocked the Union's accession to the European Convention on Human Rights.[21] More generally, the horizontal separation of powers has the effect of creating multiple veto points – the Commission, the member states in the Council, the EP and the CJEU – any of which can block the EU's consent to, compliance with, or internalization of international law.

This effect is magnified, in the EU as well as the USA, by a second separation of powers, between a federal or quasi-federal center and the constituent states. In the US context, federalism has meant in practice that the federal government must respect the rights of the various states in its negotiation of international agreements, and that individual states may complicate US compliance with such agreements by adopting policies at odds with the international legal commitments entered into by the federal government. In the EU, with its system of enumerated powers for the Union, and strong residual powers of the member states, the vertical separation of powers can similarly impair the ability of the Union to consent to international legal agreements, and to implement and internalize those agreements after the fact. The former effect is most notable in areas of "mixed competence," where the Union shares competence with the member governments. For such agreements, which include both environmental accords as well as complex trade and investment agreements (including the ACTA, TTIP and CETA

---

[17] Toby Vogel, *MEPs Reject EU-Morocco Fisheries Pact*, EUR. VOICE, Dec. 14, 2011, www politico.eu/article/meps-reject-eu-morocco-fisheries-pact/.

[18] Meissner, *supra* note 9.

[19] de Búrca, *supra* note 11.

[20] Joined Cases C-402 & 415/05P, *Kadi & Al Barakaat Int'l Found* v *Council & Commission*, 2008, E.C.R I-6351. For an excellent analysis stressing the CJEU's defense of the autonomy of the EU legal order, *see, e.g.*, Gráinne de Búrca, *The European Court of Justice and the International Legal Order After Kadi*, 51 HARV. INT'L L. J. 1 (2008).

[21] Opinion 2/13, EU:C:2014:2454, Dec. 18, 2014; Walter Michl, *Thou Shalt Have No Other Courts Before Me*, VERFBLOG, Dec. 23, 2014; 2014/12/23, http://verfassungsblog.de/thou-shalt-no-courts/; Daniel Halberstam, *It's the Autonomy, Stupid: A Modest Defense of Opinion 2/13 on EU Accession to the ECHR, and the Way Forward*, 16 GER. L. J. 105 (2015); Turkuler Isiksel, *European Exceptionalism and the EU's Accession to the ECHR*, 27 EUR. J OF INT'L L. 565 (2016).

84   *Mark A. Pollack*

agreements discussed in Sections 4.2, 4.3, and 4.4), ratification of an international agreement requires the agreement of EU institutions *as well as that of all of the individual member states*. This dramatically increases the number of veto players in the system, to include the national and even subnational parliaments of the various member states, placing further impediments to the Union's ability to consent to, comply with and internalize international law.

Taken together, the emergence of a European new sovereigntism, together with EU institutions that empower critics of international law, have resulted in a number of landmark conflicts over the EU's support for important parts of the international legal order over the past decade. I examine three such conflicts in the next three empirical sections of the chapter, summarizing the debate in each case and drawing lessons about Europe's changing relationship to public international law.

4.2 INTERNATIONAL INTELLECTUAL PROPERTY VERSUS DOMESTIC DATA PRIVACY RIGHTS: THE DEFEAT OF THE ANTI-COUNTERFEITING TRADE ACT

The Anti-Counterfeiting Trade Act, or ACTA, was a multilateral trade agreement negotiated from 2008 to 2011 among a group of mostly advanced industrial countries, which included the USA, Japan, the EU and its member states, Switzerland, Canada, Australia, New Zealand, South Korea, Singapore, Morocco and Mexico. The agreement, concluded in 2011, sought to create harmonized rules for the protection of intellectual property rights (IPR), with a focus on the digital environment of the internet, requiring all members to implement in their own domestic law a series of intellectual property protections as well as enforcement procedures and effective remedies for violations.[22]

For the EU, ACTA was a "mixed" agreement, involving the competences of both the Union and its then-twenty-seven individual member states, with the Union's interests being represented in negotiations primarily by the Commission. As a mixed agreement, ACTA would require ratification *both* by the Union, including approval by the European Council and consent of the EP, *and* by each of the member states, in order to take effect. In December 2011, the European Council unanimously endorsed the agreement. The following month, the EU and twenty-two of its member states signed ACTA in a ceremony in Japan. In an early sign of potential

---

[22] Ministry of Foreign Affairs of Japan, *Anti-Counterfeiting Trade Agreement*, www.mofa.go.jp/policy/economy/i_property/pdfs/acta1105_en.pdf.

difficulties, however, five EU member states – Germany, Cyprus, Estonia, the Netherlands and Slovakia – withheld their signatures. The subsequent ratification process, moreover, prompted vigorous opposition to the treaty, both within the EP and on the streets of many European cities, culminating in the dramatic and overwhelming rejection of ACTA by the Parliament in July 2012. For our purposes, ACTA is a case of European nonconsent to a multilateral international treaty, of a type that is commonplace in the USA but which was, at the time, relatively new for the EU. It was also, in Putnam's phrase, a case of "involuntary defection," since the EU's chief negotiator, the Commission, had negotiated and concluded a legally binding treaty with its counterparts, only to see EU and national institutions refuse to ratify the agreement after the fact.

A detailed review of the contents of ACTA, or of the debate over its ratification, is beyond the scope of this chapter,[23] yet even a brief review of the debate reveals all three of the elements discussed above, including claims that the treaty was both procedurally and substantively flawed and in conflict with core European values, as well as defiant and ultimately successful calls for the rejection of the treaty.

Procedural objections to the negotiation process for ACTA began almost immediately after the negotiations were launched. The focus at this early stage, as well as later, was on the confidential nature of the negotiations, which were conducted in secret among the delegates of the parties. In fact, the conduct of trade negotiations in secret is a long-standing tradition, designed to allow negotiators to make difficult and politically sensitive concessions in specific sectors in pursuit of an overarching agreement, yet European critics consistently referred to ACTA as a "shady back-room deal"[24] adopted behind a "veil of secrecy" under pressure from intellectual property owners, and without proper democratic oversight.[25]

---

[23] For useful reviews and analyses, see, e.g., Kimberlee Weatherall, *Politics, Compromise, Text and the Failures of the Anti-Counterfeiting Trade Agreement*, 33 Sydney L. Rev. 229 (2011); Bryan Mercurio, *Beyond the Text: The Significance of the Anti-Counterfeiting Trade Agreement*, 15 J. of Int'l Econ. L. Vol. 361 (2012); Duncan Matthews & Petra Žikovská, *The Rise and Fall of the Anti-Counterfeiting Trade Agreement (ACTA): Lessons for the European Union*, 44 Int'l Rev. of Intell. Prop & Competition L. 626 (2013); and Andreas Dür & Gemma Mateo, *Public Opinion and Interest Group Influence: How Citizen Groups Derailed the Anti-Counterfeiting Trade Agreement*, 21 J. of Eur. Pub. Pol'y 1199 (2014).

[24] Danny O'Brien, *Secret Agreement May Have Poisonous Effect on the Net*, The Irish Times, Nov. 13, 2009, at 10.

[25] Eric Pfanner, *Quietly, Nations Grapple with Steps to Quash Fake Goods*, The New York Times, Feb. 16, 2010, at B6.

86   Mark A. Pollack

These concerns about secrecy were expressed strongly in the European Parliament, which consistently sought to protect its prerogatives under the recently adopted Lisbon Treaty. In March of 2010, the EP issued a strongly worded resolution, adopted by an overwhelming vote of 663 to 13, which expressed "its concern over the lack of a transparent process in the conduct of the ACTA negotiations," and called on the Commission and the Council to grant public and parliamentary access to negotiating texts and summaries and "to engage proactively with ACTA negotiation partners to rule out further negotiations which are confidential as a matter of course."[26] Although the Commission responded by releasing a draft text of the most recent ACTA draft in April of 2010,[27] the procedural charge that the negotiations had been undertaken in secrecy, and dominated by the USA and large corporations, would continue to dog the treaty.[28]

Just as importantly for our purposes, critics of ACTA increasingly shifted from *procedural* concerns to a series of *substantive* objections centered around the claim that ACTA constituted a major threat to EU-protected rights to privacy and data protection, as well as to internet freedom. During the negotiations, amid reports that the USA was seeking strong enforcement provisions in any potential treaty,[29] critics of the proposed treaty raised the alarm about a series of rumored provisions that would criminalize individual downloading of pirated materials or make internet service providers (ISPs)

---

[26] *European Parliament Resolution of 10 March 2010 on the Transparency and State of Play of the ACTA Negotiations*, P7_TA(2010)0058, ¶¶ 2–4; see also *EU Parliament Warns ACTA Negotiators*, THE NEW ZEALAND HERALD, Mar. 11, 2010. The EP's resolution also prefigured some of the substantive concerns that would later doom the treaty, noting for example that "privacy and data protection are core values of the European Union, recognised in Article 8 ECHR and Articles 7 and 8 of the EU Charter of Fundamental Rights, which must be respected in all the policies and rules adopted by the EU," and calling for the Commission to conduct an "impact assessment of the implementation of ACTA with regard to fundamental rights and data protection, ongoing EU efforts to harmonise IPR enforcement measures, and ecommerce, prior to any EU agreement on a consolidated ACTA treaty text," which it indicated should be limited to "to the existing European IPR enforcement system against counterfeiting." *European Parliament Resolution of 10 March 2010*, ¶¶ 7, 9, and 12.

[27] Nathalie Vandystadt, *Trade/Intellectual Property: ACTA in Line with EU Legislation, Says Commission*, EUROPOLITICS INFO. SOC'Y, May 7, 2010.

[28] Nor were concerns about secrecy limited to Europe. *See, e.g.*, David Jolly, *Fresh Battle Lines Drawn over Internet Freedom: Activists in Europe Say Public Did Not Have Input on Global Copyright Pact*, THE INTER'L HERALD TRIBUNE, Feb. 6, 2012, at 13, (quoting an open letter from American law professors to President Barack Obama, criticizing the "intense but needless" secrecy of the negotiations).

[29] Michael Geist, *Anti-Counterfeiting Treaty Talks Heat Up*, THE TORONTO STAR, Mar. 30, 2009, at B02; Bobbie Johnson, *Technology: Newly Asked Questions: What Is Acta and What Should I Know About It?*, THE GUARDIAN, Nov. 12, 2009, at 2.

criminally liable for users' illegal activities.[30] One frequently mentioned concern was that ACTA could include a "three-strikes" rule, whereby individual internet users, after multiple warnings of copyright infringement, could be temporarily suspended from internet access, violating what many Europeans considered to be a fundamental human right.[31] The Commission repeatedly sought to address such fears, assuring Parliament and the public that no such provisions would appear in the final text.[32] Testifying before Parliament in July 2010, Trade Commissioner Karel de Gucht assured MEPs that, "This is not about creating a Big Brother," and that the Commission's objective was to "keep to the Community acquis."[33]

Despite these assurances, the publication of the final draft text and the signature of the treaty by the EU and twenty-two of its member states in January 2012, prompted an eruption of procedural and substantive objections to the treaty, in the EP, in national parliaments, and on the streets of European cities.

In early February of 2012, a reported 30,000 mostly young protestors took to the streets of German cities including Munich and Berlin, while other, smaller protests sprouted in Bulgaria, Romania, the Czech Republic, Hungary, Poland, Lithuania, France and the United Kingdom – a remarkable public response to a technical trade agreement.[34] Under pressure from an increasingly hostile public, national governments, including several that had already signed the agreement, renounced their support, indicating that they would not seek ratification. In Poland, for example, protesters massed in the streets of Posnan and Lublin, and the opposition Law and Justice party called for a referendum on the agreement.[35] Several days later, then-Prime Minister Donald Tusk withdrew his support of the agreement, announcing at

---

[30] Vandystadt, *supra* note 27.
[31] O'Brien, *supra* note 24, at 10; Pfanner, *supra* note 25, at B6.
[32] Vandystadt, *supra* note 27 ("For the Commission ... things are now clear: 'The ACTA will be fully in line with current EU legislation'. The aim is to combat violation of intellectual property rights 'on a commercial scale'. In other words, the agreement is not supposed to affect the peer-to-peer swapping of illegally downloaded files between two teenagers, for example. The ACTA will by no means lead to a limitation of civil liberties or to harassment of consumers,' adds the EU executive. It notes that none of the negotiating parties is proposing to introduce a graduated response' rule (two warnings and then cut-off of the connection) against users who download content illegally. Nor will access to generic medicines be hampered, as some fear").
[33] Vandystadt, *supra* note 27.
[34] Michael Steininger, *More Than 30,000 Germans Turn Out Against Anti-Piracy Treaty ACTA*, THE CHRISTIAN SCIENCE MONITOR, Feb. 13, 2012.
[35] Charles Arthur, *Acta Protests Break Out as EU States Sign up to Treaty*, THE GUARDIAN, Jan. 27, 2012.

88   *Mark A. Pollack*

a press conference that, "The opinion prepared by our officials in the course of the final months of our work on the ACTA was not well thought-out . . . It appears unarguable that the ACTA represents an attempt to enforce property rights at the expense of Internet freedom, which is too high a price . . . ."[36] Other governments followed suit in the subsequent days and weeks, including the governments of Germany, Latvia, the Czech Republic and Bulgaria.

At the EU level, ACTA sparked an equally vigorous debate, centered primarily on the EP, which would ultimately decide its fate by ratifying or rejecting the agreement. The tone was set early on when the EP's original rapporteur for the agreement, French Socialist MEP Kader Arif, resigned in protest to "denounce in the strongest manner the process that led to the signing of this agreement: no association of civil society [and] lack of transparency from the beginning." Arif also complained about the specific provisions of the treaty, which he called "very unbalanced in favour of patent holders,"[37] and "wrong in both form and substance."[38] MEPs were also under public pressure, with opponents mobilizing some 2.8 million signatures on a petition that called on the EP to reject the treaty and protect the rights of European citizens.[39]

Once again, the Commission came to the defense of the proposed treaty, reiterating its claim that no changes would be required to European legislation, and requesting an advisory opinion from the Court of Justice to assess its compatibility with European fundamental rights and freedoms.[40] Parliament's new rapporteur for the agreement, David Martin of the Socialists and Democrats group, indicated that the EP would wait for the anticipated CJEU ruling,[41] but soon the debate in the Parliament outpaced the Court, as sentiment among MEPs turned increasingly against the treaty.

MEPs brought up familiar procedural and substantive criticisms against the treaty, while also raising new and additional objections familiar from many US

---

[36]   BBC, *Polish Premier Urges European Parliament to Vote against ACTA*, BBC WORLDWIDE MONITORING, Feb. 22, 2012.

[37]   Charles Arthur, *Acta Goes Too Far, Says MEP*, THE GUARDIAN, Feb. 1, 2012.

[38]   Quoted in David Jolly, *Fresh Battle Lines Drawn over Internet Freedom: Activists in Europe Say Public Did Not Have Input on Global Copyright Pact*, THE INT'L HERALD TRIBUNE, Feb. 6, 2012, at 13.

[39]   Avaaz, *ACTA: The New Threat to the Net*, https://secure.avaaz.org/en/eu_save_the_internet/?pv=412&rc=fb.

[40]   The Commission's question to the Court, submitted on 4 April 2012, read, "Is the Anti-Counterfeiting Trade Agreement (ACTA) compatible with the European Treaties, in particular with the Charter of Fundamental Rights of the European Union?" European Commission, Press Release: "Update on ACTA's Referral to the European Court of Justice," 4 April 2012, at http://europa.eu/rapid/press-release_IP-12-354_en.htm?locale=en.

[41]   *Id.*

ratification debates. Critics, including Martin, argued that the provisions of the treaty were vague, and could potentially be interpreted in ways that could violate EU laws and EU citizens' fundamental rights. "The EP's goal and mine is to protect intellectual property rights in Europe," argued Martin, but "the problem with ACTA is its consequences. They say that the devil is in the details, but there aren't enough details in the text."[42] This view was shared by other critics, and endorsed in the Opinion of the European Data Protection Supervisor (EDPS), which criticized the treaty for the vagueness of its provisions, and noted that those provisions, "if not implemented properly," might interfere with the fundamental rights and freedoms of EU citizens.[43] Commissioner De Gucht responded forcefully to the EDPS opinion, noting that the implementation of those provisions would be left to the EU itself, and that there was no reason to assume that the Union would implement them in a way that violated fundamental rights.[44] Nevertheless, the EDPS report proved influential with MEPs, and the argument about the treaty's vagueness was widely cited in Parliament. Yet another argument familiar to veterans of US ratification debates came from European Socialists & Democrats group leader Hannes Swoboda, who objected to the treaty on the grounds that other relevant countries, like China and India, would remain outside the agreement.[45]

Gradually, over the course of multiple committee hearings and debates, MEPs and their political groups turned decisively against the agreement. On the left and center-left, the Green, Socialist and Liberal party groups in the EP all came out against the treaty, while the center-right European People's Party was divided, with many MEPs defending ACTA as a necessary agreement to protect intellectual property in the internet age.[46] Finally, in early July, 2012,

---

[42]   David Martin, quoted in Manon Malhère, *Anti-Counterfeiting Trade Agreement: MEPs Concerned About ACTA's Vagueness*, EUROPOLITICS INFO. SOC'Y, Mar. 19, 2012.

[43]   European Data Protection Supervisor, *Opinion of the European Data Protection Supervisor on the Proposal for a Council Decision on the Conclusion of the Anti-Counterfeiting Trade Agreement between the European Union and Its Member States, Australia, Canada, Japan, the Republic of Korea, the United Mexican States, the Kingdom of Morocco, New Zealand, the Republic of Singapore, the Swiss Confederation and the United States of America*, April 24, 2012, https://secure.edps.europa.eu/EDPSWEB/webdav/site/mySite/shared/Documents/Con sultation/Opinions/2012/12–04-24_ACTA_EN.pdf, paras. 33–35, 69.

[44]   Manon Malhère, *Anti-Counterfeiting Trade Agreement: De Gucht Finds Supervisor's Opinion "Unfounded"*, EUROPOLITICS INFO. SOC'Y, June 11, 2012.

[45]   Manon Malhère, *Anti-Counterfeiting Trade Agreement: S&D May Reject ACTA*, EUROPOLITICS INFO. SOC'Y, Mar. 5, 2012.

[46]   On the divisions within the EPP, and the party's efforts to delay a vote, *see* Manon Malhère, *Anti-Counterfeiting Trade Agreement: Parliament Throws Out ACTA*, EUROPOLITICS INFO. SOC'Y, July 9, 2012.

the European Parliament voted in plenary to reject the treaty, by a lopsided vote of 478 MEPs voting against the agreement, with only 39 in favor and 165 abstentions.[47] Opponents of the treaty were both jubilant and defiant. "It's a crushing victory," said the spokesman for La Quadrature du Net, a Paris-based nonprofit group advocating internet rights and freedoms. "It's a political symbol on an enormous scale, in which citizens of the world, connected by the Internet, have managed to defeat these powerful, entrenched industries."[48] Leaders in the EP were similarly celebratory. "Acta is now dead in the EU thanks to the European Parliament," said rapporteur David Martin. "I am very pleased that the parliament has followed my recommendation and rejected Acta. The treaty is too vague and is open to misinterpretation. I will always support civil liberties over intellectual property rights protection in the EU."[49] EP President Martin Schultz, for his part, celebrated ACTA's rejection as "a milestone for European democracy."[50]

Whatever one's views on the merits of ACTA, the European debate about the treaty was a watershed, not only in the EP's powers to reject international treaties, but also as the first widespread expression of a new European sovereigntism, with its deep skepticism of the process and substance of international law and its determination to defend the European legal order against intrusions that could undermine European rights, European regulations and European sovereignty. It would not, however, be the last such expression.

4.3 INTERNATIONAL TRADE AND INVESTMENT LAW: THE CAMPAIGNS AGAINST TTIP, ISDS AND CETA

The Transatlantic Trade and Investment Partnership is a proposed economic agreement, the first of its kind, between the European Union and the United States. Negotiations on the terms of an agreement began in mid-2013, with the aim of concluding an agreement before the end of President Barack Obama's final term of office in January 2017 – a deadline that was clearly missed. As its name suggests, the proposed agreement was envisioned as a comprehensive

---

[47] European Parliament Press Release, *European Parliament Rejects ACTA*, July 4, 2012, www. europarl.europa.eu/news/en/news-room/20120703IPR48247/european-parliament-rejects-acta.

[48] Jeremie Zimmermann, quoted in Eric Pfanner, *Europeans Reject Treaty to Combat Digital Piracy*, THE NEW YORK TIMES, July 5, 2012, at B5.

[49] Quoted in Charles Arthur, *Anti-Piracy Agreement Rejected by European Parliament, but Acta Could Be Revived by European Commission*, THE GUARDIAN, July 4, 2012.

[50] Martin Schultz, *European Democracy's Victory in a Treaty's Defeat*, PROJECT SYNDICATE, July 5, 2012, www.project-syndicate.org/commentary/european-democracy-s-victory-in-a-treaty-s-defeat?barrier=true.

one, incorporating both trade and investment. On the trade side, the proposed agreement would not only reduce tariffs, which were already low between the EU and the USA, but also seek to remove nontariff barriers to trade through transatlantic regulatory cooperation. On the investment side, the agreement would join a growing number of comprehensive free trade agreements and bilateral investment treaties that included protections for investment, and in particular provisions for investor-state dispute settlement, whereby investors would gain the right to challenge host-state practices that negatively impacted investment profitability.[51]

Unlike traditional trade agreements, to which opposition might take the form of old-fashioned protectionism objecting to lower tariffs and foreign competition, much of the opposition to the TTIP centered on the fear that regulatory harmonization and ISDS would undermine EU regulatory stand-ards in areas such as the food safety, environmental and consumer protection, labor and social rights.[52] Put differently, the prospect of TTIP implicated not only external tariffs but also EU regulatory sovereignty – and it was this second feature that was central to the wave of popular opposition to TTIP that flared across Europe from 2014, manifested in demonstrations across the continent as well as a "Stop TTIP" petition that secured over three million signatures.[53] Soon, the cause of opposition to TTIP was taken up by European politicians, particularly on the center-left, in both national parliaments and the EP. These opponents successfully tarred the agreement as the embodiment of American and corporate power and neoliberal values threatening EU regulations, rights,

---

[51] For general introductions to the TTIP proposals and negotiations, *see, e.g.*, Shayerah Ilias Akhtar, *Transatlantic Trade and Investment Partnership (T-TIP) Negotiations*, Congressional Research Service Report, Feb. 29, 2016; Alasdair R. Young, *Not Your Parents' Trade Politics: The Transatlantic Trade and Investment Partnership Negotiations*, 23 REV. OF INT'L POL. ECON. 345 (2016). On the prospects for regulatory cooperation under TTIP, *see* Alberto Alemanno, *The Regulatory Cooperation Chapter of the Transatlantic Trade and Investment Partnership: Institutional Structures and Democratic Consequences*, 18 J. OF INT'L ECON. L. 625 (2015); and Gregory Shaffer, *Alternatives for Regulatory Governance under TTIP: Building from the Past*, 22 COLUM. J. OF EUR. L. 403 (2016).

[52] *See, e.g.*, Philip Stephens, *US Politics Is Closing the Door on Free Trade*, FIN. TIMES, Apr. 8, 2016, at 9 ("The nature of free trade deals has changed. They used to be about tariffs. Now they focus on regulatory standards and norms, intellectual property rights, data privacy and invest-ment protection. These are issues that cut deep across national political and cultural prefer-ences. Lowering import duties is one thing; persuading voters to relax the rules on data protection or accept new rules on food safely is another"). See also the comprehensive list of grievances against TTIP on the website of the Stop TTIP Campaign, at https://stop-ttip.org /what-is-the-problem-ttip-ceta/.

[53] Stop TTIP: European Initiative Against TTIP and CETA, "Success for Stop TTIP: 3,263,920 Signatures," Oct. 7, 2015, https://stop-ttip.org/success-for-stop-ttip-3263920-million-signatures/.

sovereignty and democracy.[54] A brief survey of this opposition reveals, once again, the three elements of the new sovereigntist critique of international law.

First, as with ACTA, opponents of TTIP assailed the agreement on procedural grounds, claiming that the negotiations were being undertaken in secrecy, insulating the negotiators from either parliamentary or democratic accountability and allowing American and corporate interests to dominate. "The harsh reality," as British Labour MP Geraint Davies argued in the House of Commons, "is that this deal is being stitched up behind closed doors by negotiators, with the influence of big corporations and the dark arts of corporate lawyers." These negotiators, Davies argued further, were "stitching up rules that would be outside contract law and common law, and outside the shining light of democracy, to give powers to multinationals to sue governments over laws that were designed to protect their citizens."[55]

This last quote points to a second procedural complaint, namely that the agreement's proposed ISDS provisions would allow foreign investors to challenge and potentially overturn democratically adopted EU regulations designed to protect the citizens of Europe. European as well as American negotiators defended the inclusion of ISDS in the agreement, arguing that any comprehensive economic treaty between the EU and the USA required institutional protection of investors' rights. Opponents, however, seized upon recent ISDS challenges to national regulations, including the high-profile challenge by Swedish industrial group Vattenfall to Germany's moratorium on nuclear power, to depict investor-state dispute resolution as a corrupt practice granting extraordinary power to investors, and to unelected and nontransparent arbitral tribunals, at the expense of democratically elected parliaments. ISDS, in the eyes of its critics, "would sacrifice sovereignty on the altar of unfettered free trade, with big corporations calling the shots,"[56] transferring regulatory authority from EU institutions and governments to secretive and unelected arbitral tribunals.[57] Reflecting such concerns,

---

[54] *See, e.g.*, Georges Monbiot, *Taming Corporate Power: The Key Political Issue of Our Age*, THE GUARDIAN, Dec. 8, 2014.

[55] Quoted in "TTIP Talks Expose 'Dark Arts' of Corporate Lawyers," LEGAL MONITOR WORLDWIDE, Jan. 17, 2015.

[56] Frank McDonald, *Deal, or No Deal? What the Transatlantic Trade Deal Would Mean for Ireland*, IRISH TIMES, Oct. 14, 2014.

[57] *See, e.g.*, James Kanter, *Trade Chief for EU Calls for Prudence on U.S. Pact*, INT'L NEW YORK TIMES, Jan. 14, 2015, at 13, ("For European opponents of the investment guarantee, the concern is that if it became part of a trade agreement, it would give companies a legal opening to erode European standards in environmental protection, food quality and labor rights"); Jim Armitage, *US Firms Could Make Billions from Britain via Secret Tribunals*, THE INDEPENDENT, Oct. 10, 2014 ("Critics say the tribunals, held under the so-called investor-

The New, New Sovereigntism 93

European politicians, particularly on the center-left, turned sharply against ISDS, with the EP's Socialists and Democrats group calling in March of 2015 for the removal of ISDS from any transatlantic agreement.[58]

European concerns about ISDS shade into a second set of suspicions, namely that TTIP provisions on regulatory cooperation and harmonization, as well as ISDS, would produce lowest-common-denominator standards and undermine the EU's high regulatory standards in areas such as food safety, environmental and consumer protection, labor and social rights.[59] With respect to food safety, for example, grass-roots organizations mobilized, claiming that TTIP would result in the Union's forced adoption of regulations allowing for such American horrors as hormone-treated beef, chlorine-washed chicken, and genetically modified vegetables.[60] Others worried that either regulatory cooperation or ISDS rulings would lead Europe to harmonize down to US standards on the environment or labor rights, while British opponents of TTIP feared that agreement would force the privatization of the National Health Service, or block future efforts to renationalize privatized industries such as the railways.[61]

Reflecting these concerns and suspicions of the TTIP, opponents also displayed the third hallmark of the new sovereigntism, namely a belief that domestic sovereignty, domestic democracy and domestic laws had to be defiantly protected against TTIP, which should be comprehensively rejected. In response to these concerns and demands, the Commission, together with national governments, sought to respond to concerns about secrecy by releasing documents about the ongoing negotiations, as well as by explaining their positions and dispelling misinformation about the proposed agreement.[62] In

---

state dispute settlement (ISDS) system, subvert democratic justice, giving power over foreign citizens to big companies. Hearings are held in private, in international courts at the World Bank in Washington DC, bypassing the legal system of the country being sued, meaning details are often impossible to uncover. In some cases the very existence of the case is not made public. . . .. Unions and NGOs have claimed that TTIP will open the floodgates for ISDS cases that will overturn the decisions of democratically elected governments in Western Europe").

[58] Andrew Gardner, *Socialists Struggle over Protection for Investors*, Eur. Voice, Mar. 15, 2015.

[59] Emily Beament, *US Trade Deal "Could Weaken EU Regulation,"* The Independent, March 10, 2015.

[60] *Free Trade with US: Europe Balks at Chlorine Chicken, Hormone Beef*, US Official News, Dec. 6, 2014.

[61] George Monbiot, *The British Government Is Leading a Gunpowder Plot Against Democracy: This Bill of Corporate Rights Threatens to Blow the Sovereignty of Parliament Unless It Can Be Stopped*, The Guardian, Nov. 4, 2014.

[62] *See, e.g.*, Suzanne Lynch, *Staying Positive in Maelstrom of EU-US Trade Negotiations: Trade Commissioner Cecilia Malmstrom Has Her Work Cut Out as She Tries to Conclude the Controversial TTIP Deal with the US*, Irish Times, 4, March 27, 2015.

94   *Mark A. Pollack*

doing so, moreover, they underlined their firm commitment to protecting existing EU regulations and regulatory sovereignty. The Junker Commission and its ambassador to the USA, for example, drew clear red lines around EU regulatory policies in areas such as hormone-treated beef and genetically modified organisms, noting that the EU would keep these issues off the table of the transatlantic negotiations.[63] The governments of France and Germany, for their part, issued periodic, weak defenses of TTIP, but they also withdrew their support for ISDS, with the French Minister of State for Foreign Trade noting that, "We have to preserve the right of the state to set and apply its own standards, to maintain the impartiality of the justice system and to allow the people of France, and the world, to assert their values."[64] In Britain, the government assured citizens that the UK would not sign up to a TTIP that undermined the National Health Service, and that "it cannot, must not, and will not happen at the expense of our sovereign right to run the NHS the way we want."[65]

In the most substantive response to the growing anti-TTIP sentiment, the new European Trade Commissioner, Cecelia Malmström, conceded that "there is a huge skepticism about the ISDS instrument," and announced a suspension of talks about ISDS pending further EU consultations.[66] Later that year, the Commission proposed, in place of traditional, rotating three-member arbitral tribunals, a standing "Investment Court System" to adjudicate investment disputes. By contrast with the dominant investment arbitration system, the EU proposal envisaged a two-tiered court, including a fifteen-judge Tribunal of First Instance and a separate six-judge Appeal Tribunal. One third of the judges on each tribunal would be "nationals of" (and presumably appointed by) the United States, the EU and third countries, respectively.[67] The Commission proposal stimulated a major debate over the wisdom and

---

[63] David O'Sullivan, *Why the Transatlantic Trade Deal Will Benefit Ireland*, IRISH TIMES, Oct. 17, 2014.

[64] Patrick Harvie, *More and More People Are Becoming Aware of the Dangers of This Agreement; Why TTIP Spells Danger for Us*, EVENING TIMES (GLASGOW), Nov. 26, 2014.

[65] Deputy Prime Minister Nick Clegg, quoted in Rowena Mason & Nicholas Watt, *Nick Clegg Attempts to Calm NHS Worries Over EU-US Trade Deal*, THE GUARDIAN, Dec. 17, 2014.

[66] Quoted in Andrew Grice, *Activists Triumph as Contentious US Free Trade Deal Clause Is Suspended*, THE INDEPENDENT, Jan. 14, 2015, p. 6.

[67] For the original text of the Commission proposal, *see Transatlantic Trade and Investment Partnership*, TRADE IN SERVICES, INVESTMENT AND E-COMMERCE, CHAPTER II – INVESTMENT," Nov. 12, 2015, http://trade.ec.europa.eu/doclib/docs/2015/no vember/tradoc_153955.pdf. For an excellent analysis of the proposal, *see* Athina Fouchard Papaefstratiou, *The EU Proposal Regarding Investment Protection: The End of Investment Arbitration as We Know It?*, KLUWER ARBITRATION BLOG, Dec. 29, 2015, http://kluwerarbi

the design of its proposed Investment Court,[68] but it was not enough to calm the boil of opposition to TTIP across Europe, much less the paralysis caused by the November 2016 US presidential elections, and TTIP negotiations stalled in the second half of the year, with at best uncertain prospects under a Trump Administration.

In the interim, the TTIP was leapfrogged by a similar agreement, the Comprehensive Economic and Trade Agreement (CETA) between the EU and Canada. After years in the shadow of the larger, more high-profile and controversial TTIP, CETA rose to political prominence after 2014, when the EU and Canada reached a tentative agreement on the terms of a similar trade and investment partnership. The draft agreement bore strong resemblances to the stalled EU-US pact, yet it was also shaped in part by the controversy over TTIP, most notably in the agreement to create an alternative investor-state dispute settlement mechanism, replacing the traditional arbitral tribunals with a standing Investment Court.[69]

Despite these changes to accommodate European sovereignist concerns, CETA met with multiple legal and political challenges on its way to signature in the second half of 2016. In Germany, a group of NGOs sought an emergency injunction from the German Constitutional Court to block the government from signing the treaty, arguing that it represented an immediate threat to German constitution, the rule of law and parliamentary democracy.[70] Although the German Constitutional Court declined to block the government's signature of the treaty, it set a series of conditions on the provisional application of the treaty, and reserved the

---

trationblog.com/2015/12/29/the-eu-proposal-regarding-investment-protection-the-end-of-invest ment-arbitration-as-we-know-it/.

[68] On the controversial issue of investor-state dispute settlement in TTIP, *see, e.g.,* Mattias Kumm, *An Empire of Capital? Transatlantic Investment Protection as the Institutionalization of Unjustified Privilege,* ESIL REFLECTIONS, Vol. 4, No. 3, May 25, 2015; Gisèle Uwera, *Investor-State Dispute Settlement (ISDS) in Future EU Investment-Related Agreements: Is the Autonomy of the EU Legal Order an Obstacle?,* 15 THE LAW AND PRACTICE OF INTERNATIONAL COURTS AND TRIBUNALS 102 (2016); Ingo Venzke, *Investor-State Dispute Settlement in TTIP from the Perspective of a Public Law Theory of International Adjudication,* 17 JOURNAL OF WORLD INVESTMENT & TRADE 374 (2016); and Joseph H. H. Weiler, *European Hypocrisy: TTIP and ISDS,* EJIL TALK!, Jan. 21, 2015, www.ejiltalk.org/european-hypocrisy-ttip-and-isds/.

[69] For a good analysis, *see* Blake Cassels & Graydon LLP, *Dispute Resolution under CETA: A New Investment Court for Canada and Europe,* Dec. 15, 2016, www.lexology.com/library/detail.aspx?g=e46e5848-0761-468e-ac02-64d7a03c4edd.

[70] Stefan Wagstyl, *Protest Against EU-Canada Deal Heads to German Court,* FIN. TIMES, 4, May 31, 2016.

right to revisit the compatibility of CETA with the constitution in future cases.[71]

An equally serious and more acute challenge to CETA came during the ratification process. Following the initial signing of the treaty, the Commission had suggested that CETA fell entirely within the EU's common trade policy, which meant that the EU would have exclusive competence and ratification would involve approval by the Council and the EP, bypassing the twenty-eight individual member states and their thirty-eight national and regional parliaments.[72] In the face of considerable backlash from national parliaments and interest groups[73], however, the Commission succumbed to public pressure in July 2016, announcing that CETA would be adopted as a "mixed" agreement, requiring approval from national parliaments in all twenty-eight member states.[74] In federal Belgium, moreover, ratification would require further approval from regional parliaments in Brussels, Flanders and Wallonia.

The latter requirement nearly doomed the agreement when, in early October, the Walloon Parliament voted by a large majority (forty-six to sixteen) to reject the agreement, citing multiple objections, including most notably the provisions for ISDS, but also concerns about the impact of CETA's regulatory provisions on the right of the Union and its member states to regulate in the public interest. With the power of a veto player, the Walloon Parliament, and its Minister-President Paul Magnette, held up the treaty for weeks, demanding substantial concessions in return for its agreement.[75] The EU and Canada responded by negotiating an eleven-page "Joint Interpretive

---

[71] For a good discussion, *see* Editor Borderlex, *The EU-Canada Trade Deal and the German Constitutional Court*, Oct. 19, 2016, http://borderlex.eu/national-courts-eu-trade-policy-powers -eu-canada-trade-deal-german-constitutional-court/. For a pessimistic reading of the judgment for the future of CETA, *see* Wolfgang Münchau, *The Monstrous Battle to Secure a Trade Deal*, FIN. TIMES, Oct. 17, 2016, 11.

[72] *EU Commission to Opt for Simple Approval for Canada Deal*, REUTERS, June 28, 2016.

[73] Jim Brunsden & Duncan Robinson, *EU Spat Threatens Canada Trade Deal That Took 5 Years to Negotiate; Ratification Dispute*, FIN. TIMES, July 4, 2016.

[74] *EU Trade Deal Bows to the Power of Parliaments; Brussels Cedes Ratification of Pact with Canada to its Member States*, FIN. TIMES, July 6, 2016. See also Janyce McGregor, *Canada Gets Clarity on How Europe Will Ratify Trade Deal*, CBC NEWS, July 5, 2016, www.cbc.ca /news/politics/ceta-european-commission-ratification-mixed-competency-1.3664884 (quoting EU Trade Commissioner Cecelia Malmström suggesting that, "From a strict legal standpoint, the commission considers this agreement to fall under exclusive EU competence. However, the political situation in the council is clear, and we understand the need for proposing it as a 'mixed' agreement, in order to allow for a speedy signature").

[75] The Walloon position to the agreement reflected both local concerns, including a 16 percent regional unemployment rate, a steady stream of industrial plant closings, and the growing appeal of the Marxist Worker's Party eating into the support of the governing Socialist

Instrument"[76] which included *inter alia* detailed provisions protecting the right of each side to regulate its domestic economy[77] and to provide public services[78] as well as placing limits on regulatory cooperation[79] and detailing a variety of procedural guarantees for the investor-state dispute settlement provisions of the treaty.[80] Taken together, these provisions, and others in the

majority, and broader European concerns, with First Minister Magnette publicly calling for the European left to stand up to creeping neoliberalism. For good discussions, *see, e.g.,* Barrie McKenna, *CETA, Explained,* The Global and Mail (Canada), Oct. 25, 2016; and Konrad Yakauski, *The Walloon that Roared; Paul Magnette Didn't Set Out to Anger Canada. He Has a Much Bigger Plan – Saving the European Union from Itself,* The Globe and Mail (Canada), A13, Oct. 27, 2016.

[76] *Joint Interpretative Instrument on the Comprehensive Economic and Trade Agreement (CETA) between Canada and the European Union and Its Member States,* on-line at http://data .consilium.europa.eu/doc/document/ST-13541-2016-INIT/en/pdf.

[77] *Ibid.* para 2 ("CETA preserves the ability of the European Union and its Member States and Canada to adopt and apply their own laws and regulations that regulate economic activity in the public interest, to achieve legitimate public policy objectives such as the protection and promotion of public health, social services, public education, safety, the environment, public morals, social or consumer protection, privacy and data protection and the promotion and protection of cultural diversity").

[78] *Ibid.* para 4, noting that (a) "The European Union and its Member States and Canada affirm and recognise the right of governments, at all levels, to provide and support the provision of services that they consider public services including in areas such as public health and education, social services and housing and the collection, purification and distribution of water." (b) "CETA does not prevent governments from defining and regulating the provision of these services in the public interest. CETA will not require governments to privatise any service nor prevent governments from expanding the range of services they supply to the public." (c) "CETA will not prevent governments from providing public services previously supplied by private service suppliers or from bringing back under public control services that governments had chosen to privatise. CETA does not mean that contracting a public service to private providers makes it irreversibly part of the commercial sector."

[79] *Ibid.* para 3 ("CETA provides Canada and the European Union and its Member States with a platform to facilitate cooperation between their regulatory authorities, with the objective of achieving better quality of regulation and more efficient use of administrative resources. This cooperation will be voluntary: regulatory authorities can cooperate on a voluntary basis but do not have an obligation to do so, or to apply the outcome of their cooperation").

[80] *Ibid.* para. 6, calling *inter alia* that: (a) "CETA will not result in foreign investors being treated more favourably than domestic investors." (b) "CETA clarifies that governments may change their laws, regardless of whether this may negatively affect an investment or investor's expectations of profits." (f) "CETA moves decisively away from the traditional approach of investment dispute resolution and establishes independent, impartial and permanent investment Tribunals, inspired by the principles of public judicial systems in the European Union and its Member States and Canada, as well as and international courts such as the International Court of Justice and the European Court of Human Rights. Accordingly, the members of these Tribunals will be individuals qualified for judicial office in their respective countries, and these will be appointed by the European Union and Canada for a fixed term. Cases will be heard by three randomly selected members. Strict ethical rules for these individuals have been set to ensure their independence and impartiality, the absence of conflict of interest, bias or

98   *Mark A. Pollack*

document, sought to safeguard EU regulatory sovereignty against intrusion from CETA's provisions on nontariff barriers, regulatory cooperation and ISDS.

On the basis of these undertakings, the Walloon parliament finally signaled its approval for the Belgian government to sign the agreement,[81] and CETA was formally signed with much fanfare by Canadian and EU leaders on October 30, 2016.[82] The European Parliament followed suit in February 2017, approving the agreement by a vote of 408 to 254, with 33 abstentions, following a vigorous debate and amidst vocal protests outside the Parliament's doors.[83] Within the EP, the center-right European People's Party voted overwhelmingly in favor of the agreement, while the center-left Socialists & Democrats were split, and far left and the far right party groups remained staunchly opposed.[84] Unlike either ACTA or TTIP, therefore, CETA was allowed to pass into provisional application, although its long-term fate remained dependent on further ratification votes in the member states as well as further legal challenges before the German Constitutional Court, the CJEU and perhaps elsewhere.[85]

More importantly for our purposes here, the internal debate over CETA, and the strident European opposition to the likely dead TTIP, reveal a rising tide of suspicion towards international trade agreements, regulatory cooperation and ISDS – not only among fringe groups, but in the political center of the Union.[86] Here again, as in ACTA, we see Europeans suspicious of both the

---

appearance of bias. The European Union and its Member States and Canada have agreed to begin immediately further work on a code of conduct to further ensure the impartiality of the members of the Tribunals, on the method and level of their remuneration and the process for their selection. The common aim is to conclude the work by the entry into force of CETA."

[81] Mike Blanchfield, *Still Many Steps to Be Taken; Minister Cautious on Apparent Breakthrough on Canada-EU Trade Deal*, BARRIE EXAMINER, Oct. 28, 2016.

[82] Jason Thomson, *EU, Canada Sign Landmark Trade Deal*, THE CHRISTIAN SCIENCE MONITOR, Oct. 31, 2016.

[83] James Kanter, *E.U. Parliament Votes to Ratify Canada Trade Deal and Send Trump a Message*, THE NEW YORK TIMES, Feb. 15, 2017.

[84] Daniel Boffey, *European Parliament Passes EU-Canada Free Trade Deal amid Protests*, THE GUARDIAN, Feb. 15, 2017.

[85] *See* Catherine Stupp, *After Parliament Approval, Final Ratification Could Still Put CETA in Legal Limbo*, EURACTIV.COM, Feb. 15, 2017; and European United Left/Nordic Green Left, *The Battle over CETA Will Continue: Next, National Parliaments and Citizens Must Decide*, press release, Feb. 15, 2017, www.guengl.eu/news/article/the-battle-over-ceta-will-continue-next-national-parliaments-and-citizens-m.

[86] Writing amidst the controversy in the autumn of 2016, no less an establishment figure than Financial Times columnist Wolfgang Münchau wrote: "I would welcome the demise of Ceta and the Transatlantic Trade and Investment Partnership, a similar US-EU trade deal still under negotiation, for two reasons. First, these agreements are a focus for anti-globalisation

procedure and the substance of international law, and protective of their domestic policies, democracy and sovereignty. These concerns manifest themselves, furthermore, not only in the ratification of *new* agreements like ACTA, TTIP and CETA, but also in the implementation of and compliance with existing agreements, most notably within the World Trade Organization, as we shall see presently.

4.4 INTERNATIONAL TRADE LAW, WTO DISPUTE SETTLEMENT AND EU OBSTRUCTIONISM: FROM HORMONE-TREATED BEEF TO GMOS

If the first two cases examined above concerned the EU and its member states refusing to conclude or consent to multilateral or bilateral treaties, the third set of cases examined here represents *extended, defiant noncompliance* with international judicial rulings adopted under existing international agreements. As we have already seen in the TTIP case, food safety regulation is one of the most politically sensitive and closely guarded areas of EU policy, and where EU domestic regulations run afoul of international trade law, the EU has found itself repeatedly defending those regulations before international tribunals – and, in the high-profile cases of hormone-treated beef and genetically modified foods, failing to comply with the rulings of those tribunals.

Food safety regulation falls under the broad rubric of risk regulation, whereby governmental actors are called upon to adopt regulations regarding the acceptable degree of risk posed to society by products or by industrial processes.[87] In principle, regulators faced with a novel product or process – such as hormone-treated beef, or GM foods and crops – need to ascertain the potential harm caused by such activities, as well as the probability of such harm, before deciding on the legality or illegality of a product or process. In practice, however, regulators often take *precautionary* measures, regulating or even banning products or activities, in the presence of uncertainty about the risks posed. In areas such as food safety and environmental regulation, the EU has, in recent decades, adopted a strong version of the precautionary principle, justifying strong regulations or bans on particular products or processes, even in the absence of clear scientific evidence of risk. Much of this precautionary

---

protests. After Brexit, this is not the best time for Europe's liberal elites to double down. Second, I believe some aspects of the deals, like investor tribunals, are undemocratic and at odds with European constitutional principles." Wolfgang Münchau, "The Monstrous Battle to Secure a Trade Deal," FIN. TIMES, Oct. 17, 2016.

[87] Jonathan B. Wiener & Michael D. Rogers, *Comparing Precaution in the United States and Europe*, 5 JOURNAL OF RISK RESEARCH 317 (2002).

regulation has been driven by European public opinion, which, following a series of food-safety scandals in the 1980s and 1990s, has been strongly averse to potential food-safety risks.

Such highly precautionary domestic regulations, however, can act in practice as nontariff barriers to trade, perhaps most famously in the aforementioned examples of hormone-treated beef and GM foods. In both of these cases, EU authorities, under pressure from a strongly risk-averse public opinion, adopted domestic regulations that had the effect of banning the importation of products that had been approved as safe by US and other regulators. Under the terms of WTO law, however, and in particular under the WTO Sanitary and Phytosanitary (SPS) Agreement, the EU and other WTO signatories are required to base domestic food-safety regulations on a scientific risk assessment, so as to avoid national regulations serving as disguised restrictions on trade, and in both cases the USA challenged EU regulations for violations of WTO and SPS rules. In both cases, WTO panels ruled against the EU, but the Union failed to comply, in some cases for decades, with international legal rulings.

The US-EU dispute over hormone-treated beef can be traced back to 1989, when the EU, acting under the terms of a 1988 directive, instituted a ban on the use of synthetic growth hormones in beef cattle, and prohibited the import of animals, or meat from animals, that had been treated with these hormones.[88] Although the EU directive had been adopted primarily on the grounds of European consumer concerns about the safety of hormone-treated beef, the ban had an immediate and dramatic impact on beef producers in the United States, where some 90 percent of all beef cattle are treated with synthetic growth hormones, and where FDA studies have consistently found that hormone-treated beef is safe for human consumption.

In 1995, after the entry into force of the SPS Agreement and the Dispute Settlement Understanding, the USA initiated legal action against the EU, alleging that the EU ban on hormone-treated beef was inconsistent with the terms of the SPS Agreement because it was not based on a scientific risk assessment or agreed international standards. The EU, in response, argued that the SPS Agreement acknowledges the right of states to determine the appropriate level of health protection for their consumers, and that the ban was justified under the precautionary principle. A WTO dispute settlement

---

[88] This section draws upon a more detailed discussion in Mark A. Pollack & Gregory C. Shaffer, *The Challenge of Reconciling Regulatory Differences: Food Safety and GMOs in the Transatlantic Relationship*, TRANSATLANTIC GOVERNANCE IN THE GLOBAL ECONOMY (Mark A. Pollack & Gregory C. Shaffer, eds.), 153–78 (2001).

panel was established in May 1996, and issued its report in favor of the USA in August 1997. The EU appealed the panel's decision, and the WTO Appellate Body issued a second report in January 1998, once again in favor of the United States.

The WTO panel and appellate decisions were both complex, with the Appellate Body narrowing the scope of the panel's initial decision, but in the end it agreed with the complainant that the EU had failed to base its beef-hormone ban on a scientific risk assessment, undermining EU claims that the ban was adopted to protect human health. In response to the EU's invocation of the precautionary principle, moreover, both the panel and the Appellate Body found that the precautionary principle could not override the express requirement of a risk assessment under Article 5.1 of the SPS Agreement. In accordance with the Appellate Body's findings, the Dispute Settlement Body ruled in February 1998 that the EU ban was inconsistent with the terms of the SPS Agreement, and instructed the EU to bring its regulations into compliance by no later than May 13, 1999.

Facing continuing pressure from its own consumers, however, and hopeful of producing additional scientific findings that might justify the ban, the EU failed to act, and the USA retaliated on May 17, 1999, applying tariffs in the amount of $116.8 million targeted against specific EU products such as foie gras, Roquefort cheese and Dijon mustard. These US tariffs in turn sparked a wave of protests among French and other European farmers, including an attack in August 1999 by a group of French farmers on a McDonald's restaurant, selected as the symbol of the threat of globalization, and more specifically of American food culture, to French traditions. "McDonald's encapsulates it all," said one commentator. "It's economic horror and gastronomic horror in the same bun."[89] Although the leader of the farmers group, Jose Bové, was jailed for his part in the attack, he was later hailed as a hero in the French press for his opposition to American efforts to force upon Europeans foods that were widely seen as unwanted and unsafe, and in 2009 he was elected to the European Parliament.

EU noncompliance with the WTO ruling continued for over a decade, during which time the USA continued to apply and ratchet up its retaliatory tariffs. On January 16, 2009, for example, on the heels of an October 2008 WTO ruling that the EU had still failed to comply with the ruling and just four days before the transition to the new administration, the outgoing US Trade

---

[89] Guillaume Parmentier, quoted in J. Henley, *McDonald's Campaign Spawns French Hero: Political Activist Turned French Peasant Has Fast Food on the Run*, THE GUARDIAN, Sept. 11, 1999, at 14.

Representative, Susan Schwab, announced a change in the structure of US retaliatory tariffs, which would be altered to impose a targeted 300 percent tariff on Roquefort cheese, widely seen as an effort to pressure France, and 100 percent tariffs on thirty-four other products produced by various other member states.[90] The eventual settlement of the case came only later in 2009, when the incoming Obama administration announced a delay in the imposition of tariffs, to give time for US and EU diplomats to negotiate a solution to the dispute.[91] On May 6, 2009 US and EU negotiators announced a memorandum of understanding that would lead, in three phases, to an ultimate settlement of the dispute, in which the USA would drop its retaliatory tariffs in return for the EU granting a new, duty-free quota of 45,000 tons of so-called high-quality, hormone-free beef.[92] Although the 2009 agreement formally settled the case, the decade-long delay, and the Union's ultimately successful refusal to amend its domestic legislation, both point to the sensitivity of food safety regulation in the Union, and the difficulty it faces in complying with domestically unpopular international legal rulings.

The transatlantic dispute over the EU's policies regarding GM varieties is analytically similar to the dispute over beef hormones, but on a far larger scale. Genetic engineering is a technology used to isolate genes from one organism, manipulate them in the laboratory, and inject them into another organism. This technology first emerged in the 1970s, and by the mid-1980s, scientists and biotechnology firms were developing, patenting, growing and marketing a growing varieties of GM foods and crops. In the USA, these new technologies were generally welcomed by farmers and by the federal government, which regulated them under existing statutes through existing agencies such as the Environmental Protection Agency and the Food and Drug Administration.[93]

In Europe, by contrast, GM foods and crops were generally met with public suspicion, often flaring into hostility, and by the early 1990s the EU had

---

[90] Brian Beary, *EU/US: No End in Sight to Beef Hormone Dispute*, EUROPOLITICS, Jan. 27, 2009.

[91] Brian Beary, *EU/US: Top Trade Officials Pledge to Resolve Bilateral Disputes*, EUROPOLITICS, March 23, 2009; Brian Beary, *EU/US: Washington Postpones Sanctions in Beef Hormone Dispute*, EUROPOLITICS, April 24, 2009.

[92] Office of the United States Trade Representative, *USTR Announces Agreement with European Union in Beef Hormones Dispute*, Press Release, www.ustr.gov/about-us/press-office/press-releases/2009/may/ustr-announces-agreement-european-union-beef-hormones, accessed on 9 July 2013; Council of the European Union, *The Transatlantic Trade Dispute on "Hormones" in Beef Comes to an End*, Press Release, Luxembourg, April 26, 2012, www .consilium.europa.eu/uedocs/cms_data/docs/pressdata/en/agricult/129788.pdf.

[93] The narrative in this section is drawn from the far more extensive discussion in MARK A. POLLACK & GREGORY C. SHAFFER, WHEN COOPERATION FAILS: THE GLOBAL LAW AND POLITICS OF GENETICALLY MODIFIED ORGANISMS (2009).

developed a framework of highly precautionary and restrictive regulatory procedures for assessing and approving new GM varieties. In the first or risk assessment stage, a manufacturer or importer seeking permission to market or grow GM crops in Europe must submit an application and a risk assessment, which is examined by scientists at the European Food Safety Authority (EFSA), which in turn issues its findings to the European Commission. In the second or risk management stage, the Commission is then tasked with reviewing the EFSA findings and taking a draft decision on whether to allow the importation, sale or cultivation of the crop within the Union. The Commission is not, however, free to do as it likes at this stage, because it is supervised by representatives of the EU's intergovernmental Council of Ministers, who can object to and, by a qualified majority, potentially overturn Commission approvals of specific crops. Even after the approval of a particular food or crop, moreover, member states can, on the basis of new evidence about risks to human health or the environment, provisionally restrict or prohibit the importation, sale or cultivation of specific varieties on their territories.

As it happened, the implementation of these rules in the 1990s took place in the context of a major food safety scandal over bovine spongiform encephalopathy (or mad cow disease), followed immediately by the beef-hormones dispute, which together generated extraordinary public awareness of food safety issues and widespread public distrust of regulators and scientific assessments. In this context, the implementation of the EU's already strict regulatory system became highly politicized. Governments across Europe, under heavy public pressure to block the marketing and cultivation of GM crops even after EU scientists had pronounced them safe, repeatedly attempted to block or slow down the approval of new varieties. In June of 1999, for example, the governments of Denmark, France, Greece, Italy and Luxembourg declared the need to impose a moratorium on all approvals of GM products, and for nearly six years, from October 1998 to May 2004, no GM varieties were authorized for sale in the EU market. Furthermore, a growing number of EU member states declared national "safeguard bans" on already approved foods and crops, claiming with little or no scientific evidence that they posed a risk to human health or the environment

As in the case of hormone-treated beef, these highly precautionary and politicized EU regulations came into tension with international trade law, by effectively banning imports of GM soybeans and corn that had been found by both US and EU scientists to be safe for human consumption. Finally, in May 2003, the USA, joined by Argentina and Canada, brought a WTO complaint against the EU, alleging that its de facto moratorium on new approvals, as well as the national bans on approved varieties, constituted a violation of WTO law, and specifically of the SPS Agreement. The USA and other complainants did not challenge the EU's legislative framework for GM foods as such. Instead, the complaints focused on the EU's implementation of its own regulatory framework, challenging three specific actions: (1) the EU's de facto "general moratorium" on new approvals; (2) "product-specific moratoria," or failure to approve particular GM varieties found to be safe by the relevant EU scientific bodies; and (3) the persistent use of "safeguard bans" by some EU member states to ban GM varieties that had been approved as safe by the EU's own scientific experts. In all three cases, the complainants argued, the EU had failed to base its regulatory decisions on scientific risk assessments as required by the SPS Agreement, and those decisions were therefore inconsistent with EU obligations under WTO law.

In September 2006, the WTO dispute-settlement panel issued its decision.[94] The panel expressly avoided deciding several controversial questions, including "whether biotech products in general are safe or not." On the specific questions raised in the complaints, however, the panel found in favor of the complainants. It held that the EU had engaged in "undue delay" in its approval process in violation of the SPS Agreement. Regarding safeguards enacted by EU member states, the panel ruled that all of the national safeguard bans violated the EU's and member states' substantive obligations under the SPS Agreement because they were "not based on a risk assessment." It noted in particular that the EU's "relevant scientific committees had evaluated the potential risks . . . and had provided a positive opinion" on the GM varieties.

The WTO panel ruling put the EU in an awkward position. On the one hand, the European Commission, eager to comply with the ruling and to regularize a regulatory process that had become highly politicized and dysfunctional, sought to move ahead on three fronts: first by speeding up the approval of long-blocked GM varieties for import and marketing; second by unblocking the even more challenging process of approving GM crops for cultivation; and third by challenging the national safeguard bans that had been found to be illegal by the WTO. European public opinion, however, remained implacably hostile to GM foods and crops, and national governments channeled this opposition into the EU policy process by slowing down approvals and maintaining national safeguard bans in defiance of both the Commission and the WTO.[95]

---

[94] *Ibid.* 177–234.
[95] *Ibid.* 245–61. For an update on these efforts up to 2013, *see* Mark A. Pollack, *A Truce in the Transatlantic Food Fight: The United States, the European Union, and Genetically Modified*

With respect to approving new varieties of GM crops, the Commission finally brought an end to the six-year moratorium in May 2004, and by 2013 it had approved some thirty-seven new crops, including several of commercial significance to the USA.[96] It did so, however, only in the face of vociferous opposition from a substantial number of EU member states, and the approval process continued to lag in subsequent years, leaving dozens of GM foods and crops stuck in the regulatory pipeline even after approval by EU scientists, and potentially opening the Union to further charges of "undue delay."

On the issue of cultivation, EU policy has been even more politicized, and arguably noncompliant with WTO law. Prior to the 2006 WTO ruling, the EU had approved only a single GM crop – MON810, Monsanto's YieldGard corn – for cultivation in the EU. Other applications for cultivation of GM crops, by contrast, remained blocked in the EU's regulatory process, with member state committees and the Council unable to come to agreement, and the Commission reluctant to push through approvals on such a sensitive issue. It was not until 2011 that the Commission approved a second crop for cultivation, a genetically modified potato engineered by German chemicals firm BASF that had been blocked in the regulatory process for five years. BASF's regulatory victory, however, proved pyrrhic. Despite its formal approval, the so-called Amflora potato was deeply controversial among the member states and in public opinion, leading several member states to declare safeguard bans on cultivation, and in 2011 BASF announced that it would totally halt the test planting and marketing of the potato.[97] The following year, BASF withdrew its previous applications for EU cultivation of three other GM potato crops.[98]

Finally, in addition to the continuing delays in the approval of new GM crops for marketing and cultivation, multiple member states continued to adopt national bans on the cultivation of approved GM crops. The Commission attempted on four occasions to challenge national bans on cultivation of MON810 (which were found by EFSA to be groundless in scientific terms), but in each case a large majority of the member states supported the banning states against the Commission.[99] In March 2009, for

---

Foods in the Obama Years, (Aug. 8, 2013). Available at SSRN: https://ssrn.com/abstrac t=2295197 or http://dx.doi.org/10.2139/ssrn.2295197.

[96] Pollack, *A Truce in the Transatlantic Food Fight, supra* note 95 at 34–35.

[97] *See* Eric van Puyvelde, *Genetically Modified Organisms: BASF Halts GMO Development in Europe,* EUROPOLITICS, Jan. 18, 2012.

[98] Joanna Sopinska, *GMOs: BASF Drops EU Potato Bid,* EUROPOLITICS, Jan. 31, 2013.

[99] European Commission, *Communication from the Commission to the European Parliament, the Council, the Economic and Social Committee, and the Committee of the Regions on the*

example, the Commission attempted to challenge and overturn Austria's and Hungary's bans on the cultivation of MON810, but was supported by only five of the twenty-seven environment ministers.[100] With the Commission unable to challenge them, by early 2013 eight EU member states retained national safeguard bans on the cultivation of one or both of the two approved GM crops.[101] Faced with continuing member-state hostility toward new approvals for cultivation, as well as continuing national bans, the Commission in 2010 proposed a draft regulation, eventually adopted as Directive 2015/412, giving EU member states full control over the cultivation of GM crops on their territories, including the right to declare national bans on the cultivation of GM crops for any reason, no longer limited to the health and environmental grounds set out in existing legislation.[102]

Despite its continuing concerns, the United States has not sought to escalate the conflict by pressing for sanctions for EU noncompliance with the 2006 WTO ruling, nor has it indicated any serious intention to bring suit against the EU for its "commercially infeasible" traceability and labeling rules. Instead, as the USTR's 2013 report on SPS measures concludes, "The United States continues to engage the European Commission in an effort to normalize trade in GE products,"[103] and the two sides continued to meet in regular technical discussions of the dispute.[104]

In both the beef-hormones and GMO cases, therefore, we find an EU committed in principle to compliance with its legal obligations, including under the WTO – yet we also find a Union whose citizens and governments express a defiant critique of and resistance to international law and

> *Freedom for Member States to Decide on the Cultivation of Genetically Modified Crops*, COM (2010) 380 final, Brussels, July 13, 2010.

[100] Mark A. Pollack & Gregory C. Shaffer. *Biotechnology Policy: Between National Fears and Global Disciplines*, in POLICY-MAKING IN THE EUROPEAN UNION, 6th edition 327–51 (Helen Wallace, Mark A. Pollack & Alasdair Young, eds., 2010).

[101] Joanna Sopinska, *GMOs: BASF Drops EU Potato Bid*, EUROPOLITICS, Jan. 31, 2013.

[102] European Commission, *Communication from the Commission to the European Parliament, the Council, the Economic and Social Committee, and the Committee of the Regions on the Freedom for Member States to Decide on the Cultivation of Genetically Modified Crops*, COM (2010) 380 final, Brussels, July 13, 2010; and Directive (EU) 2015/412 of the European Parliament and of the Council of 11 March 2015 amending Directive 2001/18/EC as regards the possibility for the Member States to restrict or prohibit the cultivation of genetically modified organisms (GMOs) in their territory.

[103] United States Trade Representative, *USTR Announces Agreement, supra* note 92 at 44.

[104] *See, e.g.,* the discussion of the US/EU consultation on 20 March 2012, in *European Communities – Measures Affecting the Approval and Marketing of Biotech Products. Status Report by the European Union. Addendum,* WORLD TRADE ORGANIZATION, WT/DS291/37/Add.51, April 13, 2012, online at: http://trade.ec.europa.eu/doclib/docs/2012/april/tra doc_149347.pdf.

international judicial decisions. We have seen how, for figures like José Bové, international trade law is portrayed as being procedurally flawed due to its dominance by the USA and large corporations like Monsanto as well as its secretive system of dispute settlement by unelected panelists. In substantive terms, WTO law is seen as flawed due to its rigid insistence on scientific risk assessment as the basis for every domestic regulation, and for its inadequate recognition of the precautionary principle as a principle of customary international law.[105] Finally, while the Commission has made repeated efforts to comply with WTO rulings, we find in civil society and among the member governments a much greater willingness to openly defy the legally binding rulings of the WTO Dispute Settlement Body.

One might plausibly object at this stage that beef-hormones and GMO are uniquely sensitive issues for Europeans, outliers in an otherwise unblemished pattern of EU support for and compliance with international law. Several recent studies, however, suggest that these two cases represent the tip of the iceberg, the most visible of a broader set of cases in which EU agricultural and food safety regulations fall regularly afoul of international law, and in which the Union engages in rare but extended acts of noncompliance with international treaties and international judicial rulings. In a 2015 study, for example, Jappe Eckhardt and Manfred Elsig find that, while the USA is the subject of a disproportionate number of WTO complaints relating to trade remedies such as anti-dumping and safeguard measures, the EU is disproportionately targeted for purported regulatory violations, in which the Union is accused of adopting regulatory barriers to trade in violation of the Technical Barriers to Trade (TBT) and SPS Agreements. Indeed, the authors find that "the EU accounts for 84 percent of all SPS claims that are brought," which they take as evidence that the EU is particularly prone to violate WTO law through the application of discriminatory domestic regulations.[106]

A similarly suggestive study of WTO dispute settlement in the area of agriculture by Christina Davis finds that the EU "ranks among the least cooperative trading entities across the record of legal adjudication of trade disputes." The Union, she demonstrates, "is notorious for delaying tactics,"

---

[105] Indeed, this latter concern has led the Union to engage in an ongoing campaign of institutional proliferation and forum shopping, seeking to establish counter-norms in settings such as the Convention on Biodiversity, the Codex Alimentarius Commission, and the Organization for Economic Cooperation and Development. For a detailed exploration of this strategy in the GMO case, see, e.g., Gregory C. Shaffer & Mark A. Pollack, *Hard Law vs. Soft Law: Alternatives, Complements and Antagonists in International Governance*, 94 Min. L. Rev. 706, 743–65 (2010).

[106] Jappe Eckhardt & Manfred Elsig, *Support for International Trade Law: The US and the EU Compared*, 13 Int'l J. Con. L., 966, 975 (2015).

108 *Mark A. Pollack*

blocking or delaying panels under the pre-WTO GATT dispute settlement system, dragging out the time to settlement of disputes (forty-six months on average when the EU is a defendant, as opposed to thirty-four months for all defendants), and facing sanctions for years rather than comply with decisions in the infamous bananas case as well as beef-hormones and GMOs.[107] Davis's explanation for this outcome stresses the ways in which EU institutions diffuse responsibility for WTO violations among multiple member states, as well as the number of veto players who can block compliance with WTO rulings.[108] Davis's findings are limited to the issue-area of agriculture, and her account does not, like this one, emphasize partisan factors; but her emphasis on the large number of EU veto points, and her depiction of the long-standing, de facto legal obstructionism by a Union that prides itself on its commitment to international law, both suggest that the compliance problems manifested in beef-hormones and GMOs have broader and deeper roots in the nature of the EU as an institution.

4.5 CONCLUSIONS

What I have called the new, new sovereigntism comes primarily from the European left, rather than from the right as in the USA. Both the values it defends, and those it rejects, are different from its American variant. And yet, from a structural perspective, the same three elements are present, revealed in each of the three case studies reviewed in this chapter: first, the notion that existing international legal processes are flawed or inferior to EU processes, marred by secrecy, corporate and/or American dominance and lack of fundamental rights protection; second, the related notion that the substantive content of current or proposed international laws privileges neoliberal, free-market ideology and national security over the EU's social model and fundamental rights; and third, the concomitant, defiant rejection of at least some international laws through non-consent, noncompliance or refusal to internalize international law in the EU legal order.

The *causes* of the new European sovereigntism are complex, arising in part from developments in Europe and in part from the changing nature of the international legal order itself. Within Europe, the EU has, over the past several decades, constitutionalized a commitment to fundamental human rights, broadly conceived to include rights such as data privacy, as well as an increasingly strict regulatory *acquis* in areas such as food safety and the

---

[107] Davis, A *Conflict of Institutions, supra* note 10 at 2–4.
[108] *Ibid.* 8–13.

environment, that are increasingly in tension with proposed or established provisions of international law. The EU has thus joined the USA in being "exceptionalist" in the sense of embracing a distinctive set of domestic laws and policies which it seeks to protect from outside interference.[109] A parallel development, starting in the 1990s and escalating in the 2000s, is the rise in Europe of anti-globalist, anti-American and anti-corporatist sentiment, which sees globalization, American imperialism and neoliberal, free-market ideology as a threat not only to European laws and regulations but more broadly to the European social model and the European way of life.[110] EU institutions, meanwhile, have amplified the voices of the rising chorus of European critics, by granting veto power to a growing number of actors in Brussels, Strasbourg, Luxembourg, and in national and regional capitals to block EU consent to, compliance with, or internalization of public international law. Finally, concurrent with these developments inside Europe, public international law has famously become more comprehensive, and more intrusive, moving from a law of world order among states to a law that constrains the domestic laws and policies of its members.[111] In this sense, the growing European resistance to public international law seems overdetermined, both by changing attitudes and sclerotic institutions inside Europe and by a more intrusive body of international law outside.

There are, of course, differences between the "old" new sovereigntism coming out of the USA and the "new" new sovereigntism emerging from

---

[109] See, e.g., Anu Bradford & Eric A. Posner, *Universal Exceptionalism in International Law*, 52 HARV. INT'L L. J. 1 (2011) (arguing that all major powers are exceptionalist, "in the sense that they take distinctive approaches to international law that reflect their values and interests," and that the EU is similarly exceptionalist, seeking and insisting upon the universalization of its domestic values and interests, such as human rights and social welfare, in international law, while failing to comply with international law where it conflicts with strongly held domestic values). See also Magdalena Ličková, *European Exceptionalism in International Law*, 19 EUROPEAN JOURNAL OF INTERNATIONAL LAW 463 (2008); Sabrina Safrin, *The Un-exceptionalism of US Exceptionalism*, 41 VAN. J. TRANSNATI'L L. 1307 (2008); and Georg Nolte & Helmut Philipp Aust, *European Exceptionalism?*, 2 GLOBAL CONSTITUTIONALISM 407 (2013).

[110] On the rise of European resistance to globalization, Americanization, neoliberalism and corporate influence, see, e.g., Wade Jacoby & Sophie Meunier, *Europe and Globalization*, in RESEARCH AGENDAS IN EU STUDIES: STALKING THE ELEPHANT 354–74 (Michelle Egan, Neill Nugent, & William Patterson, eds., 2009); Peter J. Katzenstein & Robert O. Keohane, ANTI-AMERICANISMS IN WORLD POLITICS (2006); and Michaela DeSoucey, *Gastronationalism: Food Traditions and Authenticity Politics in the European Union*, 75 AM. SOCIOLOGICAL REV. 432 (2010).

[111] For foundational discussions of this transformation of international law, and its implications for domestic sovereignty, see, e.g., Philippe Sands, *Turtles and Torturers: The Transformation of International Law*, 33 N.Y.U. J. INT'L L. & POL. 527 (2001); and Kal Raustiala, *Rethinking the Sovereignty Debate in International Economic Law*, 6 J. INT'L ECON. L. 841 (2003).

Europe, and the differences are telling. First, and most obviously, European sovereigntism comes, by and large, from the left, and seeks to defend domestic rules and values very different from those of American sovereigntists, who come disproportionately from the right. Second, the targets of European sovereigntism are different, focusing primarily on international economic law and to a lesser extent security law, not environmental or human rights or criminal law as in the US case. Third, European sovereigntism is more selective, with European sovereigntists more likely to embrace the project of international law rhetorically, while identifying *specific* bodies of international law and *specific* law-making processes as threats to European values and to the European legal order. Fourth and finally, because of this feature, European sovereigntism is arguably more constructive than its American counterpart, taking the form, not (or not always) of a thorough-going rejection of international law but rather of an emerging agenda for change in international law and legal practices.

In the end, it seems clear that European opposition to substantial bodies of international law is rising, and with it a growing determination to protect the autonomy of the European legal order from the purportedly baleful effects of that law. One could object that, strictly speaking, the EU itself lacks sovereignty to protect, yet the quote from European Council President Donald Tusk that opened this chapter suggests that pro-European sentiment increasingly sees European unity as bulwark to protect the collective sovereignty of Europe against unwelcome intrusions from outside. This sentiment, together with the ability of a large number of actors to frustrate European accession to, compliance with and internalization of international law, promises to make the European Union at best an awkward participant in the international legal order in the years to come.

To this argument, the reader may raise the objection that European sovereigntism is not only newer but narrower than its American cousin, since its targets thus far have been concentrated in international trade and investment law, and its focus has been on protecting EU social and environmental regulation and fundamental rights. European sovereigntism, if it exists, does not represent an across-the-board rejection of public international law per se. Indeed, such is the optimistic interpretation of the evidence presented in this chapter, namely that the European center-left has turned its ire only on a relatively small slice of international economic law, leaving the Union's broader commitment to the international legal order intact. If this is correct, then the EU is indeed on its way to becoming an awkward international partner, but only in isolated, ring-fenced areas of economic law.

The New, New Sovereigntism

There are, however, three good reasons to believe that the new and thus-far limited European sovereigntism sketched out here may be of greater import in the future. First, while the changing European attitudes have been focused thus far primarily on trade and investment law, it seems likely that an aroused European electorate, interest groups, and parliaments are likely to rise up against the intrusions of other bodies of law that are perceived to threaten the *acquis communautaire* of EU social regulation and fundamental rights. In the cases of the SWIFT banking agreement with the USA, as well as the EU/US Passenger Name Recognition agreement, EU data privacy regulations came into conflict with bilateral counterterrorism treaties, leading to political and legal challenges to both agreements.[112] In the European Court of Justice's 2008 *Kadi* decision, moreover, EU fundamental rights appeared to clash with the international security and counterterrorism resolutions of the United Nations Security Council, and the Court responded forcefully by disallowing the implementation of Security Council rules in the EU legal order.[113] The new European sovereigntism is therefore *not* limited to international economic law, but increasingly manifests itself as resistance to international security and counterterrorism agreements as well.

Second, as the *Kadi* case suggests, opposition to the intrusion of international law may arise not only from the partisan and parliamentary actors emphasized here, but also from European courts. Within the EU, traditional scholarship has suggested that the European Court of Justice stands in marked contrast to the US Supreme Court in its openness to international law, and its willingness to accept international law as an integral part of the EU legal order. As Gráinne de Búrca has recently argued,[114] however, the ECJ has manifested a gradual hardening of its position towards public international law, and an increasing willingness to defend the autonomy of the EU legal order, beginning with its rejection of direct effect for WTO law, continuing with its defiantly dualist approach in *Kadi*, and culminating in its infamous *Opinion 2/13* which blocked EU accession to the European Convention on

---

[112] On the SWIFT agreement and its rejection by the European Parliament, *see, e.g.*, Jörg Monar, *The Rejection of the EU US SWIFT Interim Agreement*, and Katharina Meissner, *Democratizing EU External Relations*, *supra* note 9. On the European Court of Justice's invalidation of the first PNR agreement, *see, e.g.*, Javier Argomaniz, *When the EU Is the "Norm-taker": The Passenger Name Records Agreement and the EU's Internalization of US Border Security Norms*, 31 J. Eur. Integration 119 (2009); and Arthur Rizer, *Dog Fight: Did the International Battle over Airline Passenger Name Records Enable the Christmas-Day Bomber?*, 60 Cath. U. L. Rev. 77 (2010).

[113] de Búrca, *The European Court of Justice and the International Legal Order After Kadi*, *supra* note 20.

[114] de Búrca, *Internalization*, *supra* note 11.

Human Rights in an opinion widely interpreted as an effort to defend the autonomy of the EU legal order.[115] The new European sovereignty is therefore not limited to the partisan and parliamentary arenas, but is increasingly manifest in the judicial arena as well.

Third and finally, the analysis in this paper has focused primarily on resistance to public international law within the mainstream, pro-European center-left, which has led the charge against selected international legal agreements, while generally supporting European legal integration. By contrast, the European right, and in particular the extreme right whose influence is increasing rapidly in an era of rising populism, has taken the opposite tack, concentrating its opposition on *European* law and institutions in defense of *national* sovereignty, and largely ignoring, thus far, the provisions and procedures of public *international* law. Should the populist right turn its wrath on the international legal order, as Eric Posner has recently suggested it might,[116] the resulting European hostility to international law is likely to be far more virulent and less constructive than the more moderate, center-left phenomenon depicted in this chapter. What is certain is that, in these difficult times, European support for international law is being tested, and will continue to be tested, as never before.

---

[115] Halberstam, *It's the Autonomy, Stupid, supra* note 21; Isiksel, *European Exceptionalism, supra* note 21.

[116] Eric A. Posner, *Liberal Internationalism and the Populist Backlash*, CHICAGO PUBLIC LAW AND LEGAL THEORY WORKING PAPER NO. 606, Jan. 2017.

II

SPECIFIC AREAS IN INTERNATIONAL LAW: WHITHER THE WEST?

1 International Law and Constitutional Law: Is There a Final Arbiter?

5

Authority and Dialogue

State and Official Immunity in Domestic and International Courts

Chimène I. Keitner

5.1 INTRODUCTION

Structural rules of international law allocate adjudicatory authority horizontally among states. These rules include jurisdictional immunities, which operate as a defense to the exercise of foreign adjudicatory jurisdiction that would otherwise exist. Jurisdictional immunities stand at the intersection of the "domestic" and the "international," and help to mediate the relationship between these two political and juridical spheres. Like all international legal rules, the norms governing jurisdiction and immunities have evolved over time to meet the changing needs of the international community.

On the international plane, customary international law governs the contours of foreign state and foreign official immunity.[1] States have taken different approaches to incorporating relevant jurisdictional immunities into their domestic legal systems. In the context of this volume on approaches to international law in the United States and Europe, it can be instructive to examine the approaches of countries on both sides of the Atlantic. Some common law countries, such as Canada and the United Kingdom, have adopted foreign state immunity acts that codify jurisdictional immunities as a matter of domestic law.[2] The United States' domestic state immunity act codifies foreign state immunity, but not foreign official immunity.[3] National

---

[1] *Jurisdictional Immunities of the State* (Ger. v. It.: Greece intervening), 2012 I.C.J. 1 ¶ 54. The U. N. Convention on the Jurisdictional Immunities of States and Their Property, (2005) 44 I.L.M. 803, requires thirty ratifications to enter into force. Other treaties govern diplomatic and consular immunities. *See* Vienna Convention on Diplomatic Relations (adopted 18 Apr. 1961, entered into force 24 Apr. 1964), 500 U.N.T.S. 95; Vienna Convention on Consular Relations (adopted 24 Apr. 1961, entered into force 19 Mar. 1967), 596 U.N.T.S. 261.

[2] State Immunity Act, R.S.C. 1985, c. S-18 (Can.); State Immunity Act, 1978, c. 33 (U.K.).

[3] Foreign Sovereign Immunities Act, Pub. L. No. 94-583, 90 Stat. 2891 (1976) (U.S.) (codified in sections of 28 U.S.C.).

courts in these states adjudicate disputes involving jurisdictional immunities by interpreting and applying their domestic laws, against the backdrop of relevant international understandings. Other civil law countries, such as Italy, apply rules of foreign state immunity based on customary international law more directly.[4] Domestic courts in these states evaluate relevant state practice and *opinio juris* to determine whether international law permits or prohibits a particular exercise of national jurisdiction that has been challenged on immunity grounds.

This chapter considers aspects of the ongoing conversation about norms of state and official immunity among domestic and international courts. The concept of "authority" as used in the chapter's title denotes the ability to articulate and apply legal norms in a way that relevant actors understand as legitimate and binding. The term "dialogue" refers to mutual acknowledgement and citation, although not necessarily deference, among institutions charged with interpreting these norms. Because immunity norms transect the international and domestic legal spheres, adjudicating immunity claims creates opportunities for dialogue among international and domestic courts about the content of immunity norms, and about which institutions (both domestic and international) have the authority to articulate and apply them.

Deciding whether to dismiss a claim on immunity grounds involves reconciling at least two potentially conflicting norms: the individual right of access to a court on the one hand, and the norm of foreign state immunity – which reflects principles of sovereign equality and non-intervention – on the other. Depending on the forum's legal system, these norms might be grounded in either domestic or·international law, or they might have a hybrid character. For example, even jurisdictional immunities codified in domestic legislation have a distinctly international provenance; conversely, the right of judicial access might be enshrined in domestic statutory or constitutional law, as well as international instruments.[5] As a result, the distinction between domestic and international norms in this context is porous; the choice is not simply between a domestic rule and an international one, but between substantively different visions of how best to accommodate potentially conflicting values.

---

[4] Article 10(1) of the Italian Constitution provides that "the Italian juridical order conforms to the generally recognized norms of international law."

[5] Antonios Tzanakopoulos has characterized such norms as "consubstantial." *See* Antonios Tzanakopoulos, *Domestic Courts in International Law: The International Judicial Function of National Courts*, 34 LOYOLA L.A. INT'L & COMP. L. REV. 133, 143 (2011). The term "multi-sourced equivalent norms," used in the international law context, evokes a similar idea of overlapping content without a strict interpretive hierarchy for resolving conflicts. *See* Tomer Braude & Yuval Shany, eds., MULTI-SOURCED EQUIVALENT NORMS IN INTERNATIONAL LAW (2011).

In an attempt to manage this complexity, the judicial decisions canvassed in this chapter construct and invoke categorical distinctions, for example between procedural and substantive norms, and between international and domestic law. Yet the lines between these categories remain blurred, as illustrated below. Despite the judicial desire to seek clarity and impose hierarchy, doctrinal debates about jurisdictional immunities exemplify the polycentric nature of authority in the transnational legal system, which the standard tropes of "monism" and "dualism" fail adequately to capture.[6] Notably, with reference to the theme of this book, these immunity cases defy categorization along a European/North American divide. More consequentially, it is identifying the source of applicable norms (such as customary international law, a regional human rights convention, or a domestic statute) that shapes the doctrinal paths available to judges in reaching a particular result.

This chapter proceeds as follows. Section 5.2 focuses on two challenges brought before international tribunals to immunity determinations made by domestic courts in Europe: a challenge brought by individual claimants before the European Court of Human Rights (ECtHR) to the United Kingdom's determination that Saudi Arabia was entitled to jurisdictional immunity from civil claims for torture (*Jones* v. *United Kingdom*),[7] and a challenge brought by Germany before the International Court of Justice (ICJ) to Italy's determination that Germany did not enjoy jurisdictional immunity from civil claims for World War II-era crimes (*Germany* v. *Italy*).[8] Both of these cases pitted the right of access to a judicial remedy against the norm of state immunity. Domestic courts in Canada and Italy subsequently considered these international decisions in reaching their own conclusions about the scope of foreign state immunity under their domestic statutes, as explored in Section 5.3.

The Canadian Supreme Court's decision in *Estate of Kazemi* v. *Iran* illustrates normative coalescence around a conception of immunity based on a domestic statute and reinforced by international jurisprudence.[9] By contrast, the Italian Constitutional Court's Judgment 238/2014 illustrates that international decisions can also provoke "legal protectionism" – the attempt to

---

[6] On the importance of identifying "principles and mechanisms" of "coordination and reconciliation" between international and national law, *see* Daniel Bethlehem, *The Supremacy of International Law? – Part One*, at www.ejiltalk.org/the-supremacy-of-international-law-part-one/ (2 June 2016).

[7] *Jones & Ors.* v. *United Kingdom* [2014] ECHR 32.

[8] *Jurisdictional Immunities of the State* (Ger. v. It.: Greece intervening), 2012 I.C.J. 1.

[9] *See Kazemi Estate* v. *Islamic Republic of Iran* [2014] SCC 62.

shield domestic norms and institutions from foreign or international "imports."[10] Section 5.4 explores how arguments based on the supremacy of domestic constitutional law have been used in other cases beyond the immunity context to justify noncompliance with the decisions of international bodies, even when the constitution explicitly incorporates international law into the domestic legal system.[11]

From the perspective of international law, domestic law provisions do not justify or excuse noncompliance with international legal obligations.[12] Practically speaking, however, domestic rules generally control the behavior of state officials who are immediately answerable to domestic, rather than international, authorities. The only ways out of this conundrum in cases of normative conflict are substantive convergence on values (such as the widespread acceptance of the "restrictive" theory of foreign state immunity[13]), or binding agreement on final authority (such as the non-immunity provisions of the Rome Statute for the International Criminal Court[14]).

The permeability of a given domestic legal system to international determinations of the appropriate trade-off between the individual right of judicial access and the norm of foreign sovereign immunity depends on a host of historical and sociological factors that cannot be reduced to pure legal

---

[10] See Judgment 238/2014, Italian Constitutional Court (22 Oct. 2014) (official translation available at www.cortecostituzionale.it/documenti/download/doc/recent_judgments/S238_2013_e n.pdf).

[11] Other explorations of similar themes include: André Nollkaemper, *Rethinking the Supremacy of International Law*, 65 ZEITSCHRIFT FÜR ÖFFENTLICHES RECHT 65 (2010); Armin von Bogandy, *Pluralism, Direct Effect, and the Ultimate Say: On the Relationship between InterNational and Domestic Constitutional Law*, 6I*CON 397 (2008); Mattias Kumm, *The Legitimacy of International Law: A Constitutionalist Framework of Analysis*, 15 EUR. J. INT'L L. 907 (2004). For an early treatment of these questions in the context of European integration, see Joseph Weiler, *Fundamental Rights and Fundamental Boundaries: On the Conflict of Standards and Values in the Protection of Human Rights in the European Legal Space, in* THE CONSTITUTION OF EUROPE – "DO THE NEW CLOTHES HAVE AN EMPEROR" AND OTHER ESSAYS ON EUROPEAN INTEGRATION (1999).

[12] See ILC, Draft Articles on the Responsibility of States for Internationally Wrongful Acts, art. 3 (2001).

[13] U.N. Convention on Jurisdictional Immunities, *supra* note 1; *see also* Pierre-Hugues Verdier & Erik Voeten, *How Does Customary International Law Change? The Case of State Immunity*, 59 INT'L STUD. Q. 209 (2015).

[14] Rome Statute of the International Criminal Court Art. 27(2), 2187 UNTS 90 (entered into force 1 July 2002). Despite its codification in the Rome Statute, the lack of official immunity before the ICC has generated controversy in the context of the ICC's request that States parties arrest and surrender Sudanese President Omar al-Bashir. *See, e.g.,* Paola Gaeta, *The ICC Changes Its Mind on the Immunity from Arrest of President Al Bashir, But It Is Wrong Again*, at http://opiniojuris.org/2014/04/23/guest-post-icc-changes-mind-immunity-arrest-president-al-ba shir-wrong/ (23 April 2014).

Authority and Dialogue

doctrine, or to a distinction between European and North American traditions. The cases canvassed below evidence ongoing contestation about which political community possesses the authority to balance these competing values – a debate that transcends the borders between substantive and procedural, domestic and international, and common and civil law norms.

5.2 INTERNATIONAL TRIBUNALS AS THE FINAL ARBITERS (OR NOT) OF JURISDICTIONAL IMMUNITIES

5.2.1 *Sources of Law: Domestic Statutes and International Custom*

Contemporary understandings of the principles of sovereign equality and nonintervention underpin doctrines of foreign sovereign immunity, whether as a matter of comity (as in the American tradition)[15] or customary international law (under a European approach).[16] Although states have begrudgingly conceded the necessity of allowing their commercial activities (acta *jure gestionis*, or acts by right of management) to be justiciable in foreign courts in order to facilitate commerce and encourage foreign investment,[17] they jealously guard the immunity of their sovereign acts (acta *jure imperii*, or acts by right of dominion). Preserving mutual respect for this principle sometimes requires reaching uncomfortable results. For example, in *Saudi Arabia* v. *Nelson*, the US Supreme Court found that the Foreign Sovereign Immunities Act of 1976 (FSIA) did not provide jurisdiction over Scott Nelson's claims against Saudi Arabia for his wrongful arrest, imprisonment, and torture because "however monstrous such abuse undoubtedly may be, a foreign state's exercise of the power of its police has long been understood for purposes of the restrictive theory as peculiarly sovereign in nature."[18]

The Supreme Court in *Saudi Arabia* v. *Nelson* did not reach this result by interpreting and applying international law directly. Rather, it was interpreting and applying a US statute, the FSIA, which governs the immunity of foreign states.[19] The FSIA was the first of several analogous acts enacted by states in the late 1970s and mid-1980s, to codify the "restrictive" theory of foreign state

---

[15] Classically, *The Schooner Exchange* v. *McFaddon*, 11 U.S. 116, 136 (1812).
[16] *Jurisdictional Immunities of the State* (Ger. v. It.: Greece intervening), 2012 I.C.J. 1 ¶ 53.
[17] See *supra* note 13.
[18] *Saudi Arabia* v. *Nelson*, 507 U.S. 349, 361 (1993).
[19] See *supra* note 2. In *Samantar* v. *Yousuf*, 560 U.S. 305 (2010), the US Supreme Court held that the FSIA does not apply to a civil suit brought against a foreign official "in his personal capacity and seek[ing] damages from his own pockets ... because it is not a claim against a foreign state as the Act defines that term." *Id.* at 325.

immunity. Like the FSIA, these acts generally grant jurisdictional immunity to foreign states and then carve out specific categories of claims subject to domestic adjudication, such as claims based on a foreign state's commercial activities.[20] Under the UK State Immunity Act of 1978 (SIA),[21] for example, claims against foreign states for torture and other human rights violations committed outside of the United Kingdom are subject to dismissal on the grounds of foreign state immunity, because they do not fall within an enumerated statutory exception.

Within the US legal system, the Supreme Court's application of the FSIA to bar a claim against a foreign state is not directly subject to an additional layer of judicial review. By contrast, in the United Kingdom, injured parties have challenged dismissals based on immunity as disproportionately restricting their right of access to a court under the UK Human Rights Act, as well as under article 6 § 1 of the European Convention on Human Rights (ECHR). The formal protection of the right of access to a court in the ECHR provides European claimants with an additional basis for challenging jurisdictional immunity as a bar to the exercise of domestic adjudicatory jurisdiction over a foreign state.

State immunity acts give domestic effect to the structural international norm of foreign state immunity. At the same time, regional and international human rights instruments (which may themselves be "domesticated" by legislation such as the Human Rights Act) give effect to the countervailing norm of an individual's right of access to a court. The resulting clash cannot thus be characterized simply as a conflict between a domestic norm and an international one, or between a structural and a substantive (i.e., conduct-regulating) rule. Rather, the question is about the role of domestic adjudication in resolving various types of disputes between injured parties and foreign states or their officials. The rest of this chapter reviews efforts by domestic and international tribunals in Europe and the United States to delineate this evolving role in conversation with Canadian courts, and with each other.

5.2.2 Challenges to Immunity Based on the Right to Judicial Access in Europe

Unlike in the United States, the fundamental right of access to a court – part of a set of human rights codified in international instruments and domestic

---

[20] Other exceptions also exist under various state immunity acts. For example, the Canadian and US state immunity acts do not provide immunity from certain claims against designated state sponsors of terrorism. 28 USC § 1605A (US); RSC, 1985, c. S-18 § 6.1 (Can.).

[21] 1978, c. 33 § 1(1) (UK).

constitutions in the post–World War II era – is enshrined in the UK Human Rights Act, the Italian Constitution (as explored in Section 5.3.3), and the ECHR, among other instruments. Claimants in UK courts have argued that immunity-based dismissals of their claims disproportionately restrict their right of access to a court, and claimants in Italian courts have argued that certain immunity-based dismissals are incompatible with the constitutional right of access to justice. The ability to seek redress in the European Court of Human Rights (ECtHR) also provides an additional path to challenge immunity determinations as inconsistent with the right of access to a court. Notably, in *Al-Adsani* v. *United Kingdom*, the applicant asked the Grand Chamber of the ECtHR to find that the United Kingdom had violated his right of access to a court when it granted state immunity to Kuwait from civil claims for torture.[22]

In *Al-Adsani*, the applicant's access to a UK court was undeniably restricted when his claims against Kuwait were dismissed under the UK SIA without a hearing on the merits. The question for the ECtHR was whether this restriction was consistent with the United Kingdom's obligations under the ECHR. In order to pass muster under ECHR jurisprudence, a challenged restriction must pursue a legitimate aim and be proportionate to that aim. A narrow majority of the ECtHR found, by a vote of nine to eight, that the UK SIA had the legitimate aim of "complying with international law to promote comity and good relations between States through the respect of another State's sovereignty."[23] The majority reasoned further that "measures taken by a High Contracting Party which reflect generally recognised rules of public international law on State immunity cannot in principle be regarded as imposing a disproportionate restriction on the right of access to a court."[24] It opined that restrictions on the right of access to a court "generally accepted by the community of nations as part of the doctrine of State immunity" should be regarded as "inherent" restrictions on that right.[25] It also observed that the United Kingdom was not an outlier in its practice of granting foreign states immunity for their noncommercial conduct. In its view, the United Kingdom's actions therefore fell within the permissible "margin of appreciation" enjoyed by states parties to the ECHR in implementing the right of access to a court,[26] notwithstanding some contrary practice by states denying immunity for gross human rights violations.[27]

---

[22] *Al-Adsani* v. *United Kingdom* [GC], Judgment of 21 Nov. 2001, ECHR-XI.
[23] Ibid. § 54.
[24] Ibid. § 56.
[25] Ibid.
[26] Ibid. § 53.
[27] Ibid. §§ 24, 64–65.

The "margin of appreciation" doctrine in ECtHR jurisprudence accords a certain level of deference to national authorities' balancing of potentially conflicting rights or values in an attempt to protect core individual rights without unduly constraining national self-governance and diverse societal choices within the European framework.[28] Notwithstanding this doctrine, the eight dissenting judges in *Al-Adsani* would have found that the dismissal of claims against Kuwait violated the United Kingdom's obligations under the ECHR. Six of these judges would have found that the *jus cogens* or peremptory character of the prohibition on torture "deprives the rule of sovereign immunity of all its legal effects in [the international] sphere."[29] Under this theory, there can be no immunity for alleged violations of *jus cogens* norms because such rules are hierarchically superior to all other conflicting norms, including state immunity. A seventh dissenting judge would have found that the United Kingdom had a duty to contribute to the punishment of torture, and that it could not "hide behind formalist arguments" to justify treating criminal proceedings against individuals for torture (which are not barred under the UK SIA) differently from civil proceedings against states.[30] Finally, the eighth dissenting judge would have found that "any form of blanket immunity" is, by definition, a disproportionate restriction on the right of access to a court, because it does not involve any evaluation or weighing of "the competing interests in favour of upholding an immunity or allowing a judicial determination of a civil right."[31]

The Grand Chamber's decision in *Al-Adsani* involved the immunity of a foreign state, not individual foreign officials. The applicant in *Al-Adsani* had obtained a default judgment against a Kuwaiti official in the UK proceedings, but that judgment was not executed because the official had no identifiable assets in the United Kingdom.[32] Consequently, the ECtHR's decision in *Al-Adsani* did not address whether granting immunity from civil proceedings to a foreign official, rather than to the foreign state itself, would constitute a disproportionate restriction on the right of access to a court.

---

[28] Article 1 of Protocol 15 amending the Convention on the Protection of Human Rights and Fundamental Freedoms (June 24, 2013), which will come into force once all states parties to the ECHR have ratified it, adds a new recital to the Preamble of the Convention: "Affirming that the High Contracting Parties, in accordance with the principle of subsidiarity, have the primary responsibility to secure the rights and freedoms defined in this Convention and the Protocols thereto, and that in doing so they enjoy a margin of appreciation, subject to the supervisory jurisdiction of the European Court of Human Rights established by this Convention."

[29] *Al-Adsani* § 4 (joint dissenting opinion).

[30] *Al-Adsani* (dissenting opinion of Judge Ferrari Bravo).

[31] *Al-Adsani* (dissenting opinion of Judge Loucaides).

[32] *Al-Adsani* § 51.

The separate question of foreign official immunity reached the ECtHR in *Jones v. United Kingdom*.[33] As in *Al-Adsani, Jones* challenged the United Kingdom's dismissal of civil claims for torture under the SIA. The claimants in *Jones* and its companion case persuaded the UK Court of Appeal that applying the SIA to bar civil proceedings against Saudi Arabian officials for torture would disproportionately restrict their right of access to a court under the UK Human Rights Act,[34] which gives domestic effect to the ECHR. The Court of Appeal agreed with the claimants that the individual Saudi officials could not claim immunity from service,[35] but the House of Lords subsequently held that both Saudi Arabia and its officials were entitled to jurisdictional immunity under the SIA.[36]

In *Jones*, the UK House of Lords characterized its task as applying a domestic statute that was in no "relevant respect ambiguous or obscure."[37] Yet Lord Bingham still framed the question as involving the relationship between "two principles of international law": the norm of state immunity from foreign judicial authority, and the norm requiring states to suppress torture and to punish officials who engage in it.[38] His extensive citations to foreign and international sources in a judicial decision applying an unambiguous domestic statute might seem odd, but it reflects an understanding that domestic state immunity laws are embedded in a framework of evolving international standards.

The House of Lords had previously considered the question of foreign official immunity from criminal proceedings in *Ex parte Pinochet*, a case involving the Chilean ex-president's immunity from extradition to face criminal prosecution in Spain. That case had not involved consideration of the U. K. SIA, because the SIA does not apply to criminal proceedings.[39] The House of Lords found that Augusto Pinochet was not immune from extradition to face trial on charges of torture committed in Chile.[40] In *Jones*, the Court of Appeal reasoned that civil proceedings against individual foreign officials do not interfere in the "internal affairs of a foreign state"[41] any more than criminal proceedings. Unlike in *Pinochet*, the civil nature of the claims in *Jones* brought the SIA into play. The Court of Appeal concluded that while Saudi Arabia

---

[33] *Jones & Ors. v. United Kingdom* [2014] ECHR 32.
[34] 1998, c. 42 (UK).
[35] *Jones v. Ministry of Interior of Saudi Arabia* [2004] EWCA (Civ) 1394.
[36] *Jones v. Ministry of Interior for the Kingdom of Saudi Arabia & Ors.* [2006] UKHL 26.
[37] *Jones*, [2006] UKHL 26 ¶ 13.
[38] Ibid. ¶ 1.
[39] *See* State Immunity Act, 1978, c. 33, § 16(4) (UK).
[40] *Pinochet (No. 3)*, [2000] 1 A.C. 147 (HL).
[41] *Jones*, [2004] EWCA (Civ) 1394 ¶ 75.

124   *Chimène I. Keitner*

itself was immune from civil suit for torture under the SIA, individual Saudi officials were not automatically shielded by the state's immunity.

Lord Phillips, who had participated in the House of Lords' decision in *Pinochet*, wrote separately as a member of the Court of Appeal in *Jones* to emphasize that "[i]f civil proceedings are brought against individuals for acts of torture . . . [i]t is the personal responsibility of the individuals, not that of the state, which is in issue. The state is not indirectly impleaded by the proceedings."[42] Despite the strength of this reasoning, the House of Lords disagreed with this interpretation. On further appeal, the House of Lords in *Jones* held that civil proceedings against individual foreign officials do "indirectly implead" the foreign state, and are therefore subject to dismissal under the SIA.[43]

The Court of Appeal did not take the position that civil proceedings against foreign officials should invariably proceed to a hearing on the merits. Lord Mance emphasized in his opinion that:

> Quite apart from any separate principle of state immunity, the fact that a civil claim was being brought against an official or agent of a foreign state in respect of conduct in that state, and the sensitivity of any adjudication by the courts of another state upon such an issue, would rightly feature as important factors in any decision whether or not to exercise any such jurisdiction.[44]

Notwithstanding Lord Mance's cautionary language, Lord Bingham of the House of Lords characterized the Court of Appeal's decision to authorize service on the individual Saudi officials outside the United Kingdom as a "'unilateral assumption of jurisdiction by one national legal system'"[45] that impermissibly "asserted what was in effect a universal tort jurisdiction in cases of official torture."[46] Lord Mance's and Lord Bingham's approaches both acknowledged that potential foreign relations concerns can arise from suits against foreign officials for alleged human rights violations; however, they attributed different weight to the competing values of state nonintervention and individual judicial access in applying the SIA to bar to such proceedings.

The Court of Appeal and the House of Lords also diverged in their assessment of relevant principles of international law. The Court of Appeal found it "impossible to identify any settled international principle affording the state

---

[42]   Ibid. ¶ 128 (opinion of Lord Phillips of Worth Matravers).
[43]   *Jones*, [2006] UKHL 26 ¶ 31.
[44]   *Jones*, [2004] EWCA (Civ) 1394 ¶ 81.
[45]   *Jones*, [2006] UKHL 26 ¶ 34, quoting Hazel Fox, *Where Does the Buck Stop? State Immunity from Civil Jurisdiction and Torture* (2005) 121 LQR 353, 359.
[46]   *Jones*, [2006] UKHL 26 ¶ 34.

Authority and Dialogue 125

the right to claim immunity in respect of claims directed against such an official, rather than against the state itself or its head or diplomats."[47] In considering the restriction on the right of access to a court that would result from jurisdictional immunity, the Court of Appeal noted that "where there is no adequate remedy in the state where the systematic torture occurs, it might well ... be regarded as disproportionate to maintain a blanket refusal of recourse to the civil courts of another European jurisdiction[.]"[48] Reflecting on the ECtHR's judgment in *Al-Adsani*, Lord Phillips surmised that:

> Had the Grand Chamber [of the ECtHR in *Al-Adsani*] been considering a claim for state immunity in relation to claims brought against individuals [rather than against a foreign state], I do not believe that there would have been a majority in favour of the view that this represented a legitimate limitation on the right to access to a court under Article 6(1). Had the Court shared the conclusions that we have reached on this appeal, it would have held that there was no recognised rule of public international law that conferred such immunity. Had it concluded that there was such a rule, I consider that it would have been likely to have held that it would not be proportionate to apply the rule so as to preclude civil remedies sought against individuals.[49]

The later opinion of the Fourth Section of the ECtHR, composed of seven judges, did not bear out this prediction; whether or not a Grand Chamber of seventeen judges would have reached a different conclusion regarding foreign official immunity remains unknown.

The UK House of Lords in *Jones* agreed with the Court of Appeal that the SIA provides Saudi Arabia with immunity from civil claims for torture, but it rejected the Court of Appeal's conclusion that individual Saudi officials do not enjoy immunity from similar claims.[50] Following the final dismissal of their claims in UK court, the claimants in *Jones* and its companion case lodged applications with the ECtHR against the United Kingdom for violating their right of access to a court. In *Jones and Others* v. *United Kingdom*, the Fourth Section of the ECtHR agreed that "Article 6 § 1 secures to everyone the right to have any legal dispute ('contestation' in the French text of Article 6 § 1) relating to his civil rights and obligations brought before a court."[51] However, as the Grand Chamber had noted in *Al-Adsani*, states parties

---

47 *Jones*, [2004] EWCA (Civ) 1394 ¶ 83.
48 Ibid. ¶ 85; *cf. Al-Adsani* v. *United Kingdom* [GC], Judgment of 21 Nov. 2001, ECHR-XI (dissenting opinion of Judge Loucaides).
49 *Jones*, [2004] EWCA (Civ) 1394 ¶ 134 (Lord Phillips of Worth Matravers).
50 *Jones*, [2006] UKHL 26.
51 *Jones & Ors.* v. *United Kingdom* [2014] ECHR 32 ¶ 186.

enjoy a "margin of appreciation" in implementing this right, and states can limit the individual right of access to court if such limitations pursue a "legitimate aim" and bear a "reasonable relationship of proportionality" to that aim.[52] The question for the ECtHR in *Jones* was whether the application of the UK SIA to bar civil claims for torture against both a foreign state and its officials satisfied these requirements.

The Fourth Section followed the majority's reasoning in *Al-Adsani*, observing that "sovereign immunity is a concept of international law, developed out of the principle *par in parem non habet imperium*, by virtue of which one State shall not be subject to the jurisdiction of another State."[53] Consequently, "[t]he grant of sovereign immunity to a State in civil proceedings pursues the legitimate aim of complying with international law to promote comity and good relations between States through the respect of another State's sovereignty."[54] Again following the *Al-Adsani* majority,[55] the Fourth Section reasoned that "measures taken by a State which reflect generally recognised rules of public international law on State immunity cannot in principle be regarded as imposing a disproportionate restriction on the right of access to a court as embodied in Article 6 § 1."[56]

Framed this way, the question for the ECtHR became whether foreign state immunity represents a "generally recognised rule" of international law. The Fourth Section in *Jones* canvassed domestic and international jurisprudence in greater detail than the Grand Chamber had done in *Al-Adsani*. Based on this analysis, the majority found that the norm of foreign state immunity was sufficiently well established in 2006 to warrant the United Kingdom's restriction on the applicants' ability to pursue their claims against the state of Saudi Arabia at that time.[57] The majority further noted that, by contrast, state practice regarding the immunity of foreign officials from civil proceedings is "in a state of flux."[58] The variation in state practice proved favorable to the United Kingdom because, given this "state of flux," the Fourth Section was not prepared to find that the application of the UK SIA to bar civil proceedings against the named Saudi officials amounted to a disproportionate restriction on the applicants' right of access to a court.

---

[52] Ibid.
[53] Ibid. ¶ 188.
[54] Ibid.
[55] Ibid ¶ 195.
[56] Ibid. ¶ 189.
[57] Ibid. ¶ 196.
[58] Ibid. ¶ 213.

Authority and Dialogue

Like the House of Lords' reasoning in *Jones*, the Fourth Section's discussion of the immunity of individual officials collapsed the analysis of foreign official immunity into the analysis of foreign state immunity. The majority reasoned that:

> Since an act cannot be carried out by a State itself but only by individuals acting on the State's behalf, where immunity can be invoked by the State then the starting point must be that immunity ratione materiae applies to the acts of State officials. If it were otherwise, State immunity could always be circumvented by suing named officials.[59]

In adopting this reasoning, the majority did not differentiate between civil suits that do not implead the state because they seek the individual's assets, and civil suits that do implead the state because they seek the state's assets or seek to compel an individual to act on behalf of the state. Because the majority found that the United Kingdom's application of the SIA fell within the permitted margin of appreciation, it avoided the need to engage in such parsing.

Judge Kalaydjieva, writing in dissent, would have found that the United Kingdom was not justified in granting the Saudi officials immunity from civil claims, especially since these officials would not have been immune from criminal prosecution in the United Kingdom for the same conduct.[60] The majority acknowledged that "as the existence of individual criminal liability shows, even if the official nature of the acts is accepted for the purposes of State responsibility, this of itself is not conclusive as to whether, under international law, a claim for State immunity is always to be recognised in respect of the same acts."[61] As indicated above, however, the majority concluded that "[s]tate practice on the question is in a state of flux, with evidence of both the grant and the refusal of immunity ratione materiae in such cases."[62] Consequently, the House of Lords' findings on foreign official immunity "were neither manifestly erroneous nor arbitrary"[63] – which was sufficient, in the majority's view, to pass muster under the applicable standard of review.

In canvassing international practice, the Fourth Section observed that "[i]nternational opinion on the question [of foreign official immunity] may be said to be beginning to evolve, as demonstrated recently by the discussions around the work of the International Law Commission in the criminal

---

[59] Ibid. ¶ 202.
[60] Ibid. (Kalaydjieva, J., dissenting).
[61] Ibid. ¶ 207.
[62] Ibid. ¶ 213.
[63] Ibid. ¶ 214.

128 Chimène I. Keitner

sphere[,] … and further developments can be expected."[64] Ironically, however, the Fourth Section's opinion may impede the "further developments" it anticipated by signaling to states that granting foreign official immunity does not necessarily constitute a disproportionate restriction on the right of access to a court – a conclusion that did not escape the notice of the Canadian Supreme Court, as discussed in Section 5.3.[65]

5.2.3 International Law and Foreign Official Immunity Determinations in US Courts

Foreign official immunity determinations in US courts are based on the common law rather than an immunity statute interpreted to include foreign officials.[66] They therefore follow a different doctrinal path from immunity determinations made by UK and Canadian courts. Although the US executive branch historically disclaimed the ability to deprive a US court of jurisdiction over a foreign official on the grounds of *ratione materiae* immunity,[67] it has more recently asserted such authority in a series of cases involving civil claims against current and former foreign officials.[68] In making immunity determinations, the State Department takes into consideration "customary international law principles accepted by the Executive Branch in the exercise of its constitutional authority over foreign affairs."[69] The executive branch currently maintains that its determinations are binding on courts as a matter of US constitutional law.[70]

By way of example, in a case involving *ratione personae* (rather than *ratione materiae*) immunity, the Department of Justice informed the court that the State Department had "recognize[d] and allow[ed]" the defendant's immunity as follows: "Under rules of customary international law recognized and applied in the United States as a matter of common law, Sheikh Khalifa is

---

[64] Ibid. ¶ 213; for an analytical guide to the ILC's work on this topic, see http://legal.un.org/ilc/guide/4_2.shtml.

[65] See *infra* note 98 and accompanying text.

[66] See *supra* note 19.

[67] See Chimène I. Keitner, *The Forgotten History of Foreign Official Immunity*, 87 N.Y. U. L. REV. 704 (2012).

[68] See, *e.g.*, Brief for the United States as Amicus Curiae Supporting Appellants, *Yousuf v. Samantar*, No. 11-1497, 15 (4th Cir., Oct. 24, 2011) (taking the position that "[i]n the absence of a governing statute, it is the State Department's role to determine the principles governing foreign official immunity from suit").

[69] Brief for the United States as Amicus Curiae Supporting Appellee, *Habyarimana v. Kagame*, No. 11-6315, 5 (10th Cir., Apr. 30, 2012).

[70] Ibid. at 7–8.

Authority and Dialogue

immune from the Court's jurisdiction in this case. Such head of state immunity determinations are made by the Executive Branch, incident to the Executive Branch's authority in the field of foreign affairs."[71] The US Supreme Court has yet to pronounce explicitly on the degree of deference due to suggestions of immunity (or lack thereof) filed by the executive branch. Meanwhile, the Fourth Circuit Court of Appeals has agreed that "consistent with the Executive's constitutionally delegated powers and the historical practice of the courts, ... the State Department's pronouncement[s] as to head-of-state immunity [are] entitled to absolute deference."[72]

The Fourth Circuit has taken a slightly different approach to executive suggestions of conduct-based immunity:

> Unlike head-of-state immunity and other status-based immunities, there is no equivalent constitutional basis suggesting that the views of the Executive Branch control questions of foreign official immunity. ... These immunity decisions turn upon principles of customary international law and foreign policy, areas in which the courts respect, but do not automatically follow, the views of the Executive Branch.[73]

The Fourth Circuit has also found that *jus cogens* violations are not shielded by *ratione materiae* immunity under the common law, noting that "[t]here has been an increasing trend in international law to abrogate foreign official immunity for individuals who commit acts, otherwise attributable to the State, that violate *jus cogens* norms."[74] Consequently, in a decision that the US Supreme Court declined to review, it held that "under international and domestic law, officials from other countries are not entitled to foreign official immunity for *jus cogens* violations, even if the acts were performed in the defendant's official capacity."[75]

Other US courts have taken a different approach. Notably, a district court in New York deferred to the State Department's suggestion of conduct-based immunity for two Pakistani officials on the basis that, in the State Department's view, "acts of defendant foreign officials who are sued for exercising the powers of their office are treated as acts taken in an official capacity, and plaintiffs have provided no reason to question that

---

[71] Suggestion of Immunity Submitted by the United States of America, *Al Hassen v. Al Nahyan*, No. 2:09-CV-1106-DMG (C.D. Cal., 26 July 2010) at 2.
[72] *Yousuf v. Samantar*, 699 F.3d 763, 772 (4th Cir. 2012).
[73] Ibid. at 773.
[74] Ibid. at 776.
[75] Ibid. at 777.

determination."[76] The New York district court went on to opine that the Fourth Circuit's analysis of jurisdictional immunity for alleged *jus cogens* violations under the common law conflicted with an earlier Second Circuit decision finding that the FSIA provides foreign states with immunity for *jus cogens* violations, and that, according to the Second Circuit's decision, "in the common-law context, we defer to the Executive's determination of the scope of [foreign official] immunity" regardless of the severity of the allegations.[77]

In the United States, the doctrinal debate about the degree of deference owed to executive branch determinations has largely eclipsed judicial discussion of the content of applicable customary international law norms, although the State Department has publicly committed to "recognize[ing] and apply-[ing]" international law norms as part of its common-law immunity determinations. Since the US Supreme Court in *Samantar* held that the "common law" governs the immunity of foreign officials in US courts, post-*Samantar* questions of authority and dialogue have focused more on the domestic sphere. Notwithstanding the Fourth Circuit's reference to an international trend away from foreign official immunity for *jus cogens* violations, the primary locus for the direct consideration and application of international norms currently appears to reside largely inside the State Department.

To the extent that US courts are also called upon to make immunity determinations absent State Department guidance, further authoritative elucidation of the legally relevant considerations seems desirable. The reasoning adopted by foreign and international decisions may yet hold some persuasive value for US judges,[78] although the right of judicial access upon which legal challenges to immunity determinations in other courts have been based does not have a clear US analog. Instead, the predominant countervailing consideration appears to be the plenary nature of territorial jurisdiction, famously identified by Chief Justice John Marshall in his 1812 opinion finding immunity for a French ship of war docked in the port of Philadelphia whose previous American owners sought to reclaim it.[79] Given the competing interests at stake, the task of articulating clear and uniformly applicable criteria to foreign

---

[76] *Rosenberg v. Lashkar-e-Taiba*, 980 F. Supp. 2d 336, 343 (E.D.N.Y. 2013), quoting Letter from Legal Adviser Harold Hongju Koh.

[77] *Matar v. Dichter*, 563 F.3d 9, 15 (2d Cir. 2009).

[78] *See, e.g.*, Hon. Claire l'Heureux-Dubé, *The Importance of Dialogue: Globalization and the International Impact of the Rehnquist Court*, 34 TULSA L. REV. 15, 16 (1998)(observing that "More and more courts, particularly within the common law world, are looking to the judgments of other jurisdictions, particularly when making decisions on human rights issues").

[79] *The Schooner Exchange v. McFaddon*, 11 U.S. (7 Cranch) 116, 136 (1812).

official immunity determinations appears as fraught as McFaddon and Greetham's attempt to reclaim their captured ship.

5.3 NORM CONSOLIDATION AND LEGAL PROTECTIONISM IN RESPONSE TO INTERNATIONAL DECISIONS

5.3.1 The ICJ's Rejection of a Broad Human Rights Exception to State Immunity

Although the International Court of Justice's decisions in contentious cases are only binding on the parties to the dispute, domestic courts and other decision-makers often cite the ICJ's pronouncements as evidence of the content of customary international law. For example, the ECtHR's high level of confidence regarding the "generally recognised" status of state immunity for non-commercial acts in *Jones* v. *United Kingdom* was based in large part on the ICJ's 2012 decision in *Jurisdictional Immunities of the State (Germany v. Italy)*.[80] In that case, the ICJ held that Italy violated customary international law by allowing claims against Germany for World War II–era crimes committed by German armed forces to proceed in Italian courts. The ICJ ascertained the content of customary international law by looking at national legislation and domestic court decisions, as well as statements made in conjunction with the adoption of the UN Convention on Jurisdictional Immunities of States, which is not yet in force.[81] It found that the weight of state practice did not support denying jurisdictional immunity solely on account of the gravity of the alleged acts.[82] The ICJ cited the ECtHR's decision in *Al-Adsani* as further support for this conclusion.[83] It also held that the *jus cogens* or peremptory status of a substantive norm does not displace the bar of jurisdictional immunity, which it characterized as purely procedural.[84]

Judge Cançado Trindade issued a lengthy and forceful dissent from the majority's opinion, in which he emphasized the "prevalence" of the individual right of access to justice and the resulting absence of "immunities for *delicta imperii* … in the domain of *jus cogens.*"[85] Judge Yusuf also wrote a dissent in which he opined that customary international law on state immunity "remains

---

[80] *Jurisdictional Immunities of the State* (Ger. v. It.: Greece intervening), 2012 I.C.J. 1.
[81] Ibid. [77]–[78].
[82] Ibid. [85], [89].
[83] Ibid. [90].
[84] Ibid. [95]–[96].
[85] Ibid. (Diss. Op. Cançado Trindade) [5].

fragmentary and unsettled"[86] and that state immunity is "as full of holes as Swiss cheese."[87] Given the lack of alternative means of redress for the victims in this case, Judge Yusuf would have found that Italy did not violate customary international law by denying Germany's claims to immunity. Judge *ad hoc* Gaja would have found that at least some of Italy's decisions denying immunity fell within the "territorial tort" exception to state immunity. Judge Bennouna joined the majority's opinion but would have conditioned Germany's immunity on its willingness to assume international responsibility for its injurious acts and to settle the victims' compensation claims.[88]

At the time of the ICJ's decision, Philippa Webb predicted that the majority's rejection of a *jus cogens* exception to foreign state immunity would likely "have a 'chilling effect' on national courts that might otherwise have generated additional state practice and *opinio juris* narrowing the scope of foreign state immunity over time."[89] I agreed with her assessment, suggesting that "[t]he ICJ's decision will thus curtail the horizontal enforcement of certain substantive rules of international law where the defendant is a foreign state by making it more difficult (that is, less plausible in doctrinal terms and more costly in political terms) for domestic courts to deny assertions of state immunity."[90] The Canadian Supreme Court's decision in *Kazemi* v. *Iran* supported these hypotheses, as explored in Section 5.3.2. However, to the surprise of many observers, the Italian Constitutional Court's Judgment 238/2014 reached a different result on the grounds that rights-abrogating international norms, including jurisdictional immunity for German war crimes, do not enter into the Italian constitutional system and cannot be enforced by Italian courts. The Italian decision can be characterized as an instance of domestic "legal protectionism" – a phenomenon explored further in Section 5.4.

5.3.2 *Norm Consolidation in Canada's* Kazemi v. Iran

The prediction that international decisions upholding jurisdictional immunities could exercise a "chilling effect" on national courts by discouraging

---

[86]   Ibid. (Diss. Op. Yusuf) [24].
[87]   Ibid. (Diss. Op. Yusuf) [26].
[88]   Ibid. (Sep. Op. Bennouna) [14].
[89]   P. Webb, *The International Court of Justice's Judgment in Germany v. Italy: A Chilling Effect?*, at http://ilawyerblog.com/theinternational-court-of-justices-judgment-in-germany-v-italy-a-chilling-effect/ (7 March 2012).
[90]   Chimène I. Keitner, Germany v. Italy *and the Limits of Horizontal Enforcement: Some Reflections from a U.S. Perspective*, 11 J. Int'l Crim. Just.167, 172 (2013); see also the contributions in this symposium volume by Giuseppe Nesi, Micaela Frulli, Andrew Dickinson, and Lorna McGregor.

alternative approaches was borne out in *Estate of Kazemi v. Iran*, a Canadian decision that merits consideration as part of a discussion of "authority and dialogue" in the immunity context.[91] In that decision, the Supreme Court of Canada held that Canada's State Immunity Act (SIA) shields both the state of Iran and its officials from civil claims for torture. The Supreme Court found that the Canadian SIA does not violate principles of fundamental justice protected by section 7 of the Canadian Charter of Rights and Freedoms (the relevant rights-guaranteeing instrument) because Canada does not have an international obligation to provide civil redress for torture committed abroad.[92] The Court also cited the ICJ's holding that immunity is a procedural norm that does not automatically give way to the substantive *jus cogens* prohibition on torture.[93] The Canadian Supreme Court's opinion presents a clear example of a national court looking to an international tribunal to bolster its reasoning and creating additional state practice in the process. The Supreme Court's direct and explicit engagement with jurisprudence from other jurisdictions reinforces the idea of immunity as a hybrid domestic/international norm.

The Supreme Court in *Kazemi* emphasized the domestic statutory basis for its decision regarding both foreign state and foreign official immunity, as did the UK House of Lords in *Jones*. The majority applied the Canadian SIA to bar the claims against Iran and against individual Iranian officials based on the definition of the term "foreign state" in the SIA[94] and the observation that "the SIA is intended to be an exhaustive codification of Canadian law of state immunity in civil suits."[95] The majority emphasized that the SIA is a codification of "Canadian law" that "reflects domestic choices made for policy reasons" by the Canadian Parliament.[96] In the majority's view, Canada's decision to give "priority to a foreign state's immunity over civil redress for citizens who have been tortured abroad . . . is not a comment about the evils of torture, but rather an indication of what principles Parliament has chosen to promote given Canada's role and that of its government in the international community."[97] The content of customary international law would not alter this result, because "[s]hould an exception to state immunity for acts of torture have become customary international law, such a rule could

---

[91] *Estate of Kazemi v. Islamic Republic of Iran* [2014] SCC 62.
[92] Ibid. ¶ 157.
[93] Ibid. ¶ 161, citing *Jurisdictional Immunities of the State*, 2012 I.C.J. 1 ¶ 93.
[94] *Kazemi*, [2014] SCC 62 ¶ 15.
[95] Ibid. ¶ 44.
[96] Ibid. ¶ 45.
[97] Ibid. ¶ 46.

134   *Chimène I. Keitner*

likely be *permissive* – and not *mandatory* – thereby, requiring legislative action to become Canadian law."[98] In other words, even if Canada *could* deny immunity consistent with international law, it was under no obligation to do so in light of Parliament's decision to prioritize state sovereignty.

Despite emphasizing that the Canadian SIA was a product of "domestic choices," the *Kazemi* majority found support for its interpretation of this statute in the ECtHR's observation that excluding foreign officials from the purview of state immunity acts could allow claimants to circumvent foreign state immunity by naming foreign officials as defendants.[99] Because the Canadian SIA, like the UK SIA, expressly excludes criminal proceedings, the majority deemed it unnecessary to reconcile the resulting prohibition on civil proceedings against individuals with the requirement of criminal proceedings for the same conduct.[100] The majority also reasoned that the "'state of flux' of international law pertaining to foreign official immunities for *jus cogens* violations" meant that the statutory "presumption of conformity" of domestic legislation with customary international law did not apply.[101]

Justice Abella, writing in dissent in *Kazemi*, would have found that the SIA does not apply to individuals other than foreign heads of state.[102] She noted that the ICJ's holding in *Germany* v. *Italy* explicitly declined to consider "the availability of immunity for individual state officials."[103] She also observed that the ECtHR's reasoning in *Jones* "does not foreclose the possibility that torture is beyond the protection of immunity *ratione materiae*"[104] under international law. In her view, civil proceedings against individuals are more analogous to criminal proceedings than they are to civil claims against the state.[105] She would therefore have found that the SIA does not govern the *ratione materiae* immunity of foreign officials in either the civil or criminal context. In her view, "while it can be said that customary international law permits states to recognize immunity for foreign officials, ... it also does not *preclude* a state from denying immunity for acts of torture."[106] Accordingly, she would have found that the SIA does not require a Canadian court to grant immunity from

---

[98]   Ibid. ¶ 61. Emphases in original.
[99]   Ibid. ¶ 87 (citing *Jones & Ors.* v. *United Kingdom* [2014] ECHR 32 ¶ 202).
[100] *Kazemi*, [2014] SCC 62 ¶ 104.
[101] Ibid. ¶ 102.
[102] Ibid. ¶ 184 (Abella, J., dissenting).
[103] Ibid. ¶ 204.
[104] Ibid. ¶ 208.
[105] Ibid. ¶ 209.
[106] Ibid. ¶ 211 (citing *Pinochet (No. 3)*, [2000] 1 A.C. 147 (H.L.) and *Yousuf* v. *Samantar*, 699 F.3d 673 (4th Cir. 2012)).

civil proceedings for torture when the defendant is a foreign official rather than the foreign state.

Like the U.K. House of Lords' decision in *Jones*, the Supreme Court's decision in *Kazemi* turned on the interpretation and application of a domestic statute, the conclusions reached by other national courts and by international tribunals figured prominently in both opinions. The confidence with which judges can make assertions about the content of customary international law – whether as an end in itself or as support for a particular interpretation of a domestic statute – increases with their ability to cite additional decisions that reach similar conclusions. This self-reinforcing dynamic or "catalytic effect" can operate among both domestic and international courts, even in the absence of a binding system of precedent. This pattern is perhaps especially true for a norm such as jurisdictional immunity, in which state practice and *opinio juris* often takes the form of court decisions. If and when the US Supreme Court takes up the question of common-law immunity for foreign officials, it will be interesting to see whether it undertakes a similar analysis, or whether it confines itself to examining the relatively small number of US cases involving claims to *ratione materiae* immunity by foreign officials.

5.3.3 *Legal Protectionism in Italy's Judgment No. 238/2014*

The Canadian Supreme Court is not the only domestic court to have considered state immunity after the ICJ issued its decision in *Germany v. Italy*. As part of the ongoing saga involving claims arising from abuses committed during World War II, Italian courts have been called upon to resolve outstanding civil claims against Germany. In August 2012, the First Criminal Division of the Court of Cassation (Italy's highest domestic court) overruled its own earlier decisions and dismissed a reparation order for civil damages that had been issued against Germany by the Italian Military Court of Appeal.[107] Although the Italian Court of Cassation disagreed with the ICJ's reasoning in *Germany v. Italy*, it decided to comply with the ICJ's ruling "to avoid undermining Italy's international position," and in light of the current lack of widespread acceptance by other states of a *jus cogens* exception to state immunity.[108] The court took pains to emphasize that although "the new rule

---

[107] *Criminal Proceedings Against Albers*, Cass., sez. un. pen., 9 agosto 2012, n. 32139, 95 RIVISTA DI DIRITTO INTERNAZIONALE [RDI] 1196 (2012), INT'L L. DOMESTIC CTS. [ILDC] 1921 (in Ital.); *see* Filippo Fontanelli, *International Decisions – Criminal Proceedings Against Albers*, 107 AM. J. INT'L L. 632 (2013).

[108] Ibid. at 635.

of customary international law it favor[ed] has not yet emerged [it] could do so in the future."[109] That said, as suggested above, the ICJ's judgment may impede such a development in the near term.

Despite the Court of Cassation's concession, a rejection of state immunity for *jus cogens* violations was not long in coming – from another Italian court. In Judgment 238/2014, the Italian Constitutional Court found that the Italian Constitution precludes domestic implementation of the ICJ's decision in *Germany v. Italy*.[110] The Constitutional Court reached this conclusion in response to three questions posed by the Tribunal of Florence regarding the constitutionality of (1) Article 1 of Law No. 898 of August 17, 1957 (Execution of the United Nations Charter), which incorporates Article 94 of the U.N. Charter into Italian law and thereby requires Italian judges to give effect to ICJ decisions; (2) a 2013 law enacted by the Italian parliament giving effect to the decision in *Germany v. Italy* by requiring Italian courts to deny jurisdiction over claims against Germany for crimes against humanity committed by the Third Reich on Italian territory; and (3) the norm created in the Italian legal order by the incorporation, under Article 10(1) of the Italian constitution, of the customary international law of state immunity articulated in *Germany v. Italy*.

The legal basis for giving domestic effect to the ICJ's judgment is Article 1 of Law No. 898 of August 17, 1957 (Execution of the United Nations Charter), which incorporates Article 94 of the UN Charter into Italian law. The Constitutional Court deemed this legislation unconstitutional "exclusively to the extent that it obliges the Italian judge to comply with the Judgment of the ICJ of 3 February 2012, which requires that Italian courts deny their jurisdiction in case of acts of a foreign State constituting war crimes and crimes against humanity, in breach of inviolable human rights."[111] This reasoning appears to authorize the Constitutional Court to decide on a judgment-by-judgment basis whether Law No. 898 requires compliance with a decision by the ICJ, or whether compliance would amount to an unconstitutional breach of "inviolable human rights."

The Constitutional Court was careful to distinguish interpretative authority over international law, which it attributed exclusively (and perhaps

---

[109] Ibid.

[110] Judgment 238/2014, Italian Constitutional Court (22 Oct. 2014), unofficial translation by Alessio Gracis available at http://italyspractice.info/judgment-238-2014. Citations below are to this unofficial translation, which was subsequently posted on the Constitutional Court's website; an alternate translation is available at www.cortecostituzionale.it/documenti/down load/doc/recent_judgments/S238_2013_en.pdf.

[111] Judgment 238/2014 at 22.

excessively) to the ICJ, from its own paramount interpretative authority over constitutional law, which formed the basis for its ruling. This "dualist" reasoning reinforces the normative and institutional separation between international law and constitutional law. Yet, much like the ICJ's reliance on the distinction between substantive and procedural norms to elide the potential conflict between the *jus cogens* prohibitions on war crimes and crimes against humanity and the entrenched norm of state immunity, the Constitutional Court's delineation of separate judicial spheres understates the degree of interpenetration of these legal systems. In addition, on a practical level, the implementation of international law in the areas of jurisdiction and individual rights relies on domestic institutions. The doctrinal construct of "separate spheres" begs the question of where authority lies in a system of polycentric governance.

Although Italy does not have a state immunity act, it enacted a law in 2013 to effectuate its accession to the U.N. Convention on Jurisdictional Immunities (not yet in force) after the ICJ handed down its judgment in *Germany v. Italy*.[112] Article 3 of this law requires Italian judges to deny jurisdiction in "[future] cases concerning acts committed *jure imperii* by a foreign State, even when those acts constitute gross violations of international humanitarian law and of fundamental rights, such as the war crimes and crimes against humanity committed in Italy and in Germany against Italian citizens in the period 1943 to 1945 by Third Reich troops," and to "allow the revision (*revocazione*) of final judgments that did not recognize th[at] immunity."[113] These legislative provisions represented a fundamental shift in Italian policy, since the Italian government had previously deposited an interpretative declaration that "explicitly exclude[d] the application of the Convention [on Jurisdictional Immunities] and its limitations to the norm of immunity in case of damages or injuries caused by the activity of armed forces in the territory of the State of the court seized."[114] The shift from Italy's initial interpretative declaration to the language in Article 3 signaled acquiescence to the ICJ's decision by at least some organs of the Italian government.

The Tribunal of Florence also asked the Constitutional Court to evaluate the constitutionality of the 2013 legislation. The Constitutional Court deemed Article 3 unconstitutional on the grounds that it is incompatible with Articles 2 and 24 of the Italian Constitution, which safeguard the inviolability of human

---

[112] Law No. 5 (Accession of the Italian Republic to the United Nations Convention on Jurisdictional Immunities of States and their Property) (14 Jan. 2013).

[113] Judgment 238/2014 at 9; *see also* 20–21.

[114] Ibid. at 21.

dignity and protect "the right of access to justice for individuals in order to invoke their inviolable right[s]."[115] In the Constitutional Court's view (and in contrast to the ECtHR's acceptance of certain restrictions on the right of access to a court in the name of other values), "[i]t would indeed be difficult to identify how much is left of a right if it cannot be invoked before a judge in order to obtain effective protection."[116] The Constitutional Court emphasized that diplomatic remedies obtained through negotiation are not a substitute for the right of access to a court. It found that the executive branch's attempts to negotiate reparations for victims were insufficient to satisfy this constitutional imperative, and that the legislative branch's passage of the 2013 law was unconstitutional.

The Constitutional Court was also asked to clarify the effect of the ICJ's decision within the Italian domestic legal order, and the domestic legal status of the customary international law norm of state immunity identified by the ICJ.[117] The court affirmed that it has "exclusive competence over the review of compatibility with the fundamental principles of the constitutional order and principles of human rights protection."[118] By emphasizing the exclusive nature of its authority, the court established a framework for asserting the primacy of fundamental rights (derived from the "constitutional order," yet having the universal quality of "human rights") over international law principles such as state immunity. However, determining the appropriate trade-off between the values of judicial access and sovereign equality is neither an intrinsically international, nor an intrinsically domestic, function. The Constitutional Court's analytic framework purports to preserve the supremacy of the ICJ in the international sphere, but it enshrines the primacy of the domestic political community's views on the appropriate trade-off between competing values – and, within the domestic political community, the primacy of the judicial rather than the political branches.

Finally, the Constitutional Court addressed the Florence Tribunal's question about the constitutionality of the "norm created in [the Italian] legal order

---

[115] Ibid. at 15.

[116] Ibid.

[117] Although Italian law does not allow the Constitutional Court to release separate or dissenting judgments, Diletta Tega reports that "it is well known that, on this issue, there has been a bitter crossfire inside the CC, and the decision was not unanimous." Diletta Tega, *Sovereignty of Rights vs. "Global Constitutional Law": The Italian Constitutional Court Decision No. 238/2014*, at http://ukconstitutionallaw.org/2015/04/10/d iletta-tega-sovereignty-of-rights-vs-global-constitutional-law-the-italian-constitutional-court -decision-no-2382014/ (10 Apr. 2015).

[118] Judgment 238/2014, Italian Constitutional Court (22 Oct. 2014), unofficial translation by Alessio Gracis at 14.

by the incorporation, by virtue of Article 10, para. 1 of the Constitution" of the customary international law rule identified by the ICJ in *Germany v. Italy*.[119] The court held that this question was ill-founded, since the norm of state immunity for *jus cogens* violations is *not* created in the Italian legal order due to its incompatibility with fundamental rights. The court agreed with the Florentine judge that "the ICJ has 'absolute and exclusive competence' as to the interpretation of international law,"[120] which is "external to the Italian legal order."[121] It also agreed that an Italian court "must respect the principle of conformity, i.e. must follow the interpretation given [to international custom] in its original legal order, that is the international legal order."[122] However, Article 10, paragraph 1 of the Italian Constitution incorporates customary international law norms into the Italian legal order only to the extent that such norms are compatible with "the qualifying fundamental elements of the constitutional order."[123] The Constitutional Court referenced other decisions finding that "the fundamental principles of the constitutional order and inalienable human rights constitute a 'limit to the introduction . . . of generally recognized norms of international law," including European Union law, into Italian law.[124] The court's determination that the norm of state immunity for *jus cogens* violations is not incorporated into Italian law obviated the need for further constitutional review.

The Constitutional Court played at least two roles in Judgment 238/2014. First, it acted as a gatekeeper for the reception of international norms into the Italian domestic legal system. Second, it contributed to the formation and promotion of international norms, including the fundamental right of access to justice, whose entrenchment in Italian constitutional law is itself partly attributable to the recognition of international human rights in domestic constitutions in the post–World War II era. The Constitutional Court's conclusion also pushes against the idea of immunity as a purely procedural norm that has no "substantive" import or impact. It was motivated in part by the observation that "Italian courts cannot leave the protection of individuals to the dynamics of the relationships between the political organs of the States involved, since these organs have not been able to come up with a solution for decades."[125] This claim – which is both a comment on the shortcomings of

[119] Ibid.
[120] Ibid. at 9.
[121] Ibid. at 12.
[122] Ibid.
[123] Ibid. at 13.
[124] Ibid.
[125] Ibid. at 5.

140   *Chimène I. Keitner*

diplomacy and a rebuke to the Italian political branches – illustrates that overlapping conversations about immunity are taking place not only among international and domestic courts, but also among domestic institutions. By framing the issue in terms of the protection of individuals, rather than the conduct of foreign relations, the Constitutional Court asserted its own domestic institutional competence in an area that is often viewed as reserved primarily for the political branches.

The idea that constitutional values interpreted by domestic institutions trump international law values and commitments did not originate with Judgment 238/2014.[126] However, the resulting non-implementation of a clear directive from the ICJ has focused renewed attention on the hierarchy between domestic and international law, and has even led one commentator to characterize the case as "the most famous I[talian] C[onstitutional] C[ourt] judgment outside of Italy."[127] The polyphony – not to say cacophony – of courts charged with the "multi-level protection of fundamental rights,"[128] as well as the preservation of potentially countervailing judicial values such as stability and finality, fuels both normative and institutional competition.

This result was not inevitable. For example, in a 1979 case, the Italian Constitutional Court determined that pre-1948 customary international law norms (in that case, regarding diplomatic immunity) were "grandfathered" into the Italian constitutional system,[129] thereby avoiding a conflict. The court in Judgment 238/2014 declined to adopt this approach. Consequently, contrary to the prediction of some observers, the ICJ's judgment in *Germany* v. *Italy* did not in fact "put an end to the discussion"[130] regarding Germany's sovereign

---

[126]   *See*, for example, the discussion by Giuseppe Cataldi in Dinah Shelton, International Law and Domestic Legal Systems: Incorporation, Transformation and Persuasion 344–46 (2011).

[127]   Elisabetta Lamarque, *Some WH Questions About the Italian Constitutional Court's Judgment on the Rights of the Victims of the Nazi Crimes*, 6 Ital. J. Pub. L. 197, 199 (2014); *see also* the July 2016 symposium in Vol. 14, No. 3 of the Journal of International Criminal Justice on the Italian Constitutional Court's decision, with contributions from Valentina Spiga, Riccardo Pavoni, Micaela Frulli, Massimo Iovane, Gianluigi Palombella, Martin Scheinin, Raffaela Kunz, and Francesco Francioni.

[128]   Ibid. at 207; *see also* Marta Cartabia, *Fundamental Rights and the Relationship among the Court of Justice, the National Supreme Courts and the Strasbourg Court*, in CJEU, 50th Anniversary of the Judgment in Van Gend En Loos 155, 160 (2013) (observing that "[i]n a way, fundamental rights in Europe are at a crossroads between the *jus commune europaeum* and the 'constitutional identity' of each European country").

[129]   *See* Filippo Fontanelli, *Criminal Proceedings Against Albers*, 107 Am. J. Int'l L. 632, 637–38 (2013), citing Corte cost., 18 giugno 1979, n. 48 (final para.), Gazzetta Ufficiale 1979, n. 175.

[130]   Antonios Tzanakopoulos, *Preliminary Report: Principles on the Engagement of Domestic Courts with International Law* ¶ 31, www.ila-hq.org/download.cfm/docid/D022A3A9-137C-4 7B8-A6F5524FBE9FA538.

immunity in Italian courts. Instead, although the Constitutional Court took pains to defer to the ICJ's interpretation of international law, it invoked its role as guardian of Italian fundamental rights to block the integration of that interpretation into the Italian legal order under the doctrine of *controlimiti* ("counter-limits"), which curbs the ability of supranational law to infringe fundamental rights or fundamental constitutional principles.[131] Although the Constitutional Court's invocation of *controlimiti* in this case favored individual rights, a similar principle can also be invoked to block the reception of rights-promoting international norms into a domestic legal system, as illustrated in Section 5.4.

5.4 AUTHORITY, DIALOGUE, AND THE ELUSIVE "FINAL WORD"

The ultimate effect of Judgment 238/2014 remains to be seen, although neither the ICJ's judgment nor the Italian Constitutional Court's decision seems to have moved the parties closer to a negotiated settlement. Suggested next steps have included Italy substituting itself for Germany in ongoing civil proceedings, indemnifying Germany for claims, or relying on Germany's immunity from execution to shield it from having to satisfy any awards.[132] Meanwhile, the reasoning underlying the Italian decision has prompted comparisons with the Court of Justice of the European Union's (CJEU) decision in *Kadi I* and

---

[131] Enzo Cannizzaro has cautioned: "Castled in its own legal order, the Constitutional Court has fashioned a decision that, in spite of its impeccable dualist logic, will hardly serve its objectives but can seriously imperil the authority of international law and the Völkerrechtsfreundlichkeit [commitment to international law] of the Italian Constitution." Enzo Cannizzaro, *Jurisdictional Immunities and Judicial Protection: The Decision of the Italian Constitutional Court No. 238 of 2014*, 98 RIVISTA DI DIRRITO INTERNAZIONALE 126, 134 (2015). Anne Peters has noted that the German Constitutional Court relied on a similar rationale to uphold an amendment to the Income Tax Act that violated a German-Turkish dual taxation treaty. In the German court's view, "the constitutional principle of democracy (which includes the principle of discontinuity of parliament following elections) demands that the German Parliament is free to change its mind and to make or amend a law even if this violates an international treaty which had been ratified by a previous Parliament (Order of 15 Dec. 2015, paras 53–54). ... The Basic Law "'does not renounce on the sovereignty which lies in the last say of the German constitution' (para. 68)." *See* Anne Peters, *New German Constitutional Court Decision on "Treaty Override": Triepelianism Continued*, at www.ejiltalk.org/new-german-constitutional-court-decision-on-treaty-override-triepelianism-continued-2/ (29 Feb. 2016).

[132] Theodor Schilling, *The Dust Has Not Yet Settled: The Italian Constitutional Court Disagrees with the International Court of Justice, Sort of*, at www.ejiltalk.org/the-dust-has-not-yet-settled-the-italian-constitutional-court-disagrees-with-the-international-court-of-justice-sort-of/ (12 Nov. 2014).

142   *Chimène I. Keitner*

the US Supreme Court's decision in *Medellín* v. *Texas*,[133] which also blocked attempts to give effect to international decisions in a regional or national legal order. This section briefly canvasses some examples of similar decisions, as international and domestic institutions carry out overlapping mandates to protect individual rights and to balance these rights with other values. These cases illustrate domestic courts' invocation of what Joseph Weiler has called "fundamental boundaries," which express "particularized societal choice[s]" that can be either rights-enhancing or rights-restricting from the perspective of an affected individual.[134] Characterizing jurisdictional immunities as purely procedural remains unsatisfying because it avoids addressing the fundamental value conflict between the right of access to justice and the norm of sovereign equality; so too does any approach that automatically privileges either the international or the domestic legal order without addressing the particular value choice at issue.

In *Kadi I*, the applicants challenged EU Regulation 881/2002, which implemented U.N. Security Council resolutions adopted under Chapter VII by freezing the assets of certain designated persons without informing them of the basis for their designation. The CJEU annulled the Regulation insofar as it deprived the applicants of certain fundamental rights, including the right to be heard, the right to effective judicial review, and the right to property.[135] The *Kadi I* decision has been characterized as giving "priority to the constitutional identity of the EU"[136] by holding that "[a]n international obligation that is in breach of [the EU's] constitutional principles cannot form part of the EU legal order."[137] Analogously, the Italian Constitutional Court prioritized Italy's

---

[133]   *See, e.g.*, Massimo Lando, *Intimations of Unconstitutionality: The Supremacy of Italian Law and Judgment 238/2014 of the Italian Constitutional Court*, 78 Mod. L. Rev. 1028, 1034 (2015), citing *Yassin Abdullah Kadi and Al Barakaat International Foundation v. Council of the European Union and Commission of the European Communities* Joined Cases C-402/05 and C-415/05 (*Kadi I*) and *Medellín* v. *Texas*, 552 U.S. 491 (2008); *see also* Gráinne de Búrca, *The European Court of Justice and the International Legal Order After Kadi*, 51 Harv. Int'l L. J.1 (2010) (comparing *Kadi* and *Medellín*).

[134]   *See* Weiler, *supra* note 11 at 104; *See also* ibid. (noting that "[f]undamental boundaries around communities-of-value become the guarantee against existential aloneness – the protection of the *Gemeinschaft* against the *Gesellschaft*" and that "[f]undamental boundaries constitute and thus ensure different realms of power"). As Weiler notes, "fundamental rights – beyond the core [expressed in international instruments] – become an expression of the kind of particularized societal choice of which fundamental boundaries are an expression." Ibid. at 106.

[135]   *Kadi I*, 2008 E.C.R. I-6351, ¶¶ 348–49, 370.

[136]   Koen Lenaerts, *The Kadi Saga and the Rule of Law Within the EU*, 67 SMU L. Rev. 707, 709 (2014).

[137]   Ibid. at 710.

constitutional values[138] and asserted its gatekeeping role in ensuring that only legal norms compatible with those values enter into the Italian legal system. The rationale for the US Supreme Court's decision in *Medellín* was different; it did not concern a hierarchy of norms or values, but instead involved questions of treaty interpretation and federalism limits on the power of the executive branch vis-à-vis individual states. In *Case Concerning Avena and Other Mexican Nationals (Mexico v. United States)*, the ICJ found that the United States had breached its obligation under the Vienna Convention on Consular Relations to inform Mexican nationals arrested in the United States that they had the right to contact Mexican consular officers. The ICJ held that the United States was obliged to grant "review and reconsideration" of the death sentences of fifty-one Mexican nationals who had been convicted without having been notified of their right to consular access, even if such review was precluded by applicable state-level "procedural default" rules.[139] When one of these Mexican nationals invoked the ICJ decision as a basis for seeking such review, the US Supreme Court determined in that Article 94 of the UN Charter, which indicates that member states "undertake to comply" with ICJ decisions, is not "'an acknowledgement that the ICJ decision will have immediate legal effect in the courts of U.N. members 'but rather' a *commitment* on the part of UN Members to take *future* action through their political branches to comply with an ICJ decision.'"[140] This interpretation of Article 94 deprived the *Avena* decision of direct effect within the US legal system, just as Italian Judgment 238/2014 blocked the *Germany v. Italy* decision from binding domestic actors as a matter of Italian law.[141]

---

[138]   *See* Lando, *supra* note 133, at 1035 n.45.

[139]   *Avena and Other Mexican Nationals* (Mex. v. U.S.) 2004 I.C.J. 12.

[140]   *Medellín*, 522 U.S. 491 at 508 (quoting Brief for United States as *Amicus Curiae* in *Medellín I*, O.T. 2004, No. 04-5928, at 34). Emphases original.

[141]   Another possible analog to the Italian decision is the July 2015 ruling by the Russian Constitutional Court that ECtHR judgments are subordinate to the Russian Constitution. *See* Natalia Chaeva, *The Russian Constitutional Court and Its Actual Control over the ECtHR Judgement in* Anchugov and Gladkov, at http://opiniojuris.org/2016/04/25/anchugov-and-gladkov-is-not-enforceable-the-russian-constitutional-court-opines-in-its-first-ecthr-implementa tlon-case/ (25 April 2016). Like Article 10(1) of the Italian Constitution, Article 15(4) of the Russian Constitution affirms that "[t]he universally-recognized norms of international law and international treaties and agreements of the Russian Federation shall be a component part of its legal system." In its July 2015 decision, the Russian Constitutional Court asserted the authority to determine that a judgment of the ECtHR is not subject to execution if non-execution "is the only possible way to avoid violating fundamental constitutional principles." Ivan Nechepurenko, *Russian Constitutional Court Determines Moscow Not Bound to All Human Rights Court Rulings*, at www.themoscowtimes.com/news/article/russian-constitu tional-court-determines-moscow-not-bound-to-all-human-rights-court-rulings/525614.html (14 July 2015). The text of the decision (in Russian) is available at http://doc.ksrf.ru/decision/

144 Chimène I. Keitner

5.5 CONCLUSIONS

Determining the scope of jurisdictional immunity requires balancing the right to judicial access against the principle of sovereign equality, while other contested principles involve different competing values. Such value judgments are often community-specific, and can even be community-defining. Conflict-avoidance doctrines, such as the idea of a "margin of appreciation," attenuate the potential tensions inherent in a polycentric legal system, but they do not eliminate such tensions altogether.[142] Reconciling and integrating conflicting conclusions remains a core challenge for both formal and informal systems of multilayered governance.

Immunity claims are particularly interesting because they implicate both individual rights and international relations. As judicial decisions relating to jurisdictional immunities illustrate, and as scholars of legal pluralism have long observed, authority in the transnational legal system is fundamentally polycentric rather than hierarchical. Conversations among different types of actors within and between various levels of governance all contribute to the production and crystallization of applicable legal norms. In the immunity context, the fundamental right of access to justice is *both* an Italian constitutional norm *and* an international law norm.[143] Viewed from this perspective, the Italian Constitutional Court's decision prioritized domestic judicial balancing over international balancing, rather than a domestic rule over an international one.

KSRFDecision201896.pdf; a summary in English is available at www.ksrf.ru/en/Decision/Ju dgments/Documents/resume%202015%2021-%D0%9F.pdf. The court's reasoning invoked the principle of constitutional supremacy and referenced similar decisions by courts in Austria, the United Kingdom, Germany, and Italy. *See* Maria Smirnova, *Russian Constitutional Court Affirms Russian Constitution's Supremacy Over ECtHR Decisions*, at http://ukconstitutional law.org/2015/07/17/maria-smirnova-russian-constitutional-court-affirms-russian-constitutions-supremacy-over-ecthr-decisions/ (17 Jul. 2015); *See generally* Anne Peters, *Supremacy Lost: International Law Meets Domestic Constitutional Law*, 3 J. INT'L CONST. L. 170 (2009) (observing that "more and more domestic courts claim the competence to scrutinize whether international rules and court decisions are in conformity with the domestic constitution"). The referenced decisions appear to include Italian Constitutional Court Decisions Nos. 348/ 2007 & 249/2007 and German Federal Constitutional Court Decisions Nos. 92/2004 & 31/ 2011.

[142] Cf. Eyal Benvenisti, *Margin of Appreciation, Consensus, and Universal Standards*, 31 J. INT'L L. & POL. 843, 847 (1999) (cautioning against excessive reliance on the margin of appreciation doctrine where minority rights are at stake, and noting that "international human rights bodies serve an important role in correcting some of the systemic deficiencies of democracy").

[143] On this phenomenon generally, *see* Antonios Tzanakopoulos, *Judicial Dialogue in Multi-level Governance: The Impact of the* Solange *Argument, in* THE PRACTICE OF INTERNATIONAL AND NATIONAL COURTS AND THE (DE-)FRAGMENTATION OF INTERNATIONAL LAW 185, 213 (Ole Kristian Fauchald & André Nollkaemper, eds., 2014), and sources cited therein.

Courts are charged with ensuring that restrictions on rights do not unduly burden individual freedom in the name of other societal values, but there is not necessarily a "one size fits all" approach to such determinations. The question is, to whom do we entrust these trade-offs? Debates about who constitutes the relevant "we" in determining the parameters of meaningful self-governance and basic rights protection defy straightforward resolution. On a doctrinal and institutional level, simply substituting international adjudication for domestic authority carries the risk of political backlash, even if it results from a country's voluntary decision to join a treaty regime that secures substantial domestic benefits. In practical terms, the success of international challenges to national decisions relies on acceptance and implementation at the domestic level.

By conceptualizing various legal and political institutions as active interlocutors engaged in a collective process of norm articulation, we can shift the focus away from who gets the "final word" and towards the doctrinal and normative implications of this conversation for the dignity and well-being of affected groups and individuals.[144] As immunity jurisprudence illustrates, domestic courts and other actors are not passive receivers of international norms, but active shapers of those norms. Most participants in conversations about immunity recognize the dual importance of protecting individual rights and maintaining the integrity of relations between states, but some balance these conflicting values differently.

As illustrated above, identifying the source of applicable norms shapes the doctrinal paths available to judges in immunity cases. As a doctrinal matter, Canadian and UK courts view the problem of individual civil immunity through the lens of their domestic statutes, while US courts approach individual immunity primarily under the common law.

As for the jurisdictional immunity of foreign states, the Italian Constitutional Court has prioritized access to judicial remedies even at the cost of foreign relations friction, while the ICJ has prioritized diplomatic remedies even at the cost of non-recovery. A degree of normative polyphony will characterize transnational dialogue on jurisdictional immunities as long as authoritative domestic and international actors continue to hold different views about these trade-offs.

---

[144] For an overview of scholarship discussing processes of norm internalization, *see* Harold Hongju Koh, *Internalization Thorough Socialization*, 54 DUKE L. J. 975 (2005) and sources cited therein.

6

Treaty Conditions and Constitutions

Walls, Windows, or Doors?

Edward T. Swaine

In many respects, constitutions and treaties get along swimmingly. Structurally, constitutions organize domestic authority so that states can consent to treaty obligations and fulfil them. Substantively, constitutions have inspired treaty content, particularly as to human rights;[1] sometimes different constitutions incorporate that international content in return.[2] What's not to like?

Large branches (or maybe boughs) of pluralism scholarship address the challenging relationship between the international and national legal orders.[3] As to the more particular question of treaties and domestic constitutions, at least, the problem depends on one's perspective. The constitutional perspective is itself multifaceted, given national differences, but some degree of defiance seems common.[4] In the United States, those making, approving,

---

[1] *Cf.* David S. Law & Mila Versteeg, *The Declining Influence of the United States Constitution*, 87 NYU L. Rev. 762 (2012).

[2] *See, e.g.*, Zachary Elkins, Tom Ginsburg, & Beth Simmons, *Getting to Rights: Treaty Ratification, Constitutional Convergence, and Human Rights Practice*, 54 Harv. Int'l L.J. 61 (2013); Tom Ginsburg et al., *Commitment and Diffusion: How and Why National Constitutions Incorporate International Law*, 2008 U. Ill. L. Rev. 201.

[3] One might call this "external legal pluralism," as opposed to the pluralism that exists within international law. André Nollkaemper, *Inside or Out: Two Types of International Legal Pluralism*, in Jan Klabbers & Touko Piiparinen, Normative Pluralism and International Law: Exploring Global Governance 94, 94–96 (2013). Judgments vary as to the relative constraint either level imposes on the other. *See, e.g.*, Nico Krisch, Beyond Constitutionalism (2011); Armin von Bogdandy, *Pluralism, Direct Effect, and the Ultimate Say: On the Relationship between International and Domestic Constitutional Law*, 6 Int'l J. of Const'l L. 397 (2008); Matthias Kumm, *The Jurisprudence of Constitutional Conflict: Constitutional Supremacy in Europe before and after the Constitutional Treaty*, 11 European L.J. 362 (2005).

[4] Acknowledging, however, that differences may not be as cut and dried as they would at first appear. *See, e.g.*, *Krisch, supra*, ch. 4 (suggesting limits to constitutionalist depictions of certain European states in relation to the European Court of Human Rights).

and enforcing international agreements nonetheless venerate the US Constitution above any international law; its portrayal as "a machine that would go of itself" suggests both its perpetual nature and its independence from outside influences.[5] Even European states, more integrated by habit and conviction, bear this out to a degree. Courts that routinely assimilate international and supranational law remain uneasy about subordinating national constitutions, even for acknowledged international obligations, particularly when such subordination affects the equities of rights-holders.[6] Italy's constitutional court recently rejected that government's attempt to make nice with the International Court of Justice (ICJ), invoking constitutional access-to-justice rights against the customary law of state sovereignty immunity and implicating Italy's treaty obligations to respect ICJ judgments.[7] Russia's resistance has been more comprehensive. Following its judiciary's lead, it amended its constitution to give its constitutional court the power to declare international decisions non-executable based on constitutional conflicts,[8] an authority that was recently employed to frustrate a nearly $2 billion award against Russia by the European Court of Human Rights.[9] And for some time now, cases in the *Kadi* mold have taken an analogous stance in maintaining fundamental European rights against international obligations, arguably legitimating broader resistance based on national constitutions.[10]

---

[5] *Cf.* MICHAEL KAMMEN, A MACHINE THAT WOULD GO OF ITSELF: THE CONSTITUTION IN AMERICAN CULTURE (1986). As a matter of positive law, constitutional supremacy is clearly established. *See* Reid v. Covert, 354 U.S. 1, 16–18 (1957).

[6] *See, e.g.*, Anne Peters, *Supremacy Lost: International Law Meets Domestic Constitutional Law*, 3 VIENNA J. INT'L CONST'L L. 170 (2009).

[7] Corte Cost., 22 ottobre 2014, Foro it. 2015, I, 1152 (It), translated in Judgment No. 238–Year 2014, Corte Costituzionale, http://www.cortecostituzionale.it/documenti/download/doc/recentJud gments/S238_2013_en.pdf [http://perma.cc/8T86-34XX]; *see* Filippo Fontanelli, *I know it's wrong but I just can't do right: First impressions on judgment no. 238 of 2014 of the Italian Constitutional Court*, VERFBLOG, 2014/10/27, http://verfassungsblog.de/know-wrong-justcant-right-first-impressions-judgment-238-2014-italian-constitutional-court/.

[8] This attracted sustained criticism from the Venice Commission. Nevertheless, the Constitutional Court in 2016 applied the provision to limit application of European Court of Human Rights decisions. European Commission for Democracy through Law (Venice Commission), Russian Federation: Final Opinion on the Amendments to the Federal Constitutional Law on the Constitutional Court, Opinion No. 832/2015 (Strasbourg, 13 June 2016) (including, as an appendix, its Interim Opinion CDL-AD(2016)005)).

[9] Neil Buckley, *Russian Court Overrules Strasbourg on Yukos Award*, FIN. TIMES, Jan. 19, 2017, https://www.ft.com/content/e2bc9f30-de5b-11e6-86ac-f253db7791c6.

[10] Where, inter alia, the constitutional scheme is understood to inhere in the supranational European order, and the international obligation held at bay is understood to be the EU's implementation of a Security Council resolution rather than the resolution itself. *See* Case C-402/05 & C-415/05P, Kadi v. Council and Comm'n, [2008] ECR I-6351; Cases C-584, C-593 & C-595/10 P, Comm'n v. Kadi (July 18, 2013).

148   *Edward T. Swaine*

The international law side of the story, which aspires to greater universality, is also easier to generalize: international law considers itself supreme over national law, including constitutions.[11] Under the Vienna Convention on the Law of Treaties, a state party may in principle invoke a manifest violation of "a rule of its internal law of fundamental importance" (for which constitutional rules seem a prime candidate) in order to vitiate consent, but only if the rule concerns the competence to conclude treaties.[12] And if a state has actually consented to a treaty, it "may not invoke the provisions of its internal law as justification for its failure to perform a treaty."[13] The basic hierarchy is hardly surprising. Treaties often propose equivalent, reciprocal, and (optimally) effective obligations, and accommodating municipal self-exemption threatens that ideal.[14] While international law respects, at least in principle, the authority of states to establish constitutions as aspects of their sovereignty,[15] it's different when constitutions collide with international law; then, constitutions "are merely facts," requiring no more consideration than a building code.[16]

As pluralist scholarship suggests, the difficulty of assigning distinct spheres to international and national laws is only growing, making this mutual indifference – which sometimes looks like disdain – steadily harder to maintain. Even so, it is possible to gain insight by focusing on a particular means, treaty conditions, by which the particular legal forms of treaties and constitutions adapt to one another. International law and actors seeking its application seek its inclusion and even imposition on national legal orders, which domestic hierarchies and their defenders often counter; when it comes to consensual international law like treaties, and fundamental domestic constraints like constitutions, states may be pushed to withhold consent altogether.

---

[11] Applicability of the Obligation to Arbitrate Under Section 21 of the United Nations Headquarters Agreement of 26 June 1947, Advisory Opinion, 1988 I.C.J. Rep. 12, 34, ¶ 57 (Apr. 26) ("It would be sufficient to recall the fundamental principle of international law that international law prevails over domestic law"); *see also* Gerald Fitzmaurice, *The General Principles of International Law Considered from the Standpoint of the Rule of Law*, 92 RECUEIL DES COURS 68, 85 (1957).

[12] Vienna Convention on the Law of Treaties (VCLT), May 23, 1969, art. 46, 1155 U.N.T.S. 331.

[13] That rule is without prejudice to the above-described exception indicated in Article 46. VCLT, art. 27.

[14] *See, e.g.,* Applicability of the Obligation to Arbitrate Under Section 21 of the United Nations Headquarters Agreement of 26 June 1947, Advisory Opinion, 1988 I.C.J. Rep. 12, 34, ¶ 57 (Apr. 26) (noting that it is a "fundamental principle of international law that international law prevails over domestic law").

[15] Quincy Wright, *Validity of the Proposed Reservations to the Peace Treaty*, 20 COLUM. L. REV. 121, 122 & n.7 (1920).

[16] *See* Case Concerning Certain German Interests in Polish Upper Silesia, Merits, 1926 P.C.I.J. (ser. A) No. 7, at 19.

More accommodating options may be available. States attempting to reconcile treaties and constitutions often sign, ratify, or accede with conditions – a broad term used to describe reservations, understandings, declarations, and similar devices that either propose changing the international legal effect of a treaty for that state or, despite claiming lesser significance, risk doing so.[17] For this very reason, conditions are not always welcome. Reservations, in particular, are criticized as undermining the integrity and uniformity of treaties,[18] and conditions invoking constitutional impediments, here called "constitution conditions," are no more highly esteemed. In some cases, as explored later, they may attract greater scrutiny due to their nebulous, and nonnegotiable, nature.

Extra scrutiny is warranted, but so is extra sympathy. This chapter considers three possible metaphors for constitution conditions—the ways they establish walls, windows, and doors between the domestic and international domains—and evaluates each in turn, paying particular heed to the "reservations dialogue" described by the International Law Commission (ILC) and its Special Rapporteur.[19] That dialogue reveals important commonalities and a few differences in the practice of the United States, which employs conditions

---

[17] I use the broader term largely for convenience and to avoid artificial limitation, though "reservation" is used where necessary to describe accurately the metes and bounds of particular rules or prior work. The Vienna Convention, formally, speaks only to reservations, but defines a reservation as "a unilateral statement, *however phrased or named*, made by a State, when signing, ratifying, accepting, approving or acceding to a treaty, whereby it purports to exclude or to modify the legal effect of certain provisions of the treaty in their application to that State." VCLT, art. 2(d) (emphasis added). The focus on the objective rather than the name was well-advised: to take one example, states parties to the Convention on the Elimination of All Forms of Discrimination against Women (CEDAW) described the same kind of condition, an intended exemption for constitutional provisions relating to succession to the throne, either as a reservation (Lesotho and Monaco) or as a declaration (Morocco and Spain). *See* Convention on the Elimination of All Forms of Discrimination against Women, Dec. 18, 1979, Status of Reservations and Declarations, in Multilateral Treaties on Deposit with the Secretary General, Ch. VI (8), https://treaties.un.org/pages/ViewDetails.aspx?src=TREAT Y&mtdsg_no=IV-8&chapter=4&clang=_en [hereinafter CEDAW Status of Reservations and Declarations]. The International Law Commission (ILC)'s Guide to Practice suggests an elaborate set of definitions to distinguish between reservations, interpretive declarations, and other unilateral statements, but this chapter will largely ignore these niceties. Int'l Law Comm'n, Rep. of the Int'l Law Comm'n, §§ 1 et seq., U.N. Doc. A/66/10/Add.1 (2011) [hereinafter ILC Guide to Practice].

[18] For one focus on this problem, *see* Catherine Redgwell, *Universality or Integrity? Some Reflections on Reservations to General Multilateral Treaties*, 1993 BRIT. Y.B. INT'L L. 245.

[19] *See*, particularly, Annex: Conclusions on the Reservations Dialogue, in ILC Guide to Practice at 32, 601 [hereinafter Reservations Dialogue]; Special Rapporteur, Int'l Law Comm'n, Seventeenth Report on Reservations to Treaties, U.N. Doc. A/CN.4/647 (May 26, 2011) (prepared by Alain Pellet).

150   *Edward T. Swaine*

heavily, and European states, which have been more ambivalent – and the most innovative in assessing them. While these states are the focus of the chapter, other states are central players, given that they make conditions and objections that modify treaty relations with the United States and Europe and, by courting objections in their own right, play a pivotal role in constructing global norms. Overall, while the walls, or barriers, between treaties and constitutions persist, possibilities for renovation abound.

6.1 CONSTITUTION CONDITIONS AS WALLS

6.1.1 *A Domestic Wall?*

All treaty conditions propose a relationship between the preferences reflected in the treaty (and, presumptively, for the other states parties) and those of the conditioning state – although neither constituency would be entirely happy with that description.[20]

States reacting to proposed conditions might resist describing a treaty's terms as mere preferences: they may reasonably regard those terms as a negotiated bargain, one in which the conditioning state's preferences were already considered.[21] For the conditioning state, on the other hand, a treaty remains on offer. A state not yet party to a treaty is at liberty to accept or reject it *en toto*.[22] Treaties permitting reservations, moreover, give conditioning states a chance to extend the bargaining process. Other states may object, including on the ground that proposed reservations are flatly impermissible – in theory, inhibiting the conditioning state from proposing them in the first place, but which in reality requires vigilance by others. All this makes multilateral treaties rather bilateral in character, with states forging different relations with the conditioning state depending on whether they have objected and to what degree.[23]

---

[20] A conditioning state might, of course, adopt a different perspective and set of interests when contemplating another state's proposed conditions, but many manage that shift without difficulty – even without having merged the two perspectives.

[21] One might plausibly distinguish between instances in which a state actually participated in negotiations as opposed to acceding as a latecomer. This has not played a substantial role in the reservations dialogue, but participation in negotiations might at least play a role in answering demands for the general right to propose reservations, itself an answer to proposals to adopt a no-reservations clause.

[22] If a signatory, the state is obliged to respect the treaty's object and purpose until it has made clear that it does not intend to become a party to the treaty. VCLT, art. 18. It is also constrained by similar obligations derived from other sources, such as customary international law.

[23] For more by way of the international law background, *see* Edward T. Swaine, *Treaty Reservations, in* THE OXFORD GUIDE TO TREATIES 285 (Duncan B. Hollis ed., 2/e 2020); Edward T. Swaine, *Reserving*, 31 YALE J. INT'L L. 307 (2006).

While conditioning states might regard treaty terms as mere preferences, they tend to balk at describing their proposed conditions that way. Constitution conditions, particularly, are often presented as though they are non-volitional: a state's government retains a range of discretion, including as to whether to become party to the treaty, but rarely regards itself as having legal authority to change the constitution so it would be compatible with the treaty – and absent such a change, under typical municipal legal hierarchies, the constitutional rule would prevail over an inconsistent treaty obligation.[24] On these premises, constitution conditions involve preferences only in the weak sense that the state would prefer to become a party to the treaty, if it can have the benefit of its conditions, rather than staying out of the treaty altogether. And while states retain discretion as to whether to mention a constitutional limit in their conditions, it is better for a state party to acknowledge limitations that would impair treaty compliance – or so their thinking might run.[25]

Some treaty conditions suggest a kind of ideal type. For example, the United States lodged a reservation to Article 20 of the International Covenant on Civil and Political Rights (ICCPR), which regulates certain war propaganda and hate speech, stating that "Article 20 does not authorize or require legislation or other action by the United States that would restrict the right of free speech and association protected by the Constitution and laws of the United States."[26] A French declaration concerning the same Covenant – relating simply that "[i]n the light of article 2 of the Constitution of the French Republic, the French Government declares that article 27" concerning the right of

---

[24] The validity of such characterizations, including whether such conditions necessarily describe an unalterable standoff, is explored in Sections 6.2 and 6.3 below.

[25] This has been acknowledged, for example, by those generally critical of conditions. Louis Henkin, Editorial Comment, *U.S. Ratification of Human Rights Conventions: The Ghost of Senator Bricker*, 89 Am. J. Int'l L. 341, 342 (1995) ("[A] reservation to avoid an obligation that the United States could not carry out because of constitutional limitations is appropriate, indeed necessary.").

[26] US Senate Resolution of Advice and Consent to Ratification of the International Covenant on Civil and Political Rights, 138 Cong. Rec. S4783 (daily ed. Apr. 2, 1992). In a similar but vaguer vein, the United States tempered hate speech restrictions in the Race Convention "to the extent that [such speech is] protected by the Constitution and laws of the United States," *see* US Senate Resolution of Advice and Consent to Ratification of the Convention on the Elimination of All Forms of Racial Discrimination, 140 Cong. Rec. S14326 (daily ed. June 24, 1994), and attached a reservation for the Genocide Convention stipulating that "[n]othing in this Convention requires or authorizes legislation or other action by the United States of America prohibited by the Constitution of the United States as interpreted by the United States." U.S. Senate Resolution of Advice and Consent to Ratification of the Convention on the Prevention and Punishment of the Crime of Genocide, 132 Cong. Rec. S1378 (daily ed. Feb. 19, 1986); *see also* S. Exec. Rep. No. 99-2, at 20-21 (1985) (describing relationship between the Genocide Convention and First Amendment).

Edward T. Swaine

minorities to use their own language "is not applicable so far as the Republic is concerned" – arguably falls into the same category.[27] The purest example may be the US reservation stating that "nothing in the [Genocide] Convention requires or authorizes legislation or other action by the United States of America prohibited by the Constitution of the United States as interpreted by the United States."[28]

---

[27] International Covenant on Civil and Political Rights, March 23, 1976, Status of Reservations and Declarations, in Multilateral Treaties on Deposit with the Secretary General, Ch. IV (1), https://treaties.un.org/pages/ViewDetails.aspx?src=TREATY&mtdsg_no=IV-4&chapter=4& clang=_en [hereinafter ICCPR Status of Reservations and Declarations]; *see also* 1958 Const. (Fr.) art. 2. The Human Rights Committee understood the declaration as seeking a reservation, which was permissible in the absence of other states' objections. TK v France, Admissibility, Communication No 220/1987, ¶¶ 8.6–8.7, U.N. Doc. CCPR/C/37/D/220/1987, IHRL 2441 (UNHRC 8th November 1989). One might have construed the condition as alluding to the potential incompatibility of minority language rights with maintaining French as the official language (per Article 2 of the French Constitution), or to the impermissibility of distinguishing minorities in light of the equality of peoples (under Article 1); either would have asserted a constitutional conflict in a strong sense. France's explanation, however, was more that minority rights were mooted by the rights of all persons under the French Constitution. *See* U.N. Doc. CCPR/C/22/Add.2 ("Since the basic principles of public law prohibit distinctions between citizens on grounds of origin, race or religion, France is a country in which there are no minorities and, as stated in the declaration made by France, article 27 is not applicable as far as the Republic is concerned"); accord UN Doc. CCPR/C/46/Add.2. Germany also "interpret[ed] the French declaration as meaning that the Constitution of the French Republic already fully guarantees the individual rights protected by article 27." Declaration Relating to the Declaration Made by France upon Accession with Respect to Article 27, Apr. 23, 1982, 1275 U.N.T.S. 563. As explained in the text, this suggests that France's claimed incompatibility was more a claim of constitutional surrogacy than a claim that it would have been unconstitutional for France to comply with the treaty absent its condition. For a bit more discussion of the Human Rights Committee proceedings on this condition, *see* Liesbeth Lijnzaad, Reservations to UN Human Rights Treaties 218, 225, 245–47 (1994).

[28] Convention on the Prevention and Punishment of the Crime of Genocide, Dec. 11, 1946, Status of Reservations and Declarations, in Multilateral Treaties on Deposit with the Secretary General, Ch. VI (1), https://treaties.un.org/pages/ViewDetails.aspx?src=TREATY&mtdsg_n o=IV-1&chapter=4&clang=_en#EndDec [hereinafter Genocide Convention Status of Reservations and Declarations]. Another clear example, from elsewhere in the Americas, would be Colombia's reservation to the 1988 United Nations Convention against Illicit Traffic in Narcotic Drugs and Psychotropic Substances. The reservation, which Colombia withdrew in 1997, stated that "Colombia is not bound by article 3, paragraphs 6 and 9, or article 6 of the Convention since they contravene article 35 of the Political Constitution of Colombia regarding the prohibition on extraditing Colombians by birth." United Nations Convention Against Illicit Traffic in Narcotic Drugs and Psychotropic Substances, Nov. 11, 1990, Status of Reservations and Declarations, in Multilateral Treaties on Deposit with the Secretary General, Ch. VI (19), at 17, https://treaties.un.org/pages/ViewDetails.aspx?src=TREATY&mt dsg_no=VI-19&chapter=6&clang=_en [hereinafter Narcotic Convention Status of Reservations and Declarations].

Conditions of this type, which describe *direct constitutional conflicts*, seem to satisfy straightforward if stringent criteria: first, an asserted "true conflict" between what the treaty requires and what the constitution prohibits (or vice versa);[29] second, the hierarchical superiority in domestic law of the constitution over prior or subsequent treaties; and third, limits on the ability of the treaty-makers to procure accommodating changes in the constitution. An implication, if not a necessary condition, is that the condition is the only alternative to either declining to ratify the treaty or anticipating its breach.

A different type of constitution condition, which we might call *constitutional surrogates*, propose a different kind of reconciliation. For example, a state may try to substitute a constitutional standard for an international one, as when the United States asserted Eighth Amendment limitations on applying the death penalty to juveniles[30] or as to the appropriate definition of "cruel, inhuman or degrading treatment or punishment" under the Torture Convention.[31] Rather than drawing the line at what is constitutionally impermissible, a constitutional surrogate condition asserts that the state's constitution describes the full extent of the obligations it wants to assume.[32] European states responding to these reservations – as always, a small proportion of the

---

[29] For a comparable usage, *see* Hartford Fire Ins. Co. v. California, 509 U.S. 764, 798 (1993). Another in the same vein is the Maldives' reservation to CEDAW, which originally stated in part that "the Republic of Maldives does not see itself bound by any provisions of the Convention which obliges to change its Constitution and laws in any manner." CEDAW Status of Reservations and Declarations, *supra*.

[30] A US reservation to the ICCPR provided that "[T]he United States reserves the right, subject to its Constitutional constrains [sic], to impose capital punishment on any person (other than a pregnant woman) duly convicted under existing or future laws permitting the imposition of capital punishment, including such punishment for crimes committed by persons below eighteen years of age." ICCPR Status of Reservations and Declarations, *supra*.

[31] The reservation provided that "the United States considers itself bound by the obligation under Article 16 to prevent 'cruel, inhuman or degrading treatment or punishment,' only insofar as the term 'cruel, inhuman or degrading treatment or punishment' means the cruel, unusual and inhumane treatment or punishment prohibited by the Fifth, Eighth, and/or Fourteenth Amendments to the Constitution of the United States." Finland, the Netherlands, and Sweden objected. Convention against Torture and Other Cruel, Inhuman or Degrading Treatment or Punishment, June 26, 1987, Status of Reservations and Declarations, in Multilateral Treaties on Deposit with the Secretary General, Ch. IV (9), https://treaties .un.org/pages/ViewDetails.aspx?src=TREATY&mtdsg_no=IV-9&chapter=4&clang=_en.

[32] The distinction is not unlike the US approach to preemption of state law by federal statutes. The first category corresponds directly to what are known as direct conflicts, and the second resembles contentions that a statute occupies the field that state law seeks to regulate – though the US approach requires that the statute reflects and intent to occupy that field, which is more demanding. *See, e.g.*, Arizona v. United States, 567 U.S. 387, 398–400 (2012); Crosby v. National Foreign Trade Council, 530 U.S. 363, 372–73 (2000).

154   *Edward T. Swaine*

states potentially concerned, particularly with multilateral human rights conventions – were not welcoming.[33]

At the fringes perhaps, is a third type – a *constitution-plus surrogate?* – in which a state would substitute its entire panoply of domestic laws (including, but not limited to, its constitution) for a treaty terms. States do sometimes propose conditions accepting an international obligation save to the extent their laws, including statutory and other forms, provide otherwise.[34] Thus, the US Senate considered a CEDAW reservation indicating that "[t]he United States does not accept any obligation under the Convention to enact legislation or to take any other action with respect to private conduct except as mandated by the Constitution and laws of the United States,"[35] and a virtually identical reservation was proposed during Senate consideration of the Disabilities Convention.[36] In either case a narrower condition, like that used for the Genocide Convention, would have sufficed to convey any constitutional conflict,[37] but that was not the only objective; nor was a constitutional surrogate proffered, presumably because the constitution did not itself supply all the relevant law. The approach implement the view once expressed by a State Department Legal Advisor, who explained that "tak[ing] ... international legal obligations seriously" required that the United States "commit ourselves to do by treaty only that which is constitutionally and legally permissible within our domestic law."[38]

This third type of condition seems different in character from direct constitutional conflicts predicated on a sense of legal necessity, since it would impose limits according to domestic law that is not, even from a domestic perspective, hierarchically superior to international law. Perhaps the theory

[33]   Belgium, Denmark, Finland, France, Germany, Italy, the Netherlands, Norway, Portugal, Spain, and Sweden objected to the ICCPR reservation, chiefly on the ground that the provision in question was nonderogable and that the reservation was thus contrary to the treaty's object and purpose. ICCPR Status of Reservations and Declarations, *supra*. As to the Torture Convention reservation, Finland, the Netherlands, and Sweden objected. Torture Convention Status of Reservations and Declarations, *supra*.

[34]   This is distinct from issues that may be raised by doctrines of non-self-execution, which – for those states following it – may mean that a treaty obligation may, until it is separately implemented, lack domestic legal effect.

[35]   S. Exec. Rep. No. 107-9, at 11 (2002); S. Exec. Rep. No. 103-38, at 10 (1994).

[36]   S. Exec. Rep. No. 113-12, at 24 (2014).

[37]   Laurel Fletcher et al., Human Rights Violations Against Women, 15 Whittier L. Rev. 319, 339 (1994); *see* Ann E. Mayer, Reflections on the Proposed United States Reservations to CEDAW: Should the Constitution be an Obstacle to Human Rights?, 23 Hastings Const. L.Q. 727, 800–04 (1996); *see also id.* at 762 (criticizing U.S. ICCPR reservation concerning the juvenile death penalty).

[38]   *International Human Rights Treaties: Hearings Before the S. Comm. on Foreign Relations*, 96th Cong. 31 (1980) (testimony of Davis R. Robinson, former legal advisor).

Treaty Conditions and Constitutions

might be that even lesser forms of law are, ultimately, the product of a domestic constitutional order.[39] The more important point, though, concerns a weakness this third type of condition shares with the second type: unless varying from the domestic surrogate is unconstitutional – such that a direct conflict is posed[40] – any condition that substitutes a different legal standard, whether based on the constitution or not, reduces to a preference for pre-treaty law. No wonder, then, that defenders of US conditions sometimes acknowledge that "substantive reservations are based not on a constitutional conflict but rather on a political or policy disagreement with certain provisions of the treaties."[41]

As this suggests, it still remains tenable to distinguish what I have termed direct constitutional conflicts, in which conditions are motivated at least in part due to an unusually limited capacity for change. Such conditions portray a wall against which treaty obligations must break, due to incompatibility and to the municipal hierarchy of laws, in the absence of extraordinary domestic reforms. Beyond these, a condition's invocation of a constitution generally seeks to extend the argument beyond its natural domain. Like castle walls, which establish a defensive scheme benefiting not only inhabitants, but also those in the fields and villages beyond, constitutional references turn out to defend a wider swathe than first apparent.

6.1.2 *The Other Side of the Wall*

From the domestic standpoint, then, constitution conditions may – but need not necessarily – portray walls against international treaty commitments, ones that convert a domestic impediment into a proposed international exemption. Conditions relating to even the most intractable features of domestic law,

---

[39] "Permissibility" rhetoric also evokes reservations doctrine, but with an important difference: the latter is focused on a single criterion (a treaty's object and purpose) that is supreme within that treaty's scheme. Exceptionally, the Human Rights Committee has taken the view that permissibility also requires assessing compatibility with customary international law. Human Rights Committee, General Comment No. 24, ¶ 8, U.N. Doc. CCPR/C/21/Rev.1/Add.6 (Nov. 11, 1994). But see, e.g., Observations by the United States on General Comment 24 (Mar. 28, 1995) CCPR A/50/40/Annex VI 126-1343, reprinted in (1996) 3 IHRR 265, 267, ILC Guide to Practice, Guideline 3.1.5.3 ("The fact that a treaty provision reflects a rule of customary international law does not in itself constitute an obstacle to the formulation of a reservation to that provision.").

[40] Domestic legal standards might indirectly suggest conflicts of this kind. For example, the constitutional standard for presidential eligibility is plausibly exclusive, such that any attempt to add conditions by treaty would be unconstitutional. U.S. CONST. art. II, § 1, cl. 5.

[41] Curtis A. Bradley & Jack L. Goldsmith, *Treaties, Human Rights, and Conditional Consent*, 149 U. PA. L. REV. 399, 417 (2000).

Edward T. Swaine

however, are merely proposals, and depend for their effectuation on the cooperation of international law.

International law might respect and reinforce this wall by accepting some or all constitution conditions as special claims requiring accommodation. Instead, treaty law erodes that wall – or erects another, in hostile territory – by indicating that a condition's legal basis is irrelevant. Under the Vienna Convention's default regime, nothing turns on a reservation's justification: every condition is potentially wall-like (or not), regardless of whether it derives from a founding constitution or a moment's whim. The relevant characteristic, instead, is compatibility with the treaty (together with, as noted below, whether other states have opposed it, or perhaps both).[42] Proposed tests of a condition's entrenched character – for example, inquiring whether a reservation is really an essential condition of the state's willingness to be bound, as distinct from the norm in which "states have consented to having aspects of their legal system modified by international legal developments"[43] – have not been widely endorsed.

While treaties sometimes deviate from the Vienna Convention scheme, they do not generally take constitutions into account. The Council of Europe, concerned about inadmissible reservations and citing reservations of a general character as prime examples, provided states with a model response that treated claimed conflicts with "Constitution/domestic legislation/traditions" as equally irrelevant.[44] Those negotiating the American Convention on Human Rights toyed with limiting reservations to those based on constitutional provisions, but rejected that as too narrow, including on the ground that domestic legal provisions should be treated alike.[45] And a model clause that does concern a type of constitutional barrier, the "federal state" clause, is only sporadically employed.[46] While such a clause might accommodate influential states with federal systems, given limits in their constitutions on national

---

[42] This is the nub of the debate over permissibility versus opposability. *See, e.g.*, Swaine, *Reserving, supra*, at 314–17.

[43] Ryan Goodman, *Human Rights Treaties, Invalid Reservations, and State Consent*, 96 Am. J. Int'l L. 531, 556 (2002).

[44] Council of Europe, Comm. of Ministers, Recommendation No. R(99)13 of the Comm. of Ministers to Member States on Responses to Inadmissible Reservations to International Treaties, 670th Mtg. of the Ministers' Deputies (May 18, 1999), https://wcd.coe.int/com. instranet.InstraServlet?command=com.instranet.CmdBlobGet&InstranetImage=528808& SecMode=1&DocId=439658&Usage=2.

[45] For a review of the history, *see* Andrés E. Montalvo, *Reservations to the American Convention on Human Rights: A New Approach*, 16 Am. U. Int'l L. Rev. 269, 276–77 (2001).

[46] *See, e.g.*, Convention Providing a Uniform Law on the Form of an International Will, art. XIV, Oct. 26, 1973, 12 I.L.M. 1298 (providing that "[i]f a State has two or more territorial units in which different systems of law apply in relation to matters respecting the form of wills, it

power, nonfederal states have resisted them as creating asymmetrical obligations.[47] Where exemptions for federal states are secured, they may not even sound in constitutional terms, instead turning on principles of governance that may or may not have a legal basis.[48]

Absent exceptional treatment within the treaty text, the fate of constitution conditions is primarily resolved by the reaction of states according to ordinary reservations practice. If a state proposes a condition that arguably violates a treaty's object and purpose, other states may object, backstopped by some possibility that the condition will be scrutinized later by judicial tribunals or treaty bodies. Even were they to concede that a proposed constitution condition *is* consistent with the treaty's object and purpose, states may still object on another ground, or on no ground at all; other institutions play a less substantial role in these circumstances, though they may take a different view than states

---

may at the time of signature, ratification, or accession, declare that this Convention shall extend to all its territorial units or only to one or more of them, and may modify its declaration by submitting another declaration at any time," and that such declarations "shall state expressly the territorial units to which the Convention applies").

[47] Efforts in relation to World Health Organization amendments, for example, were rebuffed. See Duncan B. Hollis, *Executive Federalism: Forging New Federalist Constraints on the Treaty Power*, 79 S. Cal. L. Rev. 1327, 1374–77 (2006). Pursuing such clauses may also backfire for federal states. Following extensive consideration during the negotiation of the human rights covenants, common text wound up stating that "[t]he provisions of the Covenant shall extend to all parts of federal States without any limitations or exceptions." Article 50, Covenant on Civil and Political Rights; Article 28, Covenant on Economic, Social and Cultural Rights. See Robert B. Looper, *"Federal State" Clauses in Multilateral Instruments*, 32 Brit. Y.B. Int'l L. 162, 199 (1955–56) (noting that this result "is, of course, a federal State clause in name only," because "[i]t makes special provision for federal States only to the extent of saying they shall have no special position").

[48] Article 41 of the Cybercrime Convention, for example, states:

1. A federal State may reserve the right to assume obligations under Chapter II of this Convention consistent with its fundamental principles governing the relationship between its central government and constituent States or other similar territorial entities provided that it is still able to co-operate under Chapter III.
2. When making a reservation under paragraph 1, a federal State may not apply the terms of such reservation to exclude or substantially diminish its obligations to provide for measures set forth in Chapter II. Overall, it shall provide for a broad and effective law enforcement capability with respect to those measures.
3. With regard to the provisions of this Convention, the application of which comes under the jurisdiction of constituent States or other similar territorial entities, that are not obliged by the constitutional system of the federation to take legislative measures, the federal government shall inform the competent authorities of such States of the said provisions with its favourable opinion, encouraging them to take appropriate action to give them effect.

Council of Europe Convention on Cybercrime, art. 41, opened for signature Nov. 23, 2001, S. Exec. Rep. No. 109-06.

158   *Edward T. Swaine*

concerning what a treaty's object and purpose is and whether it has been violated.

Surveying how states react to constitution conditions, it is hard to perceive special dispensation – though it is also hard to reach any definitive conclusion at all. Acceptance tends to be tacit, so few explanations are provided.[49] Objections also provide little clarity. States often explain themselves, especially as to whether they are objecting because they regard a condition as violating a treaty's object and purpose.[50] But it is difficult to say, based on recorded objections, whether conditions are more likely to be condemned or spared based on their constitutional grounding. States do sometimes chastise them by invoking the principle that internal rules cannot justify failure to perform a treaty – which conflates an invalid excuse for nonperformance with attempts to change what the treaty requires in the first place.[51] The fit between a condition and its purported constitutional basis is rarely if ever addressed. While doing so might help distinguish direct constitutional conflicts from other domestic concerns, it would require an unlikely degree of expertise in the domestic laws of other states.

Rather than focusing on the fit with a constitutional warrant, or the constitutional basis at all, objections generally turn on the type of latitude the conditioning state seeks – both in terms of deviation from the particular treaty

---

[49] *See* VCLT, art. 20.
[50] *Id.* They also reliably indicate if they intend their objection to impair the formation of treaty relations, because it is presumed otherwise if they do not.
[51] This was the drift of objections by Denmark, Estonia, Finland, Greece, Ireland, the Netherlands, Norway, and Sweden to the U.S. reservation to the Genocide Convention, for example. Genocide Convention Status of Reservations and Declarations, *supra*; *see also* ANTHONY AUST, MODERN TREATY LAW AND PRACTICE 132 (3rd ed. 2013). For examples in the ICCPR context, see objections by Australia (to conditions by the Maldives and Pakistan), Belgium (Pakistan), Czech Republic (Maldives), Finland (United States), Hungary (Pakistan), Ireland (Botswana), Norway (Kuwait), Poland (Pakistan), and Portugal (Botswana), as well as multiple reactions to a declaration by Bahrain. ICCPR Status of Reservations and Declarations, *supra*. Some, certainly, are more nuanced. For example, France – in objecting to a reservation made by Maldives that invoked constitutional restrictions – described the problem as being subordination of the treaty to internal law, but emphasized that it was "likely to deprive a provision of the Covenant of any effect and makes it impossible for other States Parties to know the extent of its commitment." *See id. See also* Seventeenth Meeting of Chairpersons of the Human Rights Treaty Bodies, The Practice of Human Rights Treaty Bodies with Respect to Reservations to International Human Rights Treaties, ¶ 20, U.N. DOC. HRI/MC/2005/5 (reporting that a 1998 meeting of the Committee on Economic, Social and Cultural Rights considered "whether States were foreclosed from making reservations on the grounds of a State's internal religious law by the principle that failure to comply with international could not be justified by domestic law," but the chair "considered that blanket reservations would not be accepted on account of imprecision, but specific reservations would probably be acceptable").

and in broader terms. It was wholly unsurprising, for example, that European states objecting to US conditions to the ICCPR tended to single out those relating to the death penalty.[52] It is also unsurprising that reacting states likewise perceive the constitutional character of a state's condition as simply a matter of the latter's policy preference. Viewed this way, constitution conditions fit uncertainly within the objections scheme's incentive structure. The more idiosyncratic they are, the less risk that others will replicate them, which might dampen objections; at the same time, they would tend to offer little advantage if applied symmetrically and *inter se*, offering less benefit to accepting states and less reason to suppress disagreement.[53]

The most basic challenge, however, is that conditions themselves are crafted so as to generate only weak information about the acceptability of constitutional bases. Even when states explain that a condition has a domestic legal predicate, they often fail to distinguish those aspects attributable to a constitution – although they might, were they convinced that might dissuade states from objecting. States that seem fond of constitution conditions, like the United States, have failed to develop a consistent method for presenting their conditions. And they have also failed to develop a consistent way of indicating respect for others' constitution conditions, as when the United States objected – without evident embarrassment – that a declaration "purports to subordinate Colombia's obligations under the Convention to its Constitution and international treaties, as well as to that nation's domestic legislation generally."[54]

The International Law Commission, extrapolating from the Vienna Convention and practice, explained that a reservation purporting "to preserve

---

[52] Sweden, for example, explained the nature of its concerns in the aggregate (including to when a state "limits its responsibilities under that treaty by invoking general principles of national law" so as to violate a treaty's object and purpose), but did not extend its objection to the US reservation on hate speech – though it appeared vulnerable to many of the same concerns. For its part, Finland objected to the US reservation concerning cruel, inhuman or degrading treatment on the ground that it ran afoul of "the general principle of treaty interpretation according to which a party may not invoke the provisions of its internal law as justification for failure to perform a treaty"; rather than applying that reasoning to the death penalty reservation, it instead objected based on more substantive grounds. *See* ICCPR Status of Reservations and Declarations, *supra*.

[53] *Cf.* Swaine, *Reserving*, *supra*, at 342; *accord* BARBARA KOREMENOS, THE CONTINENT OF INTERNATIONAL LAW 177 (2016).

[54] Colombia's declaration, in relation to the 1988 United Nations Convention against Illicit Traffic in Narcotic Drugs and Psychotropic Substances, provided that "[n]o provision of the Convention may be interpreted as obliging Colombia to adopt legislative, judicial, administrative or other measures that might impair or restrict its constitutional or legal system or that go beyond the terms of the treaties to which the Colombian State is a contracting party." *See* Narcotic Convention Status of Reservations and Declarations, *supra*.

the integrity of specific rules of the internal law of that State in force at the time of the formulation of the reservation may be formulated only insofar as it does not affect an essential element of the treaty nor its general tenour."[55] As explored below, this suggests at least one nicety, the need to invoke "specific" rules, which may have a differential (and negative) impact on proposed constitution conditions. Otherwise, the reference to "internal law," while showing no particular animus toward constitutions, also shows no special solicitude.[56] The commentaries explained that the ILC chose "specific rules of the internal law" over "'provisions of internal law,' which might have seemed to suggest that *only* the written rules of a constitutional, legislative or regulatory nature were involved, whereas [the] guideline ... applies also to customary rules or case law."[57] The upshot is that constitutions provide no sounder excuse than any other domestic principle.

Human rights treaties, which are particularly prone to reservations and other conditions, illustrate the broader tensions. From the domestic standpoint, the relative permanence, or difficulty of changing, constitutions is an important warrant – speaking to both the genuineness of a domestic commitment and the challenge of altering it to suit a new international obligation. This is not enough to deter international scrutiny, which is a source of mutual irritation.[58] Indeed, international institutions and other states may regard such permanence negatively, and even as a basis for regarding a condition as impermissible or at least objectionable. For them, such a condition suggests that the state will be particularly unlikely to assimilate the underlying treaty obligation, meaning that the problem the treaty seeks to address will remain entrenched.[59] A constitution condition also signals that the state is likelier to

---

[55] *See* ILC Guide to Practice, *supra*, Guideline 3.1.5.
[56] Nor, although the language is somewhat unusual, do the dual criteria of preserving both "essential element[s] of the treaty" and "its general tenor."
[57] *See* ILC Guide to Practice at 383.
[58] The late Senator Jesse Helms, a powerful and inveterate critic of human rights (and other) treaties, asserted that "Anybody wanting to know why Americans are becoming increasingly fed up with the United Nations need only consider the words of one U.N. official who said, regarding the U.S. human rights report to the United Nations, 'The United States Constitution was not sacrosanct and had required some amendment over the years. The judiciary must be made aware of the evolving legal standards coming out of the application of the Covenant.' So, Mr. President, the United Nations' view of the U.S. Constitution and the U.S. Senate reservations to human rights treaties is quite clear. The United Nations, not the U.S. Senate, claims to know what is best for Americans. To which the majority of Americans will reply, and I say again: 'Bullfeathers.'" 141 CONG'L REC. 16,082 (June 14, 1995) (comments of Sen. Helms on Senate Resolution 133, relating to United Nations Convention on the Rights of the Child).
[59] *Cf.* Rep. of the Comm. on the Elimination of Discrimination against Women, 18th Sess., 19th Sess., Jan. 19–Feb. 6, 1998, June 22–July 10, 1998, at 49, U.N. Doc. A/53/38/Rev.1 (describing general concern with entrenched behavior by reserving states); General Comment No. 24, ¶

Treaty Conditions and Constitutions

resist future calls to modify or withdraw the condition – which, as discussed in the following sections, is a principal objective of the reservations dialogue for all treaties, and for many in human rights the only acceptable outcome.

6.2 CONSTITUTION CONDITIONS AS WINDOWS

International law and practice thus offer little encouragement *particular* to constitution conditions. At the same time, they are highly indulgent of conditions as a whole. Any lack of respect for constitutional walls should not distract from the fact that, behind them and around the edges, all kinds of barriers remain that serve the proposing state's ends.[60]

Why might this be, given concerns that conditions undermine treaty commitments, and potentially harm states on the receiving end? Previous work suggested one reason: a state's reservations provide information about its potential for deviating from the treaty's original terms and signal the strength of its commitment to non-reserved terms.[61] The burden of that argument, to provide a partial explanation of the regime's eccentricities and ambiguities, is greater than what is at issue here. The immediate question, instead, is whether constitution conditions function, along these lines, less as walls than as windows – ways for a state to disclose, and for others to discover, relevant information about the conditioning state's preferences and likely behavior.[62]

The problem is that constitution conditions are often distinctly opaque. National law references are leading examples of what the ILC described as "vague or general reservations" defying the principle that "[a] reservation shall be worded in such a way as to allow its meaning to be understood, in order to assess in particular its compatibility with the object and purpose of the treaty."[63] Falling short may "make it impossible for the other States parties to take a position on them."[64] The commentary cited conditions proposed by Malaysia and Thailand to ratification of Convention on the Rights of the Child alluding to the need to conform those states' obligations to their constitutions and other domestic laws (and, in the case of Malaysia, its

---

19 (expressing objective of ensuring that "reservations do not lead to a perpetual non-attainment of international human rights standards").

[60] For a description of this bias, *see* Swaine, *Reserving, supra*, at 312–23.

[61] *See generally* Swaine, *Reserving, supra*.

[62] This neglects, for reasons of clarity, the opposite perspective: that states proposing conditions may use them as windows for perceiving the reactions of other states. While conceivable, this likely has less explanatory value with regard to constitution conditions, given (by hypothesis) their relatively nondiscretionary character.

[63] ILC Guide to Practice, Guideline 3.1.5.2.

[64] *Id.*, Guideline 3.1.5.2, commentary (4), at 364–65.

162   *Edward T. Swaine*

"national policies"), to which some states objected on the ground that they were impossible to assess.[65] Unsurprisingly, constitution conditions are prone to run afoul of this norm, as they often reflect terms that were written broadly and remain prone to interpretive dispute. Indeed, because constitutional text is often construed according to dynamic, evolutionary methods entrusted to the judiciary,[66] the meaning of constitutional provisions, though fixed in some sense, are also subject to change; their relationship with treaty texts, each being forged in specialized language, is likely even more uncertain.

The solution, arguably, is to make general reservations less so, including by supporting state efforts to interrogate them. The European Convention on Human Rights, in its special regime, prohibits "[r]eservations of a general character," and suggests that reservations should identify the law concerned – implying that doing so will go toward resolving the problem of generality.[67] The Human Rights Committee, in its domain, has suggested that higher standards must be met. Its General Comment 24 indicated that, to be sufficiently non-general, a reservation "must refer to a particular provision of the Covenant and indicate in precise terms its scope in relation thereto."[68] The Committee also cautioned that "reservations should not systematically reduce the obligations undertaken only to the presently existing in less demanding standards of domestic law," "[n]or should interpretative declarations or reservations seek to remove an autonomous meaning to Covenant obligations, by pronouncing them to be identical, or to be accepted only insofar as they are identical, with existing provisions of domestic law."[69]

The United States and some European states questioned this critique,[70] in part because it was coupled with the Committee's assertion that it could

---

[65] *Id.*, Guideline 3.1.5.2, commentary (5); *see id.* n. 1661 (citing additional examples).

[66] *Cf.* Jamal Greene, *On the Origins of Originalism*, 88 Tex. L. Rev. 1 (2009) (attempting to explain unpopularity of originalism outside the United States).

[67] For a brief guide, *see* Konstantin Korkelia, *New Challenges to the Regime of Reservations Under the International Covenant on Civil and Political Rights*, 13 Eur. J. Int'l L. 437, 442–44 (2002). *See also* Sia Spiliopoulou Akermark, *Reservation Clauses in Treaties Concluded Within the Council of Europe*, 48 Int'l & Comp. L.Q.479, 488–90, 512–13 (1999) (suggesting that Council of Europe reservations practices, which "can claim to have become regional customary rules," include a preference for making reservations clauses "as detailed as possible," permitting reservations only as to legislation in force, and requesting parties to give brief accounts of such legislation).

[68] Human Rights Committee, General Comment No. 24, ¶ 19, U.N. Doc. CCPR/C/21/Rev.1/Add.6 (Nov. 11, 1994).

[69] *Id.* ¶ 19.

[70] Observations by France on General Comment 24, 4 Int'l Hum. Rts. Rep. 8 (1997); Observations by the United Kingdom on General Comment 24, 3 Int'l Hum. Rts. Rep. 261 (1996); Observations by the United States on General Comment 24, 3 Int'l Hum. Rts. Rep. 265 (1996).

Treaty Conditions and Constitutions 163

evaluate and treat as invalid impermissible objections.[71] Still, the Committee's approach to domestic excuses is reflected in at least some state practice, perhaps particularly by European states, which treats as unduly general even conditions that actually identify the domestic laws and treaty provisions concerned. Thus, Portugal objected to a US reservation to the ICCPR – which was expressed, at least in part, in terms of specific constitutional provisions – as improperly "invoking general principles of National Law [which] may create doubts on the commitments of the Reserving State to the object and purpose of the Covenant and, moreover, contribute to under-mining the basis of International Law," while Sweden condemned "general references to national legislation" (while failing, in its own lapse, specifically to reference the condition that fell short in that regard).[72] Both took aim at conditions that sought to substitute US constitutional and other laws, as opposed to those claiming a direct constitutional conflict, but they did not limit the complaint.

On this view, if other states are to gain insight from constitution conditions, the conditions must be treated with skepticism, interrogated as potentially general reservations, and tolerated (if at all) only when they are sufficiently definite as to allow evaluation. That is fine, so far as it goes. Yet it pays little attention to specific kinds of information that such conditions might commu-nicate and the incentives confronting their sponsoring states. Maintaining the window metaphor, what do constitution conditions potentially convey, and how may they be encouraged to do more?

At a minimum, constitution conditions assert that the state's proposed treatment has a legal basis, rather than being simply a political or cultural preference. By itself, that may not amount to much: conditions adverting to law may be window dressing for nonlegal preferences, and indicate in essence that a state simply prefers to stand pat. But if the condition indicates that the constitution would conflict with and override any treaty commitment, this informs other states about the problem's relative permanence. Because consti-tutions are, typically, difficult to amend, the condition provides not only a justification, which other states may accept or reject as they prefer, but also a potentially illuminating confession that the circumstance is one espe-cially unlikely to change.

As noted previously, other states (and international institutions) may well take these characteristics as unwelcome; even so, understanding them might inform and constructively influence reactions. If states realize the

[71] General Comment 24, *supra*, ¶¶ 16–18.
[72] *See* ICCPR Status of Reservations and Declarations, *supra*.

164 *Edward T. Swaine*

constitutional premises of a condition, they might reject it outright, or accept it as predetermined and unlikely to change. Alternatively, they might put greater emphasis on seeking retraction or revision of the condition, on the premise that – because overcoming a constitutional restraint requires extraordinary measures by the proposing state – it is unlikely to yield in the absence of extraordinary external pressure. In any case, knowing a condition's nature might help audiences puzzling over whether they should treat the condition as a *pre*condition for the state's participation. At least for domestic orders in which constitutions enjoy hierarchical superiority, conditions asserting a direct constitutional conflict provide a rebuttable showing that a condition requires special domestic or international accommodation before the state can join the treaty. This should be of interest to international audiences, even if they continue to resist making such claims hierarchically superior in the international order.[73]

If such information is potentially helpful, should anything be done to encourage its disclosure? Perhaps nothing is necessary. States have an interest in justifying themselves, whether encouraged by international standards or not; they may believe it dissuades sympathetic states from objecting, or need to reassure domestic audiences that the constitutional order is being preserved. Still, the impulses favoring disclosure may be dampened if the features of a constitution condition – its tendency toward generality and vagueness, and its resistance to change – attract criticism, objection, or even severance. Ironically, generality and vagueness may be encouraged if greater clarity about a condition's nature is discouraged.

Assuming one could encourage disclosure by indicating greater indulgence of constitution conditions, would it be worth it? A skeptic would note not only that the permanence of constitutions may be exaggerated – they are amended *sometimes*, and might be amended following ratification of conflicting treaty obligations — but also that permanence cannot genuinely distinguish constitution conditions from those based on other deep social features. Sharia conditions to human rights treaties are an obvious example. These too have been widely condemned as general and vague in

---

[73] For comparable reasons, they may be interested in whether domestic constitutions suggest a conflict with proposed conditions. *See, e.g.*, Rep. of the Comm. on the Elimination of Discrimination against Women, 18th Sess., 19th Sess., Jan. 19–Feb. 6, 1998, June 22–July 10, 1998, at 47, U.N. Doc. A/53/38/Rev.1 (quarreling with state reservations to Article 2 of CEDAW proposed in teeth of "national constitutions or laws [that] prohibit discrimination"). *Cf.* Wright, *supra*, at 134 (noting condemnation, by domestic constituency, of proposed condition to the Versailles Treaty on the ground that it attempted to preserve congressional authority over the use of US military forces in violation of the Commander-in-Chief clause).

character, and may reflect a commitment as permanent (if not more so) as constitutions.[74] The arbitrariness of any distinction is highlighted by the fact that some Islamic states (like Malaysia, Mauritania, and Pakistan) proposed conditions to human rights treaties that alluded to conflicts between the treaty, on the one hand, and Islamic sharia and their domestic constitutions, on the other.[75] The choice of whether one or both domestic bases were emphasized seemed almost arbitrary; European objections to those conditions, in any event, made nothing of the distinction.[76] If neither kind of condition offers more specific information – that is, by citing constitutional (or socioreligious) principles with particularity, or explaining the treaty provisions put in question – they might be treated equivalently, as under prevailing approaches. Still, constitution conditions, while indicating relative permanence, may better identify a feature that can be monitored by conventional means. If they offer, despite themselves, a potential mechanism for change, so much the better.

[74] Thus, for example, Libya's reservation upon ratification of CEDAW, which alluded to contrary Shariah obligation, drew objections from seven states; while Libya modified the reservation to render it more specific, its amended reservation cited "the peremptory norms of the Islamic *Shariah*" – and continued to be subject to objection on ground not just of generality and vagueness, but also "a reservation is also, in the view of the Government of Finland, subject to the general principle of the observance of treaties according to which a Party may not invoke the provisions of its internal law as justification for failure to perform a treaty." *See* CEDAW Status of Reservations and Declarations, *supra*; for review of the sequence, see Seventeenth Report, at 12–13.

[75] For example, Malaysia's CEDAW declaration provided that "Malaysia's accession is subject to the understanding that the provisions of the Convention do not conflict with the provisions of the Islamic Sharia' law and the Federal Constitution of Malaysia," before enumerating the affected articles. Mauritania's reservation stated that it "approved and do approve it in each and every one of [CEDAW's] parts which are not contrary to Islamic Sharia and are in accordance with our Constitution"; it was later partially withdrawn, but continued to apply to Articles 13(a) and 16. *See* CEDAW Status of Reservations and Declarations, *supra*. Pakistan's reservation to the ICCPR initially provided that "provided that '[the] Islamic Republic of Pakistan declares that the provisions of Articles 3, 6, 7, 18 and 19 shall be so applied to the extent that they are not repugnant to the Provisions of the Constitution of Pakistan and the Sharia laws'. though (like Mauritania) it later limited its application." *See* ICCPR Status of Reservations and Declarations, *supra*.

[76] For example, Finland described Mauritania's reservation as "consist[ing] of a general reference to religious or other national law," and stated that "reservations are subject to the general principle of treaty interpretation according to which a party may not invoke the provisions of its domestic law as justification for a failure to perform its treaty obligations." The Netherlands and Sweden recalled in similar terms that states were obliged to "undertake any legislative changes necessary to comply with their obligations under the treaties," not pausing over any special problems relating to making constitutional changes. *See* CEDAW Status of Reservations and Declarations, *supra*.

166   *Edward T. Swaine*

6.3 CONSTITUTION CONDITIONS AS DOORS

While the wall-like nature of constitution conditions – effectively, barricades sculpted by the domestic and international legal orders – is grudgingly acknowledged, and their capacity to serve as windows neglected, their function as doors is fully grasped on the international plane. International practice often reacts to reservations as if they are loosely chained, slightly ajar entryways to domestic premises, and the reservation regime has increasingly elaborated means by which states can respond to proposed reservations.

The objective for human rights treaties, as perceived by treaty bodies and many of the more active states, is easily stated: even if the initial value of conditions in enhancing the breadth and depth of treaty commitments has to be respected, states and others should press for their eventual withdrawal.[77] The ILC's Conclusions on the Reservations Dialogue were more nuanced, but similarly disposed; the conclusions sympathized with maintaining reservations, but also urged that states consider withdrawal or limitation of reservations "where appropriate" or "if they deem it useful."[78]

Sometimes, at least, this works. The track record, including for constitution conditions, is the most extensive for human rights treaties. Malaysia, in ratifying the Convention on the Rights of the Child, proposed reservations to multiple articles, declaring that "the said provisions shall be applicable only if they are in conformity with the Constitution, national laws and national policies of the Government of Malaysia." A number of states objected.[79]

---

[77] Seventeenth Meeting of Chairpersons of the Human Rights Treaty Bodies, The Practice of Human Rights Treaty Bodies with Respect to Reservations to International Human Rights Treaties, ¶ 2, U.N. Doc. HRI/MC/2005/5 (noting agreement "that it was appropriate for treaty bodies to request the withdrawal of reservations to the treaties they monitored"); *id.* ¶ 45 ("All treaty bodies are motivated by concern as to the existence and scope of reservations and seek, through their respective mechanisms, to restrict the scope of existing reservations and encourage the removal by States parties"). As that report indicated, supportive statements may be found in numerous publications of the treaty bodies. For other more general, representative statements, *see* Special Rapporteur, Int'l Law Comm'n, Fourth Report on Reservations to Treaties, P 12, U.N. Doc. A/CN.4/499 (Mar. 25, 1999) (prepared by Alain Pellet) (citing correspondence from the chairpersons of human rights bodies calling for limiting the number and scope of reservations); World Conference on Human Rights, June 14–25, 1993, Vienna Declaration and Programme of Action, ¶¶ I.26, II.5, II.39, II.46, U.N. Doc. A/CONF.157/23 (July 12, 1993) (urging withdrawal of reservations).

[78] Reservations Dialogue, ¶¶ 4, 7. *See also* Seventeenth Report, at 17 ¶ 33 ("Full or partial withdrawal of a reservation *that is considered invalid* is unquestionably the primary purpose of the reservations dialogue.") (emphasis added).

[79] This included Austria, Belgium, Finland, Germany, Ireland, Netherlands, Norway, Portugal, and Sweden. ICCPR Status of Reservations and Declarations, *supra*; *see also* 1958 Const. art. 2 (Fr.).

Finland was more specific than many, objecting to the invocation of national law – without distinguishing the constitutional warrant – and claiming what is sometimes known as super-maximum effect, a largely Nordic practice which treats the conditioning state as party to the treaty without any benefit of its condition.[80] Malaysia subsequently limited, without fully withdrawing, its condition.[81] Another example was Uruguay's interpretive declaration upon ratifying the Rome State establishing the International Criminal Court, which appeared to defer to its constitution in the event of conflict.[82] Under the Rome State regime, no reservations (or constructive reservations) were permissible; in the face of objections from Ireland, the United Kingdom, Denmark, and Norway, Uruguay initially sought to minimize the declaration's impact while recalling the hierarchical superiority of its constitution, but it ultimately yielded and withdrew the declaration.[83]

In light of such successes, one might think of constitution conditions as just a cautious way of cracking the door, inviting international interlocutors to encourage the necessary adaption of domestic law to allow fulfillment of agreed treaty terms. Of course, encouraging withdrawal or modification might drive down willingness to participate in multilateral treaties. That may seem like an exaggerated risk, or unwarranted reaction, to inquiries that simply check whether conditions are truly indispensable. But dialogue is taxing, and perhaps intrusive, regardless. Domestic constituencies may also be unwilling to entrust the resolution of such disputes to diplomats, and consider the safer course to be declining to participate in the first

---

[80] *See id.* For discussion of the so-called Nordic approach, and Finland's views in particular, *see* Päivi Kaukoranta, *Elements of Nordic Practice 1997: Finland*, 67 NORDIC J. INT'L L. 321 (1998); Jan Klabbers, *Accepting the Unacceptable? A New Nordic Approach to Reservations to Multilateral Treaties*, 69 NORDIC J. INT'L L. 179 (2000); Lars Magnuson, *Elements of Nordic Practice 1997: The Nordic Countries in Coordination*, 67 NORDIC J. INT'L L. 345, 350 (1998). As others have observed, this approach is not confined to Nordic countries nor to human rights treaties. *See, e.g.,* Comm'n on Human Rights, Sub-Comm'n on the Promotion and Protection of Human Rights, Reservations to Human Rights Treaties, ¶¶ 16–17, U.N. Doc. E/CN.4/ Sub.2/2004/42 (July 19, 2004) (prepared by Françoise Hampson) (citing Geneva Conventions examples)

[81] For a cautious appraisal of the sequence and the link between objections and modification, see Seventeenth Report, at 4–5.

[82] The declaration stated, in part, that "As a State party to the Rome Statute, the Eastern Republic of Uruguay shall ensure its application to the full extent of the powers of the State insofar as it is competent in that respect and in strict accordance with the Constitutional provisions of the Republic." Rome Statute, Status of Reservations and Declarations, in Multilateral Treaties on Deposit with the Secretary General, Chapter XVIII(10), https://treaties.un.org/Pages/ViewDet ails.aspx?src=IND&mtdsg_no=XVIII-10&chapter=18&clang=_en#15.

[83] *See id.; see also* Seventeenth Report, at 11–12.

place.[84] It may be simpler, all things considered, just to provide as little information as possible, and to keep the door closed. States anticipating effective interrogatories might prefer to risk less overt breaches in the fullness of time. The mere absence of conditions (or their tidying up after inquiry) hardly guarantees reform of the underlying domestic circumstance.

What can be done to better negotiate these thresholds? The baseline in the reservations dialogue remains highly skewed toward the state proposing conditions. Generally, it may insist on maintaining its condition; unless an objecting state explicitly indicates that its objection thwarts treaty relations between it and the proposing state (or asserts objections with super-maximum or other novel effect), objections still leave the conditioning state with what it wants, more or less. Beyond this, however, the reservations dialogue is biased against the proposing state. While the state may maintain or withdraw its condition, or (it appears) narrow it, it is much less clearly within its capacity to widen the condition in response to objections.[85] The ILC's Guide to Practice regards this as tantamount to the late filing of a new reservation, which is permitted only when no other state objects.[86]

There is much to commend this approach, but it is not tailored to constitution conditions, and suffers some deficiencies in that context. Constitution conditions are often prone to objection on grounds of excessive generality.[87] Anticipating this, and aware that modifications will only be permitted to narrow the condition, a conditioning state may be encouraged to begin by pitching its condition relatively broadly; reining in yet-broader conditions will remain imperfect, since most states fail to object. Other, less calculating states

---

[84] This problem has surfaced, for example, in concern by US treaty skeptics that a future president and Senate could renege on a domestic compromise, and in recurring Senate anxieties that a president could unilaterally, without consulting the Senate, withdraw reservations, understandings, and declarations transmitted while maintaining the United States as a treaty party –though some have suggested the decision would need to be made jointly. *See* CURTIS A. BRADLEY, INTERNATIONAL LAW IN THE U.S. LEGAL SYSTEM 38–39 (2nd ed. 2015).

[85] To be clear, it should be possible to widen at the time of ratification a reservation initially lodged at the time of signature.

[86] ILC Guide to Practice, Guideline 2.34; *see id.* at 187–90 (commentary). Under the rules for late reservations, unanimous consent is required, but as with acceptances of reservations generally, it may be tacit and will be assumed after twelve months. Under the normal rule for objections, however, each state speaks for itself, whereas the ILC contemplates that any one state may exercise what amounts to a veto. *Id.* Guidelines 2.3.1–2.3.2.

[87] Perhaps they are also more prone to objection on grounds of their (purported) permanence – but while that makes withdrawal less likely, it need not encumber to the same extent attempts to elicit their narrowing.

may still resist cooperating, knowing that greater specificity can only be achieved by reducing degrees of freedom. Perhaps some states will appreciate being helped toward closer approximation of treaty obligations, but the rules suggest perverse incentives for others.

One fix might be to clarify the distinction between presumptively permissible and presumptively impermissible modifications. Rather than asking whether a modification is "widening" or "narrowing," as would the ILC, the Council of Europe's Committee of Legal Advisers on Public International Law suggested that "[m]odification of a reservation is acceptable when it restricts the scope of the original reservation."[88] The European approach, while similar, would seem to permit other movement in terms of detail, such as by linking a reservation to a particular constitutional provision or judicial doctrine. The Committee went on to state, however, that "[a] modification that expands the scope of the original reservation is contrary to the rule that reservations may only be made when expressing consent to be bound," which might suggest that general reservations may be modified only when narrowed. If clarity is an important objective, in order to improve evaluation by other states, an insistence that conditions can only be narrowed – against what is often an uncertain baseline to begin with – is ill-advised.[89]

A second potential fix would be to encourage drafting contingent conditions. As previously observed, the premise of constitution conditions is that they are immutable, but that is often not strictly true; the problem is that the national agents making international agreements find it prohibitively difficult to guarantee conforming constitutional change. This does not mean, however, that the condition has to capture permanently the system's most conservative posture, or change only after ongoing and intrusive dialogue. Instead, the

---

[88] Comm. of Legal Advisers on Pub. Int'l Law (CAHDI), Practical Issues Regarding Reservations to International Treaties, 19th mtg., CM (2000) 50, App. 4 (2000), https://rm.coe.int/CoERM PublicCommonSearchServices/DisplayDCTMContent?documentId=0900001680064409.

[89] Maldives's reservation to CEDAW serves as an example. Its initial condition was extraordinarily broad, almost abstract, reserving as to "any provisions of the Convention which obliges [it] to change its Constitution and laws in any manner." It later modified that reservation, submitted upon accession and eliciting objections, to one that specifically adverted to one provision of CEDAW and one article of its constitution, but that attracted (tardy) objections from several states, including Germany's statement that "[a]fter a State has bound itself to a treaty under international law it can no longer submit new reservations or extend or add to old reservations. It is only possible to totally or partially withdraw original reservations." Maldives later withdraw part of that reservation.

Germany's approach was narrower than that urged by the ILC, which might have regarded Maldives' amendment as narrowing; regardless, its enhanced specificity contributed to the clarity of its position.

170   *Edward T. Swaine*

original version of a condition may allow for dynamic adaptation so as to take into account judicial or other developments. As a leading user of constitution conditions, the United States might take the lead. Consider, for example, its reservation to the ICCPR on free speech, which stated (in relevant part) that no legislation was authorized or required "that would restrict the right of free speech and association protected by the Constitution." The complement, implicitly, was that the United States accepts that it is required by Article 20 to restrict free speech and association that is *not* protected by the Constitution. Both notions, and the possibility of domestic change, would usefully supplement the present condition's vague sense of present incompatibility. Thus, such a reservation might add a proviso like the following: "If and to the extent the Constitution is conclusively interpreted by the U.S. Supreme Court, or amended, to permit additional regulation by the Federal Government of a kind authorized or required by Article 20, the United States will adopt such legislation and notify the treaty depositary."[90]

Even without ratcheting up legislative obligations, such solutions could help align international and constitutional obligations after domestic developments. The second US reservation to the ICCPR, for example, provided in full that "The United States reserves the right, subject to its Constitutional constraints, to impose capital punishment on any person (other than a pregnant woman) duly convicted under existing or future laws permitting the imposition of capital punishment, including such punishment for crimes committed by persons below eighteen years of age." As constitution conditions go, that is reasonably specific;[91] for that reason, once the US Supreme Court held that the execution of juveniles was unconstitutional,[92] the reservation was taken to be moot.[93] Internationally, however, the US reservation appears unaffected; if true, that would mean that any US constitutional violation

---

[90]   The US reservation to the Genocide Convention precluding "legislation or other action ... prohibited by the [US] Constitution ... as interpreted by the United States," might already permit a similar outcome, though it is less than clear. Under a conciliatory approach, the final proviso might – while retaining US autonomy over interpretation of its constitution – admit the possibility that the prevailing US interpretation would be adjusted by judicial decisions or amendment.

[91]   Whether it describes a direct constitutional conflict, however, is hazier, and depends on how "subject to its Constitutional restraints" is understood. On its face, it appears to treat the US Constitution as supplying a surrogate for the international standard; it would establish a conflict, however, if the US Constitution provides not only minimum conditions allowing the United States to take additional measures to preclude the juvenile death, but also a maximum inhibiting any such measures – for example, because of limitations on the ability to regulate state-based administration of criminal law.

[92]   Roper v. Simmons, 543 U.S. 541 (2005).

[93]   *See, e.g.*, Bradley, *supra*, at 38.

would remain immunized from the ICCPR, even though that discrepancy is an historical artefact. Such a result would be avoided if the reservation were framed elastically, permitting the United States no greater exemption than its constitution currently affords.[94]

Finally, if constitution conditions open a door between states, that allows other traffic. The Vienna Convention, recall, provides only limited upside to objecting: for normative treaties, where states are especially unlikely to disclaim treaty relations, the payoff (relative to tacit acceptance) is often unclear. States make objections anyway, however, probably because they serve additional ends – including some especially relevant for constitution conditions. When a state lodges such a condition, at least one based on a direct constitutional conflict, it is effectively claiming that it would be forced to deviate from the treaty's original terms if the circumstances governed by the condition actually arose. (The proposing state has, after all, indicated that it is constitutionally incapable of performing.) When states trouble themselves to object, they hint that such conduct is vulnerable to being called out as a breach, perhaps even a material one, by other states. Conditions and resulting objection, in this sense, take the temperature of states as to treaty performance and likely reactions to lapses; conversely, failures to object foreshadow the prospects for acquiescence.

6.4 CONCLUSION

Where, and how, do constitutions and treaties meet? This discussion understates their interplay, even accepting its metaphors. The walls separating domestic constitutions from treaty obligations are represented, additionally, by terms that each impose that are hostile to the other: for example, constitutional norms of democratic process and nondelegation that adapt imperfectly to global methods, and international obligations derived from dominant traditions that make it more difficult for other constitutional orders to play along.

Constitution conditions arguably create a means of scaling such walls, by permitting additional states to participate in multilateral treaties despite constitutional differences. To be sure, their indispensability may be less than meets the eye: just as states can overstate constraints during treaty negotiations to advance their objectives, they may exaggerate their incapacity as a means of

---

[94] Reframed, it might read "subject to its Constitutional constraints, as reckoned at the time of any sentencing" – or, if a narrower conflict-avoidance approach were favored, "to the extent required by its Constitution," so reckoned.

excusing conditions. This might become a more serious concern if treaty law paid substantially greater respect to constitutional excuses. Under existing law, however, state have little reason to articulate the basis for a treaty condition – it matters not under the Vienna Convention, as neither conditioning or objecting states need state any reason at all – so present decisions to point to constitutional grounds, at least, more plausibly suggest real limits.

Beyond breadth of participation, depth is an easily overlooked advantage. States not content to remain nonparties, and doubtful as to whether conditions will be respected, might instead try negotiating watered-down provisions.[95] Whatever the disadvantages of constitution conditions, it may be worse for all if the most acute concerns of a handful of states are extrapolated with the effect of reducing obligations for all.

What about windows, or even doors, as might exist between the domestic and international legal orders? States that successfully condition consent on constitutional bases may prove more accessible, and even malleable, than they would admit. The evolutionary potential of constitutional law – effectuated, often, through domestic interpretation by independent judiciaries – may come to reflect even a conditioned-to provision. The most famous example in the United States, at present, remains *Roper v. Simmons*, in which the majority opinion cited, as confirmatory evidence for its reading of the Eighth and Fourteenth Amendments, a provision in the ICCPR to which the United States had entered a reservation on constitutional grounds.[96] If constitutions come to be reinterpreted or clarified more in keeping with treaties, constitution conditions might finally outgrow their use. In the meantime, the United States and European states might profitably rethink how they are best advanced and best received.

---

[95] *See* Swaine, *Reserving, supra*, at 328–33.
[96] Roper v. Simmons, 543 U.S. 551, 576 (2005).

2 International Adjudication and the Development of International Law

7

International Courts and Tribunals in the USA and in Europe

The Increasingly Divided West

Chiara Giorgetti[*]

The last few years have seen significant developments in the relations of the United States and Europe towards international courts and tribunals (ICTs). With the caution that generalizations call for, it is by and large the case that, historically, while their views and relations to ICTs have never completely aligned, there has been overall a certain convergence of views between the USA and Europe towards ICTs that resolved disputes related to international economic law, such as trade and investment. At the same time, however, more divergence has traditionally existed in relation to ICTs whose jurisdiction include human rights and international criminal law. Relations with the International Court of Justice (ICJ) have often been *ad hoc* and complex on both sides.[1]

More recently, however, the situation has seen consequential changes, with the US demonstrating a much more antagonistic view towards ICTs generally, and towards ICTs that address issues related to international trade and investment particularly. The US has sought – to a large extent – to dissociates from them both. While reassessment of these fora began before the election of Donald Trump, it is with the beginning of the Trump administration in 2016 that the antagonism has taken a different pace and breadth, hand in hand with his "America First" doctrine.

---

[*] I wish to thank Ben Midas from Richmond Law School for excellent research assistance for this piece.

[1] For a thoughtful and nuanced analysis of the general issue of international law in the US and Europe, *see* Mark A. Pollack, *Who Supports International Law, and Why?: The United States, the European Union, and the International Legal Order,* 13Int'l J Const. L. 873 (2015) 873 (stating at 876 "the contrasts between the US and the EU with respect to international law are real, and cry out for explanation. Such explanations can only follow, however, from a fine-grained, discriminating analysis of US and EU attitudes and actions across various dimensions and issue-areas, and over time.").

175

176 *Chiara Giorgetti*

Differently, European countries have maintained their traditional support for international courts and tribunals, which notably are mostly based in Europe. Moreover, guided and encouraged in large part by the common policies of the European Union, they have broadly maintained their support for trade related courts, and have voiced their desire for changes in Investor-State Dispute Settlement (ISDS) mechanisms to create an investment court. In both cases, European countries have not tried to dissociate from those courts, but, rather, have argued for stronger, clearer and more permanent dispute resolution mechanisms.

On ICTs, the "West" has shifted apart. European countries and the USA are increasingly divided on their views, use and support of international courts and tribunals. This contribution explains how and why this situation occurred generally first, and by taking a variety of ICTs, and specifically the International Criminal Court, the World Trade Organization (WTO) and ISDS, as examples then.

7.1 THE USA, EUROPE AND INTERNATIONAL COURTS AND TRIBUNALS: SAME START, SEPARATE PATHS

When, in the aftermath of World War II, the ICJ was created as the principle judicial organ of the United Nations, the USA and several European Countries (such as France, Belgium, the Netherlands, Luxembourg and the United Kingdom) were both supporters and participants. In fact, they were all original members of the United Nations and so *ipso facto* parties to the ICJ statute. Many had signed the compulsory declaration to provide the ICJ with extensive jurisdiction. In that period, the position and world-view of the US and Europe were largely similar. The USA and European countries supported the creation of the ICJ and together also collaborated in the Nuremberg trials, which prosecuted Nazi leaders.

The US and European countries also walked along the same line in the second wave of courts' creation, after the Cold War. The International Criminal Tribunal for the Former Yugoslavia (ICTY) and the International Criminal Tribunal for Rwanda (ICTR) were established with the support of all "the West."[2] Though by then differences were already showing, for example in relation to human rights courts.

---

[2] *See* Doc. S/RES/827, S. C. Res. 827 of 25 May 1993, creating the ICTY which was unanimously approved and Doc. S/RES/955, SC Res. 955(1994) of 8 Nov. 1994, creating the ICTR. The resolutions passed 13–15, with all western countries in favor, Rwanda voted against and China abstained.

International Courts and Tribunals in the US and in Europe 177

Move forward another thirty years and a quantum leap seems to have occurred. Europe and the US now hold divergent views on most international courts and tribunals, from the International Criminal Court (ICC) to the WTO dispute settlement mechanism. And the Trump administration has demonstrated a clear hostility towards ICTs generally.

Given the overall similarities in economic development, political systems and to a large extent security outlook, what explains the different visions and kind of support given by European countries and the USA to international courts and tribunals?

7.1.1 *The USA and International Courts and Tribunals: From Exceptionalism to America First*

The US government's posture towards international courts has in the past been mostly based on pragmatism rather than ideology.[3] The USA has been instrumental in the creation of many international courts and tribunals since the Nuremberg and Tokyo tribunals, including the ICTR and the ICTY.[4] Yet, international courts and tribunals are in many ways just another piece in America's foreign policy strategy. As former Legal Adviser John Bellinger III explains

> Our general approach to international courts and tribunals is pragmatic. In our view, such courts and tribunals should not be seen as end in themselves but rather as potential tolls to advance shared international interests in developing the rule of law, ensuring justice and accountability and solving legal disputes. Consistent with this approach, we evaluate the contributions that proposed international courts and tribunals may make on a case-by-case basis, just as we consider the advantages and disadvantages of addressing particular matters through international judicial mechanisms rather than diplomatic or other means.[5]

---

[3]   In the persuasively clear words of Harold Koh, former Legal Adviser: "Whether pressing for or against multilateral action, in the twentieth century or the twenty-first, Americans generally tend to strike the world as pushy, preachy, insensitive, self-righteous, and usually, anti-French." Harold Hongju Koh, *On American Exceptionalism*, 55 STAN. L. REV. 1479 (2003) 1481.

[4]   *See* for example Zachary D. Kaufman, *The United States Role in the Establishment of the United Nations International Criminal Tribunal for Rwanda* in AFTER GENOCIDE: TRANSITIONAL JUSTICE, POST-CONFLICT RECONSTRUCTION, AND RECONCILIATION IN RWANDA AND BEYOND, 229, 260 (Phil Clark & Zachary D. Kaufman, eds., 2009) (republished by Oxford University Press, 2013). Clint Williamson, *The Role of the United States in International Criminal Justice*, 25 PENN ST. INT'L L. R. 819 (2007) (stating at p. 823 "the U.S. was the driving force for the creation of both courts and at the outset provided a large infusion of personnel").

[5]   John B. Bellinger III, *International Courts and Tribunals and the Rule of Law*, in THE SWORD AND THE SCALE (Cesare Romano ed., 2009).

178   *Chiara Giorgetti*

This pragmatic approach results in complex relations with the multitude of existing international courts and tribunals.[6] While the USA is generally seen as skeptical in relation to international courts and tribunals, a more sophisticated analysis shows that the relationship had varied historically in terms of the jurisdictional subject matter. It has also changed over time. For example, the USA has in the past been a supporter of tribunals that focus on international economic matters, such as trade and investment. The USA was instrumental in the success of the dispute resolution mechanism of the WTO and brought many disputes to be resolved in that forum. Similarly, on issues related to investment law, the USA has traditionally been a supporter of investment arbitration and ISDS dispute resolution mechanisms.[7]

At the same time, the USA has often criticized specific courts or decisions issued by some ICTs. For example, the USA withdrew its declaration of compulsory jurisdiction to the ICJ after the Court found it had jurisdiction in *Certain Military and Paramilitary Activities* case with Nicaragua in the 1980s.[8] Similarly, all presidents since Bill Clinton have expressed concern over the jurisdictional reach of the ICC. And even President Obama, typically seen as a proponent of a neoliberal economic global order, resisted certain WTO decisions.[9]

In the areas of human rights, the USA has not submitted itself to compulsory jurisdiction of an international court. The USA has not ratified the American Convention on Human Rights, and is not subject to the jurisdiction of the Inter-American Court of Human Rights.[10] The American government expressed a willingness to potentially enter the jurisdiction of the Court in the past, though it has not moved any closer to recognizing the compulsory jurisdiction of the Court at this time.[11]

The uneasy US relationship with the ICJ, the principle judicial organ of the United Nations, since its establishment in 1946 is another case on point.[12] The

---

[6] Steven Kull and Clay Ramsay, *American Public Opinion on International Courts and Tribunals*, in THE SWORD AND THE SCALE (Cesare Romano ed., 2009).

[7] The 2012 Model US BIT is available on the State Department site at: https://ustr.gov/sites/default/files/BIT%20text%20for%20ACIEP%20Meeting.pdf.

[8] Sean Murphy, *The United States and the International Court of Justice: Coping With Antinomies*, in THE UNITED STATES AND INTERNATIONAL COURTS AND TRIBUNALS (Cesare Romano ed., 2008).

[9] Zeeshan Aleem, *Why Trump's Plan to Defy the WTO Isn't as Reckless as It Sounds*, Vox, 8 March 2017. https://www.vox.com/policy-and-politics/2017/3/8/14766228/trump-trade-wto.

[10] Elizabeth A. H. Abi-Mershed, *The United States and the Inter-American Court of Human Rights*, in THE SWORD AND THE SCALE (Cesare Romano ed., 2009).

[11] *Id.* at 191.

[12] *See* generally, Murphy, *supra* note 8.

United States has engaged with the ICJ in more significant ways than with the Inter-American Court by nominating and getting judges elected at the Court and participating in many proceedings before the ICJ. It has also participated to all advisory proceedings to date.[13]

However, on matter of contentious cases, the USA has generally been much more skeptical and cautious. It has been suspicious of decisions of Court which are adverse to its interests.[14] It also withdrew from the compulsory jurisdiction of the Court in 1986, and withdrew from the Vienna Convention on Consular Relations after the ICJ decided three cases against it.[15] Generally, the USA is hesitant to submit itself to a process that it does not control and does not recognize the USA's role on the international stage, and would prefer to use domestic mechanisms to resolve disputes rather than submitting those disputes to the ICJ.[16]

While the relation of the USA with ICTs has often been imperfect, the presidency of Donald Trump has created important – tectonic – shifts in America's relationship with international courts. President Trump and members of his administration have been antagonistic in both words and deeds towards a variety of international courts and tribunals and have tried to undermined their legitimacy and support.[17] This antagonism is not targeted to a specific court and is not just reaction to a specific judgment. Rather, it goes to the very core and existence of international adjudication. For example, President Trump has called the ICC "illegitimate"[18] and his former national security advisor John Bolton has denounced the ICJ as "politicized and ineffective."[19] Words have also been followed by concrete actions, including

---

[13] See https://www.icj-cij.org/en/advisory-proceedings for a list of ICJ advisory proceedings. The USA has participated in each proceeding.

[14] See Murphy, *supra* note 8.

[15] *Avena and Other Mexican Nationals (Mexico v. United States of America)* Judgment, I.C.J. Reports 2004, p. 12; *LaGrand (Germany v. United States of America)* Judgment, I.C.J. Reports 2001, p, 466; *Vienna Convention on Consular Relations (Paraguay v. United States of America)* Order of 10 November 1998, I.C.J Reports 1998, p. 426.

[16] Murphy, *supra* note 8.

[17] See generally Stefan Talmon, *The United States Under President Trump: Gravedigger of International Law*, 18 Chinese J. Int'l L. 645 (2019).

[18] The White House, *Statement of the President*, 12 April 2019 ("Since the creation of the ICC, the United States has consistently declined to join the court because of its broad, unaccountable prosecutorial powers; the threat it poses to American national sovereignty; and other deficiencies that render it illegitimate.") available here: www.whitehouse.gov/briefings-statements/st atement-from-the-president-8/).

[19] Roberta Rampton, Lesley Wroughton and Stephanie van den Berg, *U.S. Withdraws from International Accord, Says U.N World Court is "Politicized"*, Reuters World News (3 October 2018) www.reuters.com.idUSKCN1MD2CP?feedType=RSS&feedName=worldNews&utm_

withdrawal from several treaties that guaranteed ICJ jurisdiction in case of disputes and denying entry visas to ICC personnel.[20] The USA has also decided not to participate in ICJ proceedings brought against it by Palestine on the issue of the relocation of the US Embassy to Jerusalem, asserting the ICJ manifestly lacked jurisdiction.[21] This decision is consequential. John Bolton also clearly stated that the evaluations on the Palestinian claims, as well as those of two other pending cases brought by Iran against the USA, had to do not only with those claims but more with the "continued consistent policy of the United States to reject the jurisdiction" of the ICJ and confirmed the policy of the Trump administration to engage in a "review of all international agreements that may still expose the United States to [the ICJ's] purported binding jurisdiction."[22]

This hostile take on ICTs is part of a broader policy shift that frames global governance as "coercion and domination" against US interest.[23] President Trump dismissed integration and proposes a view of the world in which states look inward and focus on patriotism, instead of globalism, and emphasized national sovereignty over any other interest. Trump's message, delivered at the UN General Assembly, raised the confrontation with multilateralism and global institutions to a new level. Indeed, while disagreements between the USA and international institutions have not been uncommon in the past, Trump attacks the very heart of internationalism and serves as denunciation of the post–World War II global system in favor of an introspective and confrontational posture, in line with Trump's America First doctrine.

Trump has also showed growing skepticism vis-à-vis ICTs dealing with international economic issues and harshly criticized the WTO claiming it unfairly cost American jobs.[24]

---

source=feedburner&utm_medium=feed&utm_campaign=Feed%3A+Reuters%2FworldNe ws+%28Reuters+World+News%29. – I tried that link and it did not work – this one does: www .reuters.com/article/us-usa-diplomacy-treaty/u-s-withdraws-from-international-accords-says-u-n-world-court-politicized-idUSKCN1MD2CP

[20] Scott R. Anderson, *Walking Away from the World Court*, Lawfare (Oct. 5, 2018) www .lawfareblog.com/walking-away-world-court. *See* also *John Bolton Threatens ICC With US Sanctions*, BBCNews (11 September 2018) https://www.bbc.com/news/world-us-canada -45474864.
Id.

[21] *See* ICJ, *Relocation of the US Embassy to Jerusalem (Palestine v. US)*, Order of 15 November 2018, generally and specifically at p. 3.

[22] Anderson, *supra* note 20.

[23] *Id.*

[24] Remarks by President Trump to the 73d Session of the United Nations General Assembly (25 September 2018) https://www.whitehouse.gov/briefings-statements/remarks-president-trump-73rd-session-united-nations-general-assembly-new-york-ny/:

Though it is sure to be consequential, the damage that this approach will do to the fabric of ICTs cannot yet be fully measured. This will also depend in large part on the duration of such policy and how much it will be endorsed by other states, as well as what other states will do to react to it.[25]

7.1.2 Europe and International Courts and Tribunals: Integration and Influence

In contrast to the USA, countries in Western Europe have traditionally relied on international courts and tribunals as a part of their overall foreign policy. European countries have supported the creation of such courts, have hosted and funded these courts and have urged other countries to join them.[26]

European countries have used economic and political integration as a key policy to ensure economic growth and peace after two world wars left the continent in ruins. With the end of the Cold War, this policy extended to several former Communist countries as well. With its now twenty-seven members, the European Union (EU) is capable of competing economically with much larger countries, such as the USA and China.

The EU framework created a self-contained legal system, with EU law interpreted consistently by all EU members. At the center of the EU framework lays the European Court of Justice (ECJ) to which domestic courts and member states can request advice on the interpretation of EU law. Individuals themselves can also raise relevant EU issues with their domestic courts and EU institutions have a variety of compliance mechanisms to ensure EU law is consistently applied.[27] In many areas – such as trade, commerce and foreign and security policies – EU members speak with one voice.[28] The ability to

---

[25] See generally Monika Hakimi, *Why Should We Care About International Law?* 118 MICH. L. R. (forthcoming 2020) as well as HAROLD H. KOH, THE TRUMP ADMINISTRATION AND INTERNATIONAL LAW (2018) and Harold H. Koh, *The Trump Administration and International Law: A Reply*, OpinioJuris (16 October 2018) opiniojuris.org/2018/10/16/the-trump-administration-and-international-law-a-reply/.

[26] KAREN ALTER , THE NEW TERRAIN OF INTERNATIONAL LAW – COURTS, POLITICS, RIGHTS (2014).

[27] Jed Odermatt, *The International Court of Justice and the Court of Justice of the European Union: Between Fragmentation and Universality of International Law*, forthcoming in RESEARCH HANDBOOK ON THE INTERNATIONAL COURT OF JUSTICE (Achilles Skordas ed.), Edward Elgar; iCourts Working Paper Series No. 158 (10 April 2019) ssrn.com/abstract=3369613 or http://dx.doi.org/10.2139/ssrn.3369613.

[28] Article J.1, Title V, Maastricht Treaty, provides that the common foreign and security policy of the EU is defined and implemented by the EU and that its objectives are to "Safeguard the common values, fundamental interests, independence and integrity of the Union in

group twenty-seven votes in any international negotiation gives the EU substantial leverage and power.[29]

At the same time, the EU is not the only European economic institution. There are several other regional organizations founded on cooperation and common policy. The European Free Trade Association (EFTA) for example includes Norway, Iceland, Switzerland and Liechtenstein.[30] The Council of Europe is the largest European human rights organization. Its forty-seven members include every EU member, Russia and Turkey. The Council of Europe's focus is human rights, which it enumerates in the European Convention of Human Rights (ECHR) and are enforced via the European Court of Human Rights (ECtHR).

The ECtHR is probably the most successful and important example of functional international court which grants access to individuals asserting the violations of their human rights by a State. Despite the several admissibility requirements, the ECtHR hears thousands of cases annually. Since its creation, the support given by Western European countries to the ECtHR has been strong. Indeed, the acceptance of its jurisdiction is a requirement for European Council membership.[31]

That said, there have also been voices of dissent.[32] The United Kingdom, for example, deeply criticized specific decisions of the ECtHR, especially on matters related to the right to vote of incarcerated people, and those where a person's right to family life has trumped the expulsion of foreign criminals. The UK Parliament decided not to comply with the *Hirst II* judgment on

---

conformity with the principles of the United Nations Charter; Strengthen the security of the Union in all ways; Preserve peace and strengthen international security, in accordance with the principles of the United Nations Charter, as well as the principles of the Helsinki Final Act and the objectives of the Paris Charter, including those on external borders; Promote international co-operation; Develop and consolidate democracy and the rule of law, and respect for human rights and fundamental freedoms." Article 11, Treaty on European Union (consolidated version) – Title V: Provisions on a common foreign and security policy – Article 11 – Article J.1 – EU Treaty (Maastricht 1992), Official Journal C 340, 10/11/1997 P. 0155 – Consolidated version, Official Journal C 191, 29/07/1992 P. 0058, available at: https://op .europa.eu/en/publication-detail/-/publication/44c9b4a3-60c3-462c-ac3b-775f6dod6b2d.

[29] *See*, generally, Pollack, *supra* note 1.

[30] The European Free Trade Association (EFTA) is a regional trade organization and free trade area created in 1960. It now has four members. *See* generally efta.int.

[31] Convention for the Protection of Human Rights and Fundamental Freedoms, as amended, https://www.echr.coe.int/Documents/Convention_ENG.pdf.

[32] *See* generally Mikael Rask Madsen, Pola Cebulak & Micha Wiebusch, *Backlash against International Courts: Explaining the Forms and Patterns of Resistance to International Courts*, 14 INT'L J. L. IN CONTEXT 23 (2018).

prisoners' voting rights.[33] At the initiative of the United Kingdom Chairmanship of the Committee of Ministers of the Council of Europe, a High-Level Conference met at Brighton in April 2012 and drafted Protocol 15 which introduced reference to the subsidiary principle and the doctrine of margin of appreciation.[34] The Protocol, however, requires unanimous ratification and has not yet entered into force.[35]

Europe is of course bigger and more diverse then the EU. Brexit signaled that diversity when the UK decided to leave the EU. Each European country is a sovereign with its own identity and policies. As for ICTs, this diversity is especially present in countries' relations to the ICJ. In many instances, however, the EU also represents the interests of all European countries in ICTs. For example, the EU is itself a member of the WTO and has frequently used its dispute resolution mechanism. The EU has also signaled its interest to join, as a regional organization, the ECHR and it is in the process of doing so.[36]

Because of overlapping membership in different international and regional organizations, European countries face the problem of possible overlapping jurisdiction by different courts. Additionally, issues of EU laws have been raised in front of several international tribunals, which can create conflicts and lead to inconsistent interpretation of EU law.[37] At the EU level, for example, the ECJ frequently cites judgments of the ICJ discuss issues of customary law, the application of treaties and to interpret EU law principles using international law, in areas including international humanitarian law, diplomatic

---

[33] Mikael R. Madsen, *The Challenging Authority of the European Court of Human Rights: From Cold War Legal Diplomacy to the Brighton Declaration and Backlash*, 79 L. & CONTEMP. PROBS. (2016).

[34] High Level Conference on the Future of the European Court of Human Rights, Brighton Declaration, https://www.echr.coe.int/Documents/2012_Brighton_FinalDeclaration_ENG .pdf.

[35] Protocol No. 15 amending the Convention on the Protection of Human Rights and Fundamental Freedoms, signed in Strasburg on 24 June 2013, not yet in force, available at: htt ps://www.echr.coe.int/Documents/Protocol_15_ENG.pdf. *See*, generally, ECtHR, Protocols to the Convention, available at: https://www.echr.coe.int/Pages/home.aspx?p=basictexts&c=.

[36] EU accession to the ECHR is a legal obligation under Article 6(2) of the Treaty of Lisbon. However, it has been delayed by a series of decisions of the ECJ. In October 2019, the European Council reaffirmed its commitment to the accession and agreed to additional negotiations. *See*, generally, Europe Parliament, *Legislative Train Schedule, Area of Justice and Fundamental Rights, Completion of EU Accession to the ECHR*, 15 December 2019, available at https://www.europarl.europa.eu/legislative-train/theme-area-of-justice-and-fundamental-rights/file-completion-of-eu-accession-to-the-echr.

[37] Matthew Parish, *International Courts and the European Legal Order*, 23 EUR. J. INT'L L. 141 (2012) 141–43.

184 *Chiara Giorgetti*

and consular relations, nationality and treaty law. Over time, principles of international law have also been reaffirmed as principles of EU law.[38]

The EU does not have a common position on the ICJ, the principle judicial organ of the United Nations. Each member state has its own relation. Europe enjoys a strong stature at the court. The ICJ is based in Europe and Europe has been able to get several judges elected. Interestingly, while several European countries have accepted the compulsory jurisdiction of the ICJ, others still maintain a careful relationship with this instrument.[39] Most notably, of the two European permanent members of the UN Security Council, France has not accepted the ICJ compulsory jurisdiction, and the UK has attached an important declaration to it.[40]

In sum, differently from what occurs in the USA, most European countries generally support ICTs as an instrument to advance shared foreign and security policies, and advance Europe's international standing both diplomatically and economically.

The specific examples of the ICC, the dispute settlement mechanism of the WTO and ISDS support these general conclusions.

---

[38] Odermatt, *supra* note 27.

[39] The following European countries have accepted the compulsory jurisdiction of the ICJ: Austria (19 May 1971), Belgium (17 June 1958), Cyprus (3 September 2002), Denmark (10 December 1956), Finland (25 June 1958), Germany (30 April 2008), Greece (14 January 2015), Italy (25 November 2014), Liechtenstein (29 March 1950), Luxembourg (15 September 1930), Malta (2 September 1983), Netherlands (1 August 1956), Portugal (25 February 2005), Spain (20 October 1990), Sweden (6 April 1957), Switzerland (28 July 1948), United Kingdom of Great Britain and Northern Ireland (31 December 2014). *See* https://www.icj-cij.org/en/declarations.

[40] The declaration states "1. The Government of the United Kingdom of Great Britain and Northern Ireland accept as compulsory ipso facto and without special convention, on condition of reciprocity, the jurisdiction of the International Court of Justice, in conformity with paragraph 2 of Article 36 of the Statute of the Court, until such time as notice may be given to terminate the acceptance, over all disputes arising after 1 January 1984, with regard to situations or facts subsequent to the same date, other than: (i) any dispute which the United Kingdom has agreed with the other Party or Parties thereto to settle by some other method of peaceful settlement; (ii) any dispute with the government of any other country which is or has been a Member of the Commonwealth; (iii) any dispute in respect of which any other Party to the dispute has accepted the compulsory jurisdiction of the International Court of Justice only in relation to or for the purpose of the dispute; or where the acceptance of the Court's compulsory jurisdiction on behalf of any other Party to the dispute was deposited or ratified less than twelve months prior to the filing of the application bringing the dispute before the Court; (iv) any dispute which is substantially the same as a dispute previously submitted to the Court by the same or another Party. 2. The Government of the United Kingdom also reserves the right at any time, by means of a notification addressed to the Secretary-General of the United Nations, and with effect as from the moment of such notification, either to add to, amend or withdraw any of the foregoing reservations, or any that may hereafter be added."

7.2 EUROPE, THE USA AND THE ICC: MILES APART

The different stance of European countries and the US in relation to international criminal courts and tribunals, and especially the ICC, is a telling example of the different paths taken by the USA and European countries in relations to ICTs.

Western European countries have been strong supporters of the creation of international criminal tribunals, from the ICTY and ICTR to the ICC. They have supported them legally, financially and by giving them a premise from which to operate. All Western European countries have ratified the Rome Statute.[41]

The EU has signed a collaboration agreement with the ICC which highlights the EU's commitment to supporting the functioning of the ICC and to advance the widest possible participation in the ICC.[42] The agreement also expressly stressed the fundamental importance and the priority to be given to the consolidation of the rule of law and the respect for human rights and humanitarian law, as well as the preservation of peace and the strengthening of international security, in conformity with the UN Charter and the EU Treaty. The agreement aims at facilitating the work of the ICC and increase collaboration and assistance, and with this in mind the EU created an EU Focal Point for the Court.

Moreover, the EU has also included an ICC clause in several cooperation agreements with partners countries (such Georgia, Moldova and Ukraine) as well as in the Cotonou Agreement (with African, Caribbean and Pacific countries) with the aim at increasing ratification and implementation of the Rome Statute, including expert assistance, financial support and access to information.[43]

Initially, the USA also provided key support for the creation of the ICTY and the ICTR, including budget support, and pressured States to cooperate with the tribunals to secure the custody of indictees (for example, it withheld financial assistance from Serbia).[44] The support, however, turned more

---

[41] For a list of states that have ratified the Rome Statute, *see* https://asp.icc-cpi.int/en_menus/asp/states%20parties/Pages/the%20states%20parties%20to%20the%20rome%20statute.aspx.

[42] Agreement between the International Criminal Court and the European Union on Cooperation and Assistance ICC-PRES/01–01–06, 10 April 2006.

[43] European Parliament, *Briefing – International Criminal Court: Achievements and Challenges 20 Years after the Adoption of the Rome Statute* (July 2018), www.europarl.europa.eu/RegData/etudes/BRIE/2018/625127/EPRS_BRI(2018)625127_EN.pdf.

[44] Bellinger *supra* note 5, at 9.

186   *Chiara Giorgetti*

critical with the passing of the time, as the prosecutions and conclusions of cases took a long time and the costs increased.[45]

The different stance between European countries and the USA really becomes evident with their respective postures towards the ICC. While the USA was involved in the negotiations and drafting of the ICC Statute, it later became increasingly and vocally strongly opposed to it.

President Clinton's administration was involved in the negotiation of the Rome Statute of the ICC, and signed it when he was President. He did so while expressing reservations about how the Court would exercise jurisdiction over Americans. Congress was also opposed and the Statute was never presented to the Senate for advice and consent.[46] President George W. Bush expressed much stronger concerns while he was president, especially after 9/11 and in the context of American military activities in Afghanistan.[47] President Bush went a step forward and famously "unsigned" the treaty by sending a letter announcing the USA's intention not to sign the treaty and thus confirming that it had no remaining obligations arising from its signature.[48]

American resistance to the ICC centered around the concern that the ICC might not guarantee Americans their constitutionally guaranteed protections. Critics alleged that the ICC might deprive Americans of their right to due process by prosecuting them in a way inconsistent with American ideas of criminal procedure. This concern became especially acute in relation to American troops operating in Afghanistan. While the USA had not ratified the Rome Statute, the Statute had entered into force for Afghanistan, so American troops in that country were potentially subject to ICC jurisdiction for crimes committed in Afghani territory.

---

[45]   John Cerone, *US Attitudes towards International Criminal Courts and Tribunals, in* THE SWORD AND THE SCALE (Cesare Romano ed., 2009) and John Cerone, *Dynamic Equilibrium: The Evolution of US Attitudes towards International Criminal Courts and Tribunals,* 18 EUR. J. INT'L L. 277 (2007).

[46]   ABA, *U.S. Opposition to the International Criminal Court* (16 November 2018) www .americanbar.org/publications/human_rights_magazine_home/human_rights_vol30_2003/ winter2003/irr_hr_winter03_usopposition/.

[47]   William A. Schabas, *United States Hostility to the International Criminal Court: It's All About the Security Council,* 15 EUR. J. INT'L L. 702 (2004) 703. See also, Megan A. Fairlie, *The United States and the International Criminal Court Post-Bush: A Beautiful Courtship but an Unlikely Marriage,* 29 BERK J. INT'L L, 528 (2011) and Dawn Rothe and Christopher W. Mullins, *The International Criminal Court and United States Opposition,* 45 CRIME, L. & SOC. CH. 201 (2006) 201.

[48]   *Letter from Secretary of State Bolton to the Secretary General of the United Nations* (6 May 2002) h2001-2009.state.gov/r/pa/prs/ps/2002/9968.htm.

The US also enacted laws to undermine the ICC and threatened withholding economic aid from countries who supported the ICC.[49] It also signed over 100 bilateral immunity agreements with third parties to ensure that Americans could not be extradited to face ICC jurisdiction.[50] In response to this, the EU issued guiding principles on bilateral non-surrender agreements arguing that concluding them would be inconsistent with the ICC Statute.

Upon his election, President Obama sought to reengage with the work of ICC, yet never tried to get the Rome Statute through Senate.[51] During the Obama administration, the USA cooperated with the Court in its investigation, especially in Uganda, and also delivered one suspect to the Court.[52]

It is with the election of Donald Trump, however, that things changed drastically and for the worse.[53] President Trump raised the confrontation with the ICC to a new level.[54] In his speech to the 2018 UN General Assembly, President Trump explained that

> the United States will provide no support in recognition to the International Criminal Court. As far as America is concerned, the ICC has no jurisdiction, no legitimacy, and no authority. The ICC claims near-universal jurisdiction over the citizens of every country, violating all principles of justice, fairness, and due process. We will never surrender America's sovereignty to an unelected, unaccountable, global bureaucracy. America is governed by Americans. We reject the ideology of globalism, and we embrace the doctrine of patriotism.[55]

---

[49] See, for example, the American Servicemembers' Protection Act and subsequent amendments which, inter alia, prohibited obligating funds for "use by or in support of" the ICC and requires the US to protect to "the maximum extent possible, against criminal prosecutions" by the ICC. 2002 Supplemental Appropriations Act for Further Recovery from and Response to Terrorist Attacks on the United States, Pub. L. No. 107–206, § §2001–2015, 116 Stat. 820 (2002), https://www.govinfo.gov/content/pkg/PLAW-107publ206/html/PLAW-107publ206.htm.

[50] Matthew Lee, US Relationship with International Court Crashes under Trump, AP News (10 September 2018) apnews.com/c38b08a851a84b9da1a7117c7a2eb455/US-relationship-with-international-court-crashes-under-Trump.

[51] See, for example the special briefing by Harold H. Koh and Stephen J. Rapp, US Engagement with the ICC and the Outcome of the Recently Concluded Review Conference (June 15, 2010) 2009–2017.state.gov/j/gcj/us_releases/remarks/2010/143178.htm.

[52] Lee, supra note 50.

[53] US Issues Threat to War Crimes Court BBC News (Sept. 11, 2018) www.bbc.com/news/world-us-canada-45474864.

[54] See, generally, Harold H. Koh, The Challenges and Future of International Justice, Panel Discussion at the NYU Center for Global Affairs (Oct. 27, 2010) 2009–2017.state.gov/s/l/releases/remarks/150497.htm.

[55] Remarks by President Trump to the 73rd Session of the United Nations General Assembly (Sept. 28, 2018).

188   Chiara Giorgetti

The hostility grew deeper as the ICC Prosecutor is conducting preliminary investigations for possible crimes committed by US military in Afghanistan. Former National Security Advisor John Bolton declared that the USA would use "any means possible" to protect Americans from "unjust prosecution from an illegitimate court." Bolton stated that the USA will not cooperate with the ICC as "for all intents and purposes, the ICC is already dead to us."[56] Declarations were also followed by concrete actions.[57] The Trump administration affirmed that to the extent permitted by US law, it would ban ICC judges and prosecutors from entering its territory, sanction their US funds and even prosecute them in the US criminal justice system.[58]

7.3 THE EU, THE USA AND THE IMPLOSION OF THE DISPUTE RESOLUTION MECHANISM OF THE WORLD TRADE ORGANIZATION: A WTO WITHOUT THE USA?

The WTO includes a complex and two-tiered dispute resolution mechanism, concluded by WTO members in the Dispute Settlement Understanding (DSU), and composed of a Dispute Settlement Body (DSB) and Appellate Body (AB). The DSU has been referred to as the "crown jewel" of the WTO and it has also been one of the most active international dispute resolution mechanisms in existence.[59] Since 1995, when it was reformed and given more binding powers, it has heard over 360 cases.[60] The DSU hears disputes that may arise when a WTO member alleges that another member violated an agreement or a commitment it made under the WTO, in relation to any of the trade rules it includes. It therefore only hears cases between members and not by private companies or individuals. The European Union became a member of the WTO in 1995 and has brought a number of disputes for resolution at the DSU. The US has been the most frequent user of the WTO DSU. It has brought over 120 cases and acted as responded in more than 150 cases and as a third party 150 cases. When bringing a case, the USA prevailed on over

---

[56]   See https://www.bbc.com/news/world-us-canada-45474864.

[57]   Id.

[58]   See, for example, Marty Lederman, Does Trump Have Legal Authority to Follow Through on John Bolton's Threats to the International Criminal Court? Justsecurity (Sept. 20, 2018) /www .justsecurity.org/60705/explains-boltons-threats-icc/.

[59]   Cosette D. Creamer, From the WTO's Crown Jewel to its Crown of Thorns, 113 AJIL Unbound 51 (2019).

[60]   Prior to the Uruguay Round agreement any member could veto the decision of the dispute resolution body. Now, rulings are automatically adopted unless there is a consensus to reject the ruling. See, generally, William J. Davey, The WTO Dispute Settlement System: The First Ten Years, 8 J. Int'l Econ. L. 17 (2005).

International Courts and Tribunals in the US and in Europe 189

90 percent of the adjudicated issues, while as a respondent it has lost on about 89 percent.[61] In the Fall of 2018, the USA initiated several complaints at the WTO against Russia, the European Union, Mexico, Turkey and Canada including for retaliatory tariffs imposed as a response to the US imposed steel and aluminum tariffs.[62]

The DSB is composed of all WTO members, and thus has the same composition as the General Council, just in a different guise. A case begins when a WTO Member State brings it to the DSB. After a period of mandatory consultation of sixty days, the DSB may decide to establish a panel of experts to consider the case. The Experts Panel, in an expedited procedure that takes less than one year, decides the case and issues a report, which becomes a ruling by the DSB within sixty days of issuance, unless it is rejected by consensus by the DSB. This "reverse consensus rule" – which requires all parties including the two disputing parties (and thus also the presumed winner) to block the approval of the report – makes the DSB an effective forum to resolve trade dispute.[63]

A panel ruling can be appealed by either party to the Appellate Body (AB) within sixty days of its issuance. The panel report is not considered for adoption by the DSB until after completion of the appeal.

The AB is composed of seven members, appointed by the DSB for a four-year term, renewable once. AB members are chosen among people of recognized authority who also have demonstrated expertise in international trade law and generally of the subject matters of the covered agreements.[64] They are to be broadly representative of the overall WTO membership and are required to be unaffiliated with any government. Generally, there is an AB member from the USA and one from Europe. Appeals are heard in divisions of three members selected randomly for each appeal. The AB can uphold, modify or reverse the legal finding and conclusions of the report.

---

[61] Dan Ikenson, *US Trade Laws and the Sovereignty Canard*, Forbes (March 2017) www .forbes.com/sites/danikenson/2017/03/09/u-s-trade-laws-and-the-sovereignty-canard /#754ae02e203f.

[62] See Kathleen Claussen, *Trade War Battles: The International Front*, Lawfareblog (July 27, 2018) www.lawfareblog.com/surveying-trade-war-battlefield-international-front.

[63] See generally, WTO, *Understanding the WTO: Settling Disputes*, https://www.wto.org/eng lish/thewto_e/whatis_e/tif_e/disp1_e.htm.

[64] Art. 17, Dispute Settlement Understanding, Annex 2 of the WTO Agreement, https://www .wto.org/english/tratop_e/dispu_e/dsu_e.htm. *See* also, generally, WTO, Appellate Body Members, available at: https://www.wto.org/english/tratop_e/dispu_e/ab_members_descrp_e .htm. The DSB also monitors the implementation of decisions and can authorize retaliation when a country does not comply with a ruling.

The USA has for the past several years complained of judicial overreach by the AB and its "disregard for the rules set by the WTO members and adding to or diminishing rights or obligation under the WTO Agreement."[65] The USA asserts that by doing so the AB has made US trade remedies less effective at addressing unfair dumping, countervailing duties and subsidies.[66] It also argues that the judicial overreach restricts its ability to regulate in the public interest or protect US workers and businesses against unfair trade practice. The USA has also expressed concern for the extend in which AB has used obiter dicta and made reference to their own jurisprudence.[67] Procedurally, the USA also complains that the AB is often not able to produce its reports by the mandated ninety-day period. More recently, the USA criticized the practice of allowing AB members finish working on cases after their terms had expired without prior permission form the WTO DSU.[68]

These criticisms predate the Trump administration and were shared by previous administrations, including under Presidents Bush and Obama.[69] Indeed, other members of the WTO agree with some of the criticisms, and share some of the concerns about the role of the dispute settlement mechanisms, the limited resources of the DSU and the dissatisfaction over the perceived judicial overreach of the DSU and interpretations of WTO rules which are seen as adding and diminishing the rights and obligations of its members.[70]

However, while disagreement with the DSB is not uncommon, President Trump has escalated the criticism and confrontation to a new level.[71] President Trump expressed deep concern about the World Trade

---

[65] US Trade Representative, *2019 Trade Policy Agenda and 2018 Annual Report of the President of the Unites States on the Trade Agreements Program* (March 2019) 148 https://ustr.gov/sites/def ault/files/2019_Trade_Policy_Agenda_and_2018_Annual_Report.pdf

[66] For a useful explanation, *see* Steve Charnovitz, *A Defense of the Beleaguered WTO Appellate Body*, Int'l Econ. L. & Pol'y Blog (May 9, 2019) https://worldtradelaw.typepad.com/ielpblog/ 2019/05/a-defense-of-the-beleaguered-wto-appellate-body.html.

[67] *See* Jessica Gladstone, *The WTO Appellate Body Crisis – A Way Forward*, Clifford Chance (Nov. 2019) available: https://www.cliffordchance.com/content/dam/cliffordchance/briefings/ 2019/11/the-wto-appellate-body-crisis-a-way-forward.pdf.

[68] James McBride & Andrew Chatzky, *What's Next for the WTO?* Council on Foreign Relations (Dec. 10, 2019) www.cfr.org/backgrounder/whats-next-wto.

[69] Zeeshan Aleem, *Why Trump's Plan to Defy the WTO Isn't as Reckless as It Sounds*, Vox (March 8, 2017) www.vox.com/policy-and-politics/2017/3/8/14766228/trump-trade-wto.

[70] *See*, generally, Tetyana Payosova, Gary Clyde Hufbauer & Jeffrey J. Schott, *The Dispute Settlement Crisis in the World Trade Organization: Causes and Cures*, Peterson Institute for International Economics (March 2018).

[71] David A. Gantz, *An Existential Threat to WTO Dispute Settlement: Blocking Appointment of Appellate Body Members by the United States*, AR. L. STU. DISC. 18–26, http://dx.doi.org/10 .2139/ssrn.3216633.P.7.

Organization in speeches to the UN General Assembly. He claims that the WTO is rigged against American interests and his administration will not necessarily respect the rulings that come from the WTO dispute resolution mechanism. Trump continually laments a poor record of America's success in that dispute resolution forum.[72]

Recent practice by the USA also shows a remarkable departure from the WTO framework, in terms of its acceptance of multilateral adjudication, of prohibition of counterretaliation, the regulation of remedies and norms enforcement.[73] The Trump administration has at the same time engaged in trade wars with many countries, including China, in defiance of WTO norms. President Trump also prefers bilateral treaties, rather than the regional or multinational treaties used in prior administrations. Moreover, President Trump's criticism also focuses on the DSB specifically.[74] The opposition is targeted to substantive and procedural characteristics of the institution itself, and not only the decisions it takes.[75] In this sense, it is an existential opposition to the DSB.

Indeed, after achieving considerable success and support, the DBS has changed from "the WTO's Crown Jewel to its Crown of Thorns."[76] In 2017, the USA started blocking the appointment of AB members thus "killing the WTO from the inside."[77] Because all panel reports can be appealed, and they are not considered for adoption by the DSB until the appeal is finalized, no report can become final until a decision of the AB on the appeal is issued. If the AB is unable to convene because of lack of members to constitute a quorum, then the DBS is effectively paralyzed. It cannot finalize any decision.

And indeed, in December 2019, the AB has become essentially paralyzed. The terms of two of the three remaining members (from the USA and India) expired. Members of the DSU have been unable to appoint any new members to the AB when terms expired because the US has vetoed all proposals.

---

[72] Andrew Walker, *Is Trump the WTO's Biggest Threat?* BBC News (Dec. 8, 2017) www.bbc.com /news/business-42200390.

[73] *See* generally, Rachel Brewster, *WTO Dispute Settlement: Can We Go Back Again?*, 113 AJIL UNBOUND 61–66 (2019) (concluding that "The path ahead seems like a much rockier road than the last two decades, with the prospect of protracted trade wars and uncertain trade law The WTO's ability to be an important constraint on states will be substantially weakened. Although the WTO will continue to operate, its influence is most likely to wane as the international trade system returns to more unilateral adjudication and remedies.")

[74] Gantz, *supra* note 71.

[75] Madsen, Cebulak & Wiebusch, *supra* note 32, at 220.

[76] Creamer, *supra* note 59, at 52.

[77] Philip Blekinsop, *U.S. Trade Offensive Takes out WTO as Global Arbiter*, Reuter Business News (Dec. 10, 2019) reuters.com. *See also* Eduardo Porter, *Trump's Endgame Could Be the Undoing of Global Rules*, N.Y. Times (Oct. 31, 2017) as reported in *Id.* p. 51.

192   *Chiara Giorgetti*

Appointment must be made by consensus, so it is easy to block appointments, as any member effectively holds a veto when it votes against any new appointments. Three is the minimum number of members required for the body to be able to hear and decide cases. Because of the USA's obstruction, the AB only has one member, it cannot constitute new panels. Since December 2019, the AB has only been able to continue hearing cases that had already began, but no new panel can be established. If an appeal cannot be heard, the entire DSU could come to a halt.

The USA has also repeatedly vetoed the initiation of a process to nominate and appoint new members.[78] It reiterated that it was not ready to agree to launch the process to fill the vacancies on the AB.[79] Instead, the USA urged WTO members to address its concerns.[80] Not only is the rhetoric in the Trump administration much more confrontational and acrimonious than in previous administrations, the real problem is that no negotiable (or even not negotiable) solution has been suggested for discussion and as a way to address the stalemate.[81] In its 2019 Trade Policy Agenda, US Trade Representative Robert Lighthizer did not propose any specific solutions to solve the impasse. Lighthizer foresaw that the DSB would continue to work on individual disputes, while the USA would continue to raise its "systemic concerns with Appellate Body overreaching and press for WTO Members to take responsibility to ensure the WTO dispute settlement system operates as intended and agreed in the DSU."[82] The Trade Agenda, however, does not offer specific details on how this can be done.[83] By blocking new appointments and refusing to negotiate any solutions, the USA is effectively depriving the DSU of air. The DSU is, slowly but surely, imploding. The US posture on the DSU is in an

---

[78]   *See* for example, Tom Miles, *U.S. Blocks WTO Judge Reappointment as Dispute Settlement Crisis Looms*, Reuters (Aug. 27, 2018) www.reuters.com/article/us-usa-trade-wto/u-s-blocks-wto-judge-reappointment-as-dispute-settlement-crisis-looms-idUSKCN1LC19O.

[79]   For a helpful explanation of how selection of AB members may affect the interpretation of the WTO rules, *see* Gregory C. Shaffer, Manfred Elsig & Sergio Puig, *The Law and Politics of WTO Dispute Settlement*, in THE POLITICS OF INTERNATIONAL LAW (Wayne Sandholtz & Christopher Whytock eds., 2016).

[80]   USTR, *2019 Trade Policy Agenda and 2018 Annual Report of the President of the Unites States on the Trade Agreements Program*, 148, ustr.gov/sites/default/files/2019_Trade_Policy_Agenda_and_2018_Annual_Report.pdf.

[81]   For an insightful view on possible solutions to the impasse, *see* James Bacchus, *How to Solve the WTO Judicial Crisis*, Cato Institute (Aug. 6, 2018) www.cato.org/blog/how-solve-wto-judicial-crisis.

[82]   *Id.*

[83]   *See*, for example, U.S. Statement Delivered by Ambassador Dennis Shea, *Informal Process on Matters Related to the Functioning of the Appellate Body* (May 7, 2019) https://geneva.usmission.gov/2019/05/08/ambassador-sheas-statement-at-the-wto-general-council-meeting-agenda-items-4–6-7/.

existential threat.[84] In the absence of specific actions, the DSU will most likely cease to be operational.[85] The demise of the DSU would be a seismic change that would eviscerate the core of the rule-based trade system. In the words of the EU Commissioner for Trade Cecilia Malmström "Without the WTO, there are no rules" indeed, international trade "would be anarchic. Countries would be bullied, companies would fall victim to unfair practices – there would be no reliability, no stability. So we need to repair and stand up for the system."[86]

For its part, the EU recently took the lead and proposed a set of specific reforms to address the concerns that lead to the present crisis.[87] In a Joint Communication to the WTO, the EU and other member states made some practical suggestions on how to reform the DSU, including certain amendments on specific issues related to transitional role of outgoing AB members, appellate proceedings deadlines, concerns related to AB panel reviews of panel finding on domestic law and the concerns that the AB made findings on issues not necessary to resolve a dispute. In particular, on the issue of the AB use of precedent, the Joint Communication suggested an increased "channel of communication" between the AB and the DSB with an annual meeting between the political and judicial bodies, whereby governments could express their views on jurisprudence and approach of the AB.[88] The EU is united in the effort to address the concerns raised about the DSU from within the organization itself. Recognizing that dissatisfaction with the WTO exists, the EU is moving towards a reform to the DSU to make the DSU more acceptable and ensure its continued existence. However, reform cannot be done alone.

Moreover, to bypass the implosion of the DSU, the EU has also proposed an interim appeals system based on Article 25 of the DSU by which appeals could be resolved by a panel of three arbitrators, made up of former AB members and

---

[84] See Gantz, *supra* note 71.

[85] For a possible course of action, *see* Pieter Jan Kuiper, *Guest Post from Pieter Jan Kuiper on the US Attack on the Appellate Body*, International Economic Law and Policy Blog (Nov. 15, 2017) https://worldtradelaw.typepad.com/ielpblog/2017/11/guest-post-from-pieter-jan-kuiper-professor-of-the-law-of-international-economic-organizations-at-the-faculty-of-law-of-th.html.

[86] As reported by David A. Wemer, *Europa Ready to Help with the WTO Reform*, Atlantic Council (Jan. 10, 2019) www.atlanticcouncil.org/blogs/new-atlanticist/europe-ready-to-help-with-wto-reform.

[87] WTO, *Communication from the European Union, China, Canada, India, Norway, New Zealand, Switzerland, Australia, Republic of Korea, Iceland, Singapore and Mexico to the General Council* (Joint Communication) (Nov. 26, 2018) http://trade.ec.europa.eu/doclib/do cs/2018/november/tradoc_157514.pdf.

[88] See Jessica Gladstone, *The WTO Appellate Body Crisis – A Way Forward*, Clifford Chance (Nov. 2019) https://www.cliffordchance.com/content/dam/cliffordchance/briefings/2019/11/th e-wto-appellate-body-crisis-a-way-forward.pdf.

194 *Chiara Giorgetti*

working procedurally in a way similar to the AB.[89] To implement this proposal, the EU has signed agreements with Canada in July 2019 and with Norway in October 2019. This is a viable interim solution. However, it is based on voluntary agreements and does not include the USA.

This shift in attitudes towards the DSU is a major and new difference between the USA and Europe.[90] Indeed, while WTO members agree that a reform is necessary, they disagree fundamentally on the kind of reform necessary. It seems likely that the DSU will shut down. If it did, it would be very difficult to resurrect it. The WTO may be damaged beyond repair, and its legal basis would be fundamentally undermined. Would this entail a world trade dispute resolution mechanism without the USA?

The diametrical difference in the posture of the USA and the EU in trade dispute adjudication exemplifies a new understanding of international trade policies.[91] Overall, the USA is becoming more isolationist, disengaged from Obama's preference for multilateralism and opposed to its long-standing support for free trade. Support for the Trans-Pacific Partnership (TPP), for example, vanished quickly and no candidate supported it in the 2016 Presidential campaign. It is not even an issue so far in the 2020 campaign. As Harlan Cohen observes, the new in-trade narrative on trade

> might be a type of neo-mercantilism associated most closely with Donald Trump and the populist right. In this view, trade is a zero- sum competition for resources, in which global, multilateral rules unfairly shackle entrepreneurial and enterprising states. States should be free to make the best deals they can (or to act unilaterally if need be) to maximize their own share of the spoils. [92]

He calls this the "you get what you take" theory of trade which is based on a view of trade as warfare competition, where the best competitors get the greatest share.[93]

One possibility is that members will focus on alternatives to the WTO. The USA will focus on bilateral trade agreements, while the EU will continue to

---

[89] William A. Reinsch & Jack Caporal, *Article 25: An Effective Way to Avert the WTO Crisis?* CSIS (Jan. 24, 2019) www.csis.org/analysis/article-25-effective-way-avert-wto-crisis.

[90] For an historical perspective on international trade, *see* THE EU, THE WTO, AND THE NAFTA: TOWARDS A COMMON LAW OF INTERNATIONAL TRADE? (J.H. Weiler, ed., 2001).

[91] *See* the excellent backgrounder prepared by the International Center for Trade and Sustainable Development, *WTO Members Intensify Debate Over Resolving Appellate Body Impasse* (June 28, 2018) https://www.ictsd.org/bridges-news/bridges/news/wto-members-intensify-debate-over-resolving-appellate-body-impasse.

[92] Harlan Grant Cohen, *What Is International Trade Law For?* 113 AM. J. INT'L L. 334 (2019).

[93] *Id.*

build a more multilateral and regional system.[94] Former WTO Director General Pascal Lamy has expressed concerned about a "lonesome cowboy" scenario in which the USA either quits the WTO or the remaining Members build a WTO minus the US.[95] He says "if a major power does not want to play by the rules of international discipled trade, the others will have to react."[96]

The damages sustained as a consequence of this battle may take time to heal or may completely reshape how disputes are resolved in international trade.[97]

7.4 INVESTOR-STATE DISPUTE SETTLEMENT: CONSCIOUS DECOUPLING

ISDS is a unique dispute resolution mechanism. It is a hybrid mechanism whereby an investor, an individual or a company, can bring a case against a state for violation of international law related to an investment made in that country.[98] The scope of the review is generally provided for in a bilateral investment agreement (BIT), regional agreement or, more rarely, in a contract or domestic law. The case is usually heard by an arbitral tribunal composed of three members, each party selects one arbitrator and the third (presiding) arbitrator is selected by the parties together, the selected arbitrators or a neutral appointing authority.[99] International conventions, principally the International Convention for Settlement of Investment Disputes (ICSID) and the arbitration rules of the United Nations Commission on International Trade Law (UNCITRAL), provide specific jurisdictional requirements and procedural rules.

ISDS has become an effective mechanism to resolve disputes and has enjoyed increasing levels of success, as more and more cases are filed and heard by several arbitration institutions. A record 306 cases were administered by ICSID in 2019, up from 63 in 2003.[100] Differently from trade disputes and

---

[94] European Commission, Negotiations and Agreements, http://ec.europa.eu/trade/policy/cou ntries-and-regions/negotiations-and-agreements/.

[95] *See* Tom Miles, *WTO Should Prepare for Life Without U.S., Ex-Chief Lamy Says*, Reuters (Feb. 19, 2018) www.reuters.com/article/us-usa-wto/wto-should-prepare-for-life-without-u-s-e x-chief-lamy-says-idUSKCN1G326S.

[96] *Id.*

[97] Sergio Puig, *The United States-Mexico-Canada Agreement: A Glimpse into the Geoeconomic World Order*, 113 AJIL UNBOUND 56–60 (2019).

[98] *See*, generally, Anthea Roberts, *Clash of Paradigms: Actors and Analogies Shaping the Investment Treaty System*, 107 AM. J. INT'L L. 45 (2013).

[99] *See* Chiara Giorgetti, *Who Decides Who Decides In International Investment Arbitration?*, 35 U. PA. J. INT'L L. 431 (2013).

[100] ICSID, 2019 ANNUAL REPORT, 19, icsid.worldbank.org/en/Pages/resources/ICSID-Annual-Report.aspx.

the DSU, ISDS is not a centralized system and does not have one central forum to hear disputes. Rather, these disputes are heard by *ad hoc* tribunals, with jurisdiction to hear only that case. Tribunals are *functo officio* – dissolved – after they have finally decided the one dispute they have been charged with.

Both the USA and Europe have historically been supporters and frequent users of ISDS as an effective dispute resolution mechanism.[101] As a policy choice, the USA has favored ISDS. For example, it has developed its own model BIT that has included a dispute resolution clause that offered ISDS mechanisms, including under ICSID and UNCITRAL rules.[102] It also included in the North-America Free Trade Agreement (NAFTA), which has contributed to the increased use of ISDS.[103] Similarly, European countries are parties to numerous BITs and have used ISDS frequently. While intra-EU use of ISDS is discouraged and has been ruled not compatible with EU law, most recent treaties negotiated by the EU itself with third countries offer ISDS, and aim at the creation of a permanent court to hear international investment claims.[104]

More recently, however, the USA and Europe have parted in significant ways in their support and policy towards ISDS.[105] The USA has radically changed its course, and from eager supporter of ISDS has become a skeptic. The newly negotiated US-Mexico-Canada Agreement, for example, significantly scaled back the use of ISDS as a dispute resolution mechanism available to all the parties.[106] In the final text, there is essentially no ISDS between the USA and Canada (with little exception for legacy and pending claims), and the use of ISDS between Mexico and the USA is much more limited than

---

[101] AUGUST REINISCH, ADVANCED INTRODUCTION TO INTERNATIONAL INVESTMENT LAW, Elgar Advanced Introductions series (2020).

[102] The 2012 Model US BIT is available on the State Department site at: https://ustr.gov/sites/default/files/BIT%20text%20for%20ACIEP%20Meeting.pdf.

[103] Nathalie Bernasconi-Osterwalder, *USMCS Curbs How Much Investors Can Sue Countries – Sort of*, IISD, https://www.iisd.org/library/usmca-investors.

[104] *See* Laurens Ankersmit, *Achmea: The Beginning of the End of ISDS in and with Europe?* Investment Treaty News (Apr. 28, 2018) www.iisd.org/itn/2018/04/24/achmea-the-beginning-of-the-end-for-isds-in-and-with-europe-laurens-ankersmit/ and ISSD, *Achmea judgement fall-out: 22 EU member states agree to terminate intra-EU BITs*, Investment Arbitration News (Apr. 23, 2019) (stating that twenty-two EU member states endorsed a political declaration in 2019, announcing a series of actions involving existing intra-EU BITs and upcoming or ongoing investment arbitration). For examples of new EU-negotiated treaties, see the treaty between EU and Canada (CETA), European Commission, EU-Canada Comprehensive Economic and Trade Agreement (Apr. 12, 2019) ec.europa.eu/trade/policy/in-focus/ceta/.

[105] *See*, generally, Lori Wallach, *The US Drops ISDS*, The Globalist (Jan. 24, 2020) www.theglobalist.com/united-states-european-union-trade-isds-usmca-uncitral-mic/.

[106] *Id.*

it used to be with NAFTA. Note that because Mexico and Canada are parties to other international investment treaties, they will still have access to ISDS with other countries, but not with the US. The reduced reliance over ISDS in the USMCA is therefore very much a deliberate choice of the USA. Similarly, the Trump administration notifications related to trade negotiation with the UK excludes ISDS. The Trump administration also withdrew the US support and quickly disengaged from the Trans-Pacific Partnership, which had been negotiated by the Obama administration. There have been fewer vocal criticisms of the Trump administration towards the use ISDS than for other ICTs, yet the departure from previous stands is undisputable and consequential.

ISDS as a hybrid mechanism has not been immune to criticisms. Traditionally, opposition to ISDS has focused on alleged inequality between parties (for example a wealthy investor against a small developing state), the unbalanced nature of international obligations (which mainly fall upon States, and not investor) or the contended independence and impartiality of arbitrators (who, differently from judges, are nominated by the parties themselves and continue to hold other positions which may create conflicts).[107] Such concerns have been raised mostly by civil society, smaller respondent states and other stakeholders.

Prompted in part by these concerns, UNCITRAL has initiated a process of reform of ISDS.[108] The EU has taken the lead in the reform process and has suggested the creation of a Multilateral Investment Court (MIC) which would transform ISDS into a permanent resolution mechanism, loosely modelled after the DSB of the WTO, with permanent judges available to hear investor-states disputes.[109] In doing so, the EU is representing all EU members states and has negotiated on their behalf at UNCITRAL.

The EU is the leading proponent of a permanent multilateral investment court that would replace, for extra-EU investments, the prevailing system of *ad hoc* investment treaty arbitration entirely. While UNCITRAL negotiations are occurring, the EU has included a permanent bilateral investment court system in its most recent investment and free trade agreements, including the Comprehensive Economic and Trade Agreement between the EU and

---

[107] See the insightful BACKLASH AGAINST INVESTMENT ARBITRATION (Michael Waibel, Asha Kaushal, Kyo-Hwa Chung & Claire Balchin, eds., 2010).

[108] UNCITRAL Working Group III, *Investor-State Dispute Settlement Reform*, https://uncitral .un.org/en/working_groups/3/investor-state.

[109] European Commission, *Multilateral Investment Court*, Legislative Train Schedule (Dec. 15, 2019), www.europarl.europa.eu/legislative-train/theme-a-balanced-and-progressive-trade-policy-to-harness-globalisation/file-multilateral-investment-court-(mic). See also Council of the European Union, *Negotiating Directives for a Convention Establishing a Multilateral Court for the Settlement of Investment Disputes*, 12981/17 (Mar. 1, 2018).

Canada (CETA), the EU-Singapore Free Trade Agreement (FTA) and the EU-Vietnam Free Trade Agreement.[110]

On matters of ISDS, the USA and Europe have again taken opposite sides. Both are interested in reform, but they are going on opposite directions. The EU proposal is a radical change to ISDS, a change aimed at strengthening ICTs by establishing a permanent court. Conversely, the USA is going toward less reliance on the international process, in favor of a domestic system. Though less confrontational, the change is none less consequential.

7.5 CONCLUSION: WHITHER THE WEST?

In the last twenty years, the position of the "West" vis-à-vis ICTs has increasingly diverged. While European countries generally – and the EU specifically – have embraced ICTs, the USA has been increasingly reluctant to engage and more openly opposed to ICTs. Moreover, though the USA has generally been lukewarm towards supranational human rights tribunals, its opposition to the ICC has become increasingly concrete and vocal. The new opposition towards international disputes resolutions mechanisms in the economic areas is, additionally, a major change in the US ICTs posture and deepened the divide between the USA and Europe. It is also becoming clearer that the administration of President Trump is posing an existential threat to ICTs. His opposition to all forms of international adjudications is firm and an essential feature of his "America First" policy.

What has led to this different outcome in places which, in many other aspects, behave and are similar? There are some historical and structural reasons, and also some more contingent explanations.

Europe and the USA share a common but different historical background that resulted in profoundly different attitudes to international law and ICTs. Twentieth century Europe witnessed appalling wars, fought in its territory, that devastated the continent and changed it radically. Europe was the main location not only of the fighting, but also of terrible human rights abuses of civilians. Western Europe's support for human rights and its policy towards international courts and tribunals in the areas of human rights and international criminal responsibility were shaped by its experience. Indeed, many European countries saw the establishment of international bodies that could guarantee essential human rights protections and prosecute those responsible for violations of humanitarian and international criminal law as

---

[110] *See, generally,* CHIARA GIORGETTI, THE SELECTION AND REMOVAL OF ARBITRATORS IN INVESTOR-STATE DISPUTE SETTLEMENT 18–22 (2019).

an important factor to guarantee future peace and security, as well as economic and political stability.

This historical context also influenced how Europe developed structurally. Having experienced the horrors of war firsthand, European states have been more willing to forego some level of sovereignty to ensure that disputes can be settled peacefully.[111] This logic can make adverse rulings in the ICJ, the jurisdiction of the ICC and the role of the ECtHR more acceptable. States were driven to cooperate in order to ensure security and sovereign interests.

Europe also emerged from World War II a diminished power: its economy was in ruins and it had lost most of its colonial territory. It was also a smaller political power, located between the two major super powers, with a fundamental interest in cooperation and power delegation. Many European countries recognized the benefit and added strength of espousing unity and cooperation, including in international courts and tribunals. Cooperation among states would ensure security and so also protected sovereign interests. The creation of the European Communities first and of the European Union later catalyzed those sentiments. The European Union emerged from a long trend of increasing integration where significant decisions are routinely taken by supranational institutions. Moreover, with the increasing success of the EU, additional issues and areas became ripe for cooperation and coordination, including a strong support for regional and international courts and tribunals.[112] Trust and respect for international courts and tribunals can also be explained by the fact that European states are likely more used to seeing the potential benefits of international courts as supranational courts are embedded in the European Union system.[113]

Differently, the USA emerged from World War II a stronger power both ideologically and economically, capable of influencing global politics. The USA quickly became a superpower, and then, with the end of the Cold War,

---

[111] Rosalyn Higgins, *The ICJ, the ECJ, and the Integrity of International Law*, 52 INT'L & COMP. L.Q. 1 (2003).

[112] *See* Karen Alter, *The Global Spread of European Style International Courts*, 35 W. EUR. POL. 135 (2012).

[113] *See id. See* also Murphy, *supra* note 8 (describing the institutionalist perspective as it relates to European acceptance of international courts). It is also important to recall that the USA is a federal system and this is structurally important. In an interesting twist, contrary to European states and EU, the federal structure has fostered a policy of delegation of powers centrifugally, towards individual States. A series of checks and balance makes the USA's ability to embrace international decisions, and international disputes mechanisms more broadly, difficult. Coupled with exceptionalism, USA's reticent and cautious position towards ICTs, and more specifically towards the ICJ and international human rights tribunals, and its preference for addressing certain issues, namely human rights violations, domestically rather than through international courts, can be understood through this structural prism.

the "only remaining superpower." The stronger economic and political position also led to an increased policy of exceptionalism, which is also externalized as deserving a special place in the international arena. The USA was able to design zones of influence and develop agreements to encourage free trade and economic development, and an external policy targeted at countering communism and encouraging capitalism. Its outlook was based on realism and on the realization of its hegemonic power. Realists believe that states are the principal actors in the international system, and special attention is afforded to large powers as they have the most influence on the international stage. As such, the USA is guided in its action by its desire to be and continue to be a unique power, with certain privileges as well as obligations. This has also been evident more recently, with the war on terror. The USA's policy vis-à-vis international courts and tribunals can also be explained by exceptionalism and realism. Its support for the ICTY and ICTR, but not for the ICC, are telling examples.

At the same time, exceptionalism has also translated in policy choices based on liberalism and cooperation. Thus, while pursuing national interests, these interests also include the support of international law and effective dispute resolution mechanisms. The traditional support for the WTO and ISDS should be understood with this idea in mind.

However, as the power of the USA is declining and its rivalry with China increasingly shapes its policies, new populist and inner-looking views are taking hold. Indeed, the change in US policy towards WTO and ISDS is an important shift in the US traditional positioning in international legal policy. A policy shift that moves exceptionalism towards isolationism. The presidency of Donald Trump is a clear move in that direction.

At their core, in sum, Europe and the USA have embraced divergent conceptions of specific issues related to international law.[114] This includes both in how international law is incorporated in each internal legal system and how international law is utilized externally.[115] It has also created substantial differences in their support of and engagement with ICTs.

These historical and structural differences have been compounded with a more contingent explanation brought about by the election of Donald Trump. As demonstrated in this chapter, there is increasingly little doubt that the Trump's administration represents a major shift in America's

---

[114] Guglielmo Verdirame, *"The Divided West": International Lawyers in Europe and America*, 18 EUR. J. INT'L L. 553 (2007) 554–58.
[115] M.S. *America and International Law – Why the Sheriff Should Follow the Law*, The Economist, May 23, 2014.

relationship with international courts. President Trump disregards and disparages international integration as a whole, including in ICTs.

President Trump rejects international cooperation and generally multilateralism. In his first two years of his administration, the USA has withdrawn from more international treaties, including many that included ICJ dispute resolution clause, than under any of his predecessors.[116] President Trump and his administration have harshly criticized both the WTO and the ICC, claiming the former unfairly cost American jobs and the latter was an illegitimate court, and have called the ICJ "politicized and ineffective."[117] Since his election, the USA has also blocked the nomination of DSB members, effectively blocking the working on the WTO DSU and have renounced to ISDS. The USA are also opting out of ISDS.

This unprecedent withdrawal, and often disregard for ICTs is likely to be costly. In the best of possible scenario, the USA's hostility towards ICTs will end with the Trump's administration. A new administration would reengage with the ICC, participate fully in ICJ proceedings, and reconnect with the WTO and ISDS. This seems improbable, however. The Trump's administrations set in motion certain mechanisms that will require time to stop. Its policy of undermining and disparaging international law may linger.[118] The rise of anti-globalization and populist movements in Europe will test its relationship with international courts and tribunals. The future might see some European states question ICTs and argue for a more regional approach. The WTO, the ICC, ISDS mechanisms are all undergoing reforms that will continue, and the result of which is still unknown. These reforms are likely to impactful. Of course, the hope remains that this reform will strengthen, not weaken, ICTs. The question remains if the USA will be on board.

---

[116] *See* Talmon, *supra* note 17, at 648.
[117] *See* Id. 658. *See* also *Remarks by President Trump to the 73d Session of the United Nations General Assembly* (Sept. 25, 2018) https://https://www.whitehouse.gov/briefings-statements/re marks-president-trump-73rd session united nations-general-assembly-new-york-ny.
[118] Hakimi, *supra* note 25.

8

Unravelling a Paradox of Shared Responsibility

The Disconnection between Substantive and Adjudicate Law

Andre Nollkaemper

8.1 INTRODUCTION

In this chapter I explore the paradox that when substantive principles of international responsibility increasingly accommodates situations of shared responsibility between multiple parties, international adjudication becomes less suited as a process for implementing such responsibility.

While international adjudication generally has shown remarkable development in the past decades, in various areas such growth has not kept pace with the transformations of substantive international law. One of such areas is the law on shared responsibility. International courts routinely apply various principles of responsibility.[1] However, principles relating to shared responsibility are only rarely invoked let alone applied in international adjudication. International courts rarely apply even the relatively well-established principles relating to shared responsibility, such as dual attribution,[2] aid and assistance,[3] or direction and control.[4] Moreover, they have been unable or unwilling to develop principles of shared responsibility that are still controversial, and that reflect different conceptions about what the substantive law of responsibility is or should be. Examples are the principle of circumvention[5] or, even more controversially, joint and several responsibility.[6] Among several other reasons,

---

[1] SIMON OLLESON, STATE RESPONSIBILITY BEFORE INTERNATIONAL AND DOMESTIC COURTS: THE IMPACT AND INFLUENCE OF THE ILC ARTICLES (2017).
[2] Int'l Law Comm'n, Articles on the Responsibility of International Organizations, Rep. on the Work of Its Sixty-Third Session, U.N. Doc. A/66/10, at Art. 19 (2011) [hereinafter ARIO].
[3] Int'l Law Comm'n, Articles on Responsibility of States for Internationally Wrongful Acts, Int'l Law Comm'n Y.B. 2001/II(2) Art. 16 [hereinafter ARSIWA]; ARIO, *supra* note 2, Art. 14.
[4] ARSIWA, *supra* note 3, Art. 17; ARIO, *supra* note 2, Art. 15.
[5] ARIO, *supra* note 2, Arts. 17 and 61.
[6] Roger P. Alford, *Apportioning Responsibility Among Joint Tortfeasors for International Law Violations*, 38 PEPP. L. REV. 233 (2011).

202

it appears that procedures for international adjudication often do not match the development of the substantive law of responsibility. A consequence is that international adjudicative law to some extent acts as a break on the further development of the substantive law of responsibility.

One may advance two propositions on the connection between the substantive and the adjudicative law of shared responsibility. One, and perhaps the more dominant one, is that the development of adjudicative law lags behind the development of the substantive law of responsibility, and that over time it will adjust. The other, and this is the proposition that I will explore here, is that the very development of the substantive law makes adjudication of shared responsibility claims more difficult. The substantive law is premised on the connection between multiple actors committing wrongful acts, whereas that very connection hampers adjudication. In this sense, we indeed would be able to speak of a paradox of shared responsibility.

I lay out the argument in four parts: (1) in an increasing number of situations, international responsibility is of a relational nature, (2) the substantive law of international responsibility is slowly adjusting to this relational nature, (3) procedures of international adjudication in many respects are not well suited for incorporating this relational nature, and (4) there are considerable differences between states, in terms of their willingness to submit themselves to adjudication of shared responsibility claims, event within 'the west', as a result of which responsibility will often will be shared between some states, but not all.

8.2 THE RELATIONAL NATURE OF INTERNATIONAL RESPONSIBILITY

A useful starting point for understanding the role of international courts in relation to shared responsibility is the articulation of a relational account of international responsibility. In this account, responsibility is not grounded in individual conduct but rather in the relations between actors. We can unpack the concept of "relational responsibility" by distinguishing between two constitutive elements of such a relational concept: interdependence of conduct (8.2.1) and interdependence of outcomes (8.2.2).

8.2.1 Interdependent Conduct

The first constitutive element of relational responsibility is that the conduct of the actors that contribute to harm often is interdependent. Such interdependence arises when the conduct of one state or international institution is conditional on and/or conducive to acts or omissions of other actors. Interdependent conduct may, but need not, take the form of concerted action. The observation by Lucas that "often our actions are concerted to form one coherent whole, and the action is described in terms of that whole, not of its individual constituents,"[7] captures the idea of interdependence in cases of concerted action. If cooperative conduct cannot be reduced to conduct of individual participating actors, responsibility needs to connect to the relationship between the individual actors. Individualizing responsibility may miss the point. Relational responsibility, then, does not refer to parallel individual wrongdoing, but involves interactions between actors that in combination cause harm.[8]

The extraordinary rendition practice illustrates the point: the contributions by the dozens of states that assisted the United States in extraordinary renditions would not have been sufficient in themselves to cause the outcome in terms of human rights violations. But in combination with the conduct of US agents, they were necessary for the result to occur, and on that basis both the assisting states and the United States can be held responsible.[9] We can thus speak of relational responsibility when multiple actors act together or contribute to each other's acts.[10]

The relatively well-established forms of such concerted action in the law of international responsibility, such as complicity,[11] direction and control,[12] and circumvention of responsibility,[13] are all characterized by the fact that the conduct of one actor influences or is influenced by the acts of other actors. Beyond these terms that appear in the Articles on the Responsibility of States for Internationally Wrongful Acts (ARSIWA) and the Articles on the Responsibility of International Organizations (ARIO), there are different terms that capture similar phenomena, such as contribution, collusion,

---

[7] JOHN RANDOLPH LUCAS, RESPONSIBILITY 75 (1995).

[8] LARRY MAY, SHARING RESPONSIBILITY 38 (1996). Compare also French, distinguishing between an "aggregate collectivity" – "merely a collection of people" – and a "conglomerate collectivity" – "an organization of individuals such that its identity is not exhausted by the conjunction of the identities of the persons in the organization." PETER A. FRENCH, *Collective and Corporate Responsibility* 46–47 (1984).

[9] *See* generally Helen Duffy , *Detention and Interrogation Abroad: The "Extraordinary Rendition" Programme, in* THE PRACTICE OF SHARED RESPONSIBILITYIN INTERNATIONAL LAW 89 (Andre Nollkaemper & Ilias Plakokefalos eds., 2017).

[10] MAY, *supra* note 8, at 36–38.

[11] ARSIWA, *supra* note 3, Art. 16; ARIO, note 2, Arts. 14 and 58.

[12] ARSIWA, *supra* note 3, Art. 17; ARIO, note 2, Arts. 15 and 59.

[13] ARIO, *supra* note 2, Arts. 17 and 61.

connivance, and condoning.[14] Common to such concepts is that multiple actors interact and that the conduct of each of the individual actors is dependent on, or contributes to, the actions of another.

The degree to which the conduct of actors is indeed interdependent and, accordingly, the normative justifiability of holding an individual actor responsible in connection with the acts of others, varies from case to case. The connection between actors is strong in cases where the actors act through a common organ, as in *Eurotunnel*[15] or the *Nauru* case.[16] In joint police operations the impact might be weaker, but may still be strong enough to hold one state responsible in connection with the conduct of another actor.[17] In cases where states have agreed to common obligations but do not act together, it may be that only the individual conduct is the proper unit of analysis.

8.2.2 *Interdependent Outcome*

The flipside of interdependence of conduct is that concerted action can achieve results that could not be achieved by actors alone. Concerted actions "enable their members to perform actions that they could not have performed on their own."[18] Erskine notes in this context that "agents who come together, even in an informal association, to work towards a shared goal are able to achieve things by cooperating that they would not be able to achieve independently."[19] Again, the extraordinary rendition saga is a good example. The conduct of states like Macedonia and Poland was influenced by the conduct of the United States, and in turn influenced the subsequent conduct of the United States.[20] Together they realized results that they could not have alone.

The implication is that if the harm is caused by multiple actors acting in a particular relationship, we may not be able to say that the conduct of

---

[14] *See* Chiara Lepora & Robert E Goodin, On Complicity and Compromise 36 ff. (2013).

[15] *The Channel Tunnel Group Ltd & France-Manche S.A. v. United Kingdom & France*, Case No. 2003–06, PCA Case Repository, Partial Award, (Perm. Ct. Arb. 2007), https://pcacases .com/web/sendAttach/487 [hereinafter Eurotunnel Arbitration].

[16] *Certain Phosphate Lands in Nauru (Nauru v. Austl.)*, Preliminary Objections, Judgment, 1992 I.C.J. Rep. 240, (June 26) [hereinafter *Nauru* case].

[17] Saskia Maria Hufnagel, Policing Cooperation Across Borders: Comparative Perspectives on Law Enforcement within the EU and Australia (2013).

[18] Larry May, The Morality of Groups 26 (1987).

[19] Toni Erskine, *"Coalitions of the Willing" and the Shared Responsibility to Protect*, in Distribution of Responsibilities in International Law 256 (André Nollkaemper & Dov Jacobs eds., 2015).

[20] *El-Masri v. the Former Yugoslav Republic of Macedonia*, App. No. 39630/09, 2012 Eur. Ct. H. R. 263 (2012), [hereinafter *El-Masri* case].

individual states or international organizations (IOs) is the direct and exclusive cause of the harm. In that sense, the phrase that "a State is responsible only for its *own* conduct" (as the ICJ put it in the *Genocide* case)[21] is misleading when the harm only occurs because of the involvement of other actors. The Court emphasized that there should be a sufficiently close connection "between the conduct of a State's organs and its international responsibility."[22] There certainly needs to be such a connection; however, there may well be other actors positioned between the conduct of a state's organs and the eventual harm.

Another example was the situation where Italian authorities assisted the CIA in abducting an Egyptian cleric. In that case, it can be argued that Italy committed a separate wrongful act of aiding or assisting. Yet that wrong was also a cause of the illegal abduction committed by the USA. The aid or assistance was necessary for the abduction to occur. In that case the eventual harm was the result of both the acts of both states. Neither of the two states could have produced the outcome alone.[23]

When two or more actors contribute to a particular harmful outcome, the eventual harm can be indivisible. That is, it cannot – without loss of meaning – be divided between the individual contributing actors. Multiple contributions are causally linked to the harmful outcome, but none of such contributions is by itself sufficient to produce the harmful outcome.[24] Rather, the harm may be an indivisible totality which results from the addition of various contributions and the interaction between them.

It may be argued that since, for instance, human rights are by definition held against particular states, which each owe individual obligations towards individuals under their jurisdiction, an eventual human rights violation can always be traced back to individual states rather than to "collective actors." In cases where the harmful outcome is a human rights violation, the harmful outcome would then necessarily lead to individual actors rather than to "relationships." However, it is possible to distinguish between the specific human rights violation consisting of a singular breach by one actor vis-à-vis an individual, on the one hand, and a "global harm" that consists of a cumulation

---

[21] *Application of the Convention on Prevention and Punishment of Crime of Genocide (Bosn. & Herz. v. Serb. & Montenegro)*, Judgment, 2007 I.C.J. Rep. 43, ¶ 406 (Feb. 2007), [hereinafter, *Genocide* case). Emphasis added.

[22] *Id.*

[23] Pierre d'Argent, *Reparation, Cessation, Assurances and Guarantees of Non-Repetition*, in PRINCIPLES OF SHARED RESPONSIBILITY IN INTERNATIONAL LAW: AN APPRAISAL OF THE STATE OF THE ART 225 (André Nollkaemper & Ilias Plakokefalos eds., 2014).

[24] BRIGITTE BOLLECKER-STERN, LE PRÉJUDICE DANS LA THÉORIE DE LA RESPONSABILITÉ INTERNATIONALE 267 (1973); d'Argent, *supra* note 23, at 228.

of acts of multiple actors vis-à-vis that individual. In the context of extraordinary rendition, where one state illegally arrests and then hands over an individual to another state, which then illegally detains and tortures that person, we can identify both two separate wrongs, on the one hand, and a larger, "global" wrong that results from two separate wrongs, on the other.[25]

For the above reasons, we can indeed identify situations where states and/or international institutions can achieve results by acting in concert that they could not achieve alone. If so, the proper unit of analysis in understanding responsibility is not the individual actor, but rather the relationship between the actors contributing to the harm.

8.2.3 Shared Responsibility

The interdependent nature of conduct and outcomes justifies ascribing responsibility for the harmful conduct not to one actor, but rather to "each and all of those taking part."[26] The fact that two or more actors that contributed to the harm stand in a relevant relationship to each other, and together achieve a result that could not have been achieved by themselves alone, justifies a sharing of responsibility.[27] As May observes, the concept of shared responsibility focuses attention "on the interaction of one with the other, rather than on acts of isolated agents."[28]

The defining feature of shared responsibility is that the responsibility of two or more actors for their contribution to a particular outcome is distributed between them separately, rather than resting on them collectively.[29] If the responsibility were to rest on a collectivity, it would no longer be shared, but would instead be a responsibility of the collectivity as such.[30] Somewhat counterintuitively, because the term may suggest otherwise, shared responsibility is by definition thus a responsibility that rests on individual actors for their contribution to a particular harm.

However, it follows from the above that shared responsibility is not simply the aggregation of two or more individual responsibilities. The responsibility of separate actors is connected by the interdependence of conduct and by their respective links to the same harmful outcome. The prototypical example of

---

[25] *Id.*, at 225.
[26] LUCAS, *supra* note 7, at 7.
[27] Seumas Miller, *Collective Responsibility*, 15 PUB. AFF. Q. 65 (2001).
[28] MAY, *supra* note 8, at 38.
[29] *Id.*, at 112.
[30] *Id.*, at 116.

the concept of shared responsibility is a situation where multiple actors contribute to each other's acts and thereby to the eventual outcome.[31]

This distributive understanding of shared responsibility thus presumes that when multiple actors together contribute to a harmful outcome, the responsibility of each of them should be understood in nonexclusive terms. Assignment of responsibility to one actor does not exclude the other. Such a nonexclusive concept has been defended on theoretical terms. Lucas observes that responsibility is not a material object – "I can be held responsible for an action you did, without your being thereby any the less responsible for it too."[32]

8.3 TRANSFORMATION OF THE SUBSTANTIVE LAW

If individual conduct and outcomes are explained in terms of the relations between actors in causing the harm, it follows that in principle responsibility for such harm should not be allocated to individual actors, but rather to all actors involved in such a relationship. While international law traditionally was based on the notion of independent responsibility (8.3.1), over time it is more and more recognized the relational nature of responsibility (8.3.2), though in key areas that development is incomplete and leaves open significant questions (8.3.3).

8.3.1 *The Traditional Principle of Independent Responsibility*

The dominant approach of international law to the allocation of international responsibility is based on the notion of "individual" or "independent" responsibility of states and international organizations.[33] In this account, actors are only responsible for their *own* wrong, irrespective of their connection to other actors.[34]

The dominant paradigm of individual responsibility rests essentially on two grounds. The first ground is of a methodological nature. For the purposes of

---

[31] *Id.*, at 36–38.

[32] LUCAS, *supra* note 7, at 75. Also, Zimmerman notes that "surely more than one person can be responsible for the same outcome"; *see* Michael J. Zimmerman, *Sharing Responsibility*, 22(2) AM. PHIL. Q. 115 (1985).

[33] To prevent confusion with "individual responsibility" as a term that refers to responsibility of individuals under international criminal law, in the remainder of this paper I use the term independent responsibility.

[34] Int'l L. Comm'n, Commentary to Articles on the Responsibility of States for Internationally Wrongful Acts, Int'l L. Comm'n Y.B. 2001/II 2001, [hereinafter ARSIWA Commentary], commentary to Art. 47, para. 8.

determinations of responsibility, the relevant units of analysis would be individual actors rather than collectivities of actors. This ground is premised on methodological individualism: in the final analysis all conduct is explained by the actions of individuals.[35] This approach is commonly applied to justify individual criminal responsibility.[36] Given the centrality of the sovereign state as the dominant agent in international law, this perspective can also be applied to justify the focus on individual states as agents that cause harmful effects.

The second ground underlying the paradigm of individual responsibility is of a normative nature. Just as international criminal law rejects the concepts of collective responsibility or guilt by association, instead relying on the principle of individual autonomy to limit responsibility to individuals only for their actual conduct, it would be normatively problematic to require states to be responsible for conduct other than their own.[37]

This idea of independent responsibility is reflected in the ARSIWA. The idea that individual states commit individual wrongful acts (expressed in Article 1: "every internationally wrongful act of a State entails the international responsibility of that State") underlies the ARSIWA as a whole.[38] In view of the possibility that a state might be responsible not only for its own acts but also for the acts of others, Special Rapporteur Ago suggested opting for a broader opening Article, providing that "every international wrongful act by a State gives rise to international responsibility," without specifying that this responsibility would necessarily attach to the state that had committed the wrongful act in question.[39] However, the ILC was of the opinion that the situations in which responsibility was attributed to a state other than the state that committed the internationally wrongful act were so exceptional that they should not influence the basic principle in Article 1,[40] and that following Ago's proposal would detract from the principle's basic force.[41] Thus state responsibility for

[35] Kenneth J. Arrow, *Methodological Individualism and Social Knowledge*, 84 AM. ECON. REV. 1; Steven Lukes, *Methodological Individualism Reconsidered*, 19 BRIT. J. OF SOC. 119 (1968); J. W. N. Watkins, *The Principle of Methodological Individualism*, 3 BRIT. J. FOR THE PHIL. OF SCI. 186 (1952).

[36] *See, e.g.*, Harmen van der Wilt, *Joint Criminal Enterprise. Possibilities and Limitations*, 5 J. OF INT'L. CRIM. JUST. 91 (2007).

[37] Compare *Genocide* case, *supra* note 21, ¶ 406 (critiquing on this ground the overall test as a basis for attribution of conduct).

[38] ARSIWA, *supra* note 3, Arts. 16–18 of the ARSIWA to some extent form an exception.

[39] Int'l L. Comm'n, Second Rep. on State Responsibility by Special Rapporteur Roberto Ago, U. N. Doc. A/CN.4/233 (1970), ¶¶ 29–30.

[40] Int'l L. Comm'n, Third Rep. on State Responsibility by Special Rapporteur Roberto Ago, U. N. Doc. A/CN.4/246 and Add.1-3 (1971), ¶ 47.

[41] Int'l L. Comm'n, Rep. of the Int'l L. Comm'n on the Work of its Twenty-Fifth Session, U.N. Doc. A/9010/Rev.1,176,7 May-13 (July 1973), ¶ 11.

the state's *own* wrongful conduct came to be the basic rule underlying the ARSIWA.

In the relatively scarce case law, international courts have based themselves on this principle of independent responsibility. The International Court of Justice (ICJ) focused on independent wrongdoing in *Corfu Channel*[42] and *Certain Phosphate Lands in Nauru*.[43] Likewise, the ECtHR considered the responsibility of Belgium and Greece independently in *M.S.S. v. Belgium and Greece*.[44] The Tribunal in the *Eurotunnel* case also preferred to approach international responsibility for common conduct through the lens of independent responsibility.[45]

The principle of independent responsibility applies in situations of concerted action no less than in situations where states act alone. Individual actors retain their individual obligation, even when they act in concert. In principle, the fact that more than one actor is engaged in a particular wrongful act, does not release each individual actor from its responsibilities. In the *East Timor* case, Judge Weeramantry, dissenting with the majority judgment, noted that "[e]ven if the responsibility of Indonesia is the prime source, from which Australia's responsibility derives as a consequence, Australia cannot divert responsibility from itself by pointing to that primary responsibility."[46] Australia's own role in regard to the treaty was therefore sufficient for its (independent) responsibility.

Nonetheless, the principle of individual responsibility can have shortcomings in situations of shared responsibility. A system of responsibility that disaggregates responsibility into individual cases of wrongdoing, and that does not connect well to the structure of international cooperation, may undermine key benefits of the law of responsibility. It may hinder answerability for the exercise of public authority, sustain collective action problems and legitimize harmful practices. Its most visible drawback is that it makes it difficult for persons who suffer injury to figure out who is to blame for particular harmful effects. In combination with the procedural limitations of dispute settlement, the conceptual tools of exclusive individual responsibility of states have led courts to reduce complex cooperative schemes to binary categories without engaging in principled discussions of the shared nature of

---

[42] *Corfu Channel Case*, (*U.K. v. Alb.*), Judgment 1949 I.C.J. Rep. 4 (May 1949) [hereinafter *Corfu Channel* case].

[43] *Nauru* case, *supra* note 16.

[44] *M.S.S. v. Belgium and Greece*, App. No. 30696/09 2011 Eur. Ct. H.R., 21 (2011).

[45] *Eurotunnel Arbitration*, *supra* note 15.

[46] *Concerning East Timor (Port. v. Austl.)*, Judgment, 1995 I.C.J Rep. 90 (Jun. 1995), (dissenting opinion of Judge Weeramantry), [hereinafter *East Timor* case].

responsibility.[47] A noteworthy example is the decision of the ECtHR in *Behrami*. The Court attributed all acts and omissions relating to the failed demining operations in Kosovo exclusively to the United Nations, and not its member states, without considering the possibility of a more nuanced solution in which responsibility would be shared.[48] This approach raises the question whether independent responsibility is conducive to a rule-based society in which responsibility fulfills the essential function of ensuring a return to legality and ensuring that the actors that acted in breach of international law will comply with their obligations.[49] Attributing responsibility only to one actor, even though another actor contributed to the harmful outcome, also raises normative questions. For instance, if only a directed (and not the directing) state is held responsible, do we have a proper set of principles that allow us to establish for which part of the injury to a third party it is responsible? If so, is it fair to leave the injured party with the remaining costs? If not, is it fair to hold the directed state responsible for all injury? The larger point here is that reducing situations of shared responsibility to individual responsibility may create an accountability gap that implies costs for the injured parties and the larger system and raise questions of fairness among the responsible parties.

Yet, in the light of the relational nature of responsibility as explained in Section 8.2, the foundations of independent responsibility may not be able to withstand a critical review. The idea of methodological individualism is problematic in light of the intertwined nature of conduct and outcomes. Likewise, the argument that actors should only be responsible for their own action or inaction, is less plausible when it is difficult or even outright impossible to isolate individual conduct.

8.3.2 *Emergence of the Substantive Law of Shared Responsibility*

While neither the ARSIWA nor the ARIO were designed and drafted with situations of shared responsibility in mind, both texts contain principles that addresses or allow for the possibility of international responsibility of multiple

---

[47] *See, e g , Legality of Use of Force (Serb & Montenegro v U K)*, Provisional Measures, Order, 1999 I.C.J Rep. 113 (Apr. 1999), [hereafter *Case on the Legality of the Use of Force against the U.K.*]; *East Timor* case, *supra* note 46; *Nauru* case, *supra* note 16; *Military and Paramilitary Activities in and Against Nicaragua, (Nicar. v. U.S.)*, Judgment, 1986 I.C.J Rep. 14 (Jun. 1986); *Corfu Channel* case, *supra* note 42.

[48] *Behrami v. France*, Admissibility Decision, App. No. 71412/01 & 78166/01 2007 Eur. Ct. H.R., 2 (2007).

[49] For discussion of the relationship between the rule of law and state responsibility, *see* IAN BROWNLIE, THE RULE OF LAW IN INTERNATIONAL AFFAIRS: INTERNATIONAL LAW AT THE FIFTIETH ANNIVERSARY OF THE UNITED NATIONS 79–81 (1998).

wrongdoers. The most explicit principle is the principle that where several states and/or international organizations are responsible for the same internationally wrongful act, the responsibility of each state or organization may be invoked in relation to that act.[50] This principle recognizes that several states and/or international organizations can be responsible for the same wrongful act, without expressly stating this.

It is possible to discern a marked transformation in the law of responsibility over the past few decades. This can best be illustrated by the difference between article 1 ARSIWA which, as noted, is based on the notion of independent responsibility, and Article 1 ARIO. This latter Article stipulates that the ARIO apply not only to the responsibility of an international organization for its own wrongful conduct, but rather to "the international responsibility of an international organization for *an* internationally wrongful act."[51] This concept of responsibility thus refers to a responsibility of international organizations and states that derives not only from their *own* wrongful conduct, but also for wrongful acts brought about by a cooperative action of which they were a part. Given the possibility that international organizations would contribute to the wrongful acts of member states, or vice versa,[52] the ILC found the suggestion of basing the entire law of international responsibility on individual responsibility to be unpersuasive and opted for a construction that it had rejected in relation to the responsibility of states. In this sense, the ARIO as a whole are based on a "relational account" of international responsibility.

Both the ARSIWA and the ARIO allow ample opportunities for sharing responsibility between multiple states and/or international organizations. The international law of responsibility is a flexible body of law that can be applied in, and adjusted to, a wide variety of situations, including situations involving shared responsibility. Apart from the principle on the same wrongful act, both the ARSIWA and the ARIO implicitly recognize the possibility of shared responsibility by their inclusion of "without prejudice" provisions. These provisions stipulate that attribution to, or responsibility of, one state or international organization is without prejudice to attribution to, or responsibility of, another actor and thus make clear that responsibility of one actor need not be exclusive.[53]

---

[50] ARSIWA, *supra* note 3, at Art. 47; ARIO, *supra* note 2, at Art. 48.
[51] Int'l L. Comm'n, Commentary to Art. on the Responsibility of Int'l. Org., Int'l L. Comm'n. Rep. on the Work of its Sixty-Third Session, UNGAOR 66th Sess., Supp. No. 10, UN Doc. A/66/10 (2011), ¶ 4, [hereinafter ARIO Commentary].
[52] ARIO, *supra* note 2, at Arts. 14–17.
[53] ARSIWA, *supra* note 3, at Arts. 10(3), 19, 57 and 58; ARIO, *supra* note 2, at Arts. 19, 63, and 66.

Also the principles relating to attribution are flexible and allow for a determination of shared responsibility. This holds both for attribution of conduct and attribution of responsibility. As to the former the provisions on attribution of conduct concerning a multiplicity of possibly responsible actors are largely unproblematic.[54] The ARSIWA and the ARIO enable, for instance, shared responsibility in situations involving joint organs (as supported by the *Nauru*[55] and *Eurotunnel*[56] cases), and situations where both international organizations and their member states incur responsibility.

The picture for attribution of responsibility is not any different. Both the ARSIWA and the ARIO leave open the possibility of attributing responsibility to one actor for internationally wrongful conduct committed by another actor. Indeed, it can be inferred from the very definition of attribution of responsibility, in terms of responsibility for the conduct of another, that there cannot be situations where all of the parties bear attributed responsibility. Fry thus observes that the "combination of attributed responsibility to one state or international organisation, on the one hand, and attribution of responsibility or conduct to another, on the other, might lead to multiple attribution (of responsibility, conduct, or both)."[57]

The principle of complicity is the paradigmatic example of a principle that enables shared responsibility: indeed, shared responsibility between the complicit state and the principal wrongdoing state is inherent in the very concept of complicity.[58] The aid provided may rise to a level where the aiding state becomes co-perpetrator, and thus jointly responsible with the state or organization that receives the aid. If not, the aiding state will be responsible for a separate wrong. But, either way, responsibility will only arise when the receiving state indeed commits the wrong.

The principles pertaining to reparation appear to be similarly flexible. Apart from the case of responsibility "for the same internationally wrongful act,"[59]

---

[54] The exception is transferred organs where international law does not recognize multiple attribution, *see* Francesco Messineo, *Attribution of Conduct*, in Principles of Shared Responsibility in International Law: An Appraisal of the State of the Art 60 (André Nollkaemper & Ilias Plakokefalos eds., 2014).

[55] *Nauru* case, *supra* note 16.

[56] *Eurotunnel Arbitration*, *supra* note 15.

[57] J. D. Fry, *Attribution of Responsibility*, in Principles of Shared Responsibility in International Law: An Appraisal of the State of the Art 98 (André Nollkaemper & Ilias Plakokefalos eds., 2014).

[58] V. Lanovoy, *Complicity in an Internationally Wrongful Act*, in Principles of Shared Responsibility in International Law: An Appraisal of the State of the Art 134 (André Nollkaemper & Ilias Plakokefalos eds., 2014).

[59] ARSIWA, *supra* note 3, at Art. 47; ARIO, *supra* note 2, at Art. 48.

where the responsibility of each state or organization may be invoked in relation to that internationally wrongful act, the Articles are silent in relation to shared responsibility stemming from different wrongful acts. However, this does not mean that the ARSIWA and the ARIO cannot accommodate such questions. D'Argent notes that "this silence is best explained by the fact that no specific rule is actually required in such cases and that the question of the allocation of the obligation to make reparation is simply governed by the orderly and reasoned application of the usual rules."[60]

Beyond the world of the ILC, there is a diverse practice that can be captured in terms of shared responsibility. The ILC version of the law of responsibility needs to be understood as a part of a broader process of global governance, that involves diverse principles and processes of accountability and responsibility for evaluating and adjudicating harmful conduct, and that may initiate a renewed cycle or development of rules.[61]

8.3.3 Remaining Controversies

The incorporation of shared responsibility in the positive law of responsibility still is very much work in progress. In part, the articles clearly are *lege ferenda*. This holds for instance for most articles in Part Five of the ARIO – on responsibility of states for circumvention, aid or assistance or directing and controlling an international organization.[62]

Moreover, the articles do not provide much direction for the scope and distribution of shared responsibility. The law rarely provides guidance on (often complex) questions of determination, allocation, and implementation in situations where responsibility is shared. This is in part caused by the fact that the construction of the principles of international responsibility, in relation to questions of shared responsibility could not be based on significant practice. On issues such as attribution of conduct, circumstances precluding wrongfulness, or countermeasures, hardly any practice exists in relation to multiple wrongdoers.

While to some extent such lack of guidance is not due to the specific features of shared responsibility, but rather reflects the generality of the law

---

[60] D'Argent, *supra* note 23, at 217.

[61] K. Van Kersbergen and F. Van Waarden, *"Governance" as a Bridge between Disciplines: Cross Disciplinary Inspiration Regarding Shifts in Governance and Problems of Governability, Accountability and Legitimacy* (2004) 43(2) European Journal of Political Research 143.

[62] A. Gattini, *Breach of International Obligations*, in Principles of Shared Responsibility in International Law: An Appraisal of the State of the Art 25 (André Nollkaemper & Ilias Plakokefalos eds., 2014).

of international responsibility as such, the specific nature of questions of shared responsibility, combined with the lack of practice, enhances the uncertainty in the construction and application of principles of international responsibility. This is true most of all for the problem of distribution of responsibility, and in particular, reparation between multiple actors. In those cases where it can be determined that multiple states and/or international organizations are responsible, the question will arise whether they are then responsible for the same act or omission, and to the same degree. Most ILC Articles do not differentiate between degrees of responsibility. While this is consistent with the "objective responsibility" regime the ILC sought to establish, in cases of multiple responsible states it suggested "all or nothing" solutions that might be seen as too rigid.

A key problem is the lack of a well-defined concept of causality. While in the Articles as designed by the ILC, causation is not, strictly speaking, an element of responsibility, in actual determinations of (shared) responsibility, causation will frequently be decisive. Given the definition of shared responsibility as referring to situations where different actors contribute to a single harm,[63] the determination of degrees of contribution is key not only for defining whether or not the case at hand is indeed a case of shared responsibility at all, but also for identifying degrees of responsibility. For instance, in a situation where some of the actors are bound by a negative obligation and some by a positive one, a concept of causality that would be varied according to the different kinds of obligations that were violated would permit better fine-tuning between the different responsibilities of different actors.[64] The possibility of different degrees of responsibility is also recognized by Fry, who observes that attribution of responsibility seems to be grounded on the notion of – varying – degrees of control. But there does not appear to be a coherent basis for variation.[65]

The law is largely silent on how to determine shares of reparation in those situations where causation does not provide easy answers. This holds both in situations where there is a single wrongful act, and in situations of different wrongful acts (whether concurrent or cumulative responsibility). As to the former, Article 47(2) of the ARSIWA stipulates that the principle enunciated in paragraph 1 is without prejudice to allocation of reparation between the

---

[63] A. Nollkaemper & D. Jacobs, *Shared Responsibility in International Law: A Conceptual Framework*, 34 MICH. J. OF INT'L L. 359, 366–68 (2013); A. Nollkaemper, *Introduction: Procedural Aspects of Shared Responsibility in International Adjudication*, 4 J. OF INT'L DISPUTE SETTLEMENT 277 (2013).

[64] Gattini, *supra* note 62, at 31.

[65] Fry, *supra* note 57, at 128.

responsible parties, but neither the principle nor the Commentary provides the beginning of an analysis on how this allocation should proceed. As to the latter, d'Argent notes that the ARSIWA and the ARIO only partly address the complexity stemming from situations of shared responsibility when it comes to the allocation of the secondary obligations of reparation, cessation, and assurances and guarantees of non-repetition. Furthermore they fail to consider cases where the harmful outcome is the result of several wrongful acts for which several subjects are responsible.[66]

The lack of guidance also applies to complicity. Profound questions remain as to what degrees of contribution actually trigger responsibility of the aiding state, and thereby shared responsibility, and how the law deals with possible variations in responsibility between the aiding and the aided state. Lanovoy observes that the current regime of responsibility for complicity leaves little room "for the injured party to obtain full reparation for the injury that bears an imprint of complicity."[67] He critiques the ILC for failing "to provide guidance on the causal standards governing a third party's contribution to an internationally wrongful act".[68] While d'Argent identifies several options for allocation of reparation, it is difficult to know which of those approaches is favored by international practice.[69]

8.4 INTERNATIONAL ADJUDICATIVE LAW

The paradox identified in this article is that the relational nature of responsibility that underlies principles of shared responsibility may complicate effective adjudication of claims of shared responsibility. Precisely the fact that in cases of concerted action the conduct of one actor often cannot be disconnected from that of other actors, and that the substantive law of responsibility has to accommodate such relations, may limit the power of international courts to effectively adjudicate shared responsibility claims. Factors that help explain this phenomenon are that courts are governed by a procedural logic that may lead them into different directions than the substantive logic of shared responsibility (8.4.1); that because of the structure of the international legal system often not all co-responsible parties will be before the court, with the consequence that courts have to disaggregate complex multiparty problems (8.4.2); and that questions of shared responsibility may involve such large

---

[66] D'Argent, *supra* note 23, at 249.
[67] Lanovoy, *supra* note 59, at 136.
[68] Id.
[69] D'Argent, *supra* note 23, at 230–31.

Unravelling a Paradox of Shared Responsibility

numbers of parties that such questions may be better addressed by negotiation and regulation than by adjudication (8.4.3).

8.4.1 *The Independent Logic of Adjudicative Law*

Proceedings in courts are governed by different logic than law of responsibility. International adjudication is governed by procedural rules, broadly defined. Examples of such procedural rules are rules on joinder, evidence, and fact-finding. The principles of shared responsibility, including those that relate to reparation by multiple wrongdoing actors, are better placed in the category of substantive law than in the category of procedural law (whether in the narrow or in the broad sense).[70] This also holds for reparation: to define reparation in terms of procedure would be "to confound the remedy with the process by which it is made available."[71] Indeed, the ARSIWA and the ARIO formulate reparation largely, though not entirely, in terms of substantive rather than procedural law.[72]

Where substantive law does provide for shared responsibility, there is no automatic connection with procedural law. While in some cases procedure may be seen as a facilitator of the application or development of substantive law,[73] "adjudicative law" may serve different interests and even may impede the realization of substantive law of responsibility. Particular procedural principles may lead or assist a court to formulate particular substantive principles of responsibility, or deny it the possibility to do so. It rightly has been said that "[p]rocedure is an instrument of power that can, in a very practical sense, generate or undermine substantive rights."[74]

---

[70] Also, Bentham interpreted the definition of the possible range of remedies that might be accorded for a violation of a right as being part of the substantive law. *See,* D. M. Risinger, *"Substance" and "Procedure", Revisited with Some Afterthoughts on the Constitutional Problems of "Irrebutable Presumptions,"* 30 UCLA L. Rev. 189, (1982); *Arrest Warrant of 11 April 2000 (Dem. Rep. Congo v. Belg.),* Judgment. 2002 I.C.J. Rep. 3 (Apr. 2002); *Greece Intervening: Jurisdictional Immunities of the State (Ger.v. It.),* Judgment, 2012 I.C.J. Rep. 99 (Feb. 2012), (stating that "whether a State is entitled to immunity before the courts of another State is a question entirely separate from whether the international responsibility of that State is engaged and whether it has an obligation to make reparation").

[71] *Contra* Alford, *supra* note 6, at 233, 247 (remedy is procedure).

[72] ARSIWA, *supra* note 3, at Art. 31; ARIO, *supra* note 2, at Art. 31.

[73] C. Wilfred Jenks, The Prospects of International Adjudication 184 (1964); Jeremy Bentham, *Principles of Judicial Procedure with the Outlines of a Procedure Code,* in The Works of Jeremy Bentham Vol. 2 Part 1 (John Bowring ed., 1843), cited in J. S. Martinez, *Process and Substance in the "War on Terror,"* 108 Colum. L. Rev. 1013, 1022 (2008); R. Pound, *Mechanical Jurisprudence,* 8 Colum. L. Rev. 605, 617 (1908).

[74] T. Main, *The Procedural Foundation of Substantive Law,* 87 Wash. U. L. Rev. 801, 802 (2010).

Procedural rules may have a different logic and different aims than giving effect to substantive principles of (shared) responsibility. We can recall Franck's distinction between the substantive and procedural aspects of fairness, which "may not always pull in the same direction."[75] This applies more generally to procedure in international courts. Procedural fairness, informed by equality of the parties, can conflict with what may be necessary for the implementation of shared responsibility. For instance, is it proper for a court in a procedure against state A to attribute weight to a determination of another court in a procedure against state B, if state A was not a party to the latter proceedings? The possibility that attributing such weight may help implement principles of responsibility may need to be weighed against, and may be overridden, by the procedural fairness of not burdening a party with an outcome of a procedure in which it had no part.

Moreover, procedural rules not only serve their own ends, but that they may have an impact on the status and construction of substantive rules themselves. The absence of proper procedures may cast doubt on the status and meaning of the substantive rules themselves. The fundamental point is that procedure is not just the transmitter of substance, or protective of intrinsic procedural rights, but is codeterminative of what the law is in the first place. For instance, the lack of procedural arrangements that would allow for recourse between multiple responsible parties casts doubt on the existence of joint and several liability in international law.[76]

8.4.2 Disaggregation

Procedures for international adjudication were not designed for multiparty disputes.[77] Just as the substantive principles of international responsibility developed by the ILC barely recognize the possibility of shared responsibility, the procedural rules of international courts have little to say on the situation where there is not one responsible State but multiple responsible States acting as defendants.[78] Thus, the procedural rules that apply to litigation of shared

[75] T. M. Franck, Fairness in International Law and Institutions (1995).
[76] A. Orakhelashvili, *Division of Reparation Between Responsible Entities*, in The Law of International Responsibility 663–64 (J. Crawford et. al. eds., 2010).
[77] L. Fisler-Damrosch, *Multilateral Disputes*, in The International Court of Justice at a Crossroads 376 (L Fisler-Damrosch ed., 1987).
[78] As noted by Paparinskis: "while cases of shared responsibility might illustrate the evidentiary challenges in particularly clear terms, the challenges are those of evidence in the ICJ (and international dispute settlement) more broadly and would have to be dealt with in terms of those debates." M. Paparinskis, *Procedural Aspects of Shared Responsibility in the International Court of Justice*, 4 J. of Int'l. Disp. Settlement 295 (2013).

responsibility are the ordinary procedural rules, that largely have to be adjusted to fit the specific characteristics of shared responsibility and, more generally, multilateral dispute settlement. While the powers and procedures of international courts leave leeway for broadening shared responsibility disputes beyond narrow bilateral settings, in several respects they restrict the possibility to take into account the distinctive multiparty nature of shared responsibility.[79] In particular in the ICJ there is a tension between the collective, multilateral nature of substantive principles that the Court may be asked to litigate, and the bilateral nature of its procedures.[80]

Because of the dominant role of consent, courts often can exercise jurisdiction over only a part of the co-responsible parties. The consequence may be that courts will be required to disaggregate complex issues. There may be multiple reasons why an international court will exercise jurisdiction over only part of the co-responsible parties. Often, plaintiffs will seek only redress from some, but not all (possibly) co-responsible parties. This in turn may be due to the fact that some parties offer better remedial prospects, or that the plaintiff has particular ties with one or a few, but not all defendants. It also may be due to the fact that a court will not be able to exercise jurisdiction over all co-responsible parties.[81] Here several situations need to be distinguished. The court may not be able to exercise jurisdiction over all types of actors that are co-responsible for a particular harm. Here considerable differences exist between international courts. In the ICJ only States can be parties in proceedings.[82] If a (co-)responsible party is an organization, a company, or private individual, these cannot be brought before the Court. In contrast, the dispute settlement procedures of the ITLOS are also open to "entities other than States Parties."[83] The WTO dispute settlement procedure can hear claims against States and

---

[79] Exceptions are Fisler-Damrosch, *supra* note 77, and M. Benzing, *Community Interests in the Procedure of International Courts and Tribunals*, 5 THE L. & PRAC. OF INT'L. CT. & TRIB. 369 (2006); see generally on procedural aspects of international litigation, I. Venzke, *Antinomies/ and Change in International Dispute Settlement: An Exercise in Comparative Procedural Law*, in INTERNATIONAL DISPUTE SETTLEMENT: ROOM FOR INNOVATIONS? (R. Wolfrum & I. Gätzschmann eds., 2013)

[80] Fisler-Damrosch, *supra* note 77, at 376. An example of the latter is the judgment of the ICJ in Jurisdictional Immunities, *supra* note 70.

[81] See generally on the jurisdiction of international courts, C. F. AMERASINGHE, JURISDICTION OF INTERNATIONAL TRIBUNALS (2003).

[82] Statute of the International Court of Justice (June 26, 1945, 59 Stat. 1055, 1060, 3 Bevans 1179, 1186) [hereinafter ICJ Statute], Arts. 34–35.

[83] Article 20 of the Statute of the International Tribunal for the Law of the Sea, which is Annex VI to the Law of the Sea Convention (adopted 10 December 1982, entered into force 16 November 1994) 1833 UNTS 3.

the EU.[84] The ECtHR at present can only hear claims against States, but in the future will be able to decide claims against the EU. For arbitral tribunals, everything depends on the terms of the arbitration agreement, and there is no a priori limitation to the actors that can be brought before such tribunals.

Within the category of actors that in principle can be brought before an international court, only those actors can appear as defendants that have consented to the jurisdiction of the court, through a bilateral or multilateral treaty or otherwise.[85] In some situations States and/or international organizations have given their consent before a questions of shared responsibility arises; this will apply to the ECtHR and the WTO dispute settlement procedure. However, in such cases regional limitation of jurisdiction may apply. The position of the USA in relation to the rendition cases before the ECtHR is an example. In the *El-Masri* case, the ECtHR could adjudicate questions against Macedonia, but not against the United States.[86] In situations where no such a priori consent has been given, it is likely that one or a few, but not all co-responsible parties can be brought before the court. In the ICJ, jurisdictional limitations stem in particular from the requirement of state consent to the jurisdiction.[87] The *East Timor* case,[88] the *Legality of the Use of Force* cases,[89] and *Obligations concerning Negotiations relating to Cessation of the Nuclear*

---

[84] See L. Bartels, *Procedural Aspects of Shared Responsibility in the WTO Dispute Settlement System*, 4 J. OF INT'L. DISP. SETTLEMENT 343 (2013).

[85] See, e.g., J. G. MERRILLS, INTERNATIONAL DISPUTE SETTLEMENT 119–23 (2005).

[86] See *El-Masri* case, *supra* note 20; Convention for the Protection of Human Rights and Fundamental Freedoms (Nov. 4, 1950, 213 U.N.T.S. 221, 224), Art. 1, (limiting the applicability of the Convention to the High Contracting Parties).

[87] ICJ Statute, *supra* note 82, at Art. 36

[88] *East Timor* case, *supra* note 46, at ¶104; *Greece Intervening: Jurisdictional Immunities of the State (Ger. v. It.)*, Judgment, 2012 I.C.J. Rep. 99 (Feb. 2012).

[89] See: *Legality of Threat or Use of Nuclear Weapons*, Advisory Opinion, 1996 I.C.J. Rep. 226, 270 (July 1996); *Legality of Use of Force (Yugoslavia v. U.S.)*, Request for the Indication of Provisional Measure, 1999 I.C.J. Rep. 916, 925 (June 1990); *Legality of Use of Force (Yugoslavia v. U.K)*, Request for the Indication of Provisional Measure, 1990 I.C.J. Rep. 829, 839 (June 1990); *Legality of Use of Force (Yugoslavia v. Port.)*, Request for the Indication of Provisional Measure, 1999 I.C.J. Rep. 656, 671 (June 1990); *Legality of Use of Force (Yugoslavia v. Neth.)*, Request for the Indication of Provisional Measure, 1999 I.C.J. Rep. 542, 557 (June 1990); *Legality of Use of Force (Yugoslavia v. It.)*, Request for the Indication of Provisional Measure, 1999 I.C.J. Rep. 481, 492 (June 1990); *Legality of Use of Force (Yugoslavia v. Ger.)*, Request for the Indication of Provisional Measure, 1999 I.C.J. Rep. 422, 432 (June 1990); *Legality of Use of Force (Yugoslavia v. Fr.)*, Request for the Indication of Provisional Measure, 1999 I.C.J. Rep. 363, 373 (June 1990); *Legality of Use of Force (Yugoslavia v. Can.)*, Request for the Indication of Provisional Measure, 1999 I.C.J. Rep. 259, 273 (June 1990); *Legality of Use of Force (Yugoslavia v. Belg.)*, Request for the Indication of Provisional Measure, 1999 I.C.J. Rep. 124, 139 (June 1990).

Arms Race and to Nuclear Disarmament Cessation of the Nuclear Arms Race are examples of cases where the Court was asked to adjudicate claims against some, but not all (allegedly) responsible parties.[90]

The powers of courts to determine responsibility of multiple responsible parties also may be limited by the applicable law. Given that international courts can only apply a certain set of rules, the potential responsibility of an actor under another set of rules is irrelevant for that particular court. For instance, the dispute settlement mechanism under the Law of the Sea Convention will in principle only be able to adjudicate claims under this Convention. If one of the potentially co-responsible parties has, by its contribution to the single harmful outcome, acted in contravention of a human rights treaty, that might make it co-responsible, but the LOSC DSP will not be able to adjudicate claims on that basis.

Finally, the possibility that all responsible parties may be brought before an international court may be limited by the standing of a State, or other actor, to present a claim against two or more responsible actors, over which the court in principle has jurisdiction. In the ICJ, if a State has no legal interest in the subject matter of his claim (a right that is potentially violated by a particular party), the State will lack standing and the court will not deal with the substantive questions of that particular claim.[91] While standing may at first sight seem less relevant to questions of shared responsibility, as it relates primarily to the plaintiff rather than to the responsible parties, in particular cases rules on standing can present a barrier to litigation of questions of shared responsibility. A plaintiff may have a right to bring a claim against one, but not against all responsible parties. In regard to proceedings in the ICJ, if the obligations breached by separate responsible parties are different, it may be the case that a claimant has standing vis-à-vis some responsible states but not against others. Another example is a case based on diplomatic protection, where remedies may have been exhausted in some, but not in all responsible States. In the ECtHR, the admissibility criteria contained in the Convention may prevent standing of individuals who are not under the jurisdiction of all responsible parties, or who are not a victim of breaches by all responsible States.[92]

---

[90] *Obligations concerning Negotiations relating to Cessation of the Nuclear Arms Race and to Nuclear Disarmament Cessation of the Nuclear Arms Race (Marsh. Is. v. U.K.)*, Preliminary Objections, 2016 I.C.J. Rep. 160 (2016).

[91] This may be different in other courts, such as the WTO, see EC – Regime for the Importation, Sale and Distribution of Bananas (Banana's III) WT/DS27/AB/R AB-1997-3 (rejecting a requirement of legal standing).

[92] M. Den Heijer, *Procedural Aspects of Shared Responsibility in the European Court of Human Rights*, 4 J. OF INT'L. DISP. SETTLEMENT 361 (2013).

When for any of these reasons only a part of the co-responsible parties is defendant in a particular case, a court will be forced to disaggregate shared responsibilities. Whether or not that will be problematic will depend on the circumstances of the case. In cases where the responsibility of each of the parties can be determined in isolation of the responsibility of the other parties, such disaggregation may be relatively unproblematic. But in cases where the responsibilities are intertwined, when harm is undivided, and the contributions by multiple parties are cumulative, it may be difficult to disaggregate the dispute. For instance, one court may not be able to pronounce on the responsibility of state A without considering the factual and legal position of state B, and conversely, a court's decision on state A may have implications for the assessment of the legal position of co-responsible state B.

This may be is unsatisfactory for three reasons. First, the Court may not be able to properly address, let alone resolve, the underlying problems. Second, it may not be able to provide proper remedies to plaintiffs (either in term of cessation or reparation). Indeed, the sheer complexity of doing this may lead a court to decline to determine any reparation, as in the *Genocide* case. Third, the result may be unjust between the parties, when those parties that will appear before the court will have to carry the burden for a larger group of actors that do not participate in the proceedings. If a court adjudicates the responsibility of only one actor, that actor may be held responsible, and be ordered to provide reparation for wrongs committed in whole or in part by another actor.

8.4.3 The Political Process

The more complex problems of shared responsibility become, and the more extensive and intertwined the underlying relations between actors become, the less useful the role of international adjudication becomes in handling such problems. Questions of shared responsibility relating to harmful effects of concerted action may present a complexity that exceeds the ability of international courts to address them, and more generally may be unsuited for international adjudication.

While some problems of shared responsibility may present themselves in relatively simple party-structures (e.g., a situation of extradition by a state to another state of a person in the face of risk that that person would be tortured), in other situations a high number of states can be involved. Examples are climate change, trade in endangered species, and the global financial crisis. Theoretically it may not be impossible to adjudicate claims against large numbers of parties. However, existing procedures are hardly suited for such "mass-adjudication." This may be due to the need to establish jurisdiction for each of the co-responsible parties, to differences in terms of the applicability of primary obligations, which may impact on admissibility of claims, or on evidentiary questions. But the more general point is that in complex multi-party settings, harmful outcomes will require political responses and regulation, rather than one-off adjudication. Shared responsibility problems may involve substantive obligations, rather than the allocation of ex post facto responsibility. The problem of shared responsibility in relation to the Mediterranean refugee crises is an example. While it cannot be excluded that in particular cases justiciable claims could be made against one or a few states involved in maritime operations in the area, it is quite obvious that there would be a mismatch between the judicial approach to such problems and the preeminently political questions of shared responsibility in terms of who should do what. The same can be said for climate change – one-off litigation between individual actors may well be possible. But also here there may be a mismatch between the potential outcome of such litigation and the underlying structural causes of the problem, which again required political and regulatory solutions, rather than adjudication.

It may even be said that in particular cases litigation of parts of a complex problem may be counterproductive.[93] The possibility that individual states may be brought before a court may make them less eager to engage in collective agreements that would detail obligations of multiple parties. Designing adjudication procedures in a way that would optimize litigation of shared responsibility issues (for instance by narrow interpretation of the Monetary Gold rule, flexible rules of evidence, etc.), might undermine the acceptance of shared responsibilities ex ante, which in the long run need not benefit the achievement of the particular regime in question.

None of this is unique to questions of shared responsibility. It rather is a manifestation of the fundamental tension between adjudication on the one hand, and the political process, on the other, which underlies the modest role of international adjudication in international affairs in general. However, that tension definitively will become stronger and more complex in multiparty settings, where questions of distribution of responsibility (whether ex post or ex ante) will be highly complex. Of course, it may well be possible to identify narrow legal issues in an otherwise highly political context, allowing courts to exercise either contentious or advisory jurisdiction. Shared responsibility questions will not, as a general matter, be excluded by some political questions

---

[93] D. Cole, *The Problem of Shared Irresponsibility in International Climate Law*, in *supra* note 19, at 290.

doctrine. But it may be questionable whether outcomes of such adjudication are beneficial from the perspective of the achievement of public goals, which may need to involve the wider spectrum of parties. To some extent, this indeed highlights the tension between private and public aspects of shared responsibility.[94] All of this should lead us to some modesty in terms of what we can expect from international courts in relation to shared responsibility.

8.5 DIVERSITY

The role of international adjudication in relation to shared responsibility differs widely – both between international courts and between states in terms of their willingness of states to subject themselves, or make use of, international adjudication.

As to the former, influenced by differences in the applicable law and the underlying values and constituencies, the ability of courts to handle questions of shared responsibility differs significantly.[95] For instance, while in the ICJ there is a tension between the collective nature of wrongdoing and the bilateral nature of its procedures,[96] the rules of the ECtHR and arbitral tribunals are flexible and may accommodate such complex types of adjudication. Notable differences exist in the type of actors whose shared responsibility is engaged that can be brought before the court, in the role of consent as a precondition to the exercise of jurisdiction over co-responsible States, in the scope of the applicable law as a manifestation of jurisdiction, in the requirements of standing, in the practice of joinder, in the role of the indispensable parties rule, and in the powers of the courts to obtain evidence from actors that are not party to the proceedings. Some courts are better able to handle questions of shared responsibility than others. In the ICJ, in particular the Monetary Gold principle and the rule and practice of joinder may complicate determinations on shared responsibility.[97] In the ECtHR, both these rules are less problematic, but other problems exist here, notably the requirements of a jurisdictional link and the victim requirement.[98]

---

[94] Nollkaemper & Jacobs, *supra* note 63.
[95] See e.g. for the rather particular approach of the ECtHR on questions of reparation, M. Pellonpää, *Individual Reparation Claims under the European Convention on Human Rights*, in STATE RESPONSIBILITY AND THE INDIVIDUAL: REPARATION IN INSTANCES OF GRAVE VIOLATIONS OF HUMAN RIGHTS 112–25 (A. Randelzhofer and T. Tomuschat, eds., 1999); *See* generally C. Gray, *The Choice Between Restitution and Compensation*, 10 EUR. J. OF INT'L. L.413, 418, 422–23 (1999).
[96] Fisler-Damrosch, *supra* note 77, at 376.
[97] Paparinskis, *supra* note 78.
[98] Den Heijer, *supra* note 92, at 363.

Perhaps the most important factor that accounts for such differences is that the degree in which a treaty regime protects particular public values influences the way that questions of shared responsibility will be adjudicated. In a horizontal, bilateral setting, consent in relation to jurisdiction (and joinder) remains more dominant, and the powers of courts and tribunals vis-à-vis actors that are not before the court are more limited. It is this factor that explains why the procedure in the ECtHR displays a relatively large degree of openness towards multilateral dispute settlement. However, precisely the example of the ECtHR shows that the public law nature of the regime does not provide a comprehensive explanation of the ability of the court to address questions of shared responsibility – other barriers such as jurisdiction and the victim requirement remain,[99] and call for different explanations.

There is another dimension to the diversity in international adjudication of shared responsibility problems that should be considered. This is that there are considerable differences between states that are willing and able to submit their shared responsibility disputes to international courts. Much of the practice involves a very limited number of states, in particular in "the West." But also within that group there are significant differences. The adjudication of claims in relation to extraordinary rendition provides an example. Whereas European states such as Macedonia[100] and Poland[101] were found responsible by the European Court in relation to their (shared) responsibility, the USA has always resisted attempts to be subjected to adjudication for their leading role in extraordinary rendition. The US has been able to preclude international proceedings by not accepting jurisdiction of relevant international procedures, notably the Human Rights Committee (HRC), the Committee against Torture (CAT), and the ICJ.[102] This means that no international court has authoritatively determined that the USA has committed a wrong, or determined a factual account of the conduct of the USA as part of its extraordinary rendition policy. Domestic claims in the USA were rejected on procedural grounds before reaching the merits.[103] The only case in which US agents were found responsible was an Italian decision of the Court of Appeals of Milan,

---

[99]   *Id.*, at 368.
[100]   *El-Masri* case, *supra* note 20.
[101]   *Husayn (Abu Zubaydah) v. Poland*, App. No. 7511/13, Eur. Ct. H.R. ¶ 511 (2014).
[102]   The USA is not a party to the First Optional Protocol to the ICCPR (International Covenant on Civil and Political Rights, adopted 16 December 1966, entered into force 23 March 1976, 999 UNTS 171). It withdrew the acceptance of compulsory jurisdiction of the ICJ in 1984. See the Status of Ratification Interactive Dashboard of the UN Office of the High Commissioner for Human Rights, at http://indicators.ohchr.org/.
[103]   *See, e.g., El-Masri v. Tenet*, 437 F. Supp. 2d 530 (E.D. Va. 2006), *aff'd sub nom. El-Masri v. United States*, 479 F.3d 296 (4th Cir. 2007).

which determined (in absentia) criminal liability of twenty-two CIA agents and one US military official for kidnapping Abu Omar.[104] This episode illustrates that the ability of courts to adjudicate shared responsibility claims (already limited because of the complexity of the cases, identified above), differs significantly between states – and indeed also between Europe and the United States.

8.6 CONCLUSION

The somewhat paradoxical conclusion of the above analysis is that reconstructing responsibility in a relational sense, based on the fact when acting together they can achieve things they cannot achieve alone, underpins the development of substantive law of shared responsibility, but at the same time reduces the possibility that it may be resolved through adjudication. Precisely the fact that in cases of concerted action the conduct of one actor often cannot be disconnected from that of other actors, may both justify shared responsibility, and may limit the power of international courts to effectively adjudicate shared responsibility claims.

The development of the substantive law of responsibility can call for the renewal and change of procedural law. This connection ultimately rests on the idea that it is a task of procedural law to transmit substantive obligations or rights. In particular, relatively confined, cases of shared responsibility international courts may extend their power beyond individual actors that directly caused harmful effects, and may exercise jurisdiction to co-responsible parties. Examples are rules on introduction of claims and intervention, collection of evidence in relation to absent parties and joinder. Judgments of the ECtHR in rendition cases, where it had to acquire information related to the USA, provide a good example. However, more generally there may be significant

---

[104] F. Messineo, *"Extraordinary Renditions" and State Obligations to Criminalize and Prosecute Torture in the Light of the Abu Omar Case in Italy*, 7 J. OF INT'L. CRIM. JUST. 1023, 1036, 1044 (2009); For a detailed account of the facts of the Abu Omar case see the Italian arrest warrant for involved (US) agents: Adler et al., Prosecutor, Monica Courtney Adler, Gregory Asherleigh, Gabriel Lorenzo Carrera, Eliana Castaldo, Victor Castellano, Drew Carlyle Channing, John Kevin Duffin, John Thomas Gurley, Raymond Harbaugh, Ben Amar Harty, James Robert Kirkland, Anne Lidia Jenkins, Liliana Brenda Ibanez, Robert Seldon Lady, Cyntia Dame Logan, L. George Purvis, Pilar Rueda, Joseph Sofin, Michalis Vasiliou Registro Generale Notizia di Reato No 10838/05 Registro Giudiziario Giudice per le Indagini Preliminari No 1966/05 (Tribunale de Milano, 22 June 2005), official English translation by A Bygate and N Hazzan, available at http://www.statewatch.org/cia/documents/milan-tribunal-19-us-citizens-sought.pdf. In 2012, the convictions were upheld by Italy's highest appeals court.

time-lags between the development of substantive law and the development of procedural law – certainly if the contents of the substantive law is not very clear to start with. Moreover, the fact that procedural law has its own logic may hamper the development of substantive law, and may even work in an opposite direction.

The result is that when courts do adjudicate claims of shared responsibility, they generally are forced to debundle complex situations – and steer away from any pronouncements on the responsibility of other actors involved. Thereby courts may not be able to properly address, let alone resolve, the underlying causes of harm. They also may not be able to provide proper remedies to plaintiffs (either in terms of cessation or reparation). Indeed, the sheer complexity of doing this may lead a court to decline to determine *any* reparation, as we saw in the *Genocide* case.

If a court does not seek to disaggregate a situation of multiparty responsibility, and accept that the conduct is intertwined and cannot be disconnected, this may imply that a court has to declare itself without jurisdiction. In this sense, the somewhat paradoxical outcome is that a reconstruction of responsibility in a relational sense, based on the fact that when acting together they can achieve things they cannot achieve alone, is necessary for determination of shared responsibility in a substantive sense, but may run counter the interest of a comprehensive adjudication.

The larger point is that when a court seeks to engage with a shared responsibility question in its full complexity, it will appear that the role of international adjudication in the overall scheme of shared responsibility is limited. In complex multiparty settings, possible responses to harmful outcomes will require political responses and regulation, rather than one-off adjudication. Climate change is an example. None of this is unique questions of shared responsibility. It rather is a manifestation of the fundamental tension between adjudication on the one hand, and the political process, on the other. However, that tension definitively will become stronger and more complex in multiparty settings, where questions of distribution of responsibility will be highly complex. All of this should lead us to some modesty in terms of what we can expect from international courts in relation to shared responsibility.

3 International Law and the Use of Force

9

Divergent Views on the Content and Relevance of the Jus ad Bellum in Europe and the United States?

The Case of the US-Led Military Coalition against "Islamic State"

Tom Ruys and Luca Ferro[*]

9.1 INTRODUCTION: THE TRANSATLANTIC DIVIDE – TRUTH OR CARICATURE?

The idea that Americans and Europeans hold different views on global security and on the role of international laws and institutions in this respect is *nihil nove sub sole*. The perception of a great "transatlantic divide" was particularly prominent in the wake of the 9/11 attacks, when the Bush administration declared "War on Terror" and issued its notorious 2002 National Security Strategy,[1] before embarking on its controversial intervention in Iraq. Writing in 2003, Robert Kagan stated in *Paradise and Power* that:

> It is time to stop pretending that Europeans and Americans share a common view of the world, or even that they occupy the same world. On the all-important question of power … American and European perspectives are diverging. Europe is turning away from power into a self-contained world of laws and rules and transnational negotiation and cooperation. … Meanwhile, the United States remains mired in history, exercising power in an anarchic Hobbesian world where international laws and rules are unreliable … [O]n major strategic and international questions today, Americans are from Mars and Europeans are from Venus: They agree on little and understand one another less and less.[2]

---

[*] This chapter was updated and completed in November 2017.

[1] United States of America, the White House, *The National Security Strategy of the United States of America* (Sept. 2002), *at* http://georgewbush-whitehouse.archives.gov/nsc/nss/2002/.

[2] Robert Kagan, *Paradise and Power: America and Europe in the New World Order* (London: Atlantic Books, 2003), 3.

Kagan moreover predicted that this "transatlantic divide" was not a transitory thing, but was "likely to endure."

It is not difficult to identify illustrations of the different importance allegedly attached to international law, and the rules on the use of force in particular, on both sides of the Atlantic. When, in the run-up to NATO's 1999 Kosovo intervention, UK Foreign Secretary Robin Cook informed his American counterpart, Madeleine Albright, that his legal advisors had doubts over the legality of the operation absent Security Council authorization, the latter reportedly suggested her British colleague to "get new lawyers."[3] Four years later, it was the United Kingdom that urged the United States to secure a second Security Council resolution[4] before launching the Iraq intervention. And was it not former US Secretary of State Dean Acheson who in 1963, commenting on the events surrounding the Cuban missile crisis, reminded scholars assembled at the annual meeting of the American Society of International Law that "[l]aw simply does not deal with such questions of ultimate power – power that comes close to the sources of sovereignty"?[5]

In the aftermath of the Iraq intervention, Michael Glennon, echoing the more general position of Kagan quoted above, similarly stated that

[c]ultural divisions concerning use of force do not merely separate the West from the rest, however; increasingly, they separate the United States from the rest of the West. On one key subject in particular, European and American attitudes diverge and are moving further apart by the day. That subject is the role of law in international relations.[6]

The alleged transatlantic divide concerning the content and relevance of the *jus ad bellum* plays first and foremost at the level of State authorities. In this respect, it may be observed how, following the attacks of 9/11, the Bush administration stressed in the 2002 U.S. National Security Strategy that it would "not hesitate to act alone."[7] European governments for their part, after the 2003 Iraq intervention swore by the credo of "effective multilateralism."[8]

---

[3] Reported by James Rubin, then press spokesman for US Secretary of State Albright. See: James Rubin, "Countdown to a Very Personal War," *Financial Times*, September 29, 2000.

[4] UNSC Res. 1441 (Nov. 8, 2002).

[5] Dean Acheson, "Remarks," *ASIL Proceedings* 57 (1963): 14.

[6] Michael J. Glennon, "The UN Security Council in a Unipolar World," *Virginia Journal of International Law* 44 (2003–04): 97.

[7] *US National Security Strategy* 2002 (n. 1) 6.

[8] European Union, *A Secure Europe in a Better World – the European Security Strategy* (approved by the European Council held in Brussels on December 12, 2003), *at* www .eeas.europa.eu/csdp/about-csdp/european-security-strategy/.

The divide is also thought to play at the level of international lawyers. In particular, at the methodological level, it seems that there is a stronger adherence to the traditional positivist approach to international law on the European side, whereas US scholars seem more open to alternative, policy-oriented, and other methodological approaches. Translated to the realm of the *jus ad bellum*, US scholars generally adhere to a more "expansionist" approach (which focuses primarily on (physical) State practice and, specifically, on the practice of powerful States), whereas European (as well as various other non-US scholars) adhere to a more "restrictive" approach (paying closer attention to *opinio juris* as a constitutive element of custom).[9] As far as US legal doctrine is concerned then, there may be some degree of truth in Tom Farer's assertion that "in today's legal world, purists could be placed on the list of endangered species."[10]

The different methodological approach in turn translates into different views on the actual content of the Charter rules on the use of force, for instance, on the permissibility of self-defense against attacks by non-State actors. On a related note, while there may be a more critical attitude on the part of European legal doctrine to expansionist claims concerning the permissible recourse to force, and a greater awareness for the possibility of abuse,[11]

---

[9] On the distinction between "restrictionists" and "expansionists," see: Olivier Corten, *Le Droit contre la Guerre* (Paris: Editions Pedone, 2014), 9–34. More "extensive" approaches are characterized by the dominant role of custom as a source of international law, whereby the element of State practice (rather than *opinio juris*), and, more specifically, the practice of powerful States, enjoys particular importance. As a result, custom can evolve rapidly, or even instantaneously, following State action. A more restrictive approach does not structure sources of international law hierarchically, but focuses more equally on the analysis of treaties and general principles of law. Moreover, with regard to custom, it rather emphasizes the *opinio juris* element, and, in particular, the legal conviction of the international community of States (or a significant majority thereof). Accordingly, the evolution of custom occurs more gradually. Other distinctions, largely inspired by different underlying methodological approaches are those between "bright-liners" and "balancers" (see: Matthew C. Waxman, "Regulating Resort to Force: Force and Substance of the UN Charter Regime," *European Journal of International Law* 24 (2013). See also Olivier Corten, "Regulating Resort to Force: A Response to Matthew Waxman from a 'Bright-Liner'," *European Journal of International Law* 24 (2013)) or between "purists" and "eclectics" (Tom Farer, "Can the United States Violently Punish the Assad Regime?: Competing Visions (Including that of Anthony D'Amato) of the Applicable International Law," *The American Journal of International Law* 108 (2014): 701–15.

[10] Farer (n. 9) 704. This is not to say, however, that there are no "dissenting" voices in US legal doctrine. For one example, see e.g., Mary Ellen O'Connell, "Obama's Illegal War," *Politico Magazine*, September 11, 2014, www.politico.com/magazine/story/2014/09/obamas-illegal-war -110863_Page2.html#.V_uNf_lq6Hs (referring to "America's decades of unlawful force").

[11] Reference can be made in this respect to the open letter, published at the initiative of Prof. Olivier Corten (Université Libre de Bruxelles), and signed by more than two hundreds scholars worldwide, entitled *A Plea Against the Abusive Invocation of Self-Defence as*

a number of US scholars seem focused primarily on justifying US actions to the broader international community and to provide the theoretical arguments to legally underpin these actions. Thus, to paraphrase Koskenniemi,[12] European scholars may be slightly more "utopian", while US scholars are sometimes more "apologist."

Clearly, the idea that "Americans are from Mars and Europeans are from Venus" must be unmasked for what it is: a caricature. In a similar vein, the suggestion that all European international lawyers are "restrictionists" and all US scholars "expansionists" is of course a gross misrepresentation. A few cursory observations amply illustrate that a more nuanced picture is needed. First, it must be recalled that the United States has not turned its back on the UN Charter framework on the use of force, but has generally sought to articulate legal justifications for its military operations abroad derived from this framework (albeit at times by stretching the exceptions to the prohibition on the use of force to breaking point).[13] By defending its conduct by appealing to the existing rules then, this attitude would, having regard to the International Court of Justice's position in the *Nicaragua* case, tend to "confirm rather than to weaken" those rules.[14]

Second, calls for new exceptions to the prohibition on the use of force, or for a more flexible reading of existing exceptions, do not always originate from the western side of the Atlantic. For example, in recent years, the United Kingdom

---

a Response to Terrorism. It is telling indeed that the list of signatories features dozens of European scholars, yet hardly any US-based scholars. The letter *inter alia* states that "the mere fact that, despite its efforts, a State is unable to put an end to terrorist activities on its territory is insufficient to justify bombing that State's territory without its consent. Such an argument finds no support either in existing legal instruments or in the case law of the International Court of Justice. Accepting this argument entails a risk of grave abuse in that military action may henceforth be conducted against the will of a great number of States under the sole pretext that, in the intervening State's view, they were not sufficiently effective in fighting terrorism." For both the full text of the plea (in several languages) and its signatories, see: http://cdi.ulb.ac.be/contre-invocation-abusive-de-legitime-defense-faire-face-defi-terrorisme/.

[12] Martti Koskenniemi, *From Apology to Utopia* (Cambridge: Cambridge University Press, 2005).

[13] Consider, for example, the following excerpt from the speech by US Legal Adviser Brian Egan at the 2016 ASIL Annual Meeting (Brian J. Egan, "International Law, Legal Diplomacy, and the Counter-ISIL Campaign." Speech presented at the annual meeting for the American Society of International Law, Washington DC, April 1, 2016, *at* www.state.gov/s/l/releases/remarks/255493.htm): "International law matters a great deal in how we as a country approach counterterrorism operations. . . . Based on my experience in that position, I can tell you that the President, a lawyer himself, and his national security team have been guided by international law in setting the strategy for counterterrorism operations against ISIL."

[14] *Military and Paramilitary Activities in and against Nicaragua (Nicar. v. U.S.)*, Merits, 1986 ICJ REP. 14, para. 186 (June 27).

The Case of the US-Led Military Coalition against "Islamic State"   235

has manifested itself as the staunchest proponent of the legality of unilateral humanitarian intervention absent Security Council authorization (in exceptional situations involving massive human rights abuses). It has relied on the doctrine of humanitarian intervention with regard to the creation of no-fly zones in northern Iraq in 1991 and again at the time of the 1999 Kosovo crisis. Again, following a chemical weapons attack near Damascus in August 2013, in which hundreds of civilians were killed, the British Government published a legal position in which it defended the view that military action against the Syrian regime (which it considered responsible for the attack) would be justified under this doctrine.[15] By contrast, the United States has always been very cautious with regard to humanitarian intervention. As the 2015 US Law of War Manual puts it: "Although the United Kingdom and certain other States have argued that intervention for humanitarian reasons may be a legal basis for the resort to force, the United States has not adopted this legal rationale."[16]

Third, in relation to certain controversial issues, such as, for instance, the legality of anticipatory self-defense, closer scrutiny reveals that the positions of the United States and of various European States have actually come to converge to a considerable extent, as have those of American and European legal scholars.[17] A striking illustration of such convergence is the successive affirmation of the so-called Bethlehem principles[18] on self-defense against

[15]   United Kingdom, Prime Minister's Office, *Chemical Weapons Use by Syrian Regime: UK Government Legal Position* (Aug. 29, 2003), *at* www.gov.uk/government/publications/chem ical-weapon-use-by-syrian-regime-uk-government-legal-position/chemical-weapon-use-by-syr ian-regime-uk-government-legal-position-html-version.

[16]   United States of America, Department of Defense – Office of the General Counsel, *Law of War Manual* (Jun. 2015), *at* www.dod.mil/dodgc/, 45–46. Note: in April 2017, the United States conducted missile strikes against a Syrian airfield in reaction to the Assad regime's (alleged) use of chemical weapons on the village of Khan Sheikhoun. The USA nonetheless refrained from explicitly invoking any doctrine of unilateral humanitarian intervention. See: Tom Ruys, Luca Ferro and Carl Vander Maelen, "Digest of State Practice 1 January–30 June 2017," *Journal on the Use of Force and International Law* 4 (2017).

[17]   See Tom Ruys, *"Armed Attack" and Article 51 of the UN Charter* (New York: Cambridge University Press, 2010), 25off. See also Letter dated September 7, 2015 from the Permanent Representative of the United Kingdom of Great Britain and Northern Ireland to the United Nations addressed to the President of the Security Council, UN Doc. S/2015/688 (Sep. 8, 2015) and United Kingdom, House of Lords and House of Commons, Joint Committee on Human Rights, *The Government's Policy on the Use of Drones for Targeted Killing*, Second Report of Session 2015–16, HC 574, HL Paper 141 (May 10, 2016), *at* www.publications.parliament.uk/pa/ jt201516/jtselect/jtrights/574/574.pdf.

[18]   Daniel Bethlehem, "Principles Relevant to the Scope of a State's Right of Self-Defense Against an Imminent or Actual Armed Attack by Non-state Actors," *The American Journal of International Law* 106 (2012): 770–77 (note: Bethlehem previously served as the legal adviser to the UK Foreign Office).

imminent or actual armed attacks by non-State actors by the US, the UK and Australia in the period 2016–17.[19] The goal of this chapter, however, is not to authoritatively establish the breadth of the transatlantic divide with regard to the content and relevance of the *jus ad bellum* (if at all possible). Rather, it is to take a critical look at the alleged gap by means of a case study, notably from the perspective of the recourse to force by the US-led military coalition fighting against the so-called Islamic State (IS, also known as ISIL, or Da'esh) in Iraq and Syria. At first sight, this case would seem to confirm the existence of transatlantic divide pertaining to the *jus ad bellum*, more specifically in relation to the legality of self-defense against attacks by non-State actors (such as IS) and to the validity of the so-called unable and unwilling test. A closer analysis of the intervening States' positions, however, instead reveals a gradual acceptance of the more expansionist interpretation of the legal framework first put forward by the United States as its "persistent advocate."[20]

Against this background, this chapter looks at the legal arguments put forward by the intervening States between the commencement of Operation Inherent Resolve in September 2014 and mid-2017 with a view to justifying their military operations in Iraqi and Syrian territory.[21] The purpose is not to

---

[19] See in particular the speech by U.S. Legal Adviser Brian Egan at the 2016 ASIL Annual Meeting (n. 13); United Kingdom, Attorney General's Office, *Attorney General's Speech at the International Institute for Strategic Studies* (Jan. 11, 2017), at www.gov.uk/government/speeches/attorney-generals-speech-at-the-international-institute-for-strategic-studies; George Brandis QC (Attorney-General for Australia), "The Right of Self-Defence Against Imminent Armed Attack in International Law," *EJIL: Talk!*, May 25, 2017, at www.ejiltalk.org/the-right-of-self-defence-against-imminent-armed-attack-in-international-law/. For an account of the intergovernmental talks preceding this convergence, see Victor Kattan, "Furthering the 'War on Terrorism' through International Law: How the United States and the United Kingdom Resurrected the Bush Doctrine on Using Preventive Military Force to Combat Terrorism," *Journal on the Use of Force and International Law* 4 (2017).

[20] The term is borrowed from: Christian Henderson, *The Persistent Advocate and the Use of Force* (Farnham: Ashgate Publishing Limited, 2010).

[21] This chapter does not tackle Turkish aerial and ground operations in Syria, nor Turkey's downing of a Russian warplane in November 2015, or the allegations of third-State support to Syrian rebel groups. A more detailed account of the facts and of the justificatory discourse of States can be found in the periodic Digests of State Practice published in the *Journal on the Use of Force and International Law*. See in particular: Tom Ruys and Nele Verlinden, "Digest of State Practice 1 July–31 December 2014," *Journal on the Use of Force and International Law* 2 (2015): 119–62, 131–45; Tom Ruys, Nele Verlinden and Luca Ferro, "Digest of State Practice 1 January–30 June 2015," *Journal on the Use of Force and International Law* 2 (2015): 257–98, 279ff; Tom Ruys, Luca Ferro and Nele Verlinden, "Digest of State Practice 1 July–31 December 2015," *Journal on the Use of Force and International Law* 3 (2016): 126–70, 145ff. Similarly, the chapter does not deal with US military strikes in reaction to the Syrian

The Case of the US-Led Military Coalition against "Islamic State" 237

assess the intrinsic validity of these arguments, but rather to test their divergence or convergence.

9.2 THE LAUNCHING OF THE MILITARY COALITION AGAINST IS AND THE JUSTIFICATION PUT FORWARD BY THE UNITED STATES

Although the start of the Syrian Civil War dates back to March 2011, and notwithstanding hints of military strikes against the Syrian regime by France, the United States and (initially) the United Kingdom in the wake of the chemical weapons attack near Damascus in August 2013,[22] the US-led international military campaign against IS was not launched until the summer of 2014. The immediate cause for this was the rapid advance of IS, which took control over sizeable parts of Syrian as well as Iraqi territory in June 2014, and whose ranks swelled to include several thousand foreign fighters *inter alia* from various Arab as well as European States. In addition, IS' brutalities, evidenced by the release of videos depicting the beheadings of journalists and aid workers, as well as mass executions of security forces and Shia Muslims, increasingly attracted international attention.

In a letter to the UN Security Council dated June 25, 2014, Iraq drew attention to the threat from IS, which was "carrying out organized military operations across the Syrian border" and called upon States to "assist [it] by providing military training, advanced technology and the weapons required to respond to the situation, with a view to denying terrorists staging areas and safe havens."[23]

Shortly after the IS offensive against the town of Sinjar and the persecution of its Yezidi minority, as well as the formation of a new and more inclusive Iraqi government in Bagdad – a move hailed by the UN Security Council[24] – US President Obama announced the formation of a broad coalition to combat IS. In a televised address dated September 10, 2014, he declared that "America

---

regime's (alleged) use of chemical weapons on the village of Khan Sheikhoun, see *JUFIL Digest of State Practice 2* (2017) (n. 16)

[22] The threat of military strikes was eventually staved off after Russia brokered a diplomatic deal under which Syria agreed to join the Chemical Weapons Conventions and have its chemical weapons stockpiles destroyed under OPCW supervision. See Tom Ruys and Nele Verlinden, "Digest of State Practice 1 July–31 December 2013," *Journal on the Use of Force and International Law* 1 (2014): 180–81.

[23] Annex to the letter dated June 25, 2014 from the Permanent Representative of Iraq to the United Nations addressed to the Secretary-General, UN Doc. S/2014/440 (Jun. 25, 2014), 2.

[24] Statement by the President of the Security Council, UN Doc. S/PRST/2014/20 (Sep. 19, 2014), 1.

[would] lead a broad coalition to roll back this terrorist threat," and that it would "degrade, and ultimately destroy" IS.[25]

During an open meeting of the Security Council on September 19, 2015, various States expressed their support for the US initiative and/or pledged (to consider) support (for) the envisaged operation against IS. Other States nonetheless called for caution, with some expressing concerns over the legality of unilateral action.[26]

The day following the debate, Iraq sent a letter to the Security Council, welcoming "the commitment that was made by 26 States to provide ... appropriate military assistance through the provision of air cover in coordination with the Iraqi armed forces."[27] It furthermore confirmed that the international efforts to combat "the safe haven outside Iraq's borders that is a direct threat to the security of [Iraqi] people and territory" was requested and carried out with its "express consent."[28]

On September 23, US President Obama first announced that the United States had conducted airstrikes against IS targets within Syria as part of Operation "Inherent Resolve," in cooperation with Saudi Arabia, the United Arab Emirates, Jordan, Bahrain and Qatar.[29] A number of strikes had also been undertaken against the Khorasan group, an Al-Qaeda affiliate suspected of plotting attacks against the United States and its allies.

Contrary to its Arab coalition partners, none of which put forward an express legal justification, the United States spelled out the legal basis of its operation in a short two-paragraph letter to the Security Council of the same day.[30] The first paragraph refers to the request for military support from the Government of Iraq. The Iraqi consent would indeed appear to provide a *prima facie* valid legal basis for the use of force by third-States against IS sites and military strongholds *in Iraq*. It is generally accepted that military intervention pursuant

---

[25] United States of America, the White House, *Statement by the President on ISIL* (Sep. 10, 2014), *at* www.whitehouse.gov/the-press-office/2014/09/10/statement-president-isil-1.

[26] See: UNSC Verbatim Record, UN Doc. S/PV.7271 (Sep. 19, 2014). For an overview of State positions, see: *JUFIL* Digest of State Practice 2 (2015) (n. 21), 136–38.

[27] Annex to the letter dated September 20, 2014 from the Permanent Representative of Iraq to the United Nations addressed to the President of the Security Council, UN Doc. S/2014/691 (Sep. 22, 2014), 2.

[28] *Id.*

[29] United States of America, the White House, *Statement by the President on Airstrikes in Syria* (Sep. 23, 2014), *at* www.whitehouse.gov/the-press-office/2014/09/23/statement-president-airstrikes-syria. See also the official page on Operation "Inherent Resolve" of the US Department of Defense, *at* www.defense.gov/News/Special-Reports/0814_Inherent-Resolve.

[30] Letter dated September 23, 2014 from the Permanent Representative of the United States of America to the United Nations addressed to the Secretary-General, UN Doc. S/2014/695 (Sep. 23, 2014).

The Case of the US-Led Military Coalition against "Islamic State"   239

to a valid and prior invitation by the *de jure* authorities of a State does not give rise to a use of force "between States" "in their international relations" and is accordingly excluded from the scope of Article 2(4) UN Charter.[31]

In the present case, although the Iraqi government had lost control over sizeable tracts of land, they remained in control of most of the national territory, including the capital, and continued to be recognized by the Security Council as the sole (and legitimate) government of Iraq.[32] It is admitted that a significant portion of legal doctrine, including the present authors, are of the opinion that the nonintervention principle and the right of self-determination prohibit third-State full-scale "intervention by invitation" in situations of civil war.[33] Without going into further detail, it is argued that the reliance on the Iraqi consent, which would appear not to have been challenged by other States (not participating in the military intervention in Iraq), does not necessarily conflict with this position (and accordingly need not be taken as proof that State practice permits "intervention by invitation" upon the request of the *de jure* government, including in times of civil war). In a nutshell, the main reason for this is that, rather than constituting a popular movement pursuing (political) self-determination, IS was (and is) universally regarded as a terrorist organization, which is not simply a "home-grown" Iraqi phenomenon, but counted substantial numbers of "foreign fighters" among its ranks and operated on a cross-border basis (from its safe haven in Syria).[34]

---

[31]   *Armed Activities on the Territory of the Congo (DRC v. Uganda)*, Merits, 2005 ICJ REP. 168, para. 105 (Dec. 19); Definition of Aggression, UNGA Res. 3314 (XXIX) (Dec. 14, 1974), Art. 3(e).

[32]   Statement by the President of the Security Council, UN Doc. S/PRST/2014/20, 1 (Sep. 19, 2014).

[33]   See, for example, Louise Doswald-Beck, "The Legal Validity of Military Intervention by Invitation of the Government," *British Yearbook of International Law* 56 (1985): 199–200; Erika De Wet, "The Modern Practice of Intervention by Invitation in Africa and Its Implications for the Prohibition of the Use of Force," *European Journal of International Law* 26 (2015): 979–98; Corten, *Droit contre la Guerre* (n. 9) 513–14; Christine Gray, *International Law and the Use of Force* (New York: Oxford University Press, 2008), 132–47. See also Resolution by the Institut de Droit International, *The Principle of Non-Intervention in Civil Wars*, Wiesbaden Session (Aug. 14, 1975), *at* http://justitiaetpace.org/resolutions_chrono .php?start=1969&end=1975.

[34]   On this topic, see Dapo Akande and Zachary Vermeer, "The Airstrikes against Islamic State in Iraq and the Alleged Prohibition on Military Assistance to Governments in Civil Wars," *EJIL: Talk!*, February 21, 2015, www.ejiltalk.org/the-airstrikes-against-islamic-state -in-iraq-and-the-alleged-prohibition-on-military-assistance-to-governments-in-civil-wars/; Raphael Van Steenberghe, "The Alleged Prohibition on Intervening in Civil Wars Is Still Alive after the Airstrikes against Islamic State in Iraq: A Response to Dapo Akande and Zachary Vermeer," *EJIL: Talk!*, February 12, 2015, www.ejiltalk.org/the-alleged-pro hibition-on-intervening-in-civil-wars-is-still-alive-after-the-airstrikes-against-islamic-state -in-iraq-a-response-to-dapo-akande-and-zachary-vermeer/. See also Karine Bannelier- Christakis, "Military Interventions against ISIL in Iraq, Syria and Libya, and the Legal

Either way, if the official consent by the Iraqi government put to rest most doubts regarding an adequate international mandate for forcible action against IS within Iraqi territory, "intervention by invitation" cannot serve as a legal basis for military action by third States beyond the "inviting" State's own territory. This remains so, even if it is true, as the Iraqi requests indicated, that IS had established "a safe haven *outside Iraq's borders*" securing for itself "the ability to train for, plan, finance and carry out terrorist operations *across [Iraq's] borders.*"[35] To hold otherwise would confound "intervention by invitation" as precluding a violation of Article 2(4) of the UN Charter, with the right to self-defense, in accordance with Article 51 of the UN Charter, which allows for the use of force necessary (and proportionate) to repel an armed attack across territorial boundaries.

This then explains why the US letter relies on an alternative legal basis to justify military action against IS within Syrian territory. In the second paragraph of its letter, the United States puts forward a broad interpretation of the right to self-defense, referring explicitly to Article 51 UN Charter, which would allow States to "defend themselves" against attacks by non-State actors when "the government of the State where the threat is located is *unwilling or unable* to prevent the use of its territory for such attacks."[36] Specifically, considering that the "Syrian regime has shown that it cannot and will not confront these safe havens effectively itself" the letter affirms that the USA "has initiated necessary and proportionate military actions in Syria."[37] In light hereof, the letter construes the military action against IS as an application of the right of *collective* self-defense to protect Iraqi citizens and Iraqi sovereignty. In addition, the letter also makes references to the US right of *individual* self-defense, referring specifically to "terrorist threats" that the "al-Qaeda elements in Syria known as the Khorasan Group . . . pose to the United States."[38]

Basis of Consent," *Leiden Journal of International Law* 29 (2016): 743–75; Tom Ruys and Luca Ferro, "Weathering the Storm: Legality and Legal Implications of the Saudi-led Military Intervention in Yemen," *International & Comparative Law Quarterly* 65 (2016): 61–98.

[35] Annex to the letter dated September 20, 2014 from the Permanent Representative of Iraq to the United Nations addressed to the President of the Security Council, UN Doc. S/2014/691 (Sep. 22, 2014), 2 (emphasis added).

[36] Letter dated September 23, 2014 from the Permanent Representative of the United States of America to the United Nations addressed to the Secretary-General, UN Doc. S/2014/695 (Sep. 23, 2014) (emphasis added).

[37] *Id.*

[38] *Id.*

9.3 THE LEGAL "CONTEXT" OF THE US SELF-DEFENSE ARGUMENT

The US reliance on self-defense is premised on two crucial assumptions: first, that cross-border attacks by non-State actors are capable of qualifying as "armed attacks" in the sense of Article 51 UN Charter, irrespective of any actual State involvement; and second, that such attacks justify a cross-border military reaction against the non-State group when the State from whose territory the non-State actor operates/launches its attacks is "unwilling or unable" to prevent them (this can arguably be construed as a component of the broader necessity requirement for action in self-defense).[39]

If the notion of "armed attack" has traditionally been understood as referring, not to "an incident created by irresponsible groups or individuals, but rather an attack by one State upon another,"[40] the flexible reading of the right of self-defense put forward here is not a completely novel one. Already in 1956, Israel relied on the right of self-defense to justify its controversial intervention in Egyptian territory allegedly in reaction to attacks by *Fedayeen* operating from the Sinai desert.[41] The United States for its part in the early 1980s endorsed the view that a State subjected to continuing terrorist attacks may respond with appropriate use of force to defend itself against further attacks and occasionally raised this position (also known as the Shultz doctrine) before the UN Security Council.[42] Yet, it is especially since the 9/11 attacks that the United States, as well as several other States, have come to embrace a more permissive understanding of the right of self-defense vis-à-vis non-State attacks. The United States in particular has ostensibly abandoned the need for any form of State involvement for attacks by non-State actors to qualify as

---

[39] This is also how the "unable or unwilling" doctrine is construed in e.g., the April 2016 speech by US Legal Adviser Brian Egan. See Egan (n. 13): "In particular, there will be cases in which there is a reasonable and objective basis for concluding that the territorial State is unwilling or unable to effectively confront the non-State actor in its territory so that it is *necessary to act in self-defense* against the non-State actor in that State's territory without the territorial State's consent" (emphasis added).

[40] United States of America, US Senate, Report of the Committee on Foreign Relations on the North Atlantic Treaty, Executive Report no. 8 (Jun. 6, 1949), 13; quoted in Ian Brownlie, *International Law and the Use of Force by States* (Oxford: Oxford University Press, 1963), 278. See also: Josef L. Kunz, "Individual and Collective Self-Defense in Article 51 of the Charter of the United Nations," *The American Journal of International Law* 41 (1947): 878.

[41] UNSC Verbatim Record, UN Doc. S/PV.749 (Oct. 30, 1956), 33, 36; UNGA Verbatim Record, UN Doc. A/PV.562 ((Nov. 1, 1956), 105, 145–46; UNGA Verbatim Record, UN Doc. A/PV.572 (10 Nov., 1956), 18.

[42] See Ruys, *Armed Attack* (n. 17) 421–28. See, e.g., UNSC Verbatim Record, UN Doc. S/PV.2615 (Oct. 4, 1985), para. 252.

"armed attacks" in the sense of Article 51 UN Charter.[43] This was particularly evident from a series of US official documents and statements explaining the legal rationale underlying the Obama administration's policy on targeted killings and drone strikes and which, among other, consistently rely on the so-called "unable and unwilling" doctrine.[44]

At the same time, it is observed that the two assumptions identified above are not without controversy – to put it mildly. Thus, as is well-known, in its famous *Nicaragua* judgment the International Court of Justice (ICJ), borrowing from the United Nations General Assembly (UNGA) Definition of Aggression's provision concerning "indirect military aggression,"[45] ostensibly took the view that there ought to be a close link between the non-State armed group conducting the actual attacks and another State (whether as a result of the latter's "sending" of the armed group or its "substantial involvement" therein) for these attacks to trigger the right of self-defense.[46] While this position gave rise to criticism at the time,[47] it has been observed by several scholars that it accurately reflected State practice and *opinio juris* in preceding decades.[48] Furthermore, while there has been increasing support among States for a more flexible right to take cross-border forcible action in reaction to prior attacks by non-State armed groups (and targeted against that group's presence abroad) in the wake of the 9/11 attacks and the adoption, by the UN Security Council, of resolutions 1368(2001) and 1373(2001),[49] the evidence in State practice is not unequivocal.[50] Similarly, notwithstanding increased

---

[43] Thus, the 2015 Law of War Manual stresses that the right of self-defense "applies in response to any 'armed attack', not just attacks that originate with States." *U.S. Law of War Manual 2015* (n. 16) 48–49.

[44] See, e.g., United States of America, The White House, Report on the Legal and Policy Frameworks Guiding the United States' Use of Military Force and Related National Security Operations (Dec. 2016), 10; Stephen W. Preston, "The Legal Framework for the United States' Use of Military Force Since 9/11." Speech presented at the annual meeting for the American Society of International Law, Washington DC, April 10, 2016, at www .defense.gov/News/Speeches/Speech-View/Article/606662; Egan (n. 13). For an overview and critique, see: Christine Gray, "Targeted Killings: Recent US Attempts to Create a Legal Framework," *Current Legal Problems* 66 (2013): 75–106; Kinga Tibori-Szabó, "Self-Defence and the United States Policy on Drone Strikes," *Journal of Conflict & Security Law* 20 (2015).

[45] UNGA Res. 3314 (XXIX) (n. 31), Art. 3(g).

[46] ICJ *Nicaragua* case (n. 14) para. 195.

[47] E.g., *Id.*, Dissenting Opinion of Judge Jennings, 543; Dissenting Opinion of Judge Schwebel, § 171.

[48] E.g., Gray, *Use of Force* (n. 33) 130–32 and 175–77; Pierluigi Lamberti Zanardi, "Indirect Military Aggression," in *The Current Legal Regulation of the Use of Force*, ed. Antonio Cassese (Dordrecht: Martinus Nijhoff, 1986), 113–15.

[49] UNSC Res. 1368 (Sep. 12, 2001); UNSC Res. 1373 (Sep. 28, 2001).

[50] See Ruys, *Armed Attack* (n. 17) 368ff.

The Case of the US-Led Military Coalition against "Islamic State"   243

support in legal doctrine that (grave) attacks by non-State actors may qualify as "armed attacks," irrespective of State imputability or State involvement,[51] several scholars continue to insist on a more restrictive *"Nicaragua*-style" reading of Article 51 UN Charter.[52] It may also be recalled that – to the discontent of some of its judges[53] – the ICJ has ostensibly refused to open the door (albeit in an ambiguous manner) for a broader right of self-defense against non-State attacks in its *Palestinian Wall* Opinion (2004)[54] and in its *DRC v. Uganda* judgment (2005).[55]

The controversial nature of the two assumptions mentioned above is also reflected in the reactions of an – admittedly limited – number of States who questioned the legality of the coalition strikes against IS in Syria. For example, Russia's Foreign Ministry held that the legitimacy of the strikes was "questionable," "because such actions can only be taken with a UN sanction and clear agreement of the government of the country where they are undertaken, in this case the Damascus government."[56] A similar position was voiced by

---

[51]   See, e.g., Elizabeth Wilmshurst, *Principles of International Law on the Use of Force by States in Self-Defence*, CHATHAM HOUSE (Oct. 1, 2005), *at* www.chathamhouse.org/publications/pap ers/view/108106, 13; "Leiden Policy Recommendations on Counter-terrorism and International Law," Annexed to Larissa van den Herik and Nico Schrijver (eds.), *Counter-Terrorism Strategies in a Fragmented International Legal Order* (Cambridge: Cambridge University Press, 2013), 706–26, paras. 38–39; Bethlehem (n. 18) 774; Advisory Committee on Issues of Public International Law (Netherlands), *Advisory Report on Armed Drones*, Advisory Report No. 23 (Jul. 2013), *at* http://cms.webbeat.net/ContentSuite/upload/cav/doc/ CAVV_advisory_report_on_armed_drones_(English_translation_-_final)_(2).pdf, 14.

[52]   Corten, *Droit contre la Guerre* (n. 9) 717–58; Christine Gray, "Targeted Killings: Recent US Attempts to Create a Legal Framework," *Current Legal Problems* 66 (2013); Albrecht Randelzhofer and Georg Nolte, "Article 51," in *The Charter of the United Nations*, ed. Bruno Simma, et al., vol. 2 (Oxford: Oxford University Press, 2012), 1414–19. See also *A Plea Against the Abusive Invocation of Self-Defence as a Response to Terrorism* (n. 11).

[53]   Legal Consequences of the Construction of a Wall in the Occupied Palestinian Territory, Advisory Opinion, 2004 ICJ REP. 136 (July 9), Separate Opinion Judge Kooijmans, para. 35, Declaration of Judge Buergenthal, para. 6, and Separate Opinion of Judge Higgins, para. 33; ICJ *Armed Activities* case (n. 33), Separate Opinion Judge Kooijmans, para. 25 and Separate Opinion Judge Simma, para. 8.

[54]   ICJ *Wall* Advisory Opinion (n. 53) para. 139 (*Compendium* 951).

[55]   ICJ *Armed Activities* case (n. 31) paras. 146–47.

[56]   Russia, Ministry of Foreign Affairs, *Comment by the Information and Press Department of the Russian Ministry of Foreign Affairs regarding US Air Strikes at Terrorists in Syria and Iraq* (Sep. 24, 2014), *at* http://archive.mid.ru/BDOMP/Brp_4.nsf/arh/EAD701F21FAB067044257D5 E0038D682?OpenDocument. See also: "Russia Condemns US Strikes on Islamic State Without Syria's Approval," *The Moscow Times*, September 25, 2014, www .themoscowtimes.com/news/article/russia-condemns-u-s-strikes-on-islamic-state-without-syria -s-approval/507784.html. Consider also: Michelle Nichols, "Russia's Lavrov Questions Legality of US Airstrikes on Syria," *Reuters*, September 26, 2014, http://in.reuters.com/art icle/2014/09/26/syria-crisis-russia-lavrov-idINKCN0HL2KB20140926. Moreover, in its own letter to the President of the UN Security Council, on October 15, 2015, Russia explicitly relied

Iran.[57] A number of countries such as Cuba or Venezuela stressed the need to respect the sovereignty of Syria.[58] Syria itself did not – at least initially – submit a formal complaint to the UN Security Council following the launch of Operation Inherent Resolve,[59] but nonetheless insisted on multiple occasions that, absent approval by, and coordination with, the Syrian authorities, the intervention was "illegal."[60] In a letter dated September 17, 2015, Syria moreover explicitly attacked what it perceived as a "distorted reading" of this "important and sensitive paragraph of the Charter" [i.e., Article 51 UN Charter].[61]

If the reactions above suggest that the flexible interpretation of the right of self-defense vis-à-vis attacks by non-State armed groups and the concomitant "unable and unwilling" doctrine remain controversial, they also raise the related, yet distinct, question as to whether Syria could effectively be regarded

on the "request from the President of the Syrian Arab Republic, Bashar al-Asad, to provide military assistance in combating the terrorist group Islamic State in Iraq and the Levant (ISIL)" to justify the launch of air and missile strikes by late-September 2015. Annex to the letter dated October 15, 2015 from the Permanent Representative of the Russian Federation to the United Nations addressed to the President of the Security Council, UN Doc. S/2015/792 (Oct. 15, 2015), 2.

[57] Iran, *Statement by Hassan Rouhani, President of Islamic Republic of Iran, in a Meeting with Directors of US Media in New York* (Sep. 23, 2014), at www.president.ir/en/81134; "No Legal Standing for US Strikes in Syria: Rouhani," *Press TV*, September 24, 2014, www.presstv.ir/detail/2014/09/24/379908/us-strikes-in-syria-not-legal/.

[58] See the official page of the UN General Assembly General Debate: September 24–30, 2014, at www.un.org/en/ga/69/meetings/gadebate/. See also: UNSC Verbatim Record, UN Doc S/PV.7419 (Mar. 27, 2015) 24 (Venezuela); Hazem Sabbagh, "South African Ambassador: Syria Is an Independent Sovereign State, Can Handle Its Own Affairs," SANA, June 22, 2015, http://sana.sy/en/?p=45877.

[59] Syria did, however, submit formal complaints on other occasions, e.g. with regard to Turkish operations on its soil. See Identical letters dated October 3, 2014 from the Chargé d'affaires a.i. of the Permanent Mission of the Syrian Arab Republic to the United Nations addressed to the Secretary-General and the President of the Security Council, UN Doc. A/69/426-S/2014/719 (Oct. 8, 2014), 1.

[60] E.g., Régis Le Sommier, "Our Full Interview with Syrian President Bashar Al-Assad," *Paris Match*, December 3, 2014, www.parismatch.com/Actu/International/Our-Interview-with-Syrian-President-Bashar-al-Assad-661984 "Syria's President Speaks—A Conversation with Bashar al-Assad," *Foreign Affairs*, March/April 2015, www.foreignaffairs.com/interviews/2015-01-25/syrias-president-speaks. See also: Hala Jaber, "Britain's Airstrikes Are Doomed to Fail," *The Sunday Times* (Dec. 6, 2015), at www.thesundaytimes.co.uk/sto/news/focus/article1641838.ece.

[61] Identical letters dated September 17, 2015 from the Permanent Representative of the Syrian Arab Republic to the United Nations addressed to the Secretary-General and the President of the Security Council, UN Doc. S/2015/719 (Sep. 21, 2015), 1. See also: Identical letters dated 21 September 2015 from the Permanent Representative of the Syrian Arab Republic to the United Nations addressed to the Secretary-General and the President of the Security Council, UN Doc. A/70/385-S/2015/727 (Sep. 22, 2015).

The Case of the US-Led Military Coalition against "Islamic State" 245

as "unwilling" to confront IS and its safe haven in Syria. While there can be little doubt that the Assad regime had lost control over significant parts of Syrian territory and was accordingly "unable" to prevent cross-border operations by IS into Syria (as the United States has claimed[62]), its message (whether genuine or not) was that it was nonetheless "willing" to do so and, more specifically, that it was willing to accept military operations against IS in its territory as long as these were coordinated with the Syrian authorities.[63] Accordingly, Operation "Inherent Resolve" also raises a fundamental question as to the concrete application of the "unable and unwilling" doctrine – whose operationalization, all things considered, remains shrouded in mystery.

Against this background, it is worth having a closer look at the position of European States, specifically of those States contributing to the US-led operation. It is noted in this respect that, while a number of European States had occasionally spoken out, implicitly or explicitly, in favor of an extension of Article 51 UN Charter to attacks by non-State actors, up until the launching of Operation Inherent Resolve, they did so in a cautious manner only.[64] In particular, up until the launch of the operation, no European State had explicitly invoked the "unable and unwilling" test to justify military operations abroad.[65] Nor, it seems, were there any examples of European States explicitly embracing this test *in abstracto*, for example by including it in their military manuals. Hence, it remains to be seen whether European States opted for a more traditional and restrictive understanding of the right of self-defense or rather chose to copy the US reasoning.

---

[62] See, for example, Egan (n. 13): "By September 2014, the Syrian government had lost effective control of much of eastern and northeastern Syria, with much of that territory under ISIL's control."

[63] See e.g., UNSC Verbatim Record, UN Doc. S/PV.7418 (Mar. 26, 2015), 5 (Syria); Identical letters dated May 25, 2015 from the Permanent Representative of the Syrian Arab Republic to the United Nations addressed to the Secretary-General and the President of the Security Council, UN Doc. A/69/912–S/2015/371 (Jun. 1, 2015); UNSC Verbatim Record, UN Doc S/PV.7476 (Jun. 29, 2015), 4 (Syria).

[64] See, in particular: The Netherlands, Ministry of Defence, Netherlands Defence Doctrine (Sep., 2005), at www.government.nl/binaries/government/documents/leaflets/2010/01/12/neth erlands defence doctrine/defence-doctrine-eng pdf, 33; France, Secrétariat Général de la Défense Nationale, *La France face au terrorisme: Livre Blanc du Gouvernement sur la sécurité intérieure face au terrorisme*, (Oct., 2006), www.ladocumentationfrancaise.fr/rapports-publics /064000275/, 95. Further: Ruys, *Armed Attack* (n. 17) 443–46.

[65] It is observed, however, that in the wake of the 9/11 attacks NATO for the first time activated Article 5 of the NATO Treaty in light of the fact that an attack had been "directed from abroad" against the US. *Statement by NATO Secretary-General Lord Robertson* (Oct. 2, 2001), reprinted in *International Legal Materials* 41 (2001): 1267; *Statement by the North Atlantic Council, NATO Press Release No. 124* (Sep. 12, 2001), *at* www.nato.int/docu/pr/2001/p01-124e .htm.

It is noted in the margin that the US arguments, spelled out in the letter to the Security Council of 23 September 2014, present an additional challenge from a legal perspective. Indeed, inasmuch as the United States relied not only on *collective* self-defense (to protect Iraq from ongoing attacks), but also on *individual* self-defense, this opens another proverbial can of worms. In particular, the letter does not suggest that the United States itself has been the subject of an "armed attack" triggering the right of self-defense, but instead refers to the "threat" to the United States (and its allies) "posed" by the so-called Khorasan group.[66] It follows that the invocation of individual self-defense rests on a third assumption, additional to the two assumptions identified earlier, notably that it is lawful to engage in anticipatory self-defense preceding the occurrence of an armed attack.

The permissibility of anticipatory action nonetheless remains a subject of considerable debate.[67] It is noted that the (admittedly growing number of) proponents of anticipatory self-defense generally insist on the requirement that the threat of an armed attack be "imminent" to justify action in self-defense. In the present case, the letter to the Council merely refers to a "threat" without further ado. A news release of the Department of Defense in turn stated that the "United States ... took action to disrupt the imminent attack plotting (sic) against the United States and Western interests conduct by ... the Khorasan Group."[68] To the authors' knowledge, however, no further information was made public supporting the existence of an "imminent" threat of attack against the USA.[69]

9.4 THE POSITION OF EUROPEAN AND OTHER WESTERN MEMBERS VIS-À-VIS THE COALITION AGAINST IS

9.4.1 *The Early Months of the Campaign against IS*

When Operation "Inherent Resolve" was launched in September 2014, it received support not only from a number of Arab States, but also from several European States and other western countries. In particular, the United

---

[66] Letter dated September 23, 2014 from the Permanent Representative of the United States of America to the United Nations addressed to the Secretary-General, UN Doc. S/2014/695 (Sep. 23, 2014).

[67] Further: Ruys, *Armed Attack* (n. 17) 305ff.

[68] United States of America, Department of Defense, *U.S. Military, Partner Nations Conduct Airstrikes in Syria* (Sep. 23, 2014), *at* www.defense.gov/News-Article-View/Article/603301.

[69] But see, for a critical opinion: Kevin Jon Heller, "The Invention of the Khorasan Group and Non-Imminent Imminence," *Opinio Juris*, September 29, 2014, http://opiniojuris.org/2014/09/29/invention-khorasan-group-non-imminent-imminence/.

Kingdom, France, Belgium, the Netherlands and Denmark all agreed to contribute to the campaign, as did Canada and Australia.

What is remarkable, however, is that, whereas the Arab coalition partners participated in air strikes against IS targets in Syrian territory, the aforementioned countries all limited their actions to Iraqi territory. While this choice may be explained by a variety of politico-strategic and military reasons, a number of elements suggest that it may also have been inspired in part by the perception that the legal case for intervention in Syria was weaker – put differently, by a desire to steer clear from troubled legal waters.

First, it appears that these countries primarily justified their participation in the coalition by reference to the "intervention by invitation" doctrine. Thus, the Dutch government justified the troop deployment on the basis of the Iraqi requests for military support of June 25 and September 20, 2014.[70] These requests were stated to provide a sufficient legal basis for the deployment of forces within Iraq. France similarly stressed that the action was undertaken pursuant to a request from the Iraqi authorities and aimed at restoring Iraqi sovereignty.[71] According to a policy paper of the British government released on September 25, "the consent of Iraq" was equally considered to provide "a clear and unequivocal basis for the deployment of UK forces … to take military action to strike ISIL sites and military strongholds in Iraq."[72] A resolution adopted by the Canadian House of Commons and supporting the government's decision to take part in the aerial campaign against IS similarly placed considerable emphasis on the request from the government of Iraq for military support against IS.[73] The fact that these States sought to rely primarily on the "intervention by invitation" doctrine, rather than the more controversial flexible reading of self-defense and the so-called unable and willing doctrine, is also corroborated by the fact that none of them submitted a report to the UN Security Council (as would normally be expected (and

---

[70] The Netherlands, *Brief van de Ministers van Buitenlandse Zaken, van Defensie en voor Buitenlandse Handel en Ontwikkelingssamenwerking*, 2014–15, 27925, No. 506, 4 (Sep. 24, 2014).

[71] "Premier Bombardement Français contre l'Etat Islamique en Irak," *Le Monde*, September 19, 2014, *at* www.lemonde.fr/proche-orient/article/2014/090/19/premieres-frappes-francaises-contre-l-ei-en-irak_4490645_3218.html. See also the statement by Prime Minister Valls during the session of the Assemblée nationale of September 24, 2014, *at* www.assembleenationale.fr /14/cri/2013-2014-extra3/20143001.asp.

[72] United Kingdom, Prime Minister's Office, *Policy Paper, Summary of the Government Legal Position on Military Action in Iraq against ISIL* (Sep. 25, 2014), *at* www.gov.uk/government/ publications/military-action-in-iraq-against-isil-government-legal-position/summary-of-the-government-legal-position-on-military-action-in-iraq-against-isil.

[73] Canada, House of Commons, Vote No. 252, 41st Parliament, 2nd Session (Oct. 7, 2014).

required) from a State exercising the right of self-defense pursuant to Article 51 UN Charter). Only the United Kingdom submitted a letter to the UN Security Council reporting its actions, and then only in late November, that is, two months after it originally decided to deploy troops in Iraq.[74]

Second, a number of States actually acknowledged, implicitly or explicitly, that the legal case for airstrikes against IS in Syria was less straightforward. The UK Foreign Secretary, for instance, mid-September 2014 reportedly noted that the legal environment and military permissiveness in Syria and Iraq were very different, stressing that "Britain will not be taking part in air strikes in Syria."[75] The Dutch government for its part, observed in a letter to Parliament that there "currently [existed] no international consensus as to whether there [was] a mandate under international law for military deployment in Syria. . . . The Dutch troop deployment is therefore limited to Iraq."[76] In turn, then Canadian Prime Minister Stephen Harper explicitly stated that Canada would "strike ISIL where – and only where – Canada has the clear support of the government of the country in question."[77] He admitted that "[a]t present this is only true in Iraq. If it were to become the case in Syria, we will participate in air strikes against ISIL in that country also."[78] The message implicit in this statement is that the lack of consent of the Syrian government (in Damascus) constituted the decisive reason why Canada confined its involvement to Iraqi territory.

At first sight, the foregoing considerations would seem to confirm that the European States involved in Operation "Inherent Resolve," as well as, for instance, Canada, took a more cautious approach than the United States and steered clear from contributing to a precedent in favor of a more expansionist reading of the right of self-defense. Put differently, the decision of these States to take part in military operations exclusively in Iraqi territory and to couch such actions in terms of intervention by invitation, would ostensibly confirm

---

[74] Identical letters dated November 9, 2015 from the Permanent Representative of the Syrian Arab Republic to the United Nations addressed to the Secretary-General and the President of the Security Council, UN Doc. S/2015/851 (Nov. 16, 2015).

[75] Stephen Brown and Erik Kirschbaum, "Germany, Britain Say Won't Take Part in Anti-IS Air Strikes in Syria," *Reuters*, September 11, 2014, www.reuters.com/article/iraq-crisis-germany-b ritain/germany-britain-say-wont-take-part-in-anti-is-air-strikes-in-syria-idUSB4N0QV00920140911.

[76] The Netherlands, *Brief van de Ministers van Buitenlandse Zaken, van Defensie en voor Buitenlandse Handel en Ontwikkelingssamenwerking*, year 2014–15, 27925 No. 506 (Sep. 24, 2014), 4–5 (translation provided by the authors).

[77] Canada, House of Commons, Debates, 41st Parliament, 2nd Session, Hansard, Vol. 147, No. 122 (Oct. 3, 2014), at 8227 (emphasis added).

[78] *Id.*

The Case of the US-Led Military Coalition against "Islamic State"   249

the existence of a divide, albeit not a strictly "transatlantic" one, between the United States and "the rest of the West."

The considerations spelled out above only tell part of the story, however, and the provisional conclusion hardly holds on closer scrutiny. This is so for three reasons. First, a number of countries, even if they chose not to intervene in Syria (or not to take part in Operation Inherent Resolve altogether), nonetheless expressed support for the strikes against IS in Syrian territory, including in legal terms. Thus, even if British Foreign Secretary Philip Hammond hinted at the different legal environment in Syria and Iraq (see *supra* note 75), he was (almost immediately) rebuffed by the Prime Minister's Office.[79] Before the UK House of Commons, Prime Minister Cameron insisted that, even if "the Syrian situation [was] more complicated than the Iraqi situation," there was no "legal barrier" against military action against IS within Syria.[80] In its letter to the Security Council dated November 26, the United Kingdom moreover expressed support for the coalition's strikes against "ISIL sites and military strongholds in Syria, as necessary and proportionate measures."[81] Other European powers, such as France and Germany, also did not see any legal impediment to military action in Syria either. The French Minister for Foreign Affairs, for example, affirmed that "[i]l n'y a pas à notre sens d'empêchement juridique à ce que les attaques de Daech fassent l'objet de réactions aussi bien en Irak qu'en Syrie. Cela nous semble faire partie . . . de la possible légitime défense, au titre de l'article 51."[82] Germany, for its part, recognized that US attacks against IS within Syria were "about helping the Iraqi government to defend Iraq against attacks carried out by IS from Syria."[83] It specifically appeared to rely in this context on the alleged tacit consent given

---

[79] United Kingdom, Prime Minister's Office, *Press Briefing: Afternoon 11 September 2014* (Sep. 11, 2014), *at* www.gov.uk/government/news/press-briefing-afternoon-11-september-2014 (stressing that the United Kingdom "had not ruled anything out").

[80] United Kingdom, House of Commons, Hansard Record of Commons Debate (Sep. 26, 2014) Columns 1259, Column 1264, Column 1623 (referring to the right of collective self-defense and, it appears, humanitarian intervention, as possible legal bases for action in Syria).

[81] Identical letters dated November 25, 2014 from the Permanent Representative of the United Kingdom of Great Britain and Northern Ireland to the United Nations addressed to the Secretary-General and the President of the Security Council, UN Doc. S/2014/851 (Nov. 26, 2014).

[82] France, France Diplomatie, *Syrie – Irak – Conférence de presse de M. Laurent Fabius, ministre des Affaires étrangères et du Développement international* (Sep. 22, 2014), *at* http://basedoc .diplomatie.gouv.fr/vues/Kiosque/FranceDiplomatie/kiosque.php?fichier=bafr2014-09-23. html#Chapitre13.

[83] Stephen Brown, "Berlin Voices Support for Air Strikes on Islamic State in Syria," *Reuters*, September 26, 2014, www.reuters.com/article/us-mideast-crisis-germany-idUSKCN0HL1BU20140926.

by the Assad regime: "The Syrian government was advised beforehand [of the attacks] and has made no protest."

Second, a number of States did not, or at least not exclusively, rely on "intervention by invitation," but instead relied, at least in part, on the right of self-defense. For example, a resolution of the Belgian Parliament approving the deployment of several fighter jets in Iraqi territory, in its preamble referred – rather ambiguously – to the request for assistance from the Iraqi authorities "which suffices under international law to justify a military action against IS within Iraq (in accordance with Article 51 of Chapter VII of the UN Charter)."[84] And while the United Kingdom initially relied on the consent of Iraq, in its letter to the Security Council of November 26 it instead framed its actions as "measures in support of the collective self-defense of Iraq."[85] It follows that, even if these countries did not explicitly embrace the "unable and unwilling" doctrine, they did take the view that the cross-border activities of IS gave rise to an "armed attack" triggering the right of self-defense – even though it is clear that IS was not "sent by or on behalf of" Syria and that Damascus was not "substantially involved" in the group's activities.

On a related note, if the position of the Dutch government mentioned above appears to explicitly question the legality of US strikes against IS in Syrian territory, a closer reading reveals that it actually *endorses* the "unable and unwilling" test, but questions whether this test was ultimately fulfilled in the case under consideration. The relevant passage merits being restated in full:

> There currently exists no international consensus as to whether there is a mandate under international law for military deployment in Syria. ... The Cabinet expresses its understanding for the efforts of the United States. This air campaign is conducted in cooperation with a number of countries in the region, but does not entail any cooperation with the Syrian regime.
>
> The United States ... rely on the right of collective self-defense .... The exercise of this right is subject to strict requirements, especially where an (imminent) armed attack emanates from an armed group such as ISIS. Whether Syria is able or willing to tackle such attacks is decisive in such case. At this moment, it cannot be ascertained whether or not self-defense

---

[84] Belgium, Chambre des Représentants de Belgique, *Résolution sur la Situation en Irak et la Participation de la Belgique à la Coalition Internationale contre l'EI*, Parl Doc 54, 0305/004, 3 (Sep. 26, 2014) (translation provided by the authors).

[85] Identical letters dated November 25, 2014 from the Permanent Representative of the United Kingdom of Great Britain and Northern Ireland to the United Nations addressed to the Secretary-General and the President of the Security Council, UN Doc. S/2014/851 (Sep. 26, 2014). The resolution of the Canadian parliament (n. 73) referred not only to the request from Iraq, but also to the fact that IS had called on its members to target Canada and Canadians at home and abroad, and to the threat posed by IS to international peace and security.

The Case of the US-Led Military Coalition against "Islamic State"   251

provides an international legal basis. The Dutch troop deployment is therefore limited to Iraq.[86]

In other words, the Dutch government did not quash the "unable and unwilling" rationale *on substance*, it was merely unconvinced that its conditions were met *in practice* at the time (without, however, explaining why).

9.4.2 *Extension of Military Operations to Syrian Territory and Shifting Justificatory Discourse*

In subsequent months, several western coalition partners of the United States decided to expand their military operations to Syrian territory. In parallel, the discourse of States in the course of 2015 further shifted towards the position "persistently advocated" by the United States, and even more so following the Paris attacks of November 2015.

First, in a remarkable volte-face, Canadian PM Stephen Harper late March 2015 tabled a motion before the House of Commons providing for an expansion of Canadian operations to targeting IS "safe havens" within Syria.[87] In stark contrast to prior statements that action in Syria was excluded absent approval from Damascus, it was now asserted that Canada would "not seek the express consent of the Syrian government."[88] Speaking for the House of Commons, the Defense Minister specifically referred to the legal position "taken by President Obama's administration" to conclude that action against IS in eastern Syria was lawful "in part at the invitation of the government of Iraq under Article 51 of the United Nations Charter to give practical expression to the collective right of self-defense."[89] A few days letter, Canada submitted a letter to the Security Council copying in full the US position.[90] It is worth

---

[86] The Netherlands, *Brief van de Ministers van Buitenlandse Zaken, van Defensie en voor Buitenlandse Handel en Ontwikkelingssamenwerking*, year 2014–15, 27925, No. 506, 5 (Sep. 24, 2014) (translation provided by the authors).

[87] Canada, House of Commons, Debates, 41st Parliament, 2nd Session, Hansard, Vol. 147, No. 188 (Mar. 24, 2015), at 12207ff.

[88] *Id.*, at 12208. The motion was passed shortly hereafter: Canada, House of Commons, Vote No. 368, 41st Parliament, 2nd Session (Mar. 30, 2015).

[89] Canada, House of Commons, Debates, 41st Parliament, 2nd Session, Hansard, Vol. 147, No. 190, (Mar. 26, 2015), at 12358.

[90] Letter dated March 31, 2015 from the Chargé d'affaires a.i. of the Permanent Mission of Canada to the United Nations addressed to the President of the Security Council, UN Doc. S/2015/221 (Mar. 31, 2015): "In accordance with the inherent rights of individual and collective self-defence reflected in Article 51 of the United Nations Charter, States must be able to act in self-defence when the Government of the State where a threat is located is unwilling or unable to prevent attacks emanating from its territory." Following his election late 2015, the new Canadian Prime Minister Justin Trudeau put an end to Canadian air strike operations in Iraq

observing that the Canadian letter not only expressly endorses the "unable and unwilling" doctrine, but also follows the US approach by invoking both *collective* and *individual* self-defense. The invocation of the right of individual self-defense is not explained, save for a general reference to the "threat [posed by IS] not only to Iraq, but also to Canada and Canadians"[91] – suggesting the endorsement of a broadly construed right of anticipatory self-defense as well.[92]

In another interesting – albeit less radical – volte-face, the Dutch Foreign Minister in June 2015 informed Parliament that it could "now be concluded with sufficient certainty that there is a legal basis under international law for the use of force against ISIS in Syria."[93]

If the Dutch Foreign Minister concluded that action against IS in Syria was lawful under the 'unable and unwilling' doctrine, he ultimately explained that the Dutch government chose not (yet) to deploy its forces in Syria for political reasons. By contrast, several other coalition members did expand their military operations to Syrian territory. The United Kingdom, for instance, on 21 August 2015, conducted a single precision strike against "an ISIL vehicle in which a target known to be actively engaged in planning and directing imminent armed attacks against the United Kingdom was travelling."[94] The action

and Syria in February 2016. See, e.g.: Canada, Prime Minister, *Canada's New Approach to Addressing the Ongoing Crises in Iraq and Syria and Impacts on the Region: Promoting Security and Stability* (Feb. 8, 2016), at http://pm.gc.ca/eng/news/2016/02/08/canadas-new-approach-addressing-ongoing-crises-iraq-and-syria-and-impacts-region. Canada nonetheless continued to participate in operation Inherent Resolve i.a. through reconnaissance missions and refueling sorties. See, e.g.: www.forces.gc.ca/en/operations-abroad-current/op-impact.page.

[91] Letter dated March 31, 2015 from the Chargé d'affaires a.i. of the Permanent Mission of Canada to the United Nations addressed to the President of the Security Council, UN Doc. S/2015/221 (Mar. 31, 2015).

[92] Note: Even though Canada had been stunned by two shooting incidents allegedly involving "ISIL-inspired terrorists" in October 2014 (see: "Canada's PM Says Parliament Shooting Was Terrorism," *Al Jazeera America*, October 22, 2014, http://america.aljazeera.com/articles/2014/10/22/canada-parliamentshooting.html), it was not claimed that Canada had somehow been subject to a prior "armed attack."

[93] The Netherlands, *Kamerbrief inzake Nader Advies Extern Volkenrechtelijke Adviseur Geweldgebruik tegen ISIS in Syrië*, MinBuza-2015-333470 (Jun. 26, 2015), at www.rijksover heid.nl/documenten/kamerstukken/2015/06/26/kamerbrief-inzake-nader-advies-extern-volken rechtelijke-adviseur-geweldgebruik-tegen-isis-in-syrie, 1 (translation provided by the authors); The Netherlands, *Kamerbrief over Verlenging Nederlandse Bijdrage aan de Internationale Strijd tegen ISIS*, DVB/CV/097/15 (Jun. 19, 2015), at www.rijksoverheid.nl/documenten/kam erstukken/2015/06/19/kamerbrief-over-verlenging-nederlandse-bijdrage-aan-de-internationale-strijd-tegen-isis, 6.

[94] Letter dated September 7, 2015 from the Permanent Representative of the United Kingdom of Great Britain and Northern Ireland to the United Nations addressed to the President of the Security Council, UN Doc. S/2015/688 (Sep. 8, 2015). Further, see: UK Joint Committee on Human Rights, *Report* (n. 17).

The Case of the US-Led Military Coalition against "Islamic State"   253

was reported to the UN Security Council on 7 September as a "necessary and proportionate exercise of the individual right of self-defence of the United Kingdom."[95] The same day French President Hollande announced that France would start conducting reconnaissance flights over Syrian territory so as to pave the way for possible strikes against IS.[96] The move from the Elysée was accompanied by a letter to the Security Council referring to the Iraqi request for assistance, as well as to Article 51 UN Charter, and the "direct and extraordinary threat to the security of France" posed by ISIL.[97] No mention was made, however, of the "unable and unwilling" doctrine.

On September 9, 2015, another coalition member, Australia, decided to expand its scope of operations from Iraq to Syria, announcing that it was taking measures against IS in Syria, "in support of the collective self-defence of Iraq."[98] In its report to the Security Council, Australia also endorsed the view that:

> States must be able to act in self-defence when the Government of the State where the threat is located is unwilling or unable to prevent attacks originating from its territory. The Government of Syria has, by its failure to constrain attacks upon Iraqi territory originating from ISIL bases within Syria, demonstrated that it is unwilling or unable to prevent those attacks.[99]

Meanwhile, following a terrorist attack on July 20, 2015 that claimed the lives of thirty-two citizens in the Turkish city of Suruç, and was allegedly committed by a Turkish national with ties to IS,[100] Turkey for its part had launched a large-scale military operation against IS, as well as, even more controversially, against Kurdish PKK targets. It reported to the Security Council that it was "under a clear and imminent threat of continuing attack from Daesh."[101] It too stressed, once again, that "the regime in Syria is neither capable of nor

---

[95] Id.

[96] "Ce Qu'Il Faut Retenir de la Conférence de Presse de François Hollande," Le Monde, September 7, 2015, at www.lemonde.fr/les-decodeurs/article/2015/09/07/ce-qu-il-faut-retenir-de-la-conference-de-presse-de-francois-hollande_4748072_4355770.html.

[97] Identical letters dated September 8, 2015 from the Permanent Representative of France to the United Nations addressed to the Secretary-General and the President of the Security Council, UN Doc. S/2015/745 (Sep. 9, 2015).

[98] Letter dated September 9, 2015 from the Permanent Representative of Australia to the United Nations addressed to the President of the Security Council, UN Doc. S/2015/693 (Sep. 9, 2015).

[99] Id.

[100] Ceylan Yeginsu, "Suicide Bomber in Suruc Is Said to Be a Turk With Possible Ties to ISIS," The New York Times, July 22, 2015, at www.nytimes.com/2015/07/23/world/europe/turkey-suruc-bombing.html.

[101] Letter dated July 24, 2015 from the Chargé d'affaires a.i. of the Permanent Mission of Turkey to the United Nations addressed to the President of the Security Council, UN Doc. S/2015/563 (Jul. 24, 2015), 1.

254   *Tom Ruys and Luca Ferro*

willing to prevent these threats emanating from its territory, which clearly imperil the security of Turkey and the safety of its nationals. Individual and collective self-defence is our inherent right under international law, as reflected in Article 51 of the UN Charter."[102]

9.4.3 Evolutions Following the Paris Attacks of November 13, 2015 and the Terrorist Attacks in Brussels of March 22, 2016

The terrorist attacks in Paris of November 13, 2015 and the Brussels attacks of March 22, 2016 further pushed a number of European States to embrace an expanded reading of self-defense. The Paris attack, targeting cafés, restaurants, a music venue and sports stadium, brought the IS horror to the heart of Europe and sent a shockwave throughout the continent. The Brussels bombings, targeting the Zaventem airport and Maalbeek metro station, further amplified Europeans' sense of insecurity and need for decisive (military) action.

A few days after the attack in France, the French President made an emotional speech to the *Assemblée Nationale* in Versailles, announcing that France had responded by conducting air strikes against an IS command post in the city of Raqqa and that it would further beef up its operations against IS in Syria. In language remarkably reminiscent of US President Bush's rhetoric in the aftermath of the 9/11 attacks, President Hollande stated that France was the victim of aggression, and thus considered itself to be at war with IS (that is, a non-State armed group).[103] For the first time ever, he also activated the collective defense clause enshrined in Article 42(7) of the Treaty on European Union.[104] In accordance with Article 35 of the French Constitution, the *Assemblée Nationale* on 25 November approved the prolongation of the French troop deployment against IS.[105] In the preceding debate, the French Minister of Defense clarified that, while France had initially relied primarily on collective self-defense in support of Iraq, this legal basis was now

---

[102] *Id.*

[103] France, Sénat, *Address of François Hollande, President of the French Republic, to the French Parliament* (Nov. 16, 2015), *at* www.senat.fr/evenement/archives/D46/hollande.html: "Les actes commis vendredi soir à Paris et près du Stade de France, sont des actes de guerre. Ils ont fait au moins 129 morts et de nombreux blessés. Ils constituent une agression contre notre pays, contre ses valeurs, contre sa jeunesse, contre son mode de vie."

[104] *Id.* The text of Article 42(7) TEU reads, in part, as follows: "If a Member State is the victim of armed aggression on its territory, the other Member States shall have towards it an obligation of aid and assistance by all the means in their power, in accordance with Article 51 of the United Nations Charter."

[105] France, Assemblée Nationale, Vote en Application de l'Article 35, Alinéa 3, de la Constitution, XIVe Législature, Session Ordinaire de 2015–2016 (Nov. 25, 2015).

The Case of the US-Led Military Coalition against "Islamic State" 255

complemented with the right of individual self-defense.[106] At the same time, no reference was made to the "unable and unwilling" doctrine.

Another element that was invoked by the French Minister of Defense to support the 'legitimacy' of the intervention in Syria and Iraq concerned the resolution adopted by unanimity by the UN Security Council on 20 November 2015. Inspired by deadly terrorist attacks by IS in Paris, as well as in Sousse (Tunisia), Ankara, the Sinai desert and Beirut, the Council asserted that "the Islamic State in Iraq and the Levant ... constitutes a global and unprecedented threat to international peace and security."[107] In a carefully worded operative paragraph, the Council further

> [called] upon Member States that have the capacity to do so to take all necessary measures, in compliance with international law, in particular with the United Nations Charter ... to redouble and coordinate their efforts to prevent and suppress terrorist acts committed specifically by ISIL ... and to eradicate the safe haven they have established over significant parts of Iraq and Syria.[108]

Inasmuch as (1) the resolution was not explicitly adopted under Chapter VII of the UN Charter, (2) merely called upon States to take measures without effectively authorizing or deciding any type of action, and (3) added the reservation that measures taken ought to be in compliance with the UN Charter, the language is deliberately circular and a conspicuous example of so-called constructive ambiguity. As Akande and Milanovic have pointed out, the resolution was deemed to be "constructed in such a way that it can be used to provide political support for military action, without actually endorsing any particular legal theory on which such action can be based or providing legal authority from the Council itself."[109] In sum, the call for eradication of an IS safe haven in Syria nudges Member States to take action in Syria, without, however, providing any autonomous legal authority to do so.

Shortly after the Paris attacks and the adoption of resolution 2249(2015), both the United Kingdom and Germany obtained parliamentary approval for military action in Syria on December 2 and 4 respectively.[110] On December 3, 2015, the United Kingdom – which had hitherto conducted only a single strike

---

[106] Id.
[107] UNSC Res. 2249 (Nov. 20, 2015), 1.
[108] Id. para. 1.
[109] Dapo Akande and Marko Milanovic, "The Constructive Ambiguity of the Security Council's ISIS Resolution," EJIL: Talk!, November 21, 2015, at www.ejiltalk.org/the-constructive-ambiguity-of-the-security-councils-isis-resolution/ (emphasis added).
[110] United Kingdom, House of Commons, Hansard Record of Commons Debate (Dec. 2, 2015), Column 321ff; Germany, Deutscher Bundestag, Bundestagsbeschlüsse am 3. und 4.

in Syrian territory (see *supra* notes 94 and 95) – officially informed the UN Security Council that it was "taking necessary and proportionate measures against ISIL/Daesh in Syria, as called for by the Council in resolution 2249 (2015), in exercise of the inherent right of individual and collective self-defence."[111] Even though the letter did not refer to the unwilling and unable test, Prime Minister David Cameron, in the run-up to the Parliamentary vote, stated that the "legal basis for military action against ISIL in Syria … is the collective self-defence of Iraq." Moreover, he invoked "a solid basis of evidence on which to conclude … that the Assad regime is unwilling and/or unable to take action necessary to prevent ISIL's continuing attack on Iraq – or indeed attacks on us."[112]

The German *Bundestag* for its part on December 4 voted a resolution put forward by the Government paving the way for the deployment of Germany's armed forces – in particular for the deployment of surveillance and reconnaissance planes[113] – against IS in Syria until the end of 2016.[114] The resolution concerned primarily refers to the right of collective self-defense in support of Iraq, yet also contains references to Security Council resolution 2249(2015) as well as to France's invocation of Article 42(7)TEU. The resolution moreover notes that several States have for some time conducted military operations against IS in Syria in light of the latter country's being unable or unwilling to prevent attacks from its territory.[115] On December 10, 2015, Germany also

Dezember (Dec. 4, 2015), *at* www.bundestag.de/dokumente/textarchiv/2015/kw49-angenommen-abgelehnt/397844. However, it is worth noting that Germany did not join other countries in conducting airstrikes, but limited its operations to contributing reconnaissance jets, a frigate to help protect a French aircraft carrier, refueling aircraft and up to 1,200 military personnel: "German Parliament Approves Military Campaign against Islamic State in Syria," *Reuters*, December 5, 2015, *at* www.reuters.com/article/us-mideast-crisis-germany /german-parliament-approves-military-campaign-against-islamic-state-in-syria -idUSKBN0TN0ZM20151205.

[111] Letter dated December 3, 2015 from the Permanent Representative of the United Kingdom of Great Britain and Northern Ireland to the United Nations addressed to the President of the Security Council, UN Doc. S/2015/928 (Dec. 3, 2015).

[112] United Kingdom, Prime Minister's Office, *PM Statement Responding to FAC Report on Military Operations in Syria*, Prime Minister David Cameron (Nov. 26, 2015), *at* www .gov.uk/government/speeches/pm-statement-responding-to-fac-report-on-military-operations-in-syria.

[113] Lizzie Dearden, "Germany to Send Up to 1,200 Troops to Middle East after Bundestag Approves Military Action against ISIS in Syria," *Independent*, December 4, 2015, *at* www .independent.co.uk/news/world/europe/germany-votes-to-approve-military-action-against-isis -in-syria-a6760131.html.

[114] Germany, Deutscher Bundestag, Drucksache 18/6866 (Dec. 1, 2015).

[115] *Id.* ("In diesem Zusammenhang werden auch militärische Maßnahmen auf syrischem Gebiet durchgeführt, da die syrische Regierung nicht in der Lage und/oder nicht willens ist, die von ihrem Territorium ausgehenden Angriffe durch IS zu unterbinden.").

The Case of the US-Led Military Coalition against "Islamic State"   257

informed the Security Council of its military operations in the following wording:

ISIL has occupied a certain part of Syrian territory over which the Government of the Syrian Arab Republic does not at this time exercise effective control. States that have been subjected to armed attack by ISIL originating in this part of Syrian territory, are therefore justified under Article 51 of the Charter of the United Nations to take necessary measures of self-defence, even without the consent of the Government of the Syrian Arab Republic. Exercising the right of collective self-defence, Germany will now support the military measures of those States that have been subjected to attacks by ISIL.[116]

The reference to Syria's internationally recognized government not being able to exercise "effective control" over part of its territory, seems a (barely concealed) reference to it not being able to prevent attacks occurring from its territory against neighboring, or even more distant, States. Especially when read together with the resolution of the *Bundestag*, it would appear that Germany too came to endorse the "unable and unwilling" test.

Finally, in the course of 2016, four more European States followed suit and expanded military operations to include Syria. Denmark, the Netherlands and Norway sent Article 51 letters to the United Nations, relying on the right of collective self-defense as the justification for its "necessary and proportionate measures" against "Islamic State" in Syria in order to eradicate its "safe haven" in Iraq and Syria.[117] All three States also referred to Security Council resolution 2249 (2015), although it is not entirely clear what legal value they attached thereto.[118] Similarly, Belgium relied on the right to collective self-defense as the international legal justification, while also drawing attention, like Germany before it,[119] to the fact that IS had "occupied a certain part of

---

[116]   Letter dated December 10, 2015 from the Chargé d'affaires a.i. of the Permanent Mission of Germany to the United Nations addressed to the President of the Security Council, UN Doc. S/2015/946 (Dec. 10, 2015).

[117]   Letter dated January 11, 2016 from the Permanent Representative of Denmark to the United Nations addressed to the President of the Security Council, UN Doc. S/2016/34 (Jan. 13, 2016); Letter dated February 11, 2016 from the Chargé d'affaires a.i. of the Permanent Mission of the Netherlands to the United Nations addressed to the President of the Security Council, UN Doc. S/2016/132 (Feb. 10, 2016); Letter dated June 3, 2016 from the Permanent Representative of Norway to the United Nations addressed to the President of the Security Council, UN Doc. S/2016/513 (Jun. 3, 2016).

[118]   *Id.*

[119]   See n. 116.

258   Tom Ruys and Luca Ferro

Syrian territory over which the Government of the Syrian Arab Republic does not, at this time, exercise effective control."[120]

9.5 CRITICAL OBSERVATIONS

It follows from the foregoing that the position of western members of the US-led coalition against IS (other than the United States itself) underwent a marked evolution after September 2014.

First, if initially all of these countries limited their involvement exclusively to operations in Iraqi territory, Australia, Canada, the United Kingdom, France, Denmark, Norway and Belgium all gradually extended their scope of activities to Syrian territory,[121] while Germany similarly joined the coalition with a view to conducting operations in Syria.[122] If the Netherlands initially expressed doubts over the legality of operations in Syrian territory, it later revoked these doubts, while stressing that its decision not to intervene in Syria was due to political reasons instead – only to abandon those political objections later.

Second, if initially justifications focused on the consent of the Iraqi authorities, in the end, all of the countries under examination embraced the self-defense argument, thus (at least implicitly) qualifying the conduct of IS as constituting an "armed attack" in the sense of Article 51 UN Charter. In their correspondence with the UN Security Council, Australia, Canada and the United Kingdom[123] eventually all invoked the "unable and unwilling doctrine" originally put forward by the United States – as did Turkey. The Dutch government did the same in its correspondence with parliament. In a similar vein, Germany and possibly Belgium would appear to have embraced the doctrine as well.

A number of States moreover combined their reliance on the right of *collective* self-defense, with a reliance on *individual* self-defense. While France did so only after the attacks on its soil on November 13,[124] the United

---

[120]   Letter dated June 7, 2016 from the Permanent Representative of Belgium to the United Nations addressed to the President of the Security Council, UN Doc. S/2016/523 (Jun. 9, 2016).

[121]   But, see the announcement by new Prime Minister, Justin Trudeau (n. 90).

[122]   But, see the limitation of the German military operations (n. 110).

[123]   UK Joint Committee on Human Rights, *Report* (n. 17), para. 3.22: "To be entitled to rely on self-defence against non-state actors, the State from whose territory the armed attack is being launched or prepared for must be unable or unwilling to prevent the attack."

[124]   It is noted, however, that France did refer to the "direct and extraordinary threat to the security of France" in its letter to the UN Security Council dated September 9, 2015, see: UN Doc. S/2015/745. It does not follow from the letter, however, whether France is relying on collective

Kingdom and Canada did so as well. These two countries' position thus signals an acceptance of a broad reading of Article 51 UN Charter as including anticipatory action. This is especially true for Canada, which (contrary to the United Kingdom) did not even identify an imminent threat of attack, but instead relied in general terms on the threat posed by IS to Canada and to Canadians abroad.

What explains for this remarkable shift? The idea that a fundamental change in the facts on the ground – as relevant for the legal analysis – is responsible for the changing attitude and justificatory discourse of the States concerned appears unconvincing. For instance, France relied on Article 51 UN Charter to support an extension of its operations to Syrian territory well before the Paris attacks in November 2015. What about the Dutch volte-face? It is recalled that in September 2014 the Dutch government, applying the unable and unwilling test, took the view that "[a]t this moment, it cannot be ascertained whether or not self-defense provides an international legal basis."[125] In June 2015, however, the government declared that there was now "sufficient certainty that there is a legal basis under international law for the use of force against ISIS in Syria."[126] Interestingly, in order to explain its changed insights and conclusions, the Foreign Minister referred to the fact that

> [c]ontrary to what was true in September 2014, there is now sufficient factual evidence that there are continuous armed attacks from Syria against Iraq, directed by ISIS headquarters in Raqqah, Syria. In addition, there is a continuous flow of fighters and weapons from Syria to Iraq for purposes of deployment in the battle in Iraq. It is also evident that the Syrian authorities are incapable of stopping these armed attacks.[127]

All things considered, however, the factors invoked here hardly qualify as novel elements that were insufficiently certain in September 2014. Indeed, these elements were arguably well established when the US-led coalition

---

    self-defense in support of Iraq only, or also on individual self-defense (the letter only refers to Article 51 UN Charter in general terms).

[125] The Netherlands, *Brief van de Ministers van Buitenlandse Zaken, van Defensie en voor Buitenlandse Handel en Ontwikkelingssamenwerking*, 2014–15, 27925, No. 506 (Sep. 24, 2014), 5 (translation provided by the authors).

[126] The Netherlands, *Kamerbrief inzake Nader Advies Extern Volkenrechtelijke Adviseur Geweldgebruik tegen ISIS in Syrië*, MinBuza-2015-333470 (Jun. 26, 2015), *at* www.rijksoverheid.nl/documenten/kamerstukken/2015/06/26/kamerbrief-inzake-nader-advies-extern-volkenrechtelijke-adviseur-geweldgebruik-tegen-isis-in-syrie, 1 (translation provided by the authors).

[127] *Id.* (translation provided by the authors).

against IS was launched in September 2014.[128] They were broadly reported in the media and in reports of think tanks and NGOs, and were at the heart of the US and Iraqi argumentation. The impression that the supposedly novel "factual evidence" invoked by the Dutch Foreign Minister was put forward *pour le besoin de la cause* is further reinforced by the fact that the legal opinion of the expert advisor (Professor Nollkaemper) that is annexed to, and forms the inspiration for, the letter of the Foreign Minister, actually invokes wholly different reasons for explaining the shift in position, including – rather controversially – the view that Syria did not (or no longer?) appear to object against strikes against IS on its territory, which would allegedly make it a *sui generis* case.[129]

Similar reservations can be made in respect of Canada. Whereas Canada initially relied strongly on Iraqi consent and asserted that it would not operate in Syrian territory absent green light from Damascus, mere months later it copied the US legal justification in full. The changed position of the Canadian government may well have been triggered by the brutalities of IS, with the awareness that "continuing to degrade ISIL [would] require striking its operations and infrastructure where they are located, including in Syria" (as the motion tabled by the government observed), or, possibly, with electoral reasons.[130] Yet, it remains unclear what (legally relevant) factors might account for the government's sudden turnaround. In the debate before the House of Commons, the Minister of Defence referred to "the legal advice received from our own Judge Advocate General and the position taken by

---

[128] Consider, e.g., the statement by US Legal Advisor Egan that "[b]y September 2014, the Syrian government had lost effective control of much of eastern and northeastern Syria, with much of that territory under ISIL's control." See: Egan (n. 13).

[129] The Netherlands, *Kamerbrief inzake Nader Advies Extern Volkenrechtelijke Adviseur Geweldgebruik tegen ISIS in Syrië*, MinBuza-2015-333470 (Jun. 26, 2015), *at* www .rijksoverheid.nl/documenten/kamerstukken/2015/06/26/kamerbrief-inzake-nader-advies-exte rn-volkenrechtelijke-adviseur-geweldgebruik-tegen-isis-in-syrie, Annex, paras. 1–6, 16. The expert opinion essentially refers to two factors, why military actions against IS in Syria are now (as opposed to in September 2014) deemed compatible with the "unable and unwilling" test. The first concerns the finding that "recent statements" would appear to indicate that Syria is not objecting to strikes against IS on its territory. The second element is that the serious human rights violations would allegedly rule out any coordination of air strikes against IS with Damascus. Yet, the latter element – leaving aside its intrinsic validity – would not appear to be a new element, nor one related to the "unable and unwilling" test proper. The first element in turn would seem to ignore repeated statements by the Syrian authorities stressing the illegality of unauthorized strikes on its territory. See *supra* nn. 60–62). No reference is made in the letter of the Foreign Minister to the willingness or unwillingness of Syria to fight IS.

[130] In this sense, see: Canada, House of Commons, Debates, 41st Parliament, 2nd Session, Hansard, Vol. 147, No. 190, (Mar. 26, 2015), at 12339ff.

President Obama's administration" to support the invocation of the right of self-defense. Yet, to the discontent of several MPs, the former legal advice was not made public. As for the US legal position, it was observed by some that this position was already known late September 2014 when the deployment of armed forces against IS was first debated, and was never mentioned at the time.[131] This led one MP, Craig Scott (a human rights lawyer and law professor) to conclude that "the ministers, did not have a clue about what the legal basis would be that they were going to be putting forward" and that what this suggested was that "legality is an afterthought. Not knowing and not reading whatever legal opinion they purport to have in order to know how they are allowed to go into Syria, so as to then know what the purpose of the mission can be in law, suggests that it does not matter to them. They are going in for other reasons."[132]

In light of the foregoing, what the present case illustrates is that the post-9/11 idea of a transatlantic divide with regard to the normative framework on the use of force is perhaps more fiction than reality, and should at least be taken *cum grano salis*. Indeed, western countries, cognizant of the importance of tackling the IS presence in both Iraq *and* Syria for purposes of destroying the group, did not hesitate to adopt an expansionist reading of Article 51 UN Charter, which they had hitherto by and large refrained from subscribing to. This move took place against the background of growing concerns over IS at the political level and in public opinion, influenced by the influx of asylum seekers *inter alia* from Syria and Iraq, as well as by several terrorist attacks on European soil and growing concerns that returned foreign fighters or IS sympathizers in Europe might commit further attacks. If all of international law is ultimately a compromise between interests and norms,[133] the case then undermines the perception that the United States is necessarily more drawn to an interest-centered interpretation of (often fairly indeterminate) legal norms, whereas other (less powerful) western States (in particular in Europe) will follow an inspiration that is rather guided by normative considerations instead of considerations of utility.

Put differently, European States are not necessarily more utopian. Nor are they necessarily more sensitive to the risk of establishing precedents that may lend themselves to abuse – overall, the States examined here indeed paid little or no attention to the potentially far-reaching implications and the

---

[131] *Id.*, at 12367.
[132] *Id.*
[133] Further, see, e.g., Janina Dill, *Legitimate Targets? Social Construction, International Law and US Bombing* (Cambridge: Cambridge University Press, 2014), 45ff.

concomitant risk of abuse of the unable and unwilling doctrine in other settings (a fact which is all the more remarkable if one considers, for instance, that the Belgian municipality of Molenbeek, located in the Brussels region, was widely branded a terrorist "safe haven" in the media in the aftermath of the Paris attacks, with the Belgian minister of the interior publicly suggesting that the government did not "have control over the situation in Molenbeek").[134] This attitude is markedly different from the position of most western States at the time of NATO's controversial Kosovo intervention in 1999. *In illo tempore*, most States (save for the United Kingdom and, arguably, Belgium) steered clear from expressly subscribing to the legality of unilateral humanitarian intervention (absent Chapter VII authorization) for fear of setting a precedent (many scholars in turn adopted an "unlawful but legitimate" analysis).[135] No such precedent-averse attitude was present in the case examined here.[136]

The period between the launch of the US-led coalition against IS in September 2014 and the expansion of the operation in 2015 and the first half of 2016 saw a marked convergence of the legal positions of the United States and other western countries. Several other western States in particular shifted their stance towards a position that the United States ostensibly copied from Israel in the late 1970s and early 1980s, and that it began defending more vigorously after the 9/11 attacks revealed the increased destructive potential of transnational terrorist groups in the twenty-first century. It could be seen as an example of "persistent advocacy" on the part of the United States of a more expansionist reading of the right of self-defense – and a successful one at that (more successful in any case (at least so far) than the UK's advocacy in support

---

[134] Lisa De Bode, "Molenbeek: Belgium's Haven for Foreign Fighters," *Al Jazeera America*, November 16, 2015; *at* http://america.aljazeera.com/articles/2015/11/16/molenbeek-known-as-safe-haven-for-foreign-fighters-social-workers-say.html; Kimiko De Freytas-Tamura and Milan Schreuer, "Belgium Minister Says Government Lacks Control Over Neighborhood Linked to Terror Plots," *The New York Times*, November 15, 2015, *at* www.nytimes.com/live/paris-attacks-live-updates/belgium-doesnt-have-control-over-molenbeek-interior-minister-says/.

[135] Further: Gray, *Use of Force* (n. 33) 42–46.

[136] It may be observed in this respect that Belgium was alone in explicitly drawing attention, in its letter to the Security Council, to the "exceptional" nature of the situation. See: Letter dated June 7, 2016 from the Permanent Representative of Belgium to the United Nations addressed to the President of the Security Council, UN Doc. S/2016/523 (Jun. 9, 2016): "ISIL has occupied a certain part of Syrian territory over which the Government of the Syrian Arab Republic does not, at this time, exercise effective control. In the light of this exceptional situation, States that have been subjected to armed attack by ISIL originating in that part of the Syrian territory are therefore justified under Article 51 of the Charter to take necessary measures of self-defence."

The Case of the US-Led Military Coalition against "Islamic State"   263

of the humanitarian intervention doctrine). Several western States indeed appear have to mirrored their legal justification after the one put forward by the United States. Particularly telling, for example, is the Canadian minister of defense's express reliance on the legal "position taken by President Obama's administration" before the Canadian House of Commons, or the reference to the US position in the Dutch government's letter to parliament of September 2014.[137] In this respect, analogies can arguably be drawn with the US persistent advocacy in support of anticipatory self-defense in the wake of the 9/11 attacks, and its insistence, for example, in the 2002 US National Security Strategy that "[f]or centuries, international law [has] recognized that nations need not suffer an attack before they can lawfully take action to defend themselves against forces that present an imminent danger of attack."[138] Here too, it appears that US advocacy has been partly successful and has resulted in a growing number of States, including European States, endorsing a doctrine which has nonetheless been highly controversial (and lacking of support in State practice) throughout the entire Cold War era.[139] It is worth noting in the margin that the British letter of September 7, 2015 appears to mark the first time the UK expressly justified its actions to the UN by relying on self-defense against allegedly imminent armed attacks.[140]

In the end, the case of the US-led military coalition against IS strikes as one where European States as well as several other western States originally steered clear from murky legal grounds only to find themselves ultimately embracing an extensive reading of the right of self-defense, and relying for the first time, whether explicitly or implicitly, on the controversial "unable and unwilling" doctrine to justify military operations abroad.

Whether, more than fifteen years after the 9/11 attacks, which first gave broader impetus to calls for a more flexible interpretation of the right of self-defense vis-à-vis attacks by non-State armed groups, the coalition against IS (and its legal underpinning) signals the conclusive breakthrough for the "unable and unwilling" doctrine is open to debate. The present contribution has not sought to provide a conclusive answer. At the same time, one can ignore neither the acquiescent attitude of numerous UN Member States, nor

---

[137] See *supra* nn. 86 and 89.
[138] *US National Security Strategy* 2002 (n. 1) 15.
[139] See Ruys, *Armed Attack* (n. 17) 318ff. More generally, on the US role as a "persistent advocate" in the *jus ad bellum*, see: Henderson, *The Persistent Advocate and the Use of Force* (n. 20).
[140] Letter dated September 7, 2015 from the Permanent Representative of the United Kingdom of Great Britain and Northern Ireland to the United Nations addressed to the President of the Security Council, UN Doc. S/2015/688 (Sep. 8, 2015). See also *supra* n. 19 on the UK's confirmation of the Bethlehem principles (n. 18).

the more critical, or outright condemnatory position of several others (such as Russia).[141] Nor can one *a priori* dismiss the suggestion that the Assad regime's own record of war crimes and human rights violations precluded the need for consent from the *de jure* government and turns the coalition against IS into a *sui generis* case, as some have suggested.[142]

[141] See *supra* nn. 56–63. It is nonetheless worth noting that Russia itself has previously relied on a broad reading of Article 51 UN Charter in the face of non-State attacks. See: Ruys, *Armed Attack* (n. 17) 445.

[142] In this sense, see the advice of Nollkaemper, annexed to the letter of the Dutch Foreign Minister of June 26, 2015, *supra* n. 93. Consider also: Claus Kreß, "The Fine Line Between Collective Self-Defense and Intervention by Invitation: Reflections on the Use of Force against 'IS' in Syria", *Just Security*, February 17, 2015, www.justsecurity.org/20118/claus-kreb-force-isil-syria/#more-20118.

CPSIA information can be obtained
at www.ICGtesting.com
Printed in the USA
LVHW080920030821
694401LV00004B/303